Higehiro: After Being Rejected, I Shaved and Took in a High School Runaway Vol. 01
(HIGE O SORU. SOSHITE JOSHIKOSEI O HIRO. Vol.1)
© Shimesaba, Booota 2019
© Imaru Adachi 2019
First published in Japan in 2019 by KADOKAWA CORPORATION, Tokyo. English
translation rights arranged with KADOKAWA CORPORATION, Tokyo.

ISBN: 978-1-64273-144-6

Original story by Shimesaba
Manga by Imaru Adachi
Character design by booota
Translated by Eric Margolis
English Edition Published by One Peace Books 2021

Printed in USA
2 3 4 5 6 7 8 9 10

One Peace Books
43-32 22nd Street STE 204 Long Island City New York 11101
www.onepeacebooks.com

surprised me the most (well, the number one thing is of course how wonderful the drawings are) was the way he handled the story. I thought that when a story gets adapted for manga, a lot ends up on the cutting room floor. But far from keeping information to its minimum, Imaru modified the flow of the story in comic form to be smooth and easily understandable. I thought, "This is more than just a pretty good one." And every time I got the storyboard, I could tell that he had created the manga perfectly to satisfy fans.

As the original author, I couldn't be more pleased with the result. I want the manga edition to reach many readers and for all of the fans of the original novel to get to know Imaru. And if it becomes an opportunity for new fans of the manga to get to know the much-inferior original, then that's all I could ask for.

I pray that the manga version becomes a success. I also hope to continue to work alongside Imaru. And with that, I'll bring my afterword to an end here.

Shimesaba

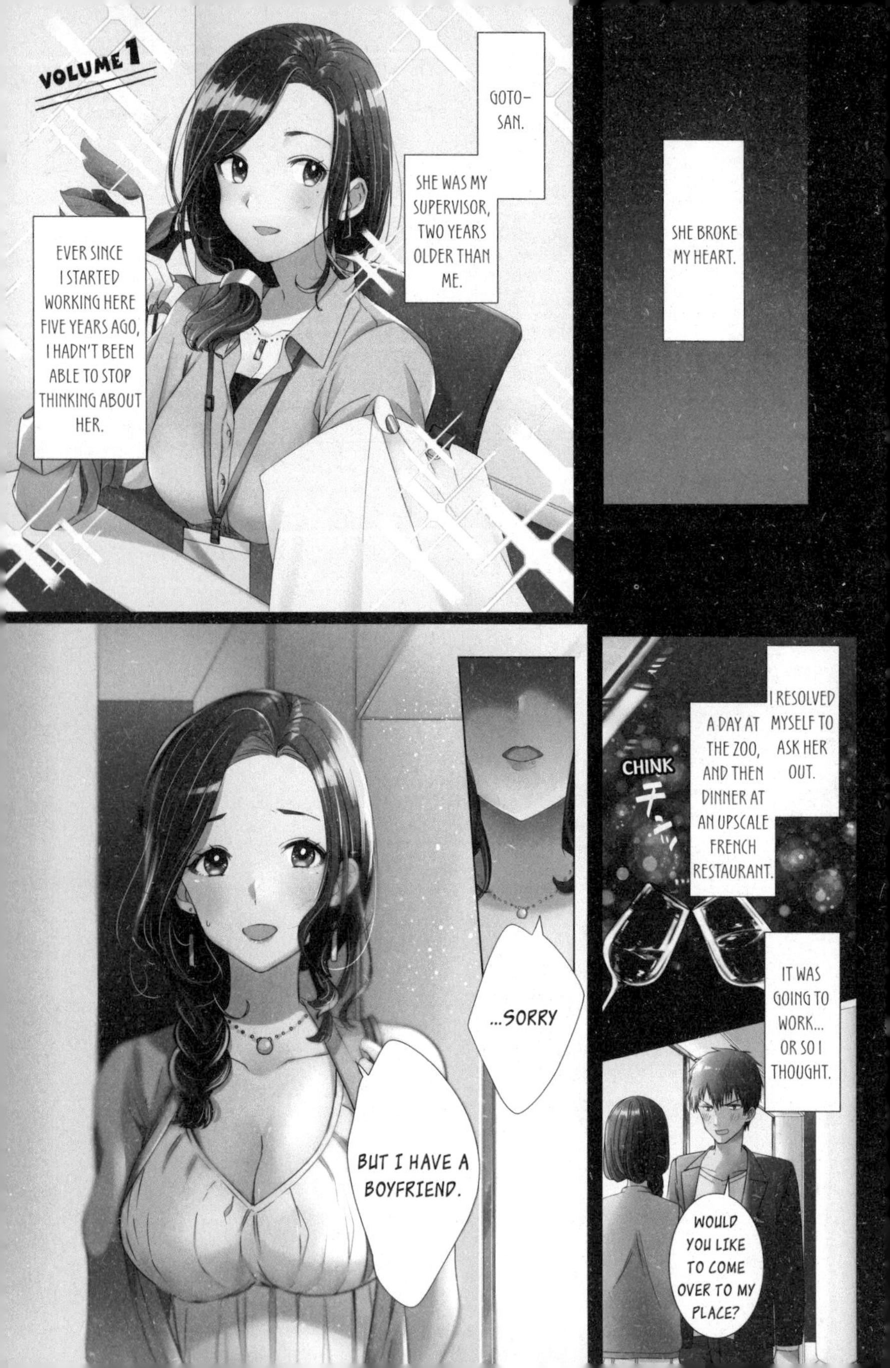
VOLUME 1
SHE BROKE MY HEART.
GOTO-SAN.
SHE WAS MY SUPERVISOR, TWO YEARS OLDER THAN ME.
EVER SINCE I STARTED WORKING HERE FIVE YEARS AGO, I HADN'T BEEN ABLE TO STOP THINKING ABOUT HER.
I RESOLVED MYSELF TO ASK HER OUT.
A DAY AT THE ZOO, AND THEN DINNER AT AN UPSCALE FRENCH RESTAURANT.
CHINK
チン
IT WAS GOING TO WORK... OR SO I THOUGHT.
WOULD YOU LIKE TO COME OVER TO MY PLACE?
...SORRY
BUT I HAVE A BOYFRIEND.

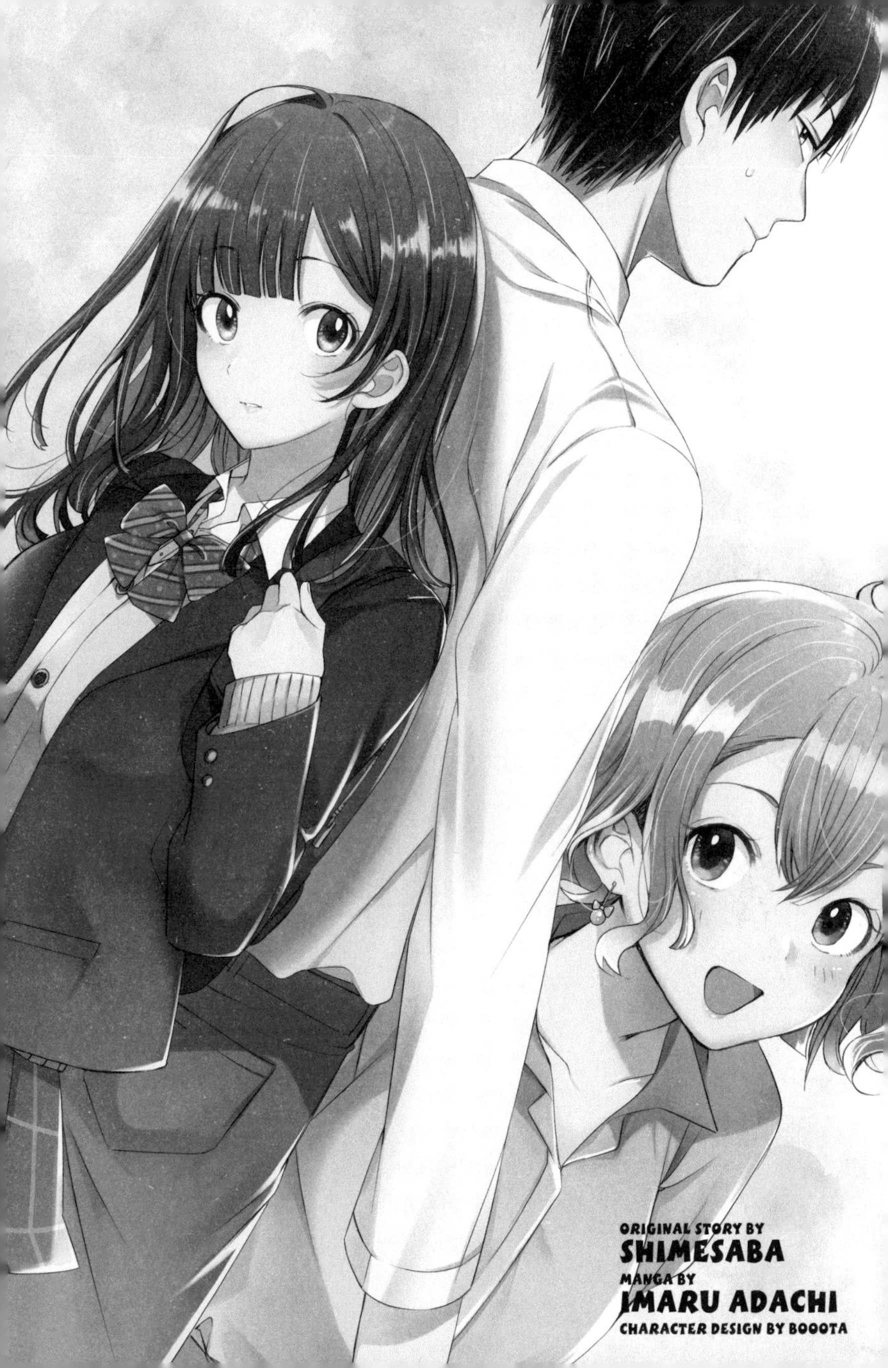
ORIGINAL STORY BY
SHIMESABA
MANGA BY
IMARU ADACHI
CHARACTER DESIGN BY BOOOTA

HIGE HIRO

After Being Rejected, I Shaved and Took in a High School Runaway

1

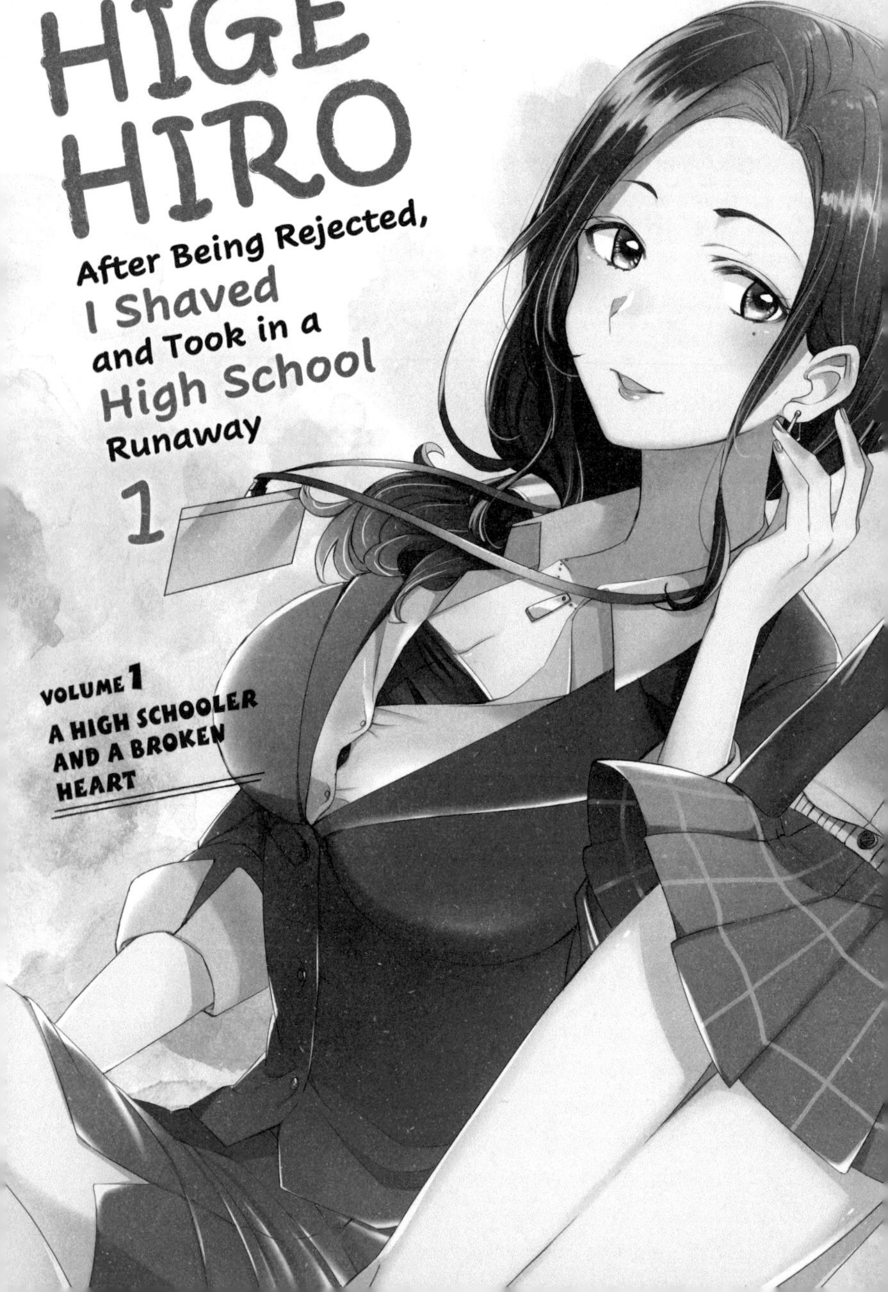

VOLUME 1

A HIGH SCHOOLER AND A BROKEN HEART

HIGEHIRO

**After Being Rejected,
I Shaved and Took
in a High School Runaway** **1**

TABLE OF CONTENTS

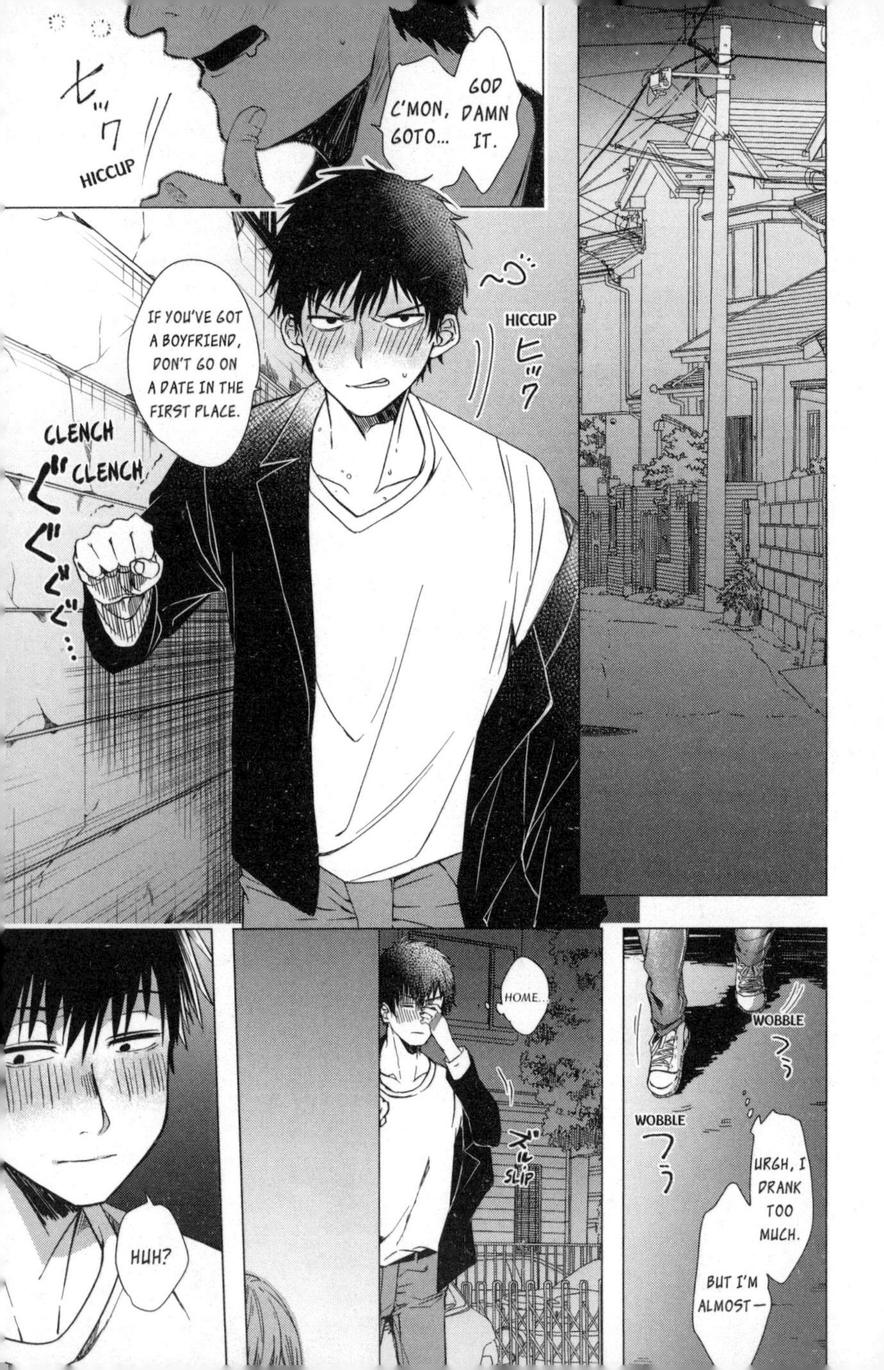
C'MON, GOTO... GOD DAMN IT.
ヒック
HICCUP
~ッ
HICCUP
ヒック
IF YOU'VE GOT A BOYFRIEND, DON'T GO ON A DATE IN THE FIRST PLACE.
CLENCH CLENCH
ぐぐぐ…
WOBBLE
フラ
WOBBLE
フラ
URGH, I DRANK TOO MUCH.
BUT I'M ALMOST—
HOME...
ズル
SLIP
HUH?

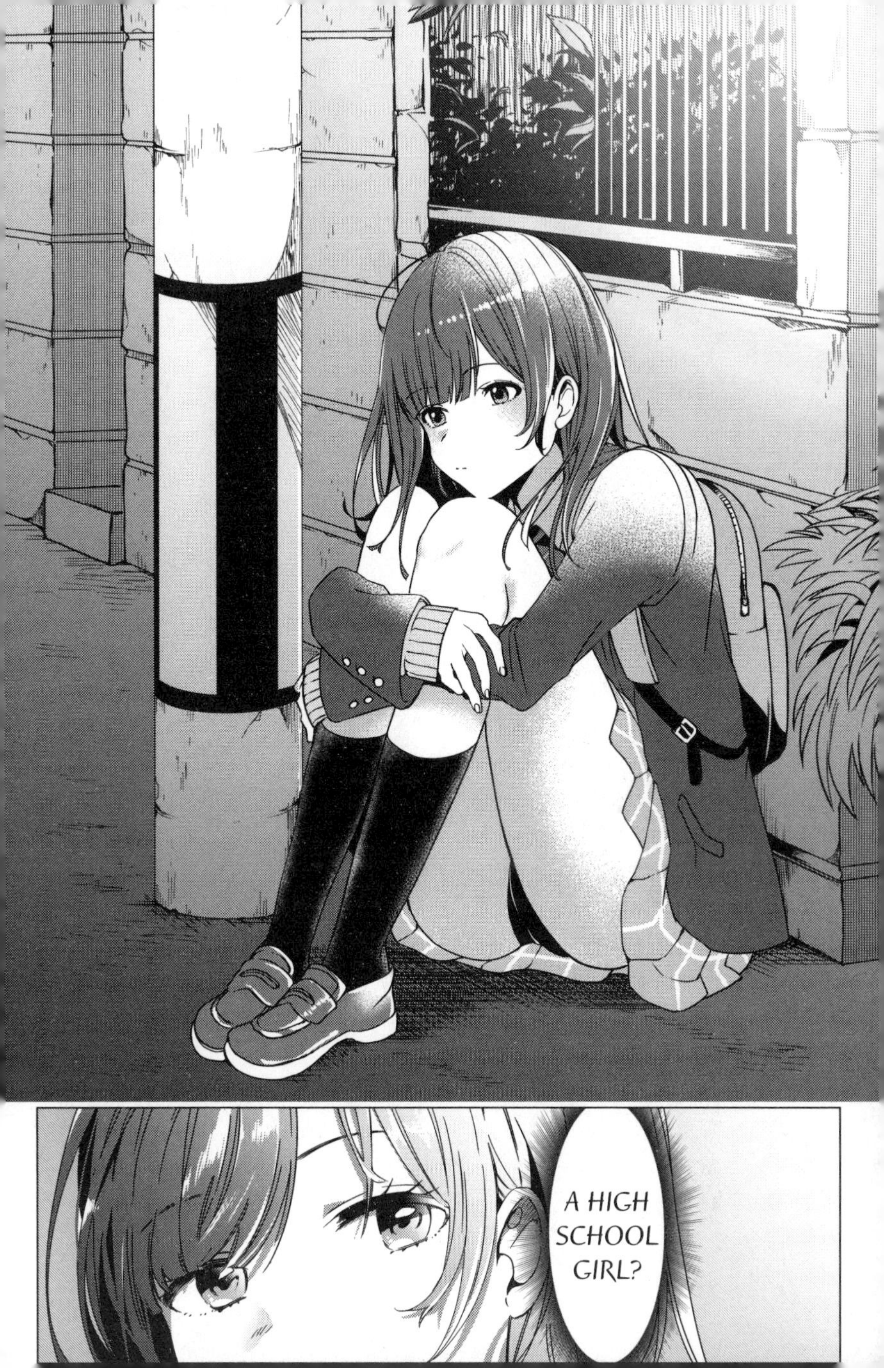
A HIGH SCHOOL GIRL?

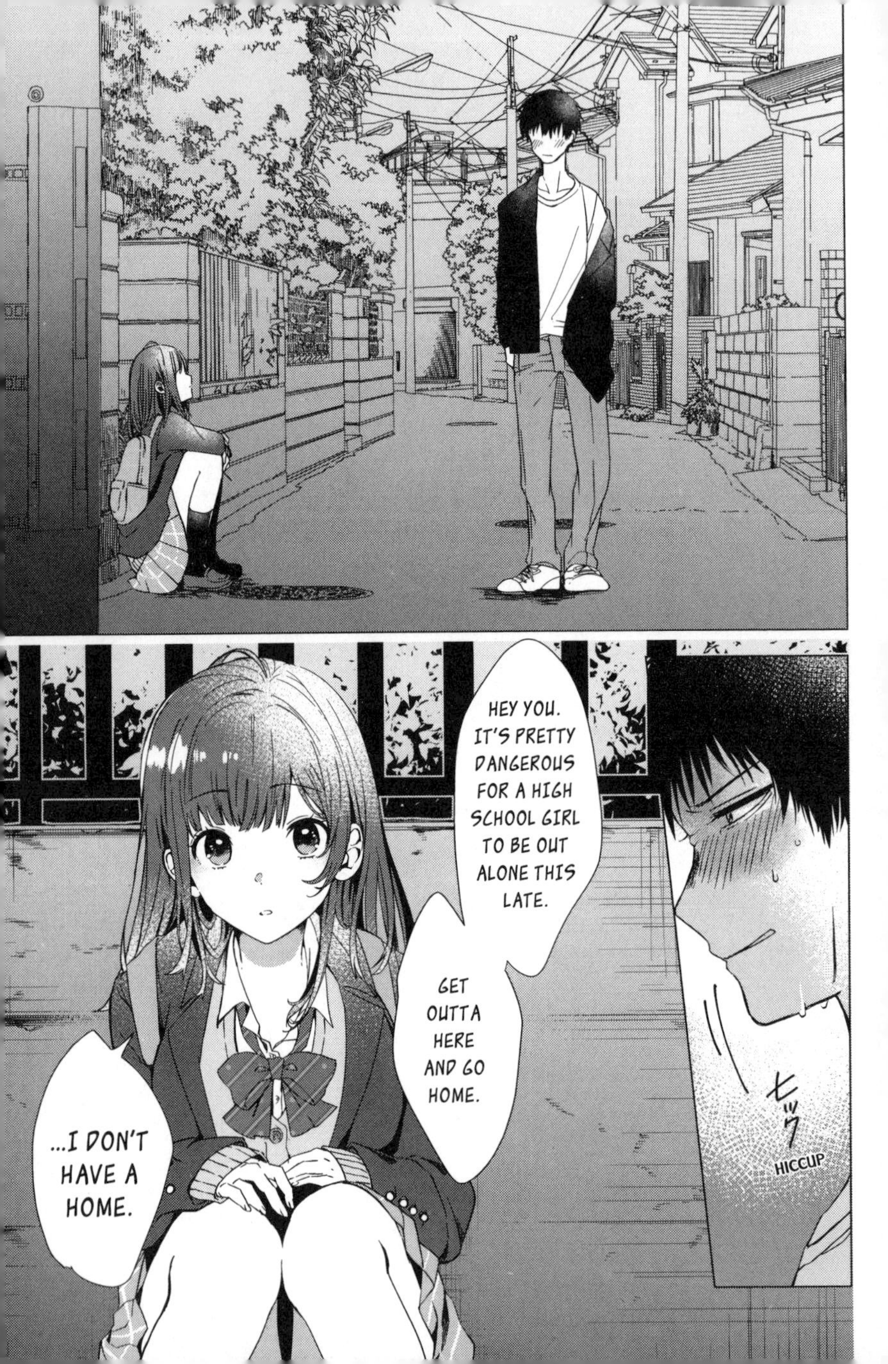
HEY YOU. IT'S PRETTY DANGEROUS FOR A HIGH SCHOOL GIRL TO BE OUT ALONE THIS LATE.
GET OUTTA HERE AND GO HOME.
ヒック
HICCUP
...I DON'T HAVE A HOME.

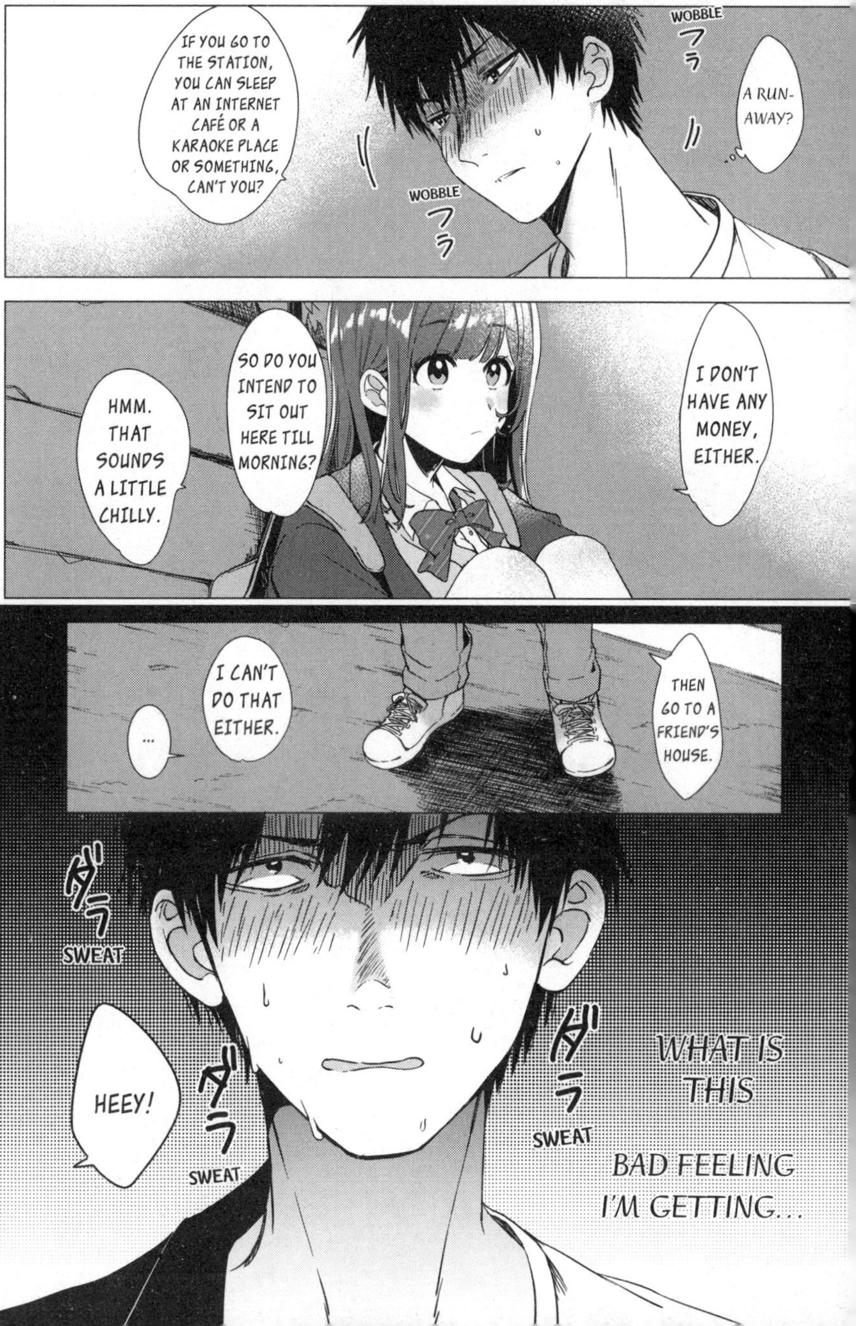
WOBBLE
フラ
A RUN-AWAY?
IF YOU GO TO THE STATION, YOU CAN SLEEP AT AN INTERNET CAFÉ OR A KARAOKE PLACE OR SOMETHING, CAN'T YOU?
WOBBLE
フラ
I DON'T HAVE ANY MONEY, EITHER.
SO DO YOU INTEND TO SIT OUT HERE TILL MORNING?
HMM. THAT SOUNDS A LITTLE CHILLY.
THEN GO TO A FRIEND'S HOUSE.
I CAN'T DO THAT EITHER.
...
WHAT IS THIS BAD FEELING I'M GETTING...
ダラ
SWEAT
ダラ
SWEAT
HEEY!
ダラ
SWEAT

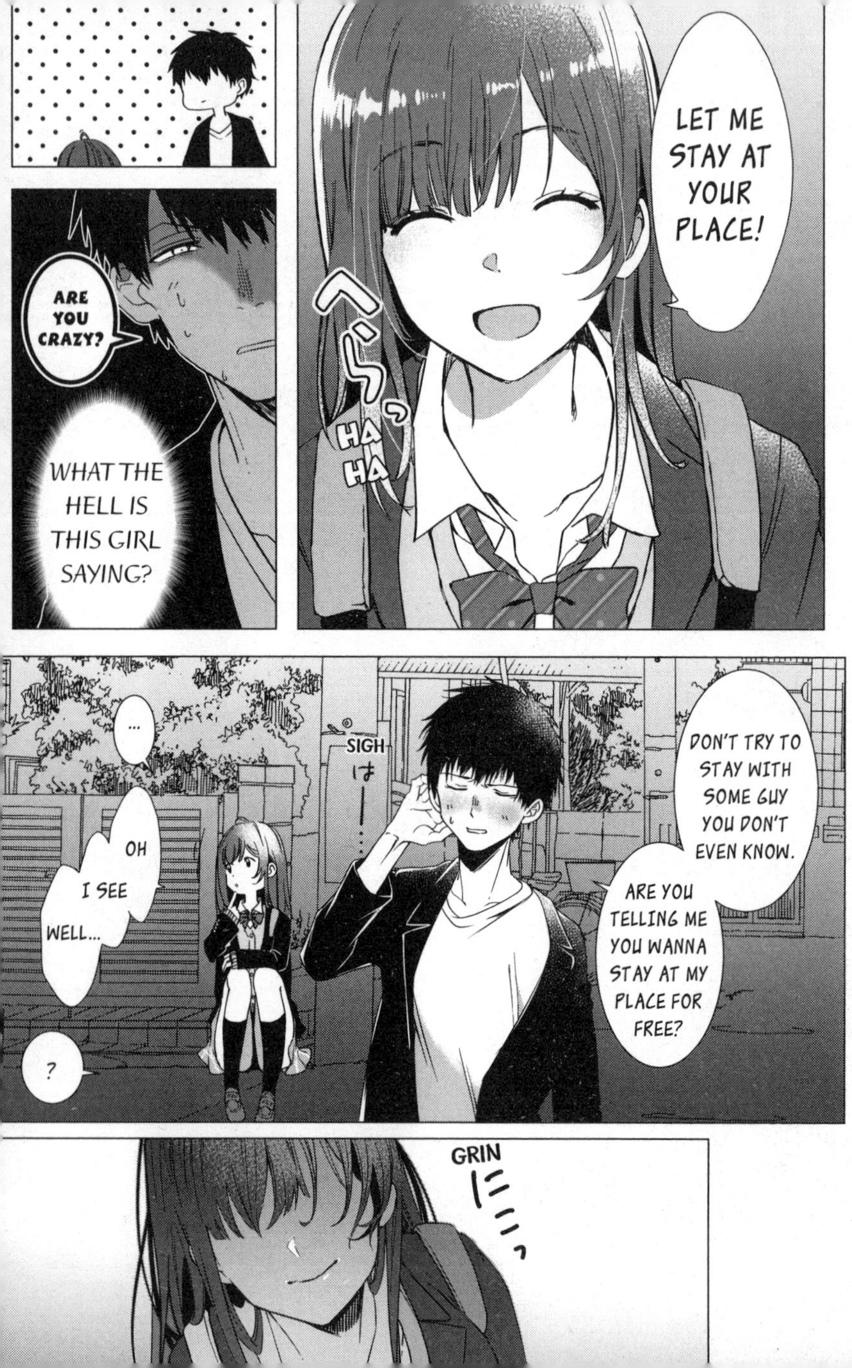
LET ME STAY AT YOUR PLACE!
HA HA
へらっ
ARE YOU CRAZY?
WHAT THE HELL IS THIS GIRL SAYING?
DON'T TRY TO STAY WITH SOME GUY YOU DON'T EVEN KNOW.
ARE YOU TELLING ME YOU WANNA STAY AT MY PLACE FOR FREE?
SIGH
はー…
...
OH I SEE
WELL...
?
GRIN
にっ

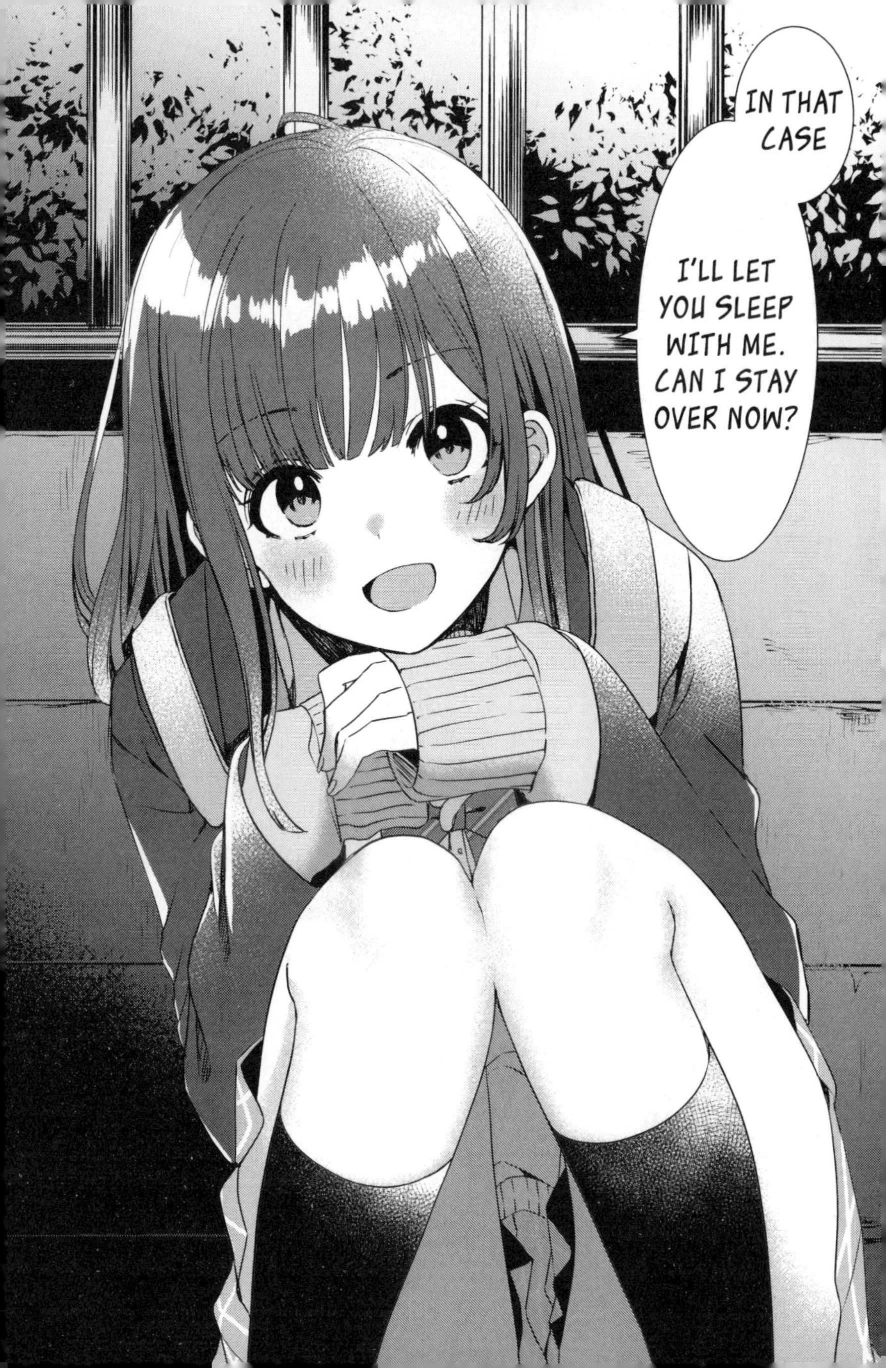
IN THAT CASE
I'LL LET YOU SLEEP WITH ME. CAN I STAY OVER NOW?

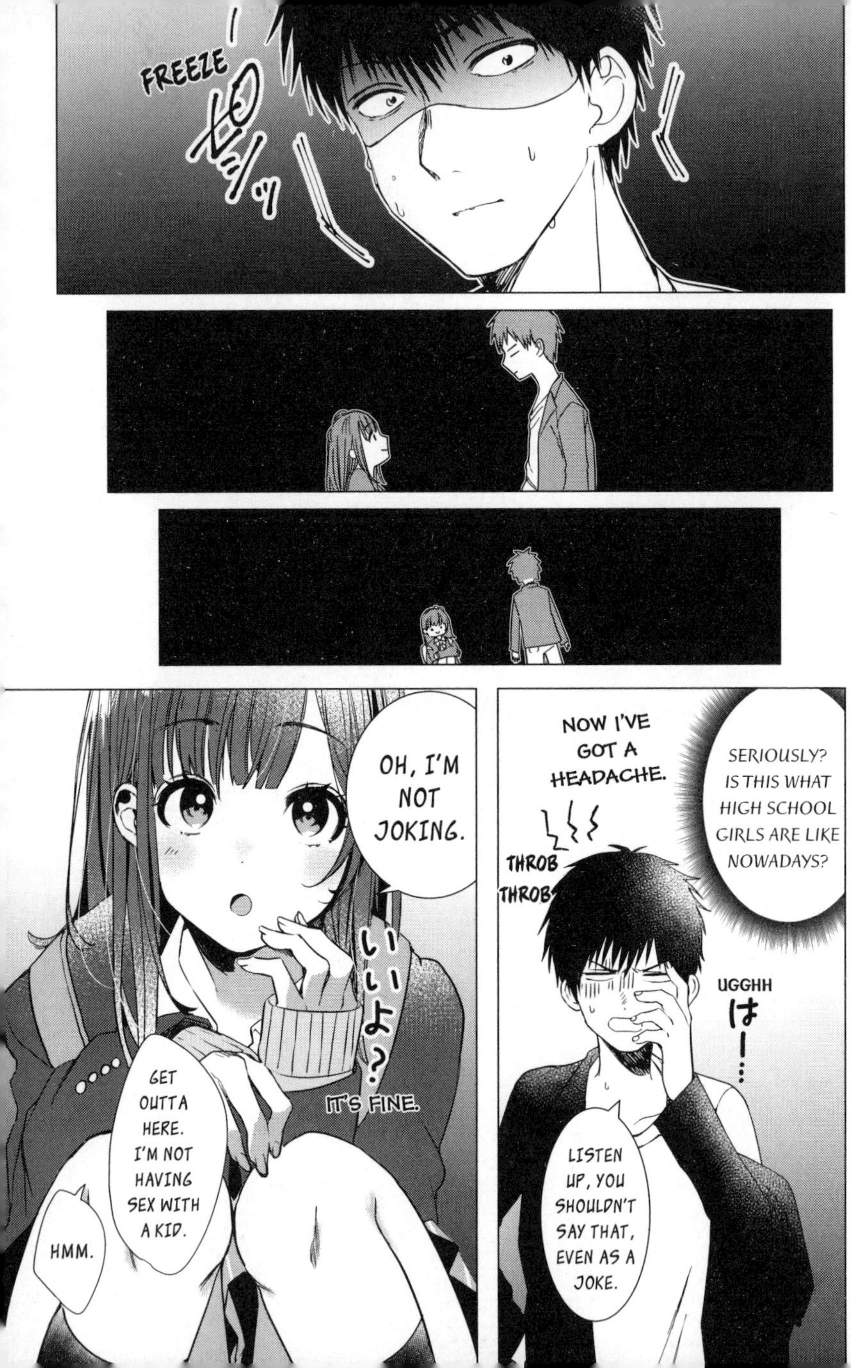
FREEZE
SERIOUSLY? IS THIS WHAT HIGH SCHOOL GIRLS ARE LIKE NOWADAYS?
NOW I'VE GOT A HEADACHE.
THROB THROB
UGGHH
はー…
LISTEN UP, YOU SHOULDN'T SAY THAT, EVEN AS A JOKE.
OH, I'M NOT JOKING.
いいよ？
IT'S FINE.
GET OUTTA HERE. I'M NOT HAVING SEX WITH A KID.
HMM.

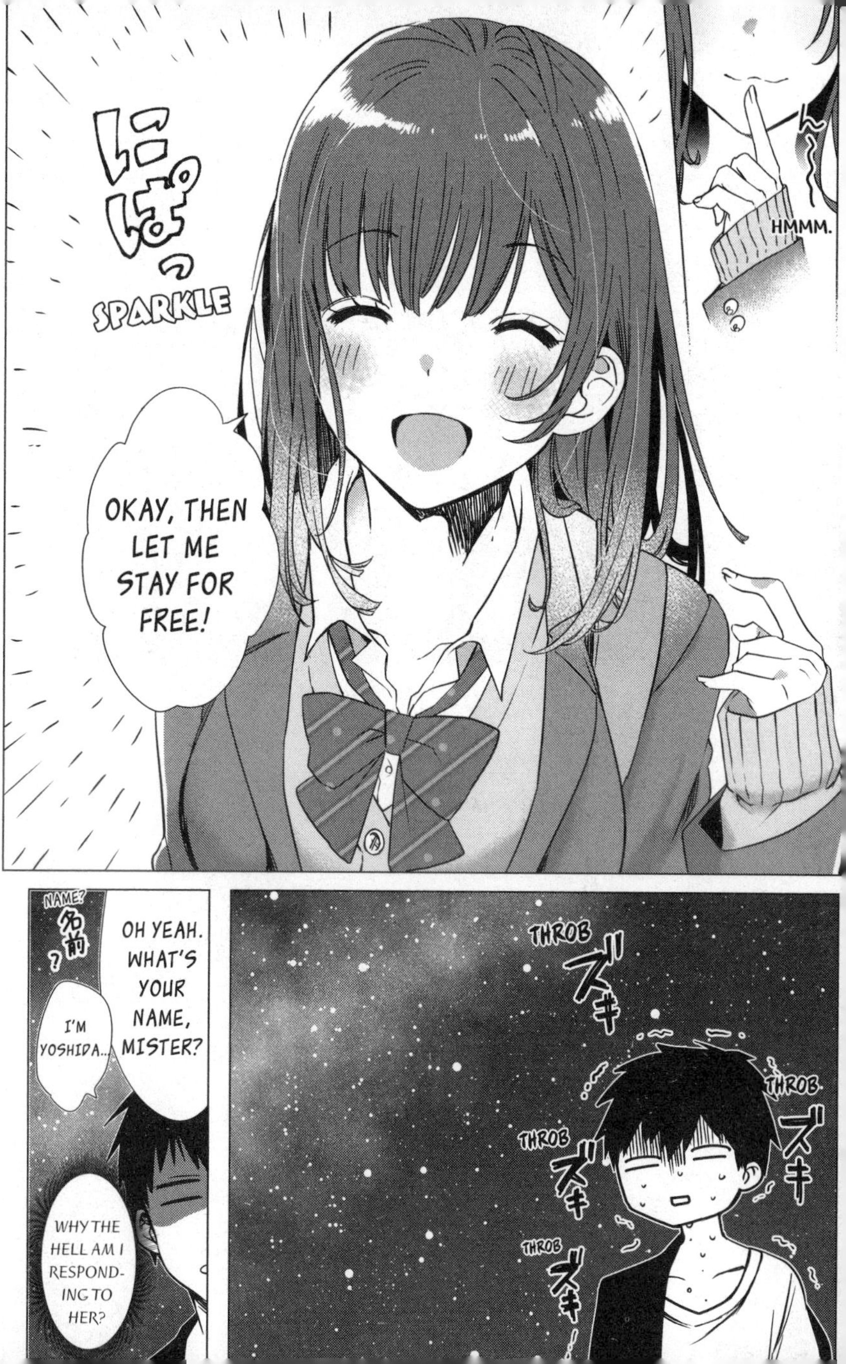

んー~
HMMM.
にぱっ
SPARKLE
OKAY, THEN LET ME STAY FOR FREE!
THROB
ズキ
THROB
ズキ
THROB
ズキ
THROB
ズキ
NAME?
名前?
OH YEAH. WHAT'S YOUR NAME, MISTER?
I'M YOSHIDA...
WHY THE HELL AM I RESPOND-ING TO HER?

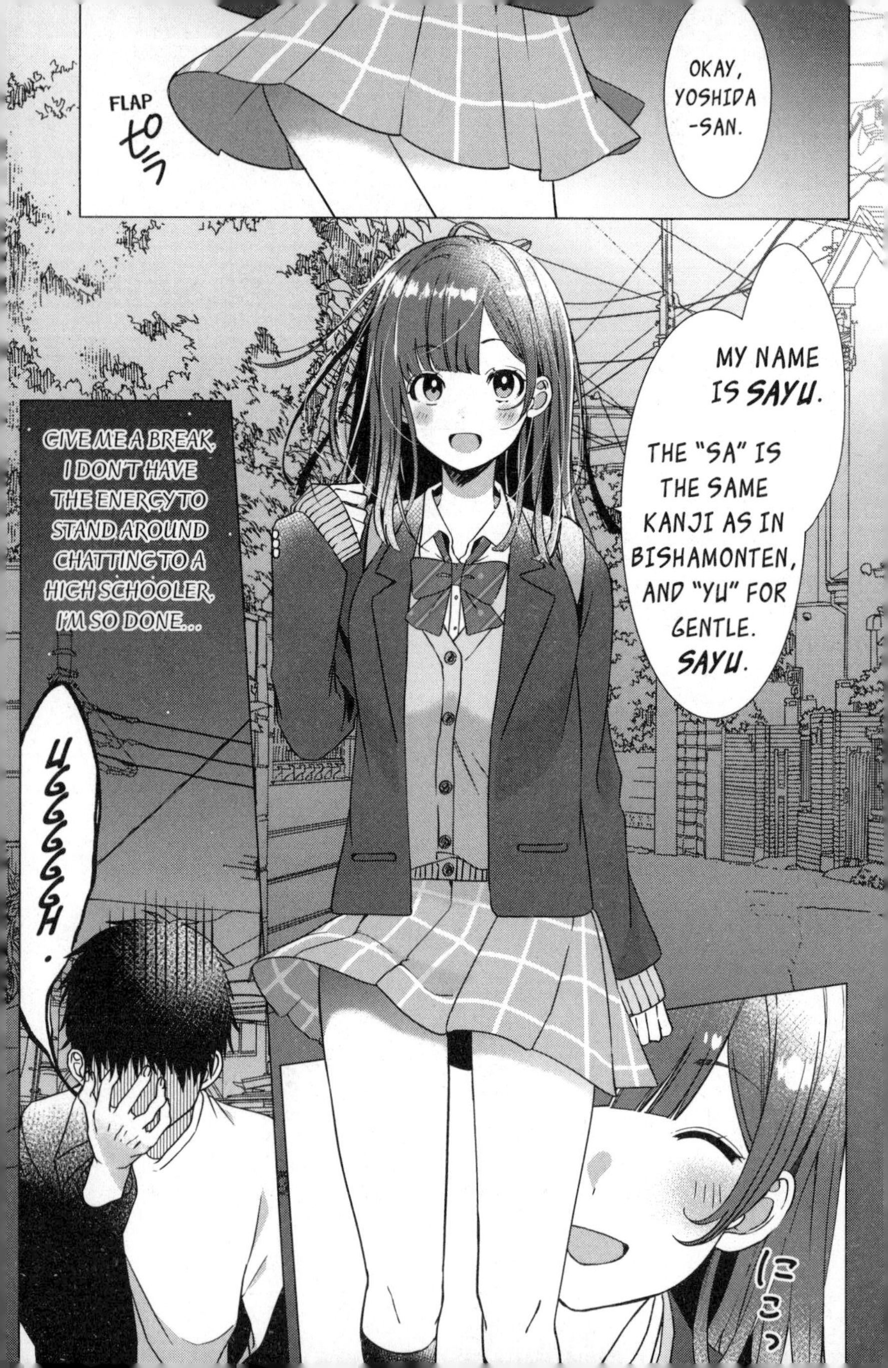
OKAY, YOSHIDA -SAN.
FLAP
MY NAME IS SAYU.
THE "SA" IS THE SAME KANJI AS IN BISHAMONTEN, AND "YU" FOR GENTLE. SAYU.
GIVE ME A BREAK, I DON'T HAVE THE ENERGY TO STAND AROUND CHATTING TO A HIGH SCHOOLER, I'M SO DONE...
UGGGGGGH.
にこっ

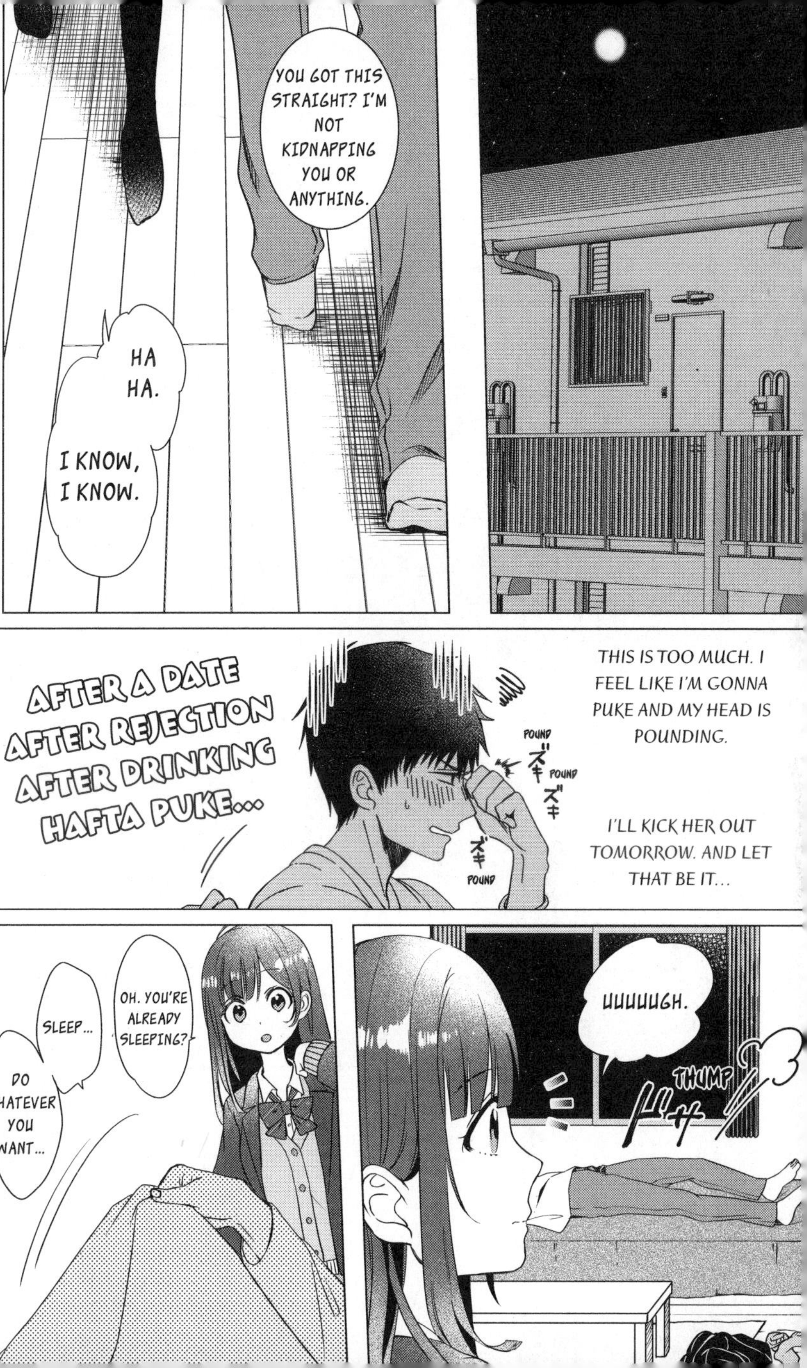
YOU GOT THIS STRAIGHT? I'M NOT KIDNAPPING YOU OR ANYTHING.
HA HA.
I KNOW, I KNOW.
THIS IS TOO MUCH. I FEEL LIKE I'M GONNA PUKE AND MY HEAD IS POUNDING.
POUND
POUND
POUND
I'LL KICK HER OUT TOMORROW. AND LET THAT BE IT...
AFTER A DATE
AFTER REJECTION
AFTER DRINKING
HAFTA PUKE...
UUUUUGH.
THUMP
OH. YOU'RE ALREADY SLEEPING?
SLEEP...
DO WHATEVER YOU WANT...

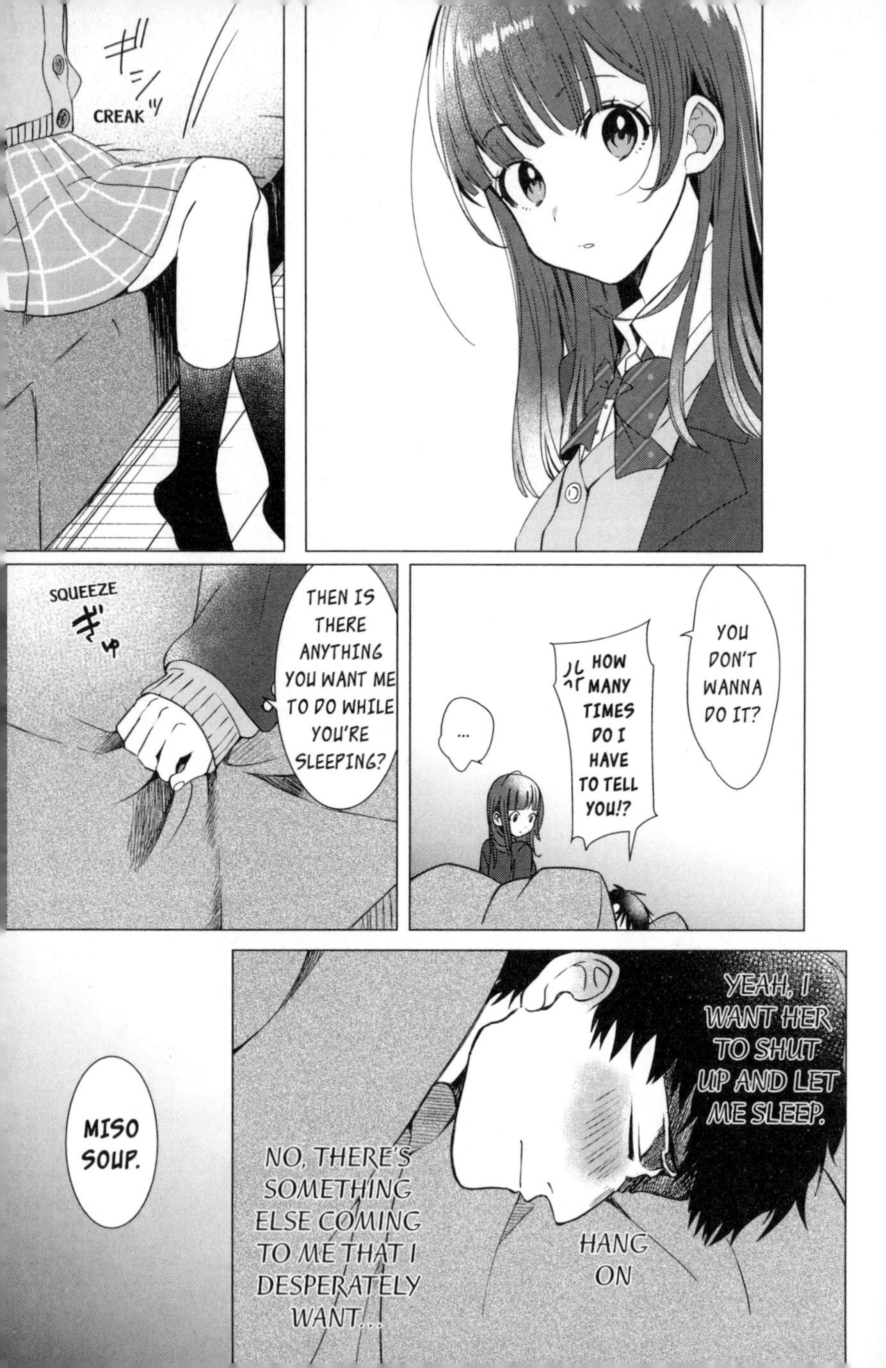
ギシッ
CREAK
YOU DON'T WANNA DO IT?
HOW MANY TIMES DO I HAVE TO TELL YOU!?
...
THEN IS THERE ANYTHING YOU WANT ME TO DO WHILE YOU'RE SLEEPING?
SQUEEZE
ぎゅ
YEAH, I WANT HER TO SHUT UP AND LET ME SLEEP.
HANG ON
NO, THERE'S SOMETHING ELSE COMING TO ME THAT I DESPERATELY WANT...
MISO SOUP.

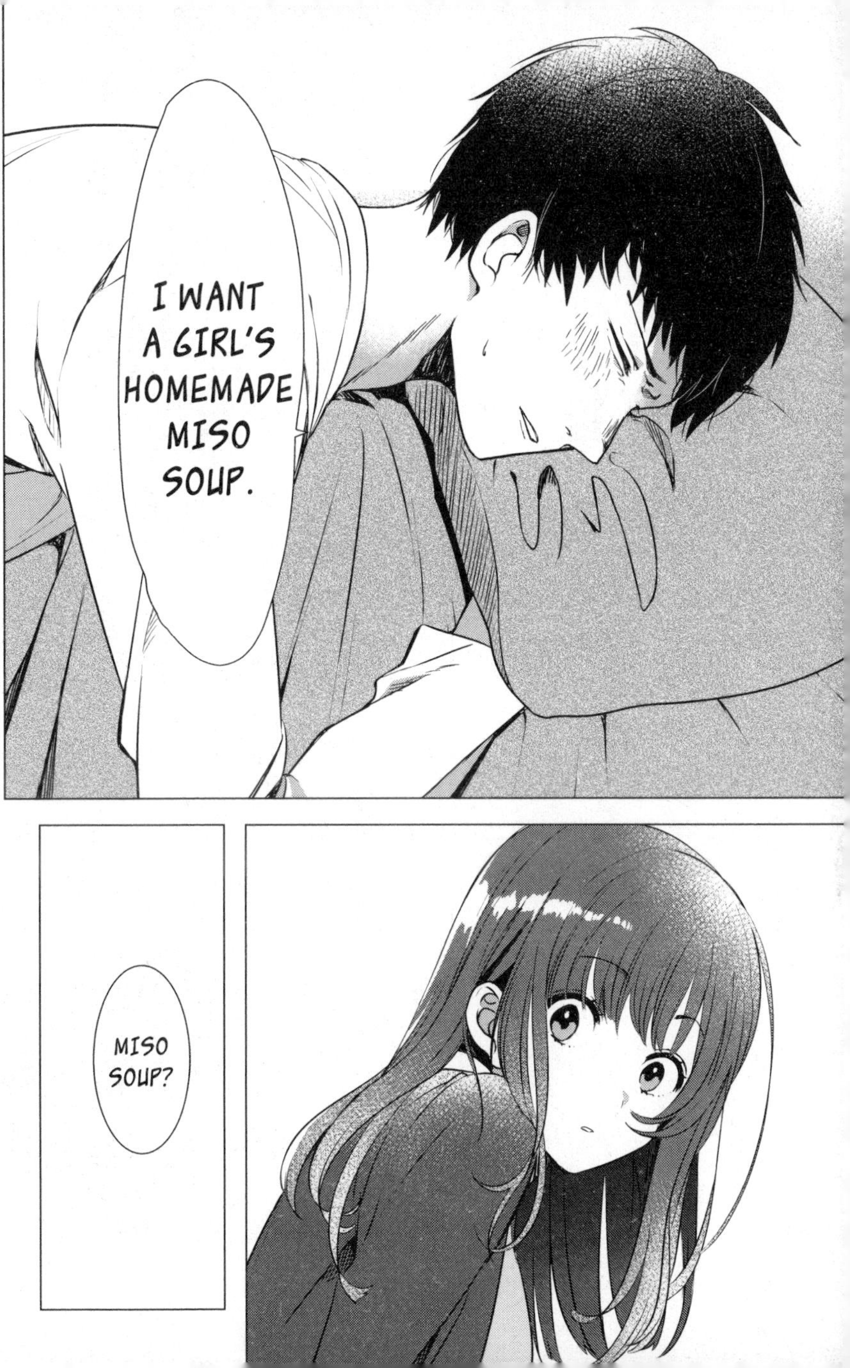
I WANT A GIRL'S HOMEMADE MISO SOUP.
MISO SOUP?

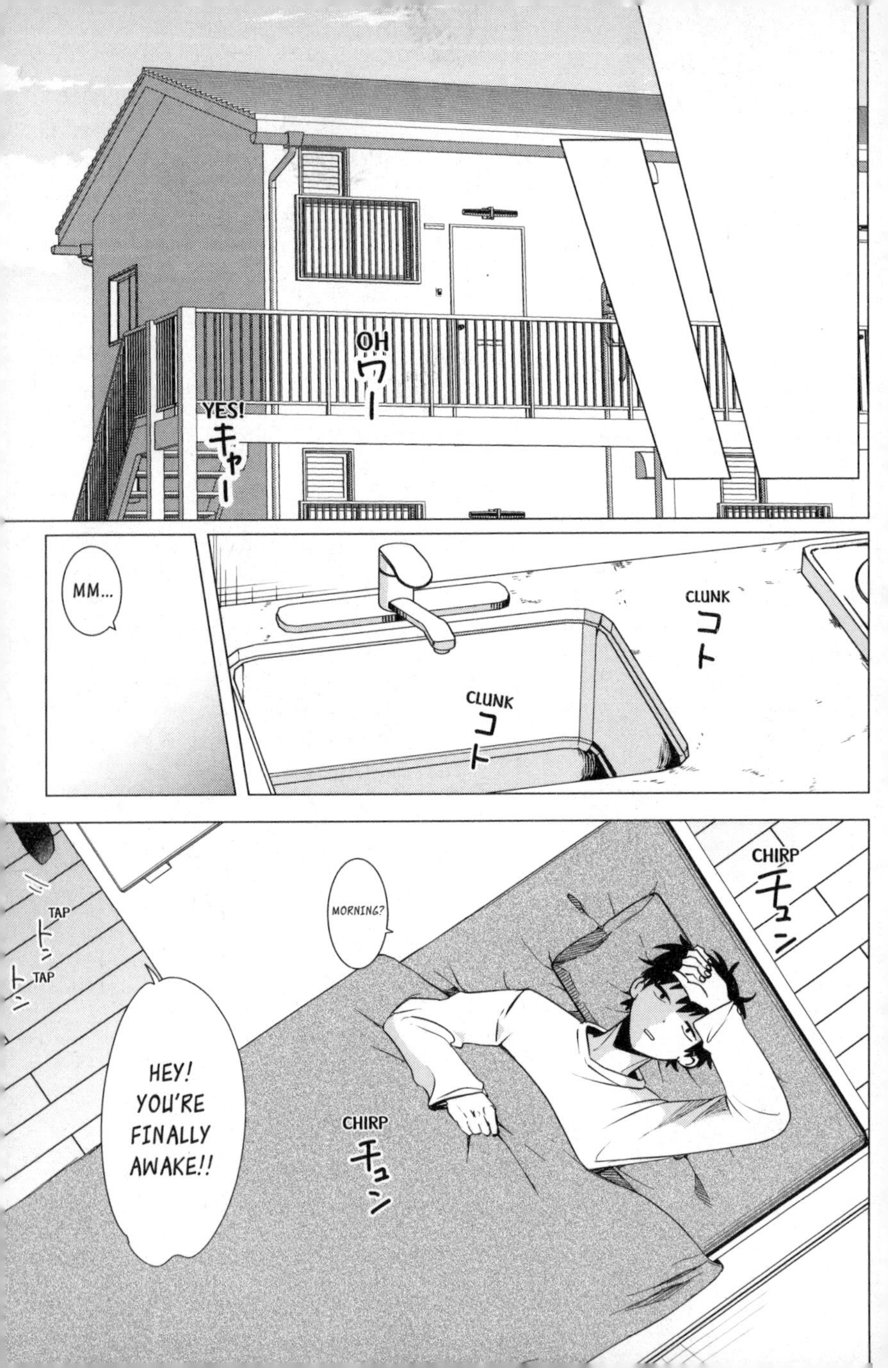

OH
ワー
YES!
キャー
CLUNK
コト
CLUNK
コト
MM...
CHIRP
チュン
MORNING?
CHIRP
チュン
HEY! YOU'RE FINALLY AWAKE!!
TAP
TAP

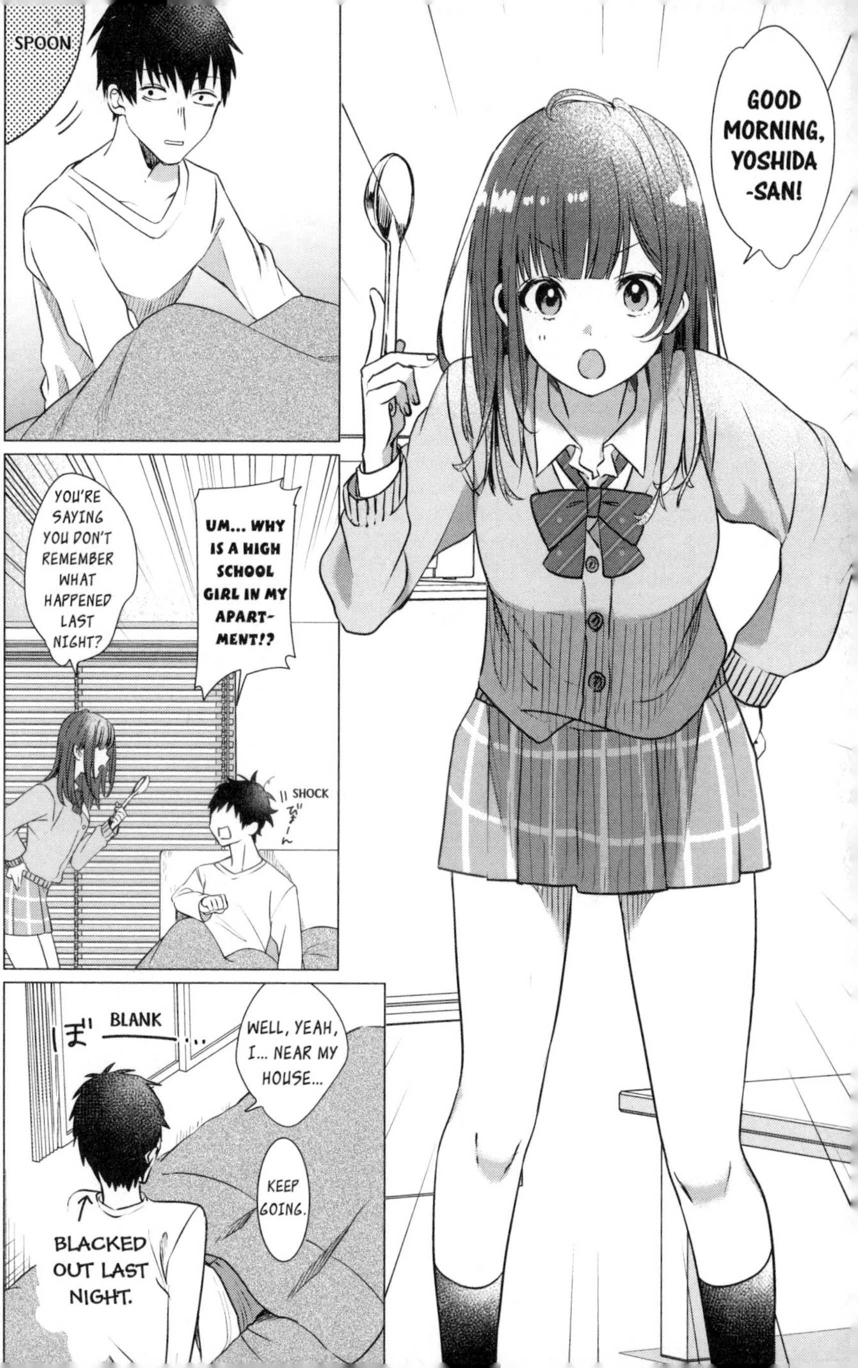
GOOD MORNING, YOSHIDA -SAN!
SPOON
UM... WHY IS A HIGH SCHOOL GIRL IN MY APART- MENT!?
YOU'RE SAYING YOU DON'T REMEMBER WHAT HAPPENED LAST NIGHT?
SHOCK
BLANK
WELL, YEAH, I... NEAR MY HOUSE...
KEEP GOING.
BLACKED OUT LAST NIGHT.

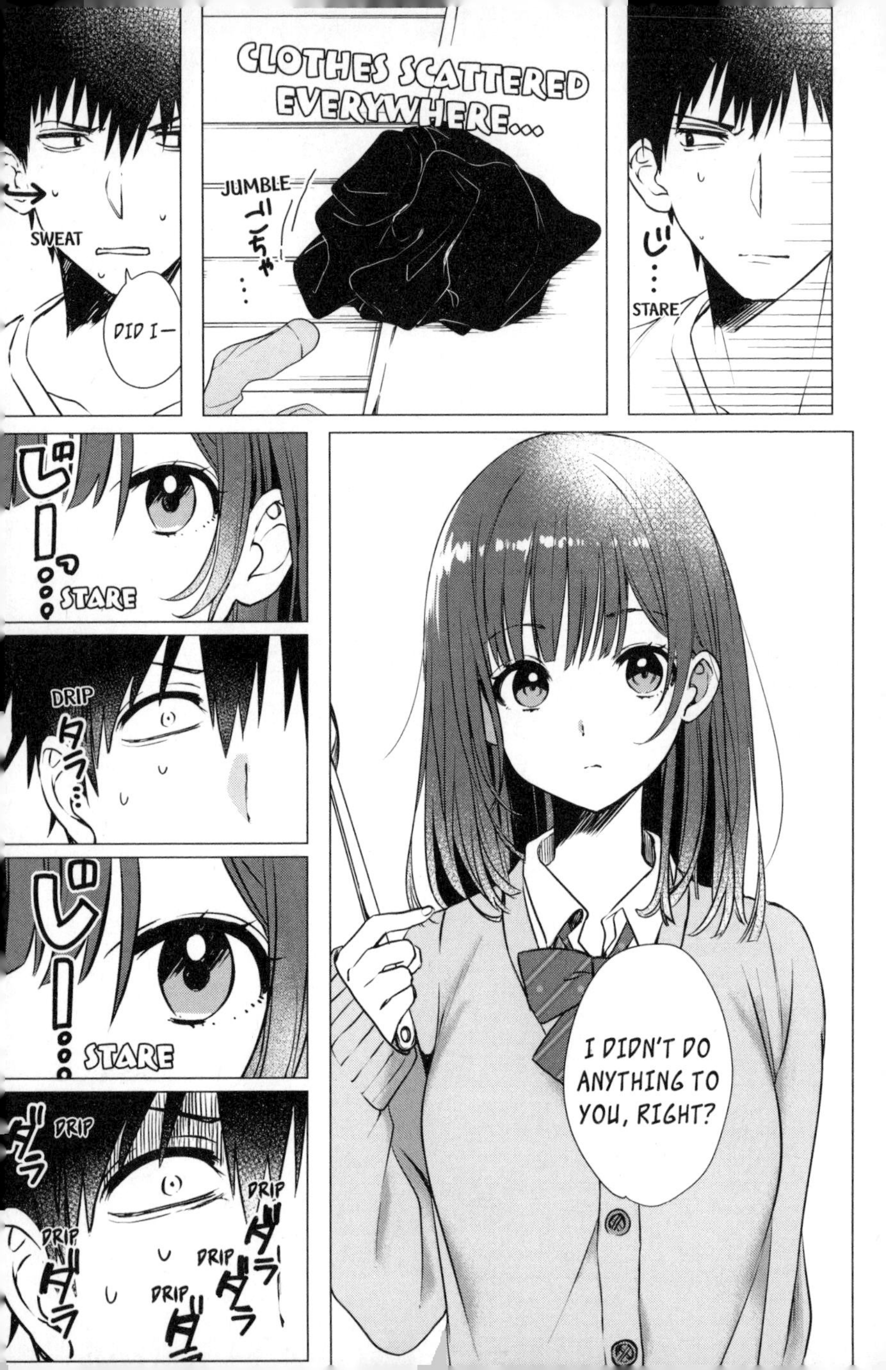

じ…
STARE
CLOTHES SCATTERED EVERYWHERE...
JUMBLE
ごちゃ…
SWEAT
DID I—
I DIDN'T DO ANYTHING TO YOU, RIGHT?
じー…
STARE
DRIP
タラ…
じー…
STARE
DRIP
ダラ
DRIP
ダラ
DRIP
ダラ
DRIP
ダラ
DRIP
ダ

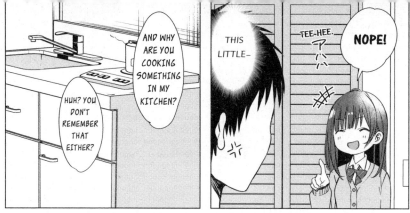

NOPE!
TEE-HEE.
アハハ
THIS LITTLE-
AND WHY ARE YOU COOKING SOMETHING IN MY KITCHEN?
HUH? YOU DON'T REMEMBER THAT EITHER?
STEAM
ほか
STEAM
ほか
MISO SOUP!
YESTERDAY YOU SAID, "MAKE ME MISO SOUP EVERY DAY!"
I WHAT!? NO I DIDN'T!
SOUNDS LIKE A PROPOSAL!
AHAHA.
ANYWAY, DRINK UP.

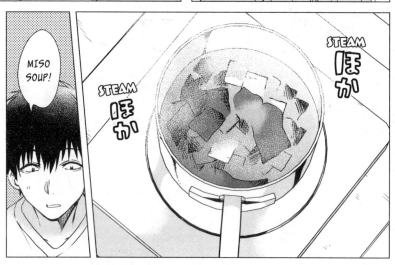

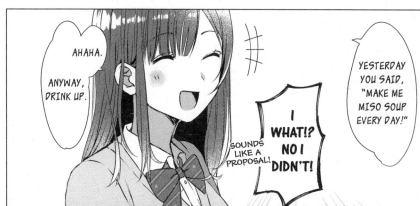

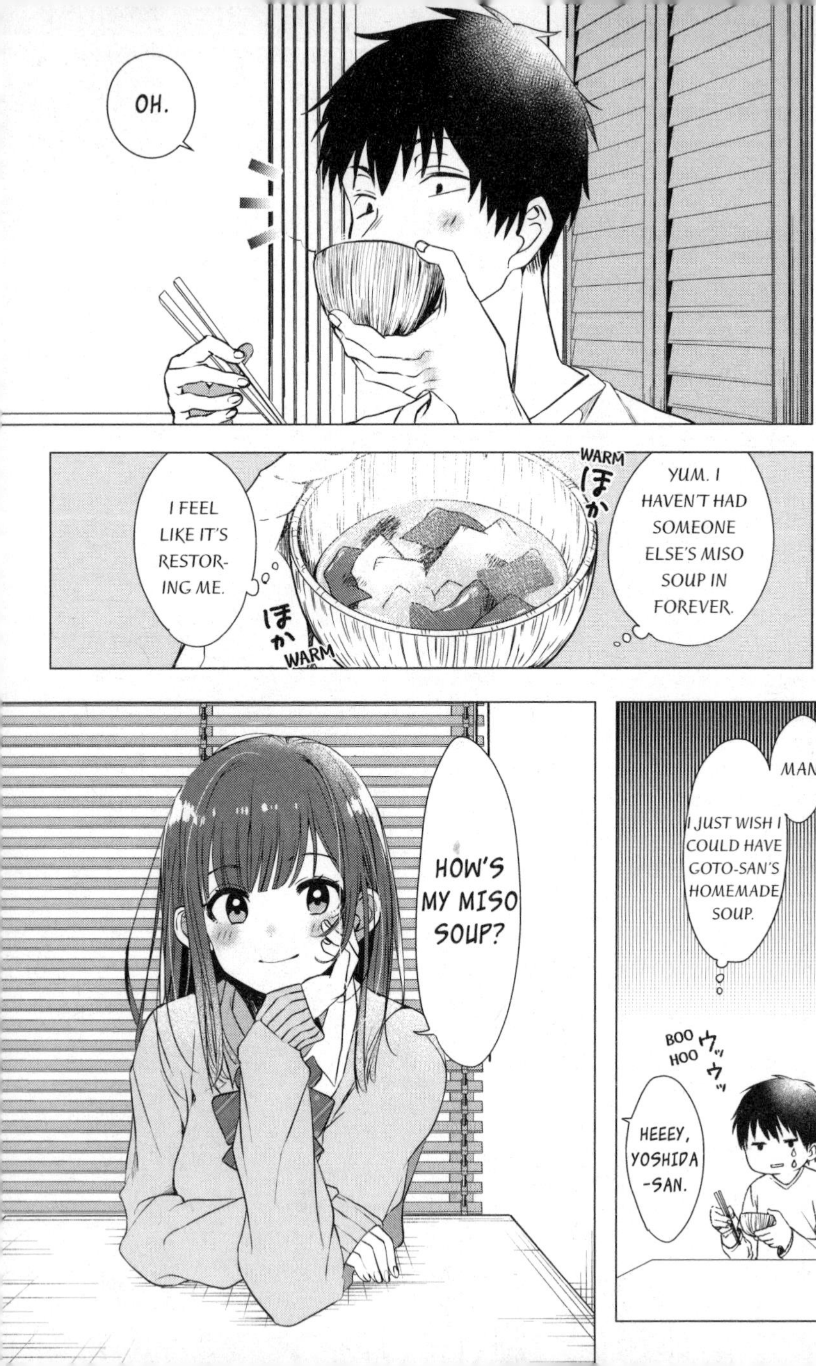
OH.
WARM
ほか
YUM. I HAVEN'T HAD SOMEONE ELSE'S MISO SOUP IN FOREVER.
I FEEL LIKE IT'S RESTOR-ING ME.
ほか
WARM
MAN.
I JUST WISH I COULD HAVE GOTO-SAN'S HOMEMADE SOUP.
BOO HOO
ウッウッ
HEEEY, YOSHIDA-SAN.
HOW'S MY MISO SOUP?

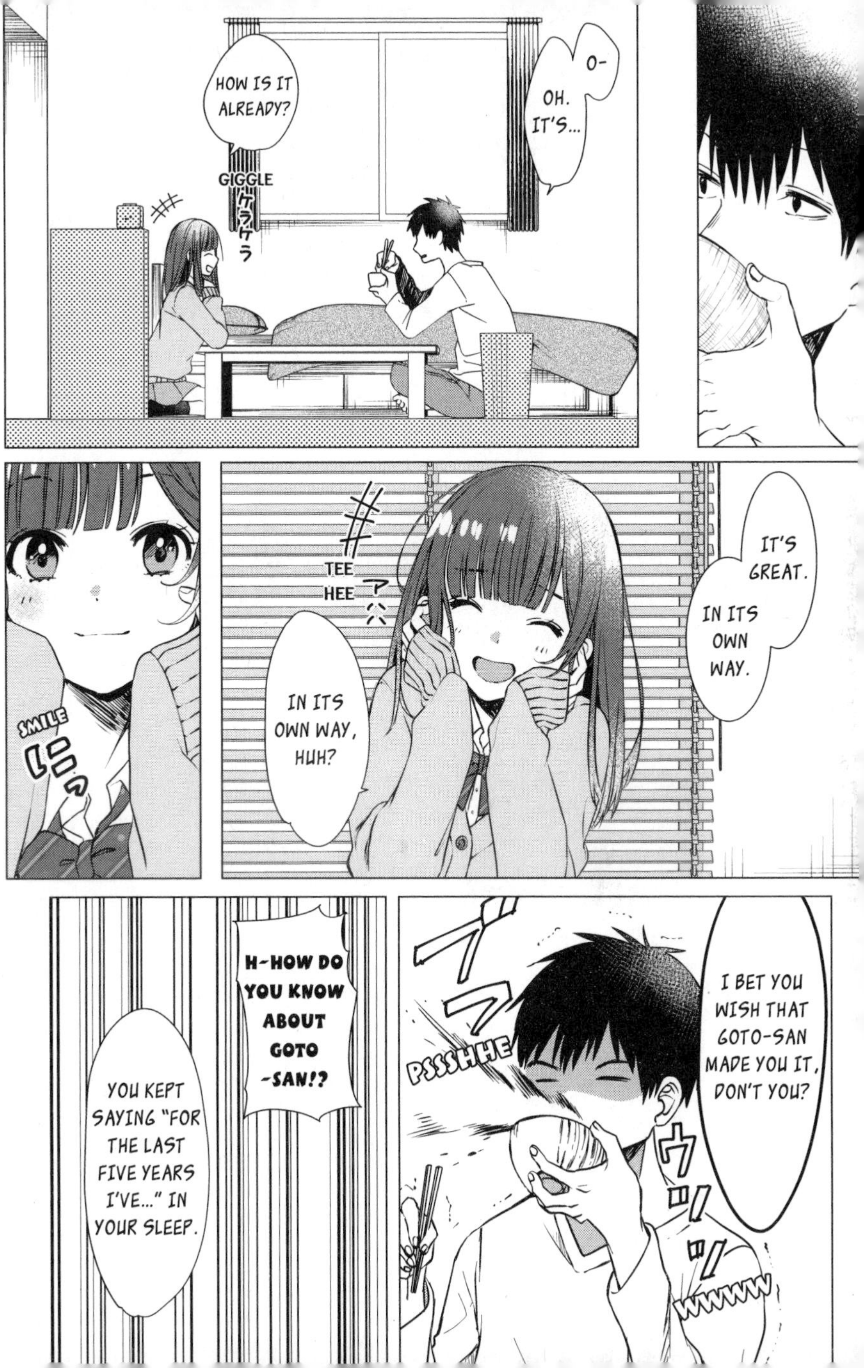
O-
OH. IT'S...
HOW IS IT ALREADY?
GIGGLE
ケラケラ
IT'S GREAT.
IN ITS OWN WAY.
TEE HEE
アハ
IN ITS OWN WAY, HUH?
SMILE
I BET YOU WISH THAT GOTO-SAN MADE YOU IT, DON'T YOU?
PSSSHHE
WWWW
H-HOW DO YOU KNOW ABOUT GOTO-SAN!?
YOU KEPT SAYING "FOR THE LAST FIVE YEARS I'VE..." IN YOUR SLEEP.

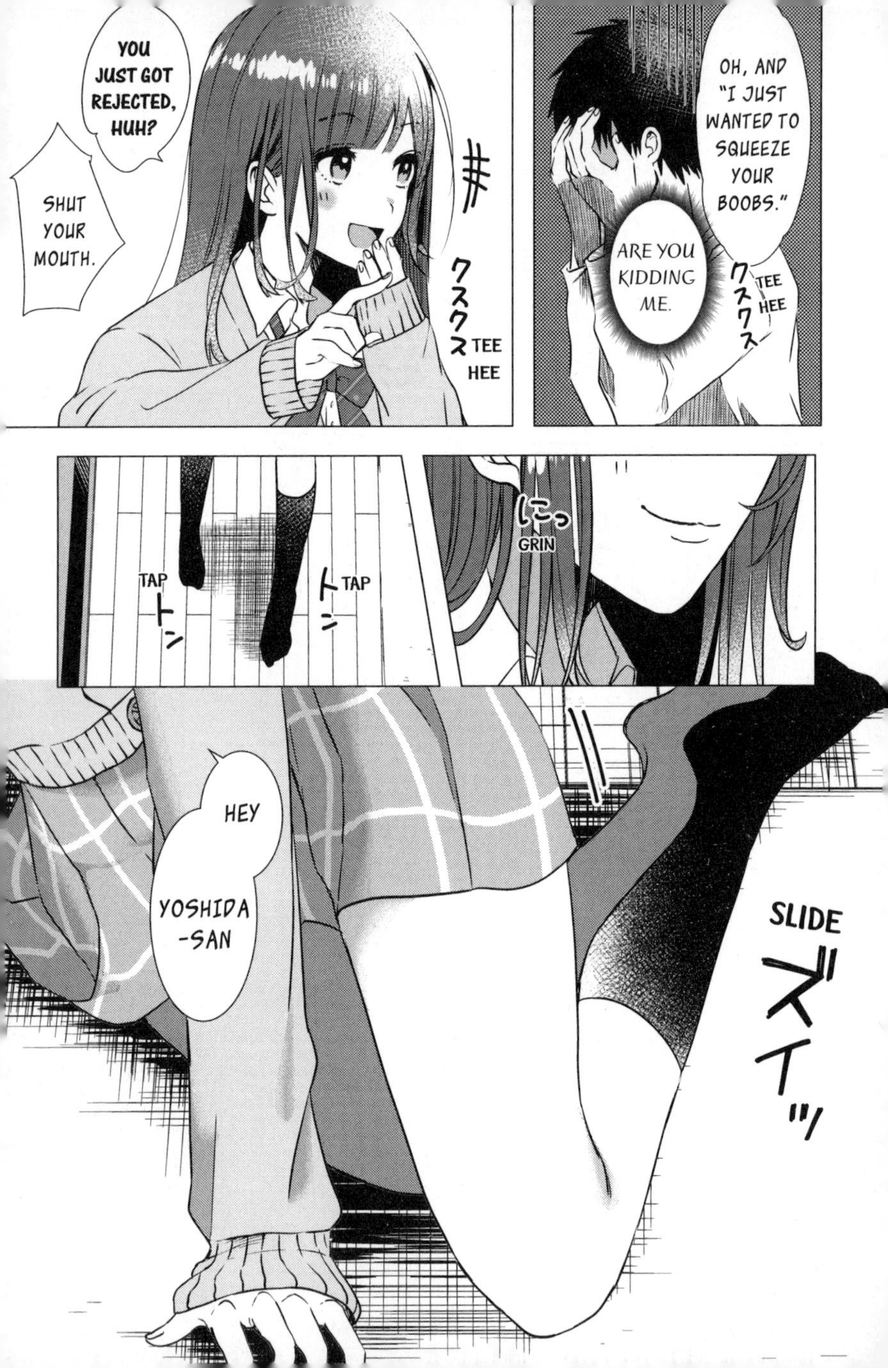
OH, AND "I JUST WANTED TO SQUEEZE YOUR BOOBS."
ARE YOU KIDDING ME.
クスクス TEE HEE
YOU JUST GOT REJECTED, HUH?
SHUT YOUR MOUTH.
クスクス TEE HEE
にっ GRIN
トン TAP
トン TAP
HEY
YOSHIDA-SAN
SLIDE
ズイッ

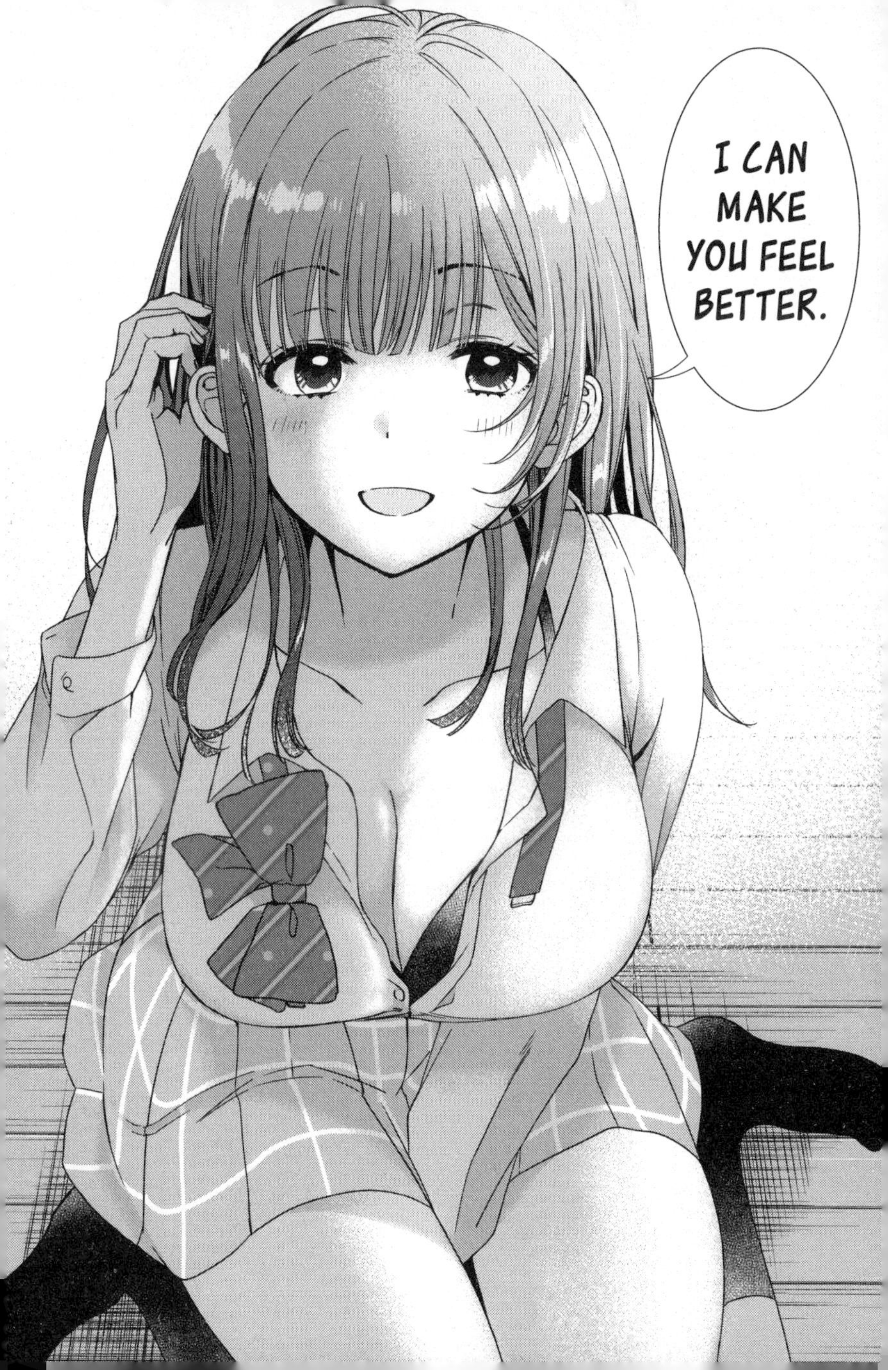
I CAN MAKE YOU FEEL BETTER.

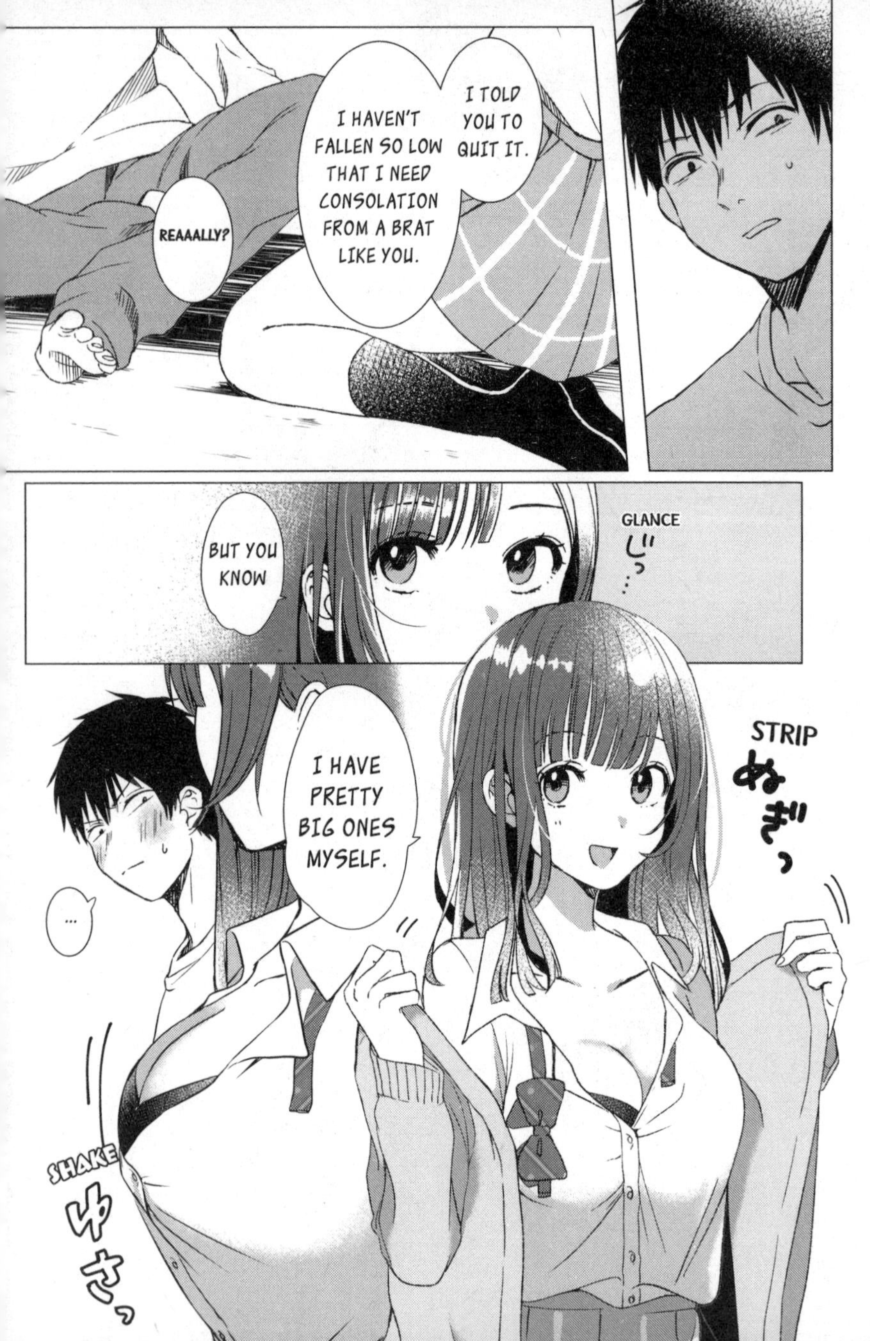
I TOLD YOU TO QUIT IT.
I HAVEN'T FALLEN SO LOW THAT I NEED CONSOLATION FROM A BRAT LIKE YOU.
REAAALLY?
GLANCE
じっ…
BUT YOU KNOW
STRIP
ぬぎっ
I HAVE PRETTY BIG ONES MYSELF.
...
SHAKE
ゆさっ

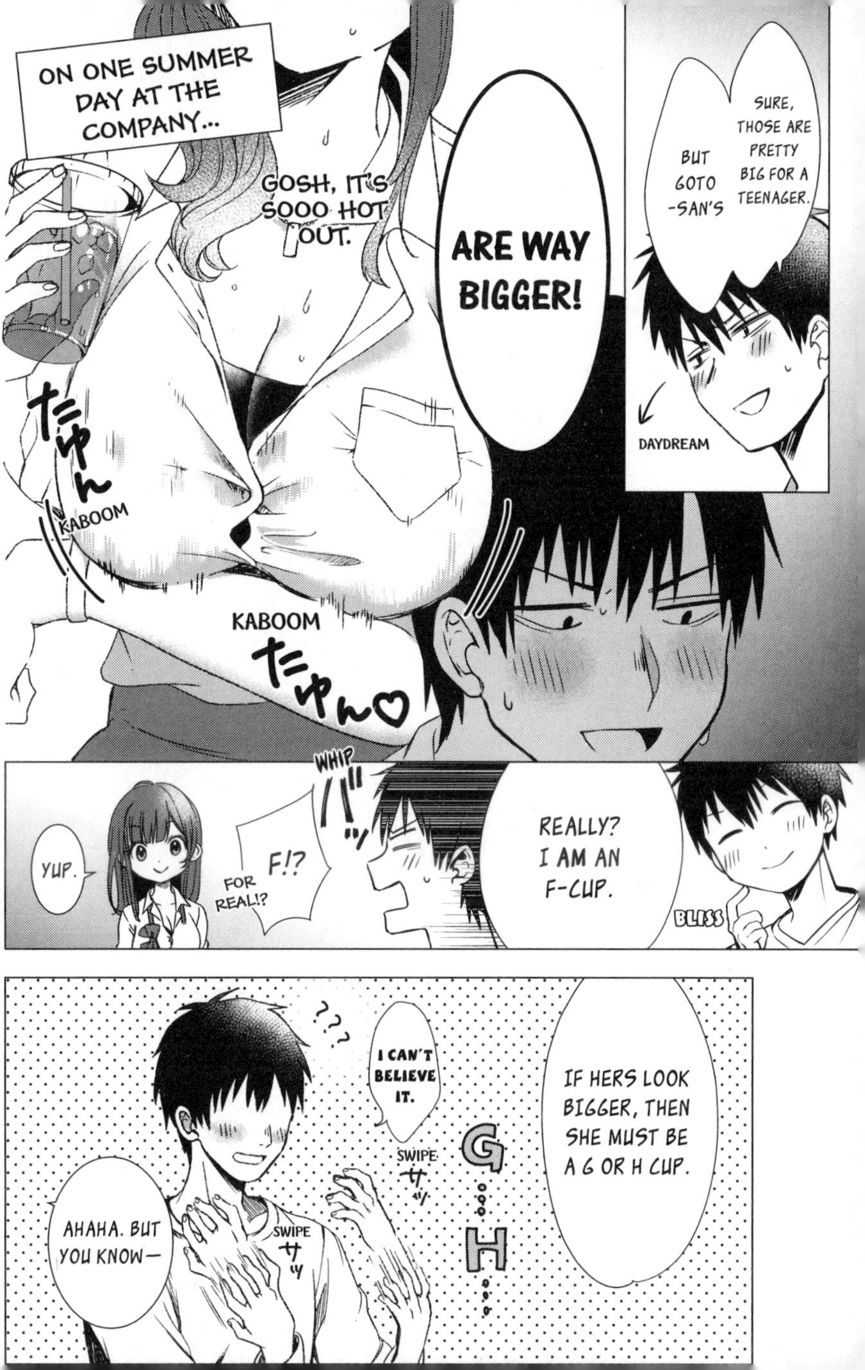

SURE, THOSE ARE PRETTY BIG FOR A TEENAGER.
BUT GOTO-SAN'S
DAYDREAM
ARE WAY BIGGER!
ON ONE SUMMER DAY AT THE COMPANY...
GOSH, IT'S SOOO HOT OUT.
たゆん
KABOOM
KABOOM
たゆん♡
REALLY? I AM AN F-CUP.
BLISS
WHIP
バッ
F!?
FOR REAL!?
YUP.
IF HERS LOOK BIGGER, THEN SHE MUST BE A G OR H CUP.
G...
H...
I CAN'T BELIEVE IT.
???
SWIPE
サッ
AHAHA. BUT YOU KNOW—
SWIPE
サッ

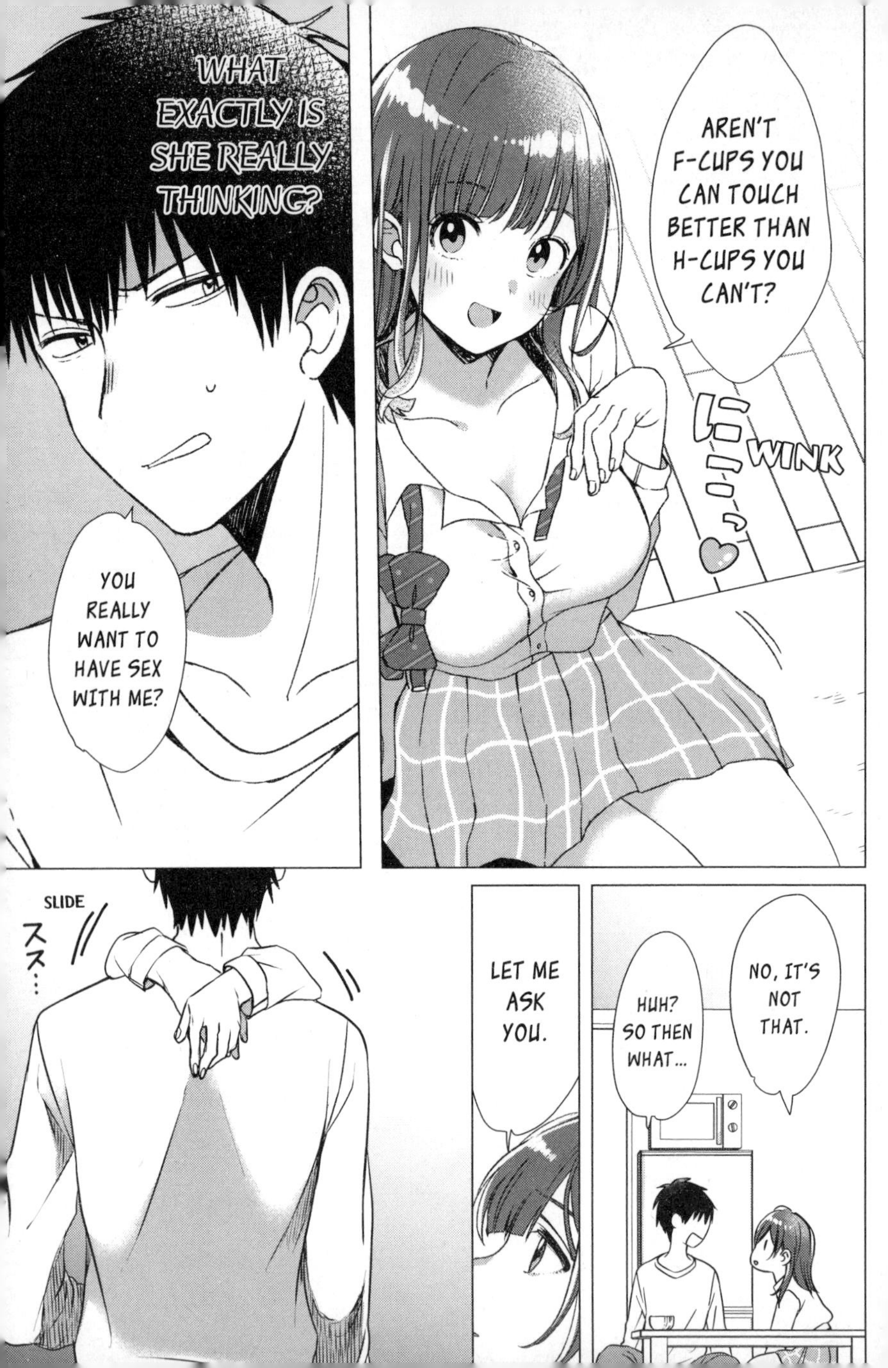
AREN'T F-CUPS YOU CAN TOUCH BETTER THAN H-CUPS YOU CAN'T?
WINK
WHAT EXACTLY IS SHE REALLY THINKING?
YOU REALLY WANT TO HAVE SEX WITH ME?
NO, IT'S NOT THAT.
HUH? SO THEN WHAT...
LET ME ASK YOU.
SLIDE
スス…

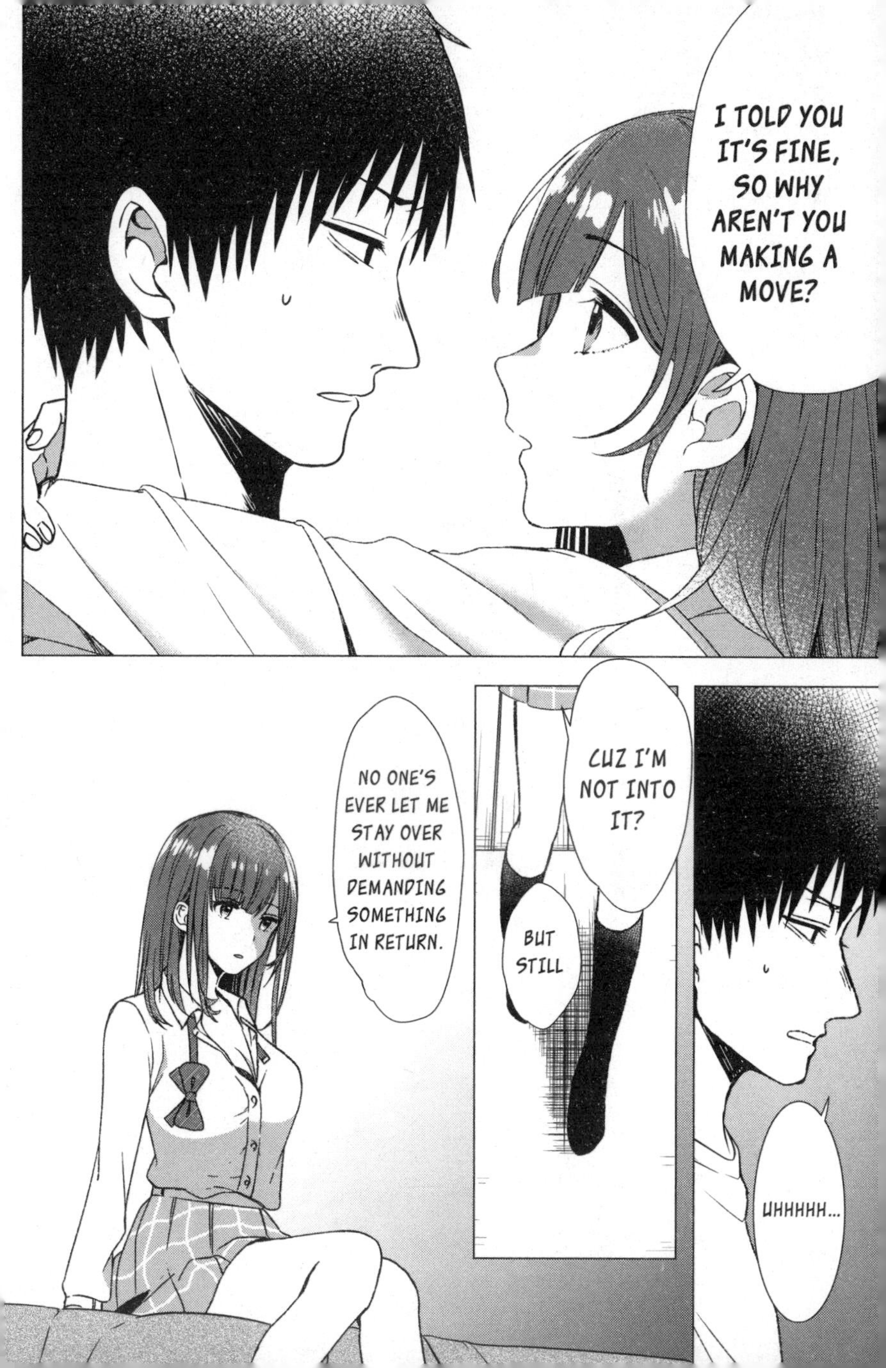
I TOLD YOU IT'S FINE, SO WHY AREN'T YOU MAKING A MOVE?
UHHHHH...
CUZ I'M NOT INTO IT?
BUT STILL
NO ONE'S EVER LET ME STAY OVER WITHOUT DEMANDING SOMETHING IN RETURN.

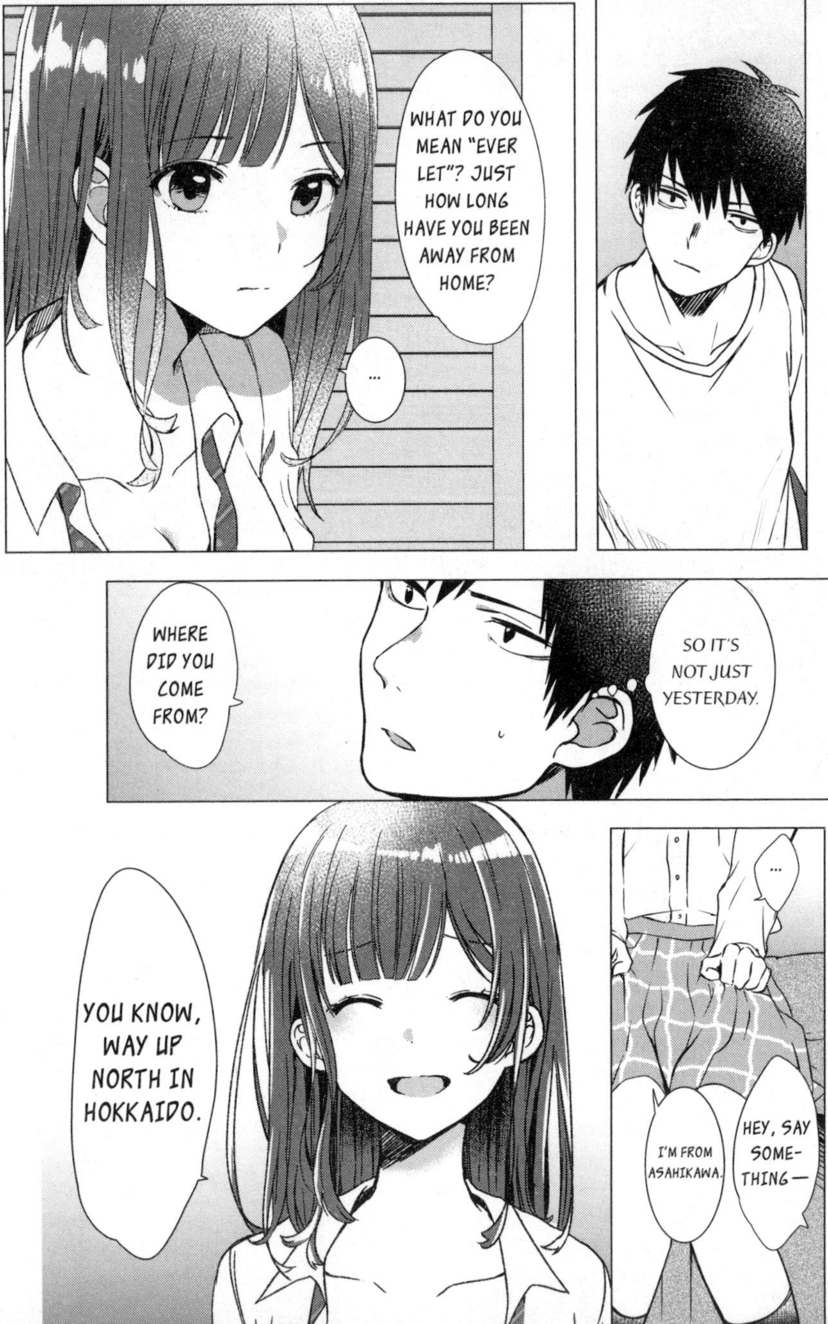
WHAT DO YOU MEAN "EVER LET"? JUST HOW LONG HAVE YOU BEEN AWAY FROM HOME?
...
SO IT'S NOT JUST YESTERDAY.
WHERE DID YOU COME FROM?
...
HEY, SAY SOME-THING—
I'M FROM ASAHIKAWA.
YOU KNOW, WAY UP NORTH IN HOKKAIDO.

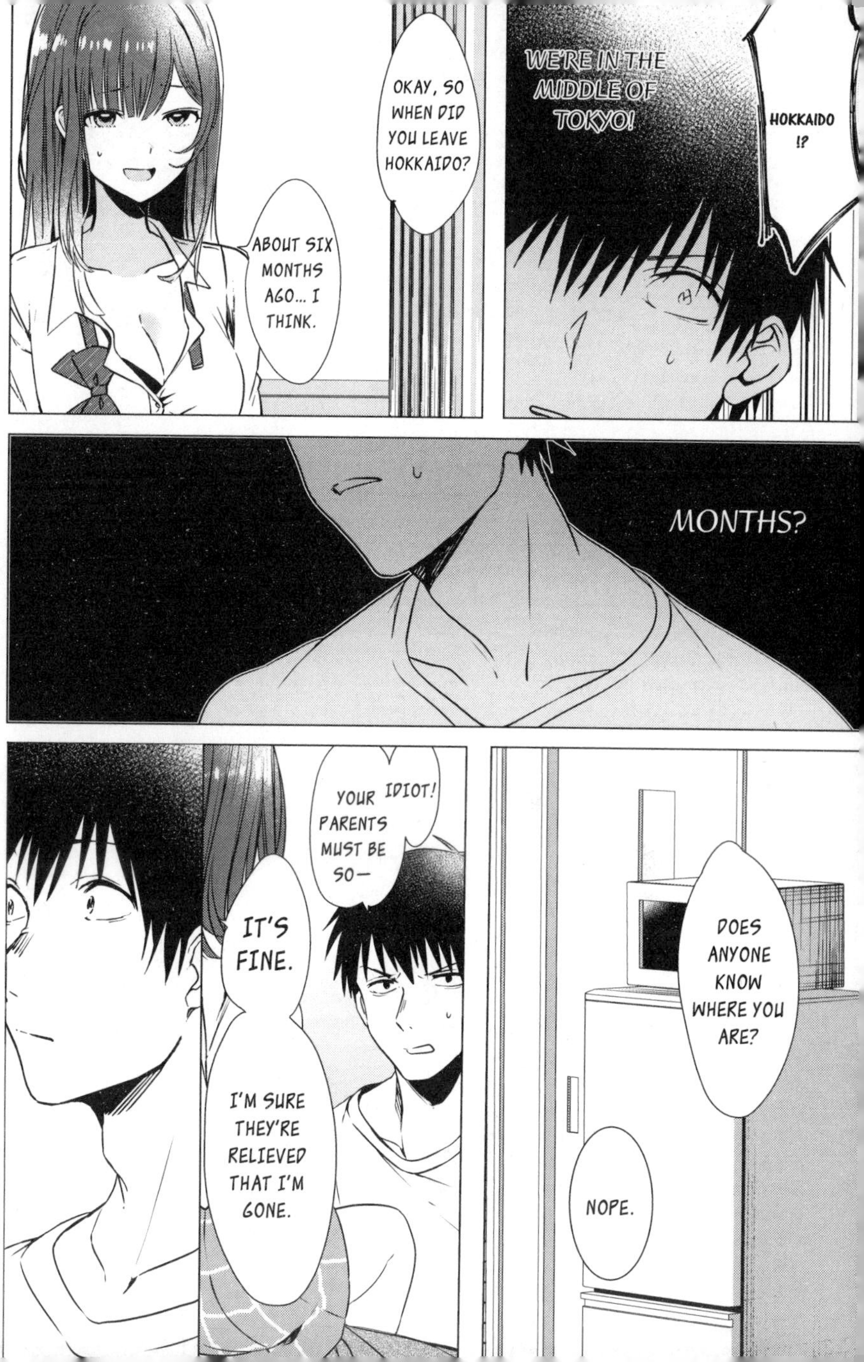
HOKKAIDO!?
WE'RE IN THE MIDDLE OF TOKYO!
OKAY, SO WHEN DID YOU LEAVE HOKKAIDO?
ABOUT SIX MONTHS AGO... I THINK.
MONTHS?
DOES ANYONE KNOW WHERE YOU ARE?
NOPE.
YOUR PARENTS MUST BE SO—
IDIOT!
IT'S FINE.
I'M SURE THEY'RE RELIEVED THAT I'M GONE.

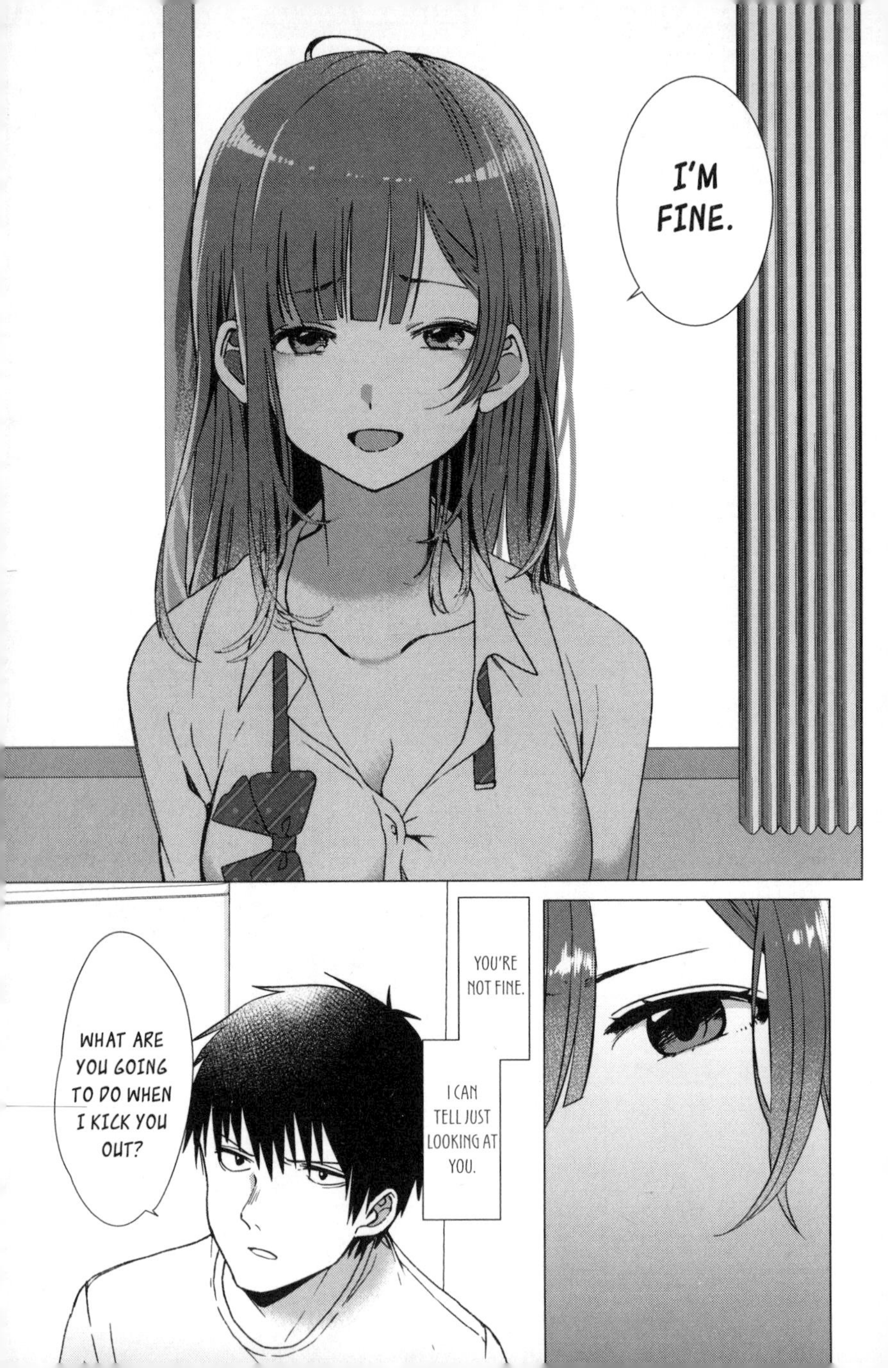
I'M FINE.
YOU'RE NOT FINE.
I CAN TELL JUST LOOKING AT YOU.
WHAT ARE YOU GOING TO DO WHEN I KICK YOU OUT?

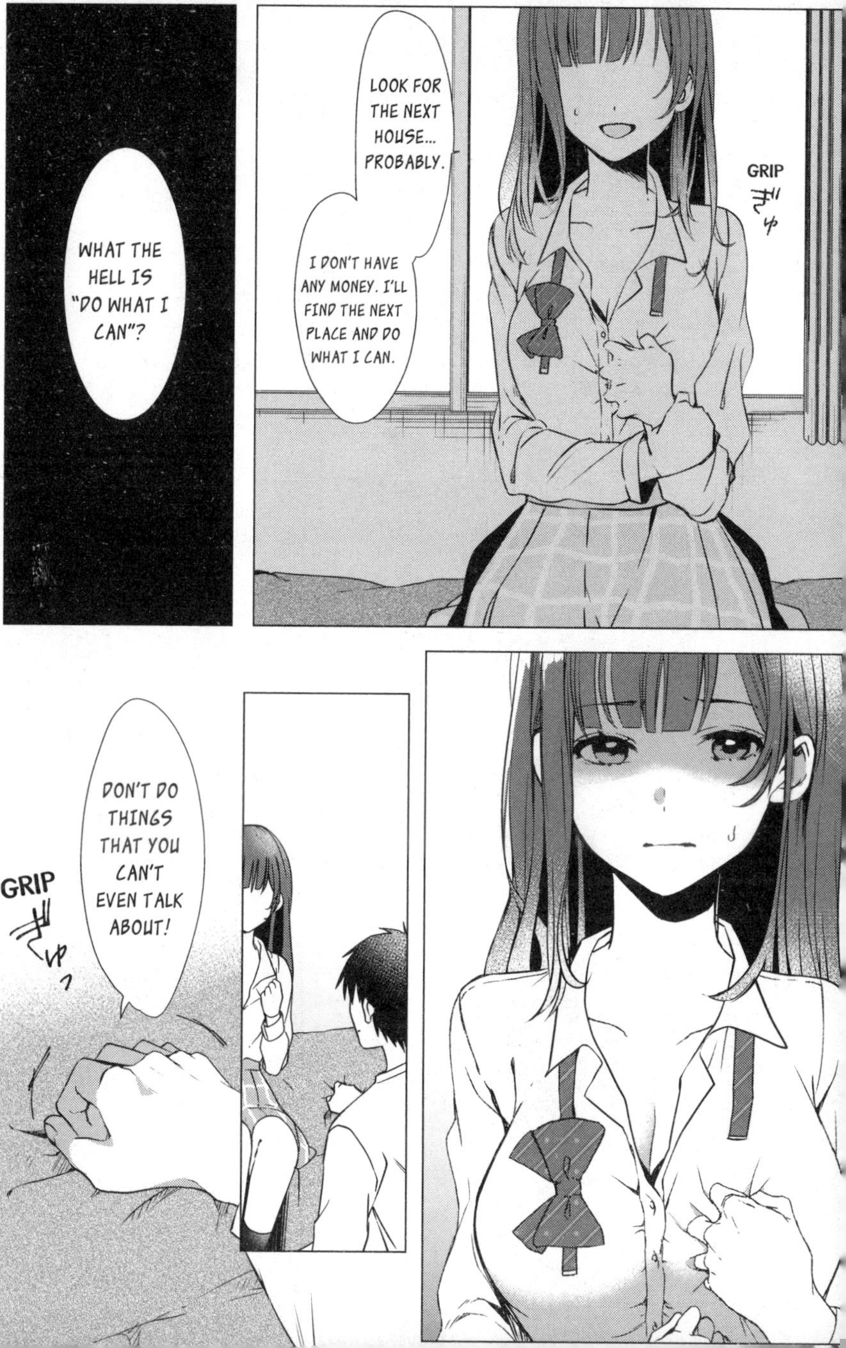
LOOK FOR THE NEXT HOUSE... PROBABLY.
I DON'T HAVE ANY MONEY. I'LL FIND THE NEXT PLACE AND DO WHAT I CAN.
GRIP
ぎゅ
WHAT THE HELL IS "DO WHAT I CAN"?
DON'T DO THINGS THAT YOU CAN'T EVEN TALK ABOUT!
GRIP
ぎゅっ

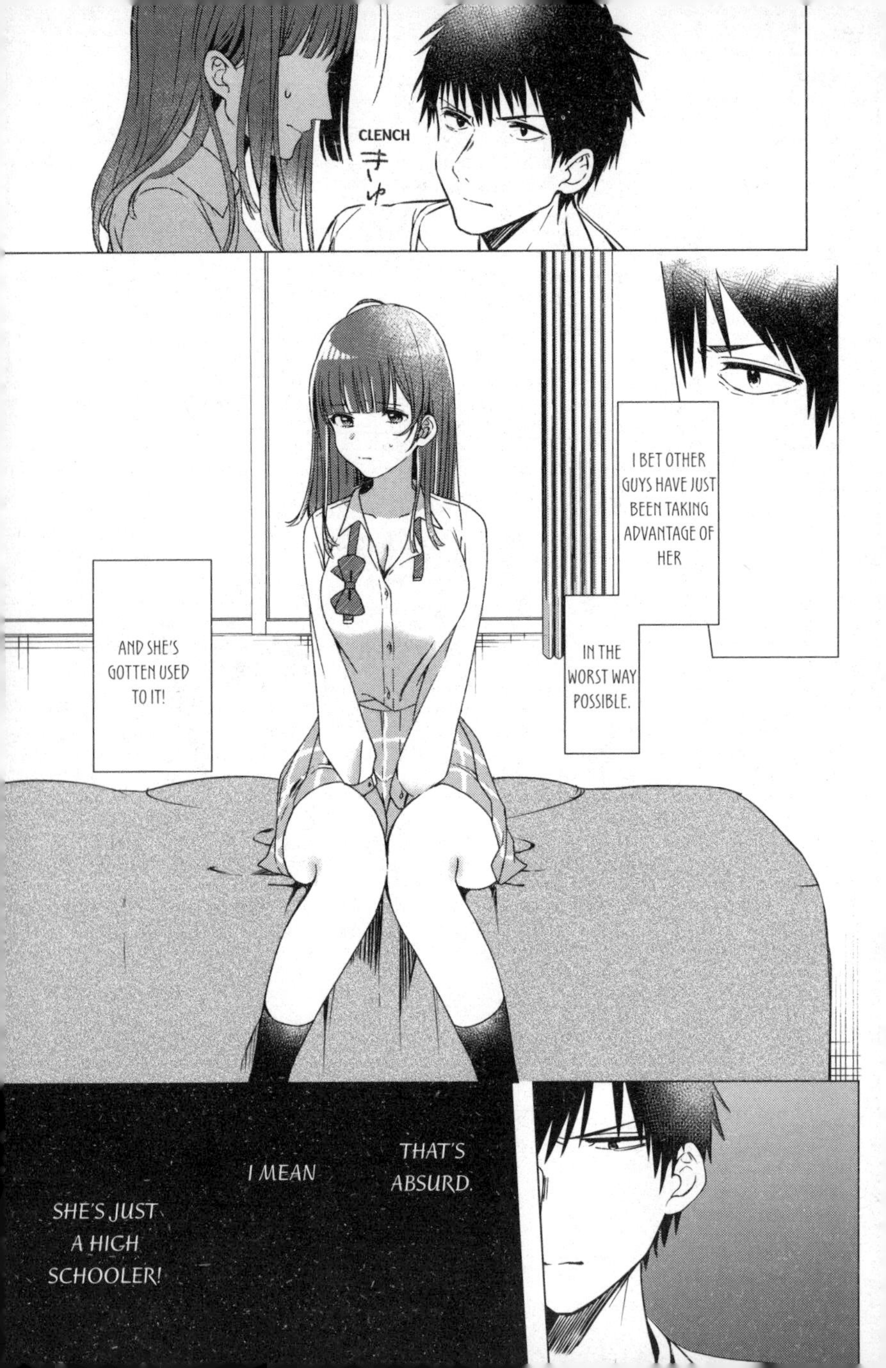
CLENCH
きゅ
I BET OTHER GUYS HAVE JUST BEEN TAKING ADVANTAGE OF HER
IN THE WORST WAY POSSIBLE.
AND SHE'S GOTTEN USED TO IT!
THAT'S ABSURD.
I MEAN
SHE'S JUST A HIGH SCHOOLER!

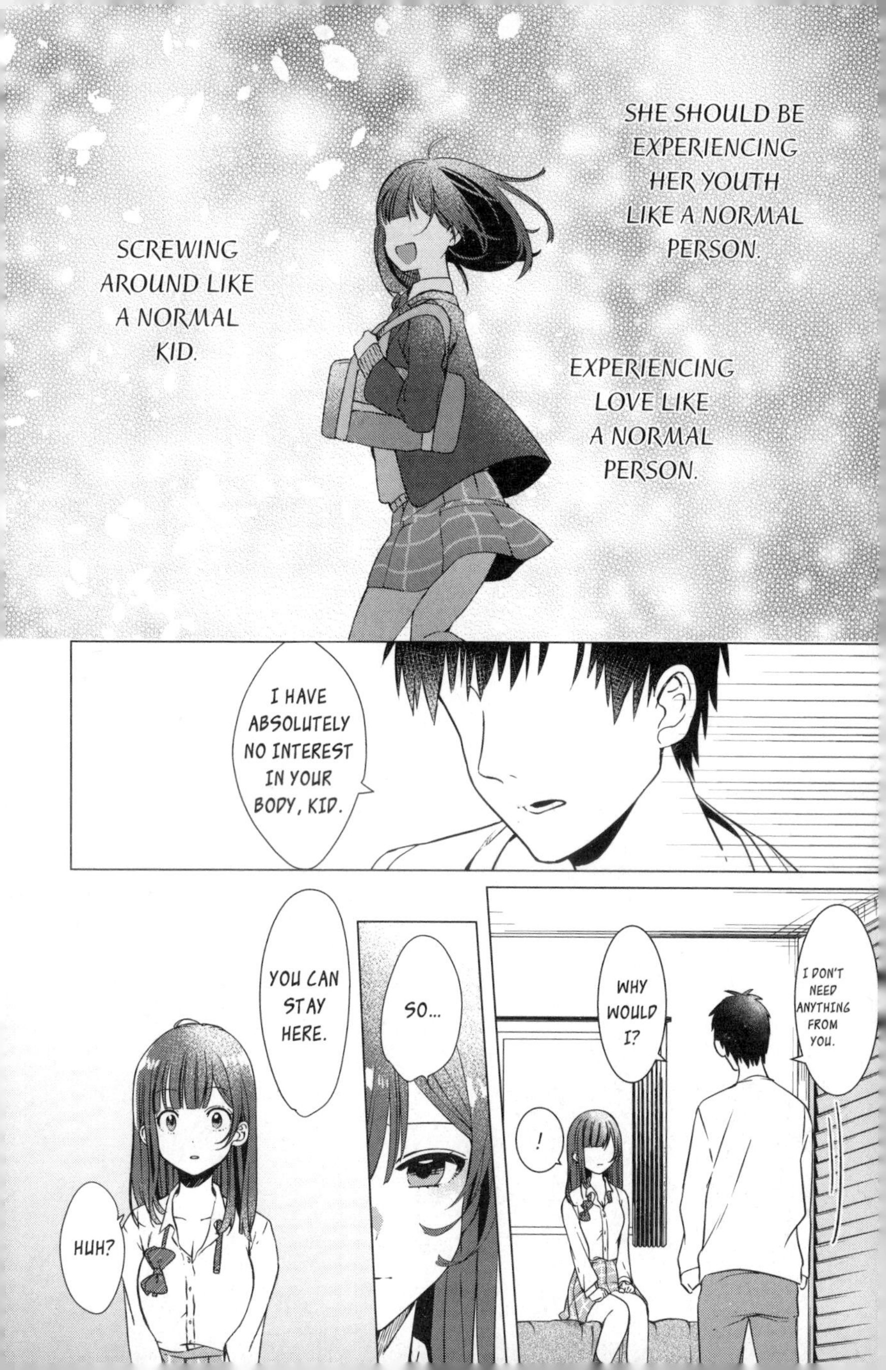
SHE SHOULD BE EXPERIENCING HER YOUTH LIKE A NORMAL PERSON.
EXPERIENCING LOVE LIKE A NORMAL PERSON.
SCREWING AROUND LIKE A NORMAL KID.
I HAVE ABSOLUTELY NO INTEREST IN YOUR BODY, KID.
I DON'T NEED ANYTHING FROM YOU.
WHY WOULD I?
!
SO...
YOU CAN STAY HERE.
HUH?

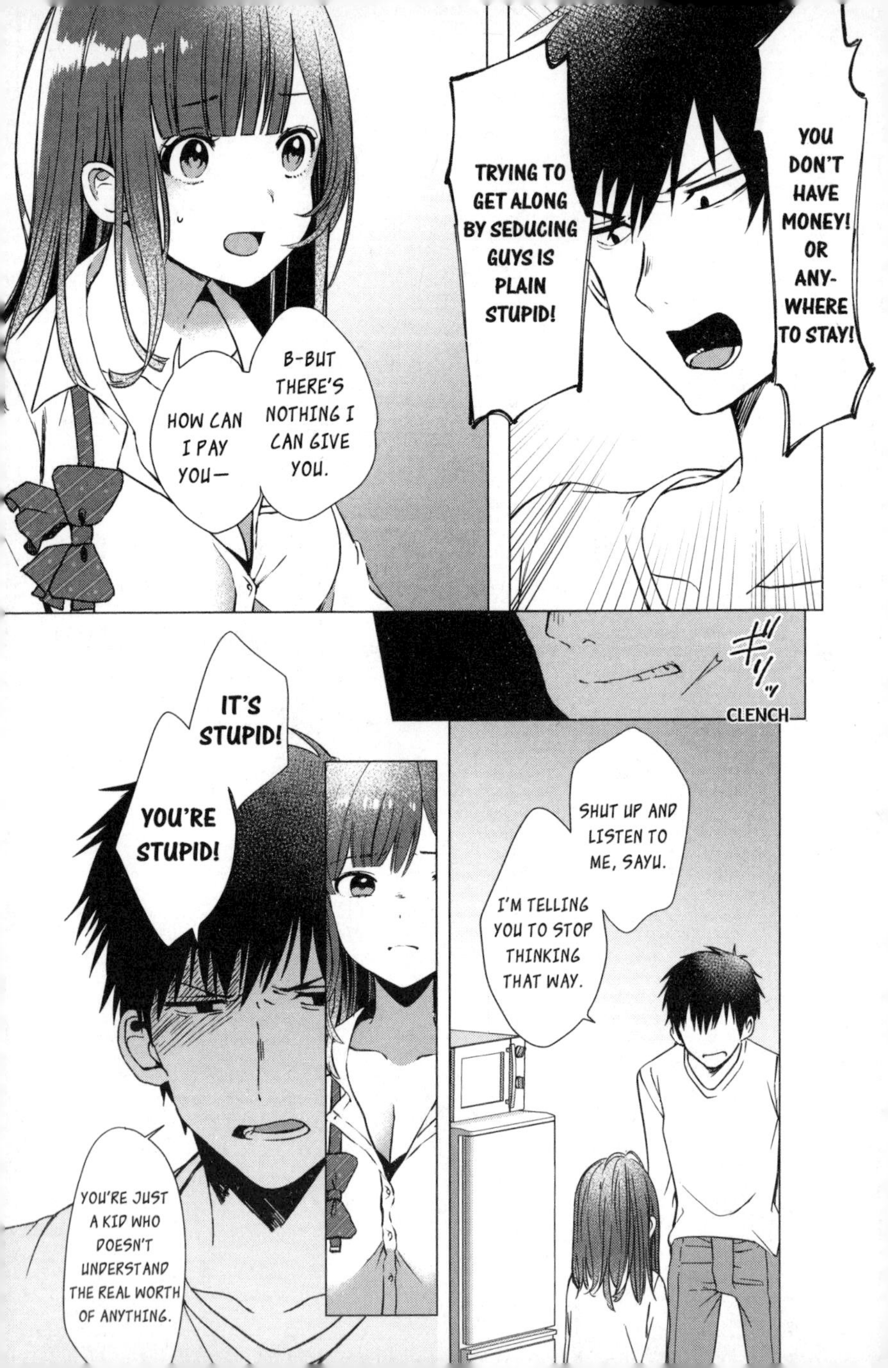
YOU DON'T HAVE MONEY! OR ANYWHERE TO STAY!
TRYING TO GET ALONG BY SEDUCING GUYS IS PLAIN STUPID!
B-BUT THERE'S NOTHING I CAN GIVE YOU.
HOW CAN I PAY YOU—
ギリッ
CLENCH
SHUT UP AND LISTEN TO ME, SAYU.
I'M TELLING YOU TO STOP THINKING THAT WAY.
IT'S STUPID!
YOU'RE STUPID!
YOU'RE JUST A KID WHO DOESN'T UNDERSTAND THE REAL WORTH OF ANYTHING.

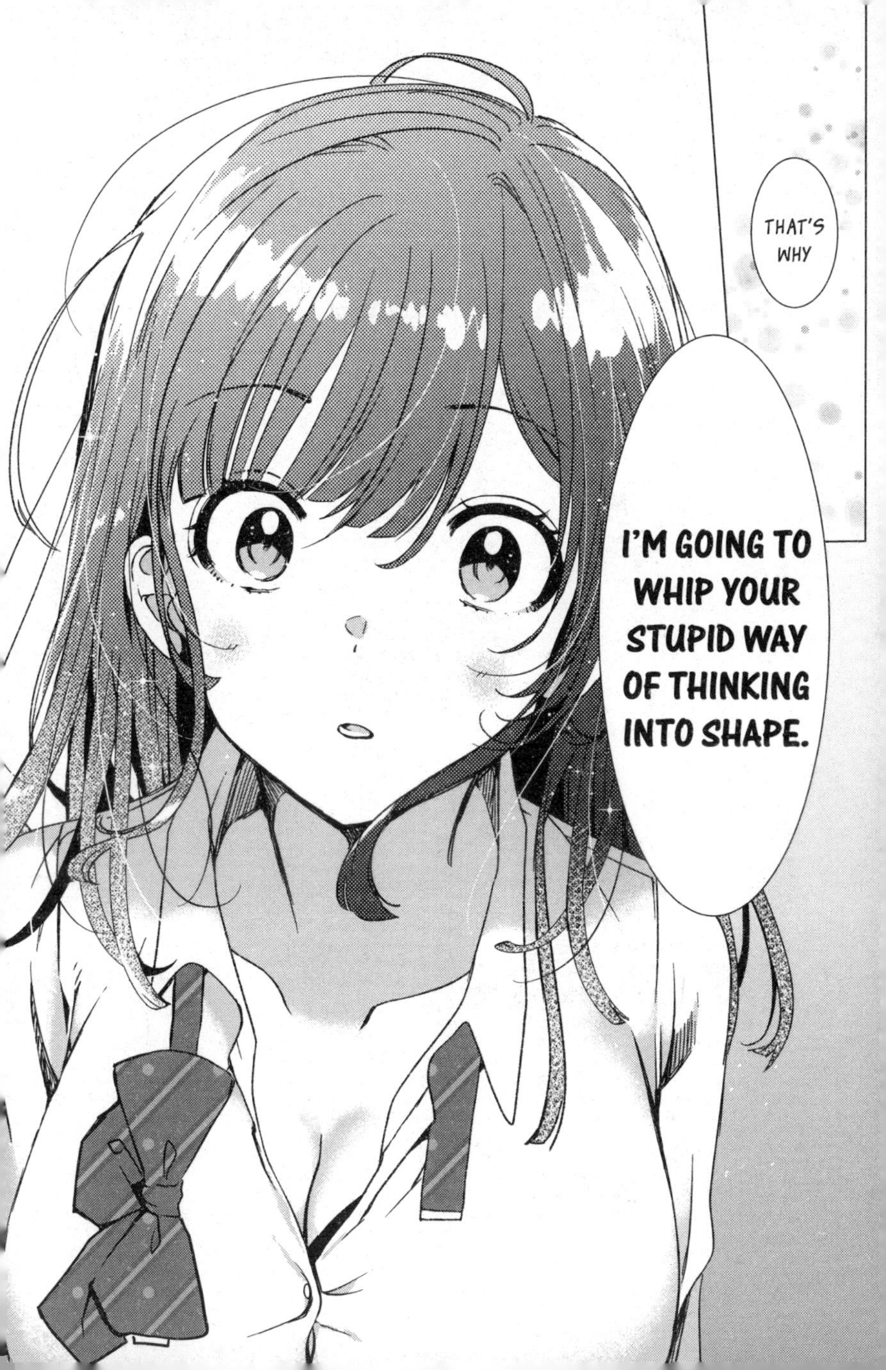
THAT'S WHY
I'M GOING TO WHIP YOUR STUPID WAY OF THINKING INTO SHAPE.

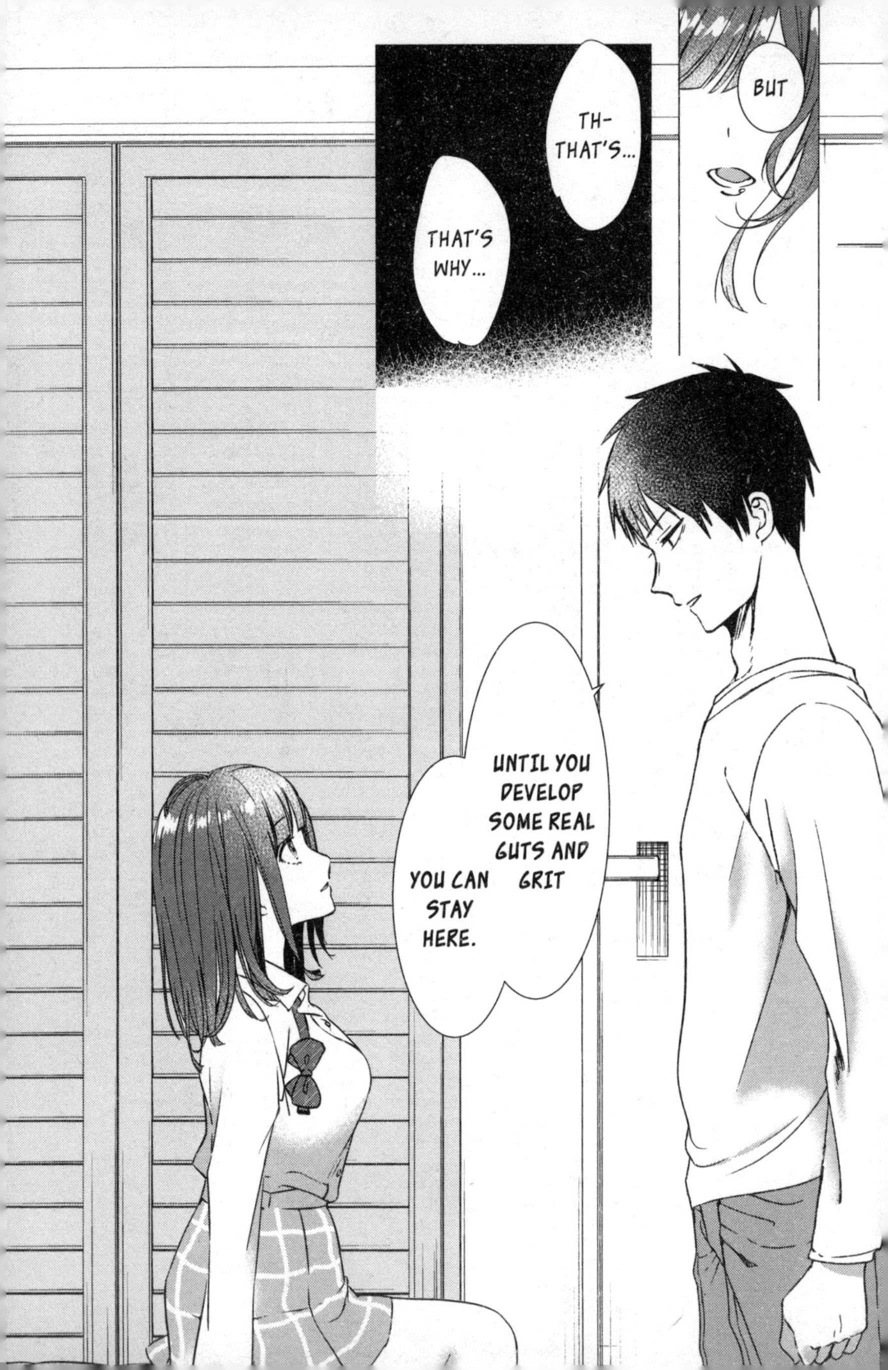
BUT
TH- THAT'S...
THAT'S WHY...
UNTIL YOU DEVELOP SOME REAL GUTS AND GRIT YOU CAN STAY HERE.

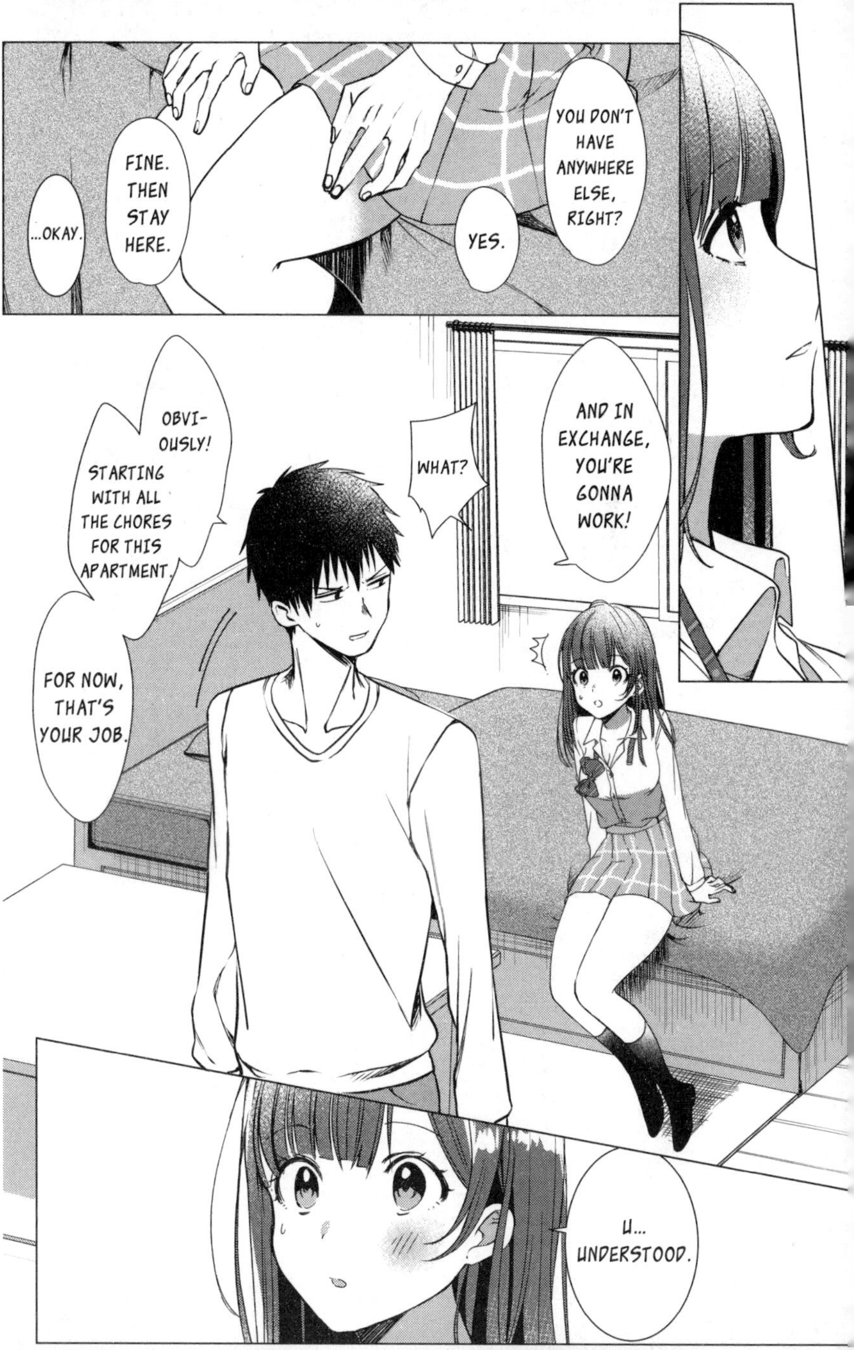
YOU DON'T HAVE ANYWHERE ELSE, RIGHT?
YES.
FINE. THEN STAY HERE.
...OKAY.
AND IN EXCHANGE, YOU'RE GONNA WORK!
WHAT?
OBVI-OUSLY! STARTING WITH ALL THE CHORES FOR THIS APARTMENT.
FOR NOW, THAT'S YOUR JOB.
U... UNDERSTOOD.

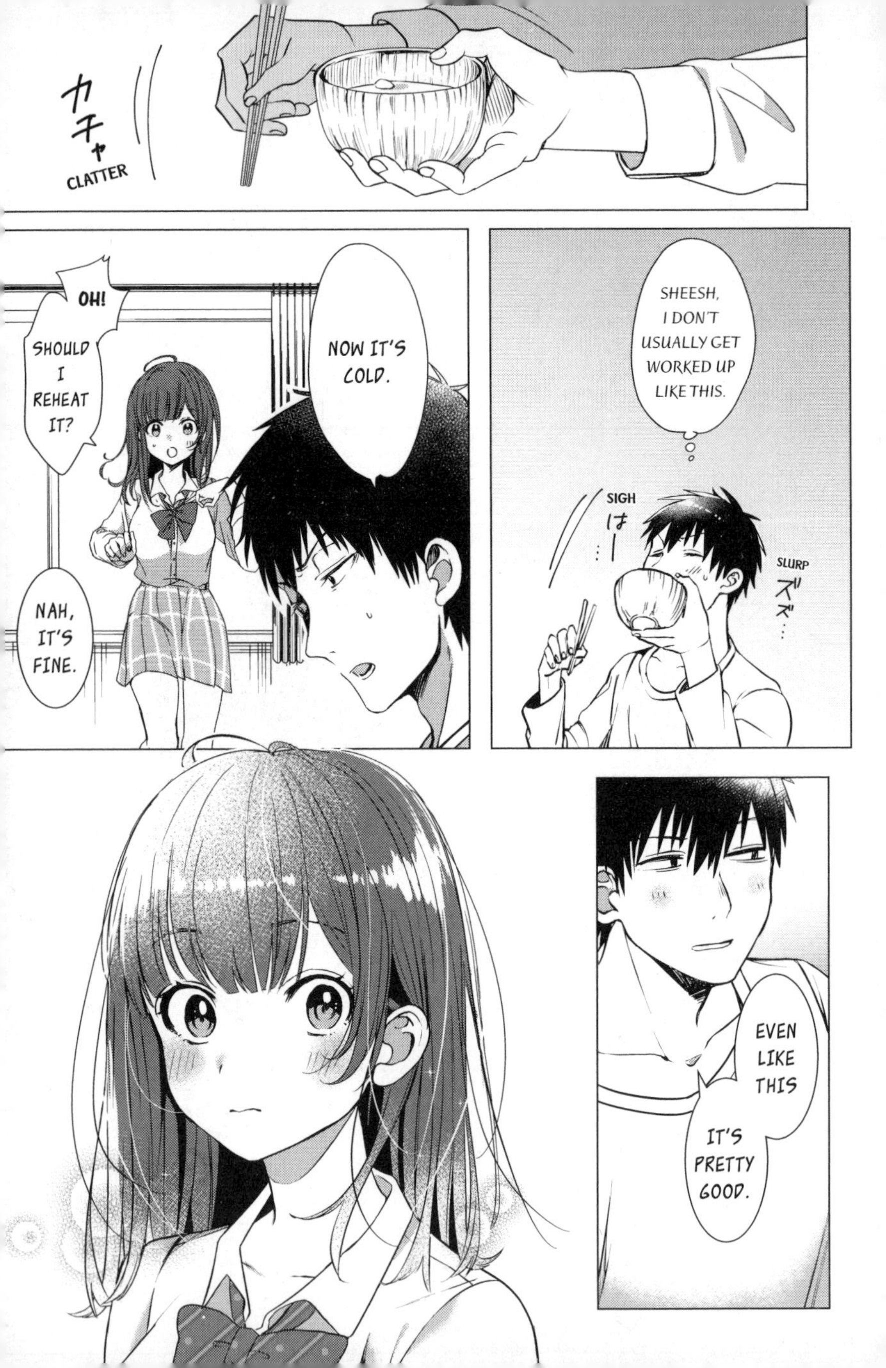
カチャ
CLATTER
SHEESH, I DON'T USUALLY GET WORKED UP LIKE THIS.
SIGH
はー…
SLURP
ズズ…
NOW IT'S COLD.
OH!
SHOULD I REHEAT IT?
NAH, IT'S FINE.
EVEN LIKE THIS
IT'S PRETTY GOOD.

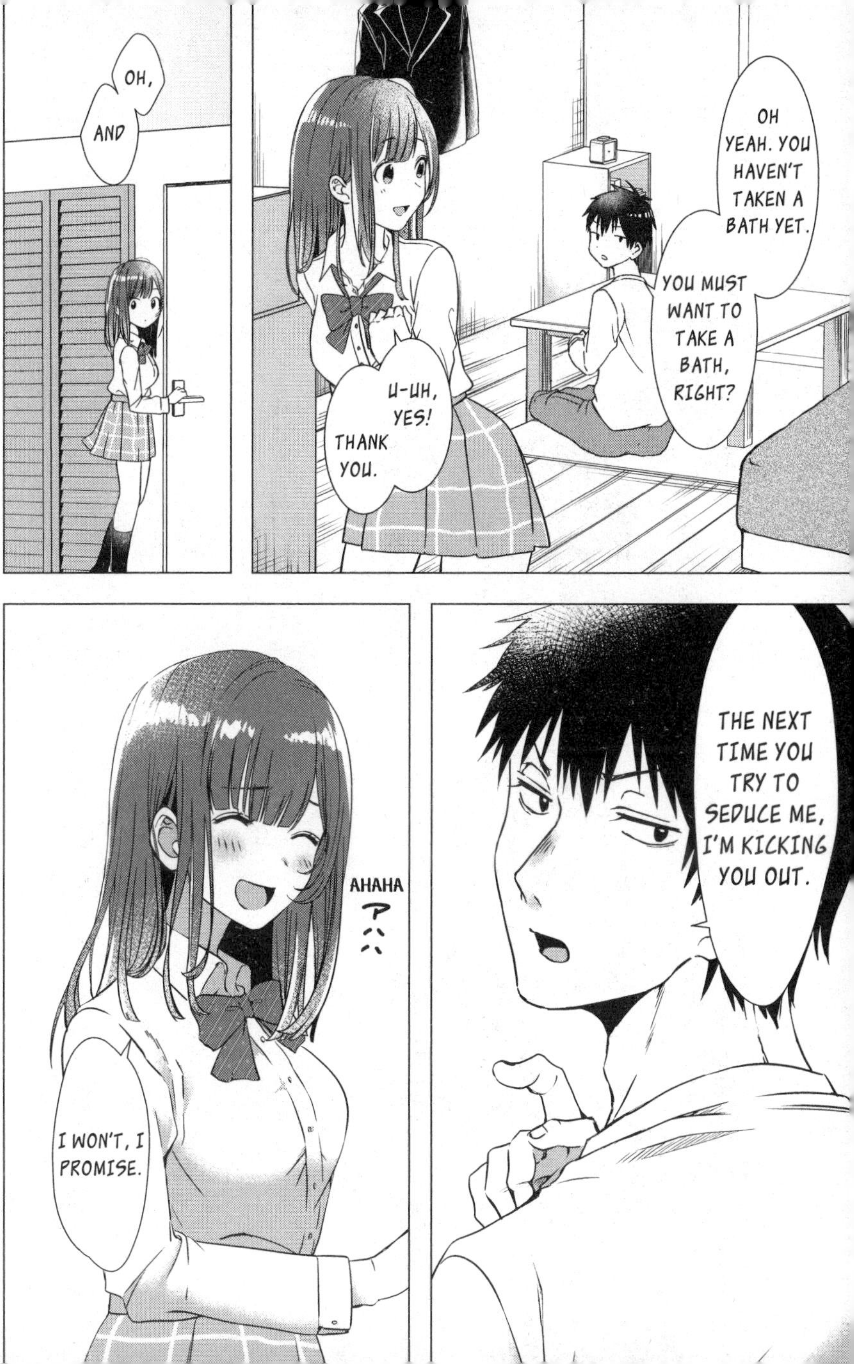
OH YEAH. YOU HAVEN'T TAKEN A BATH YET.
YOU MUST WANT TO TAKE A BATH, RIGHT?
U-UH, YES! THANK YOU.
OH, AND
THE NEXT TIME YOU TRY TO SEDUCE ME, I'M KICKING YOU OUT.
AHAHA
I WON'T, I PROMISE.

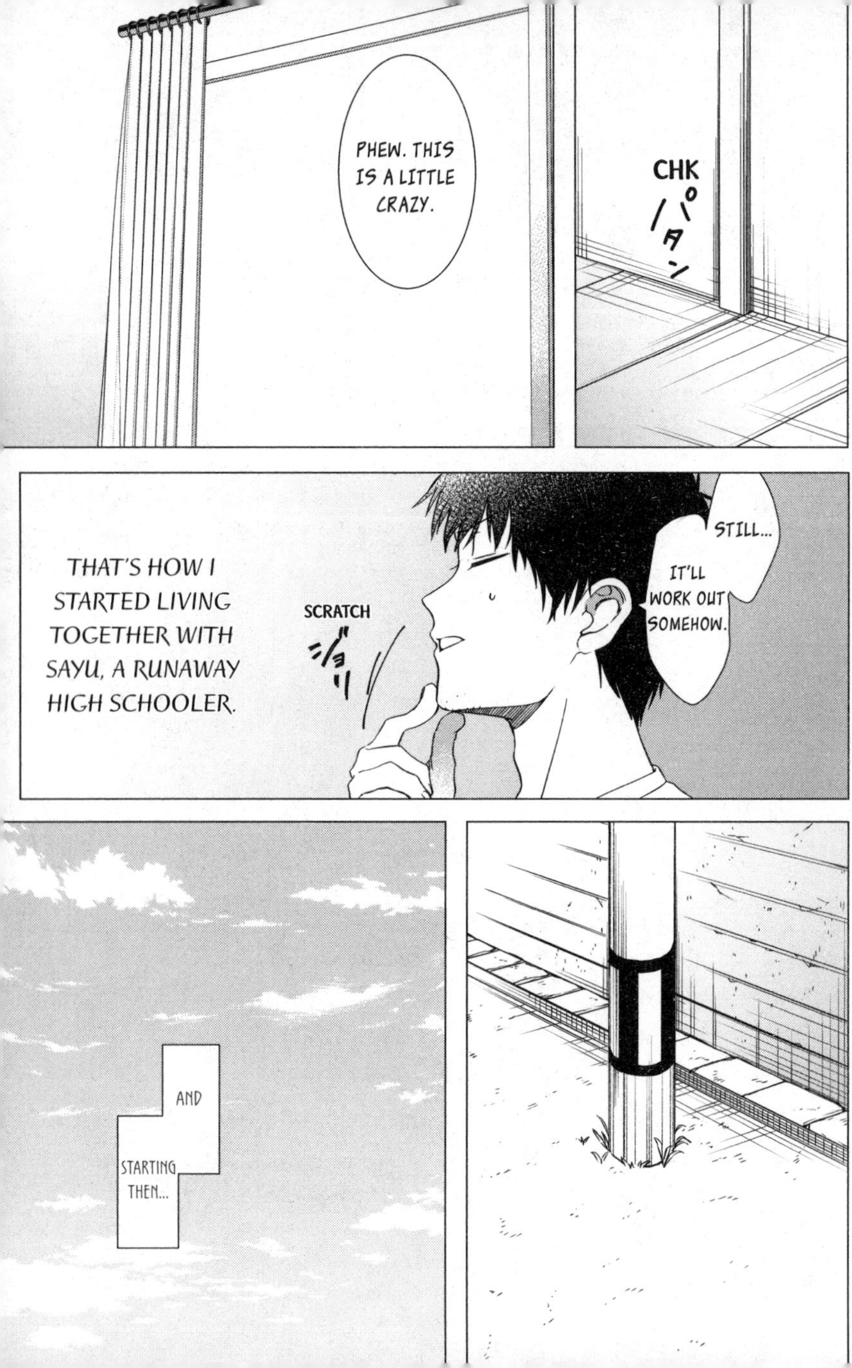
CHK
パタン
PHEW. THIS IS A LITTLE CRAZY.
STILL...
IT'LL WORK OUT SOMEHOW.
SCRATCH
ジョリ
THAT'S HOW I STARTED LIVING TOGETHER WITH SAYU, A RUNAWAY HIGH SCHOOLER.
AND
STARTING THEN...

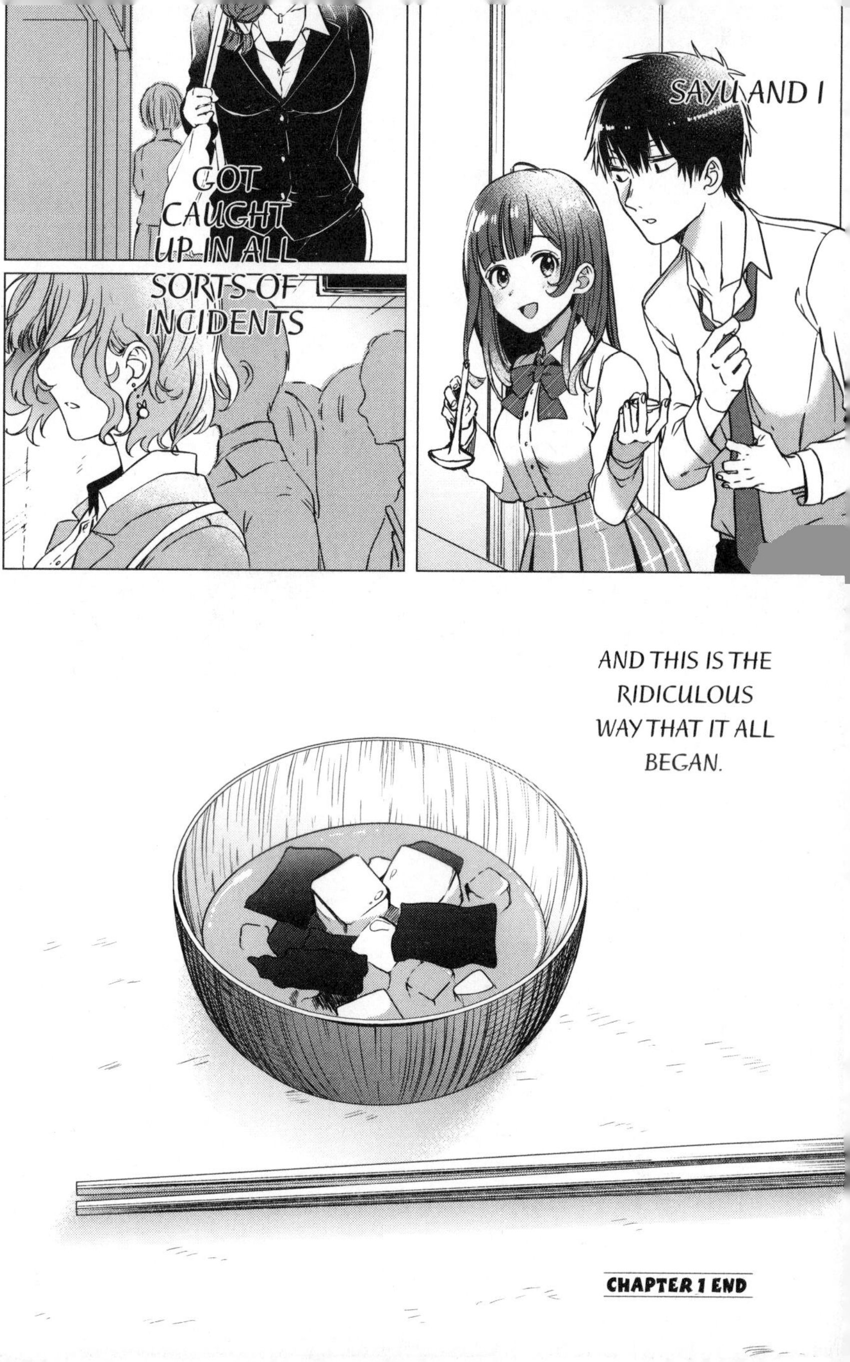
SAYU AND I
GOT CAUGHT UP IN ALL SORTS OF INCIDENTS
AND THIS IS THE RIDICULOUS WAY THAT IT ALL BEGAN.
CHAPTER 1 END

[CHAPTER 2]

DAILY LIFE AND DAILY RESTRAINT

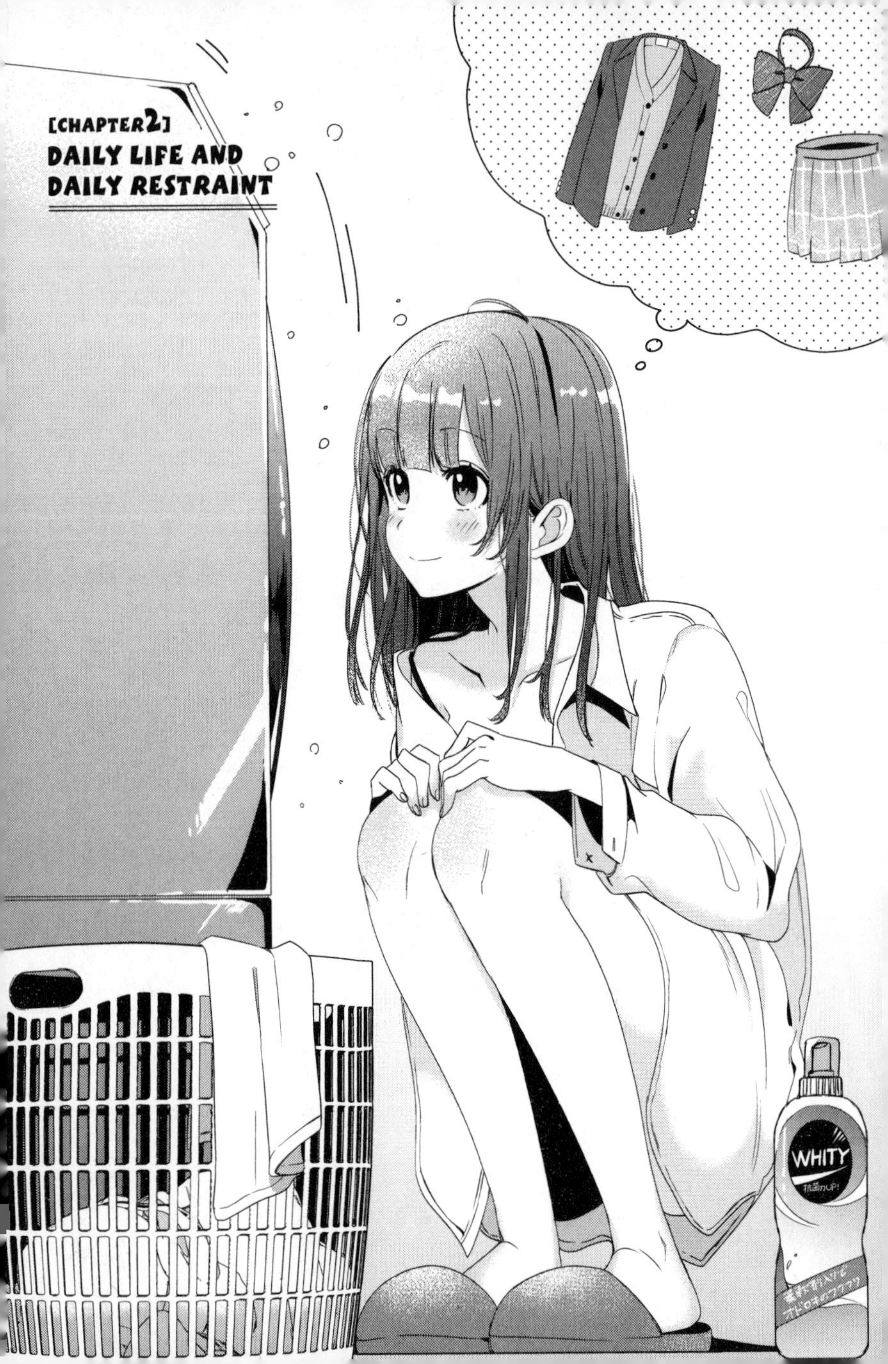
WHITY

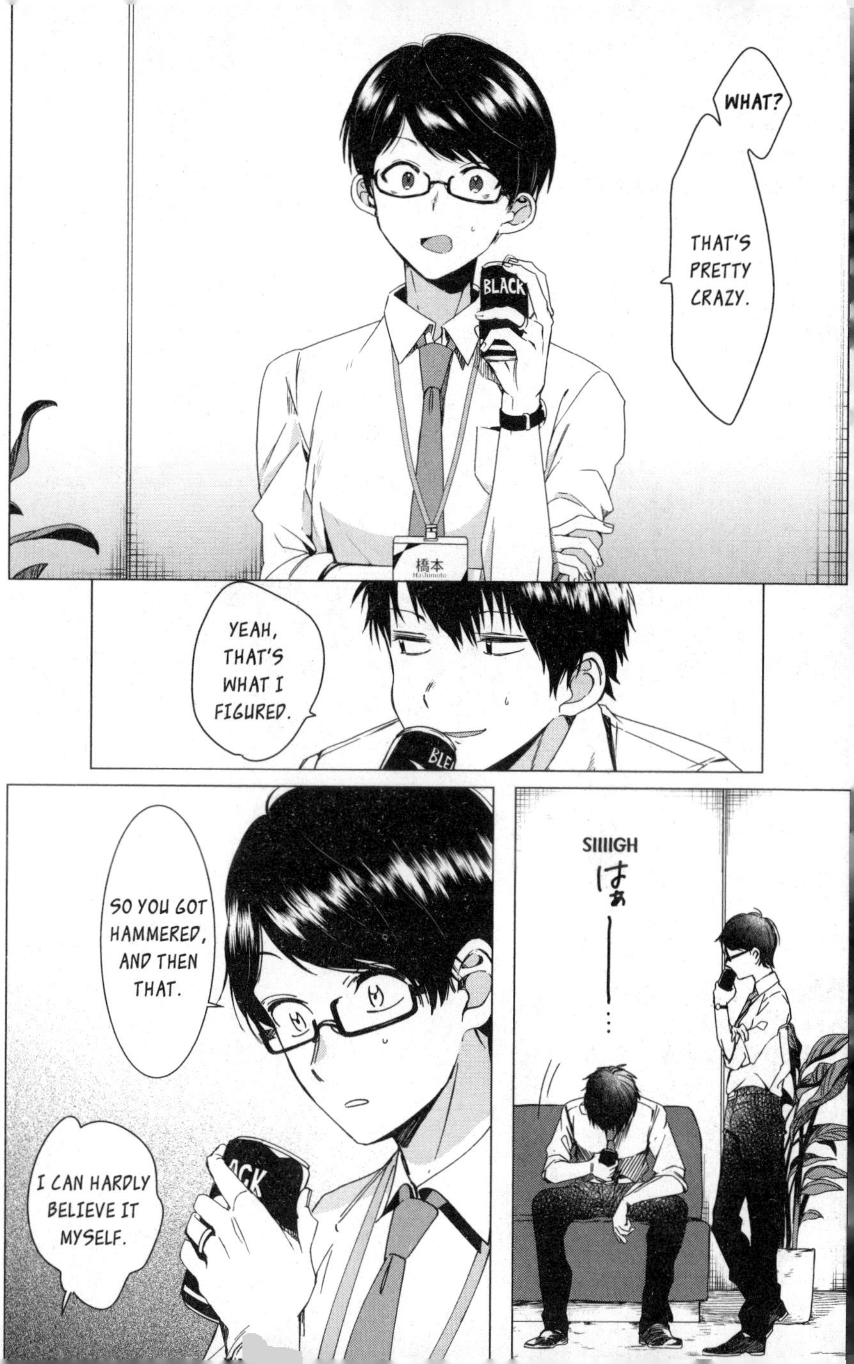
WHAT?
THAT'S PRETTY CRAZY.
橋本 Hashimoto
BLACK
YEAH, THAT'S WHAT I FIGURED.
SIIIGH
はぁ—…
SO YOU GOT HAMMERED, AND THEN THAT.
I CAN HARDLY BELIEVE IT MYSELF.

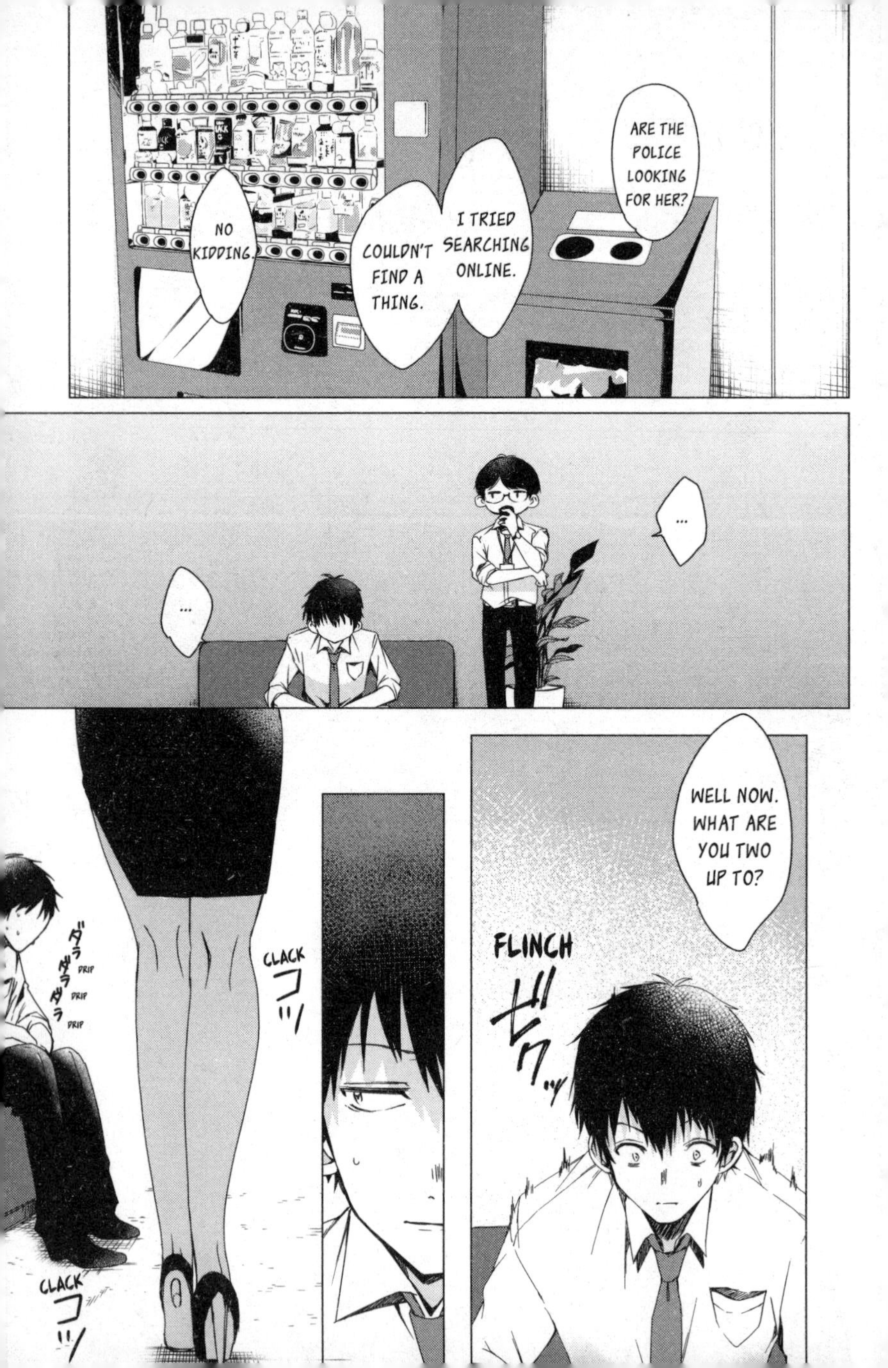
ARE THE POLICE LOOKING FOR HER?
I TRIED SEARCHING ONLINE.
COULDN'T FIND A THING.
NO KIDDING.
...
...
WELL NOW. WHAT ARE YOU TWO UP TO?
FLINCH
ゾクッ
CLACK
コツ
ダラ DRIP
ダラ DRIP
ダラ DRIP
CLACK
コツ

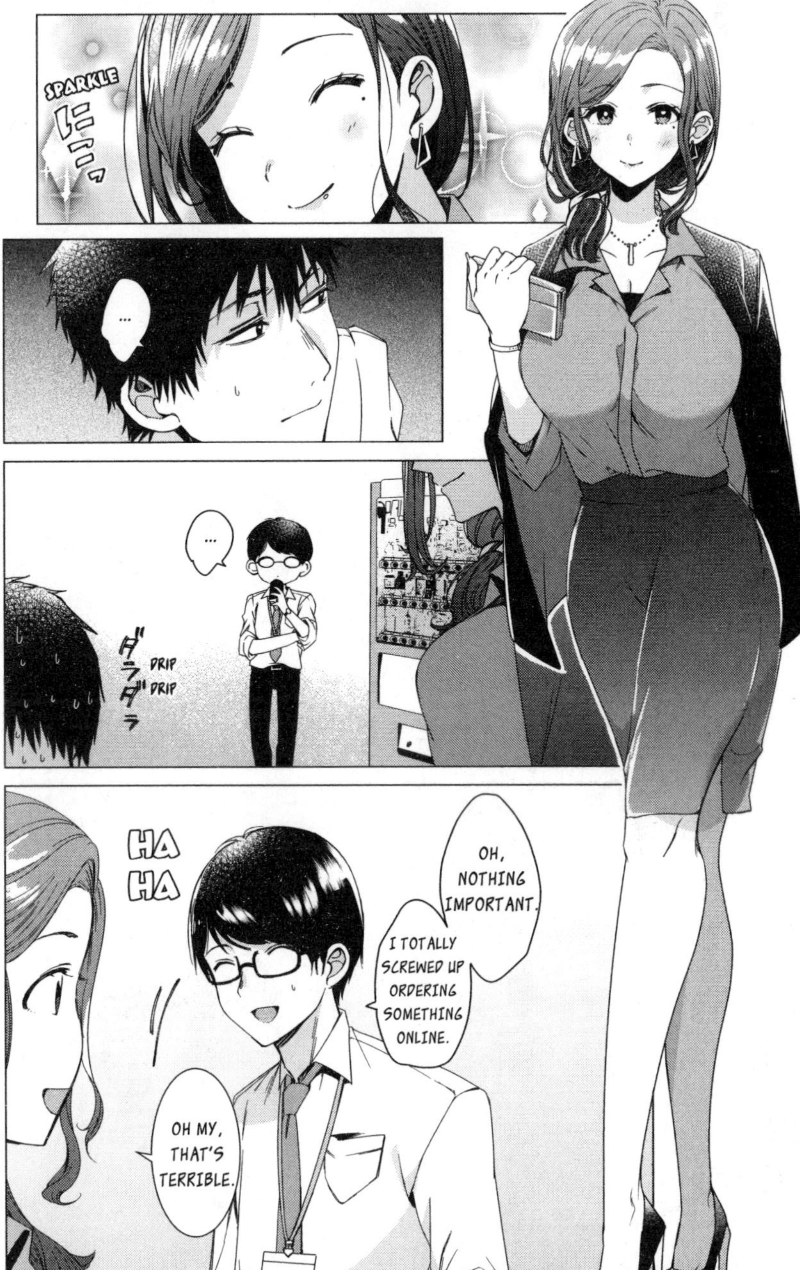
SPARKLE
...
...
DRIP DRIP
OH, NOTHING IMPORTANT.
I TOTALLY SCREWED UP ORDERING SOMETHING ONLINE.
HA HA
OH MY, THAT'S TERRIBLE.

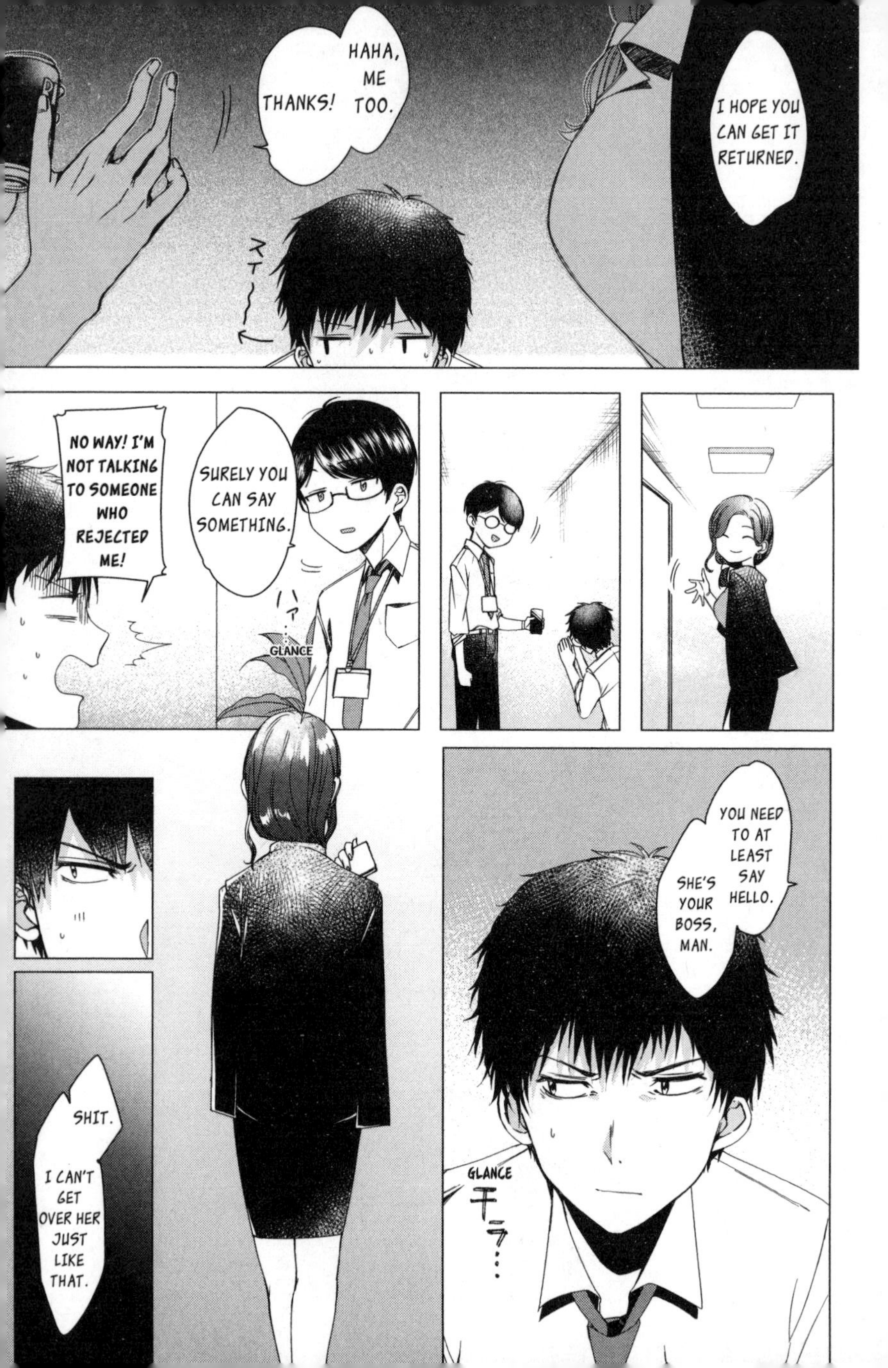
I HOPE YOU CAN GET IT RETURNED.
HAHA, ME TOO.
THANKS!
SURELY YOU CAN SAY SOMETHING.
GLANCE
NO WAY! I'M NOT TALKING TO SOMEONE WHO REJECTED ME!
YOU NEED TO AT LEAST SAY HELLO.
SHE'S YOUR BOSS, MAN.
GLANCE
SHIT.
I CAN'T GET OVER HER JUST LIKE THAT.

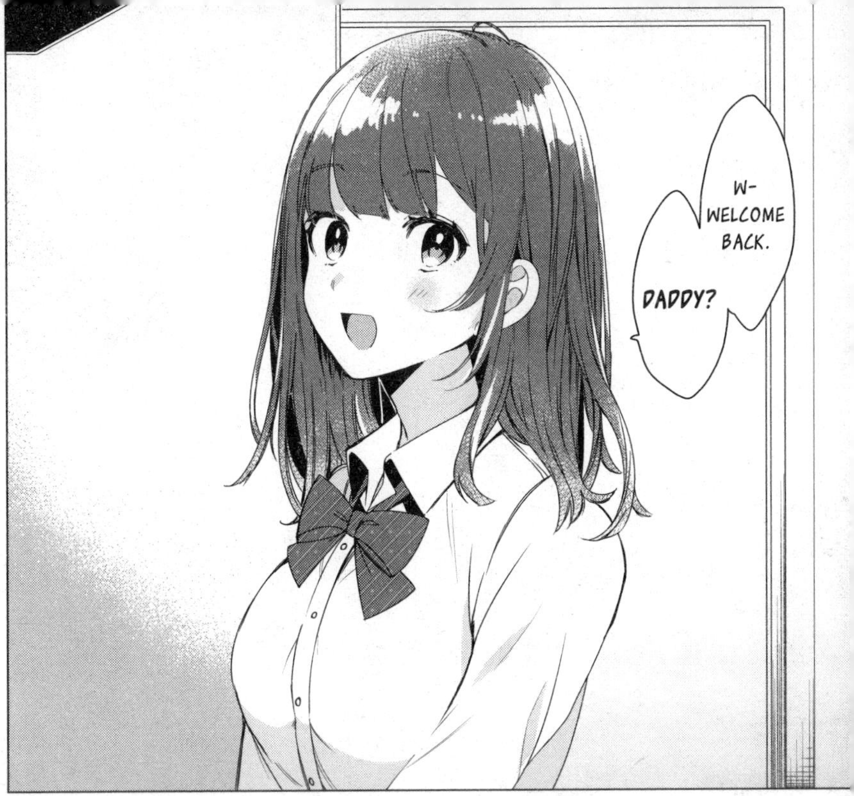
W-WELCOME BACK.
DADDY?
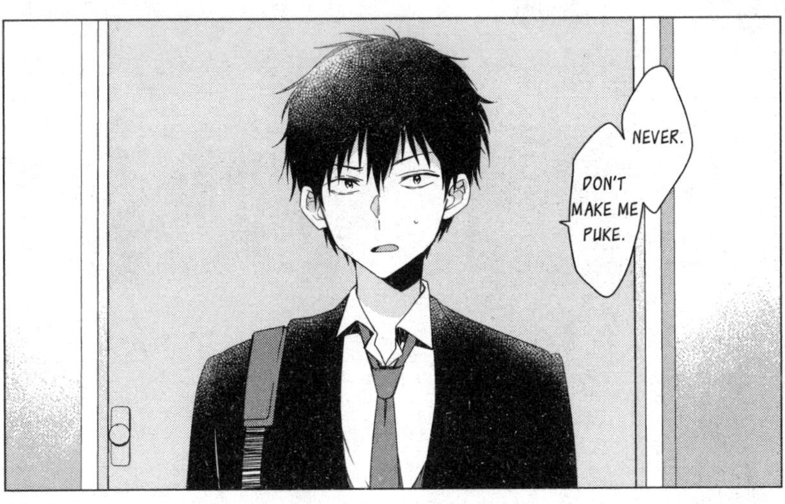
NEVER.
DON'T MAKE ME PUKE.

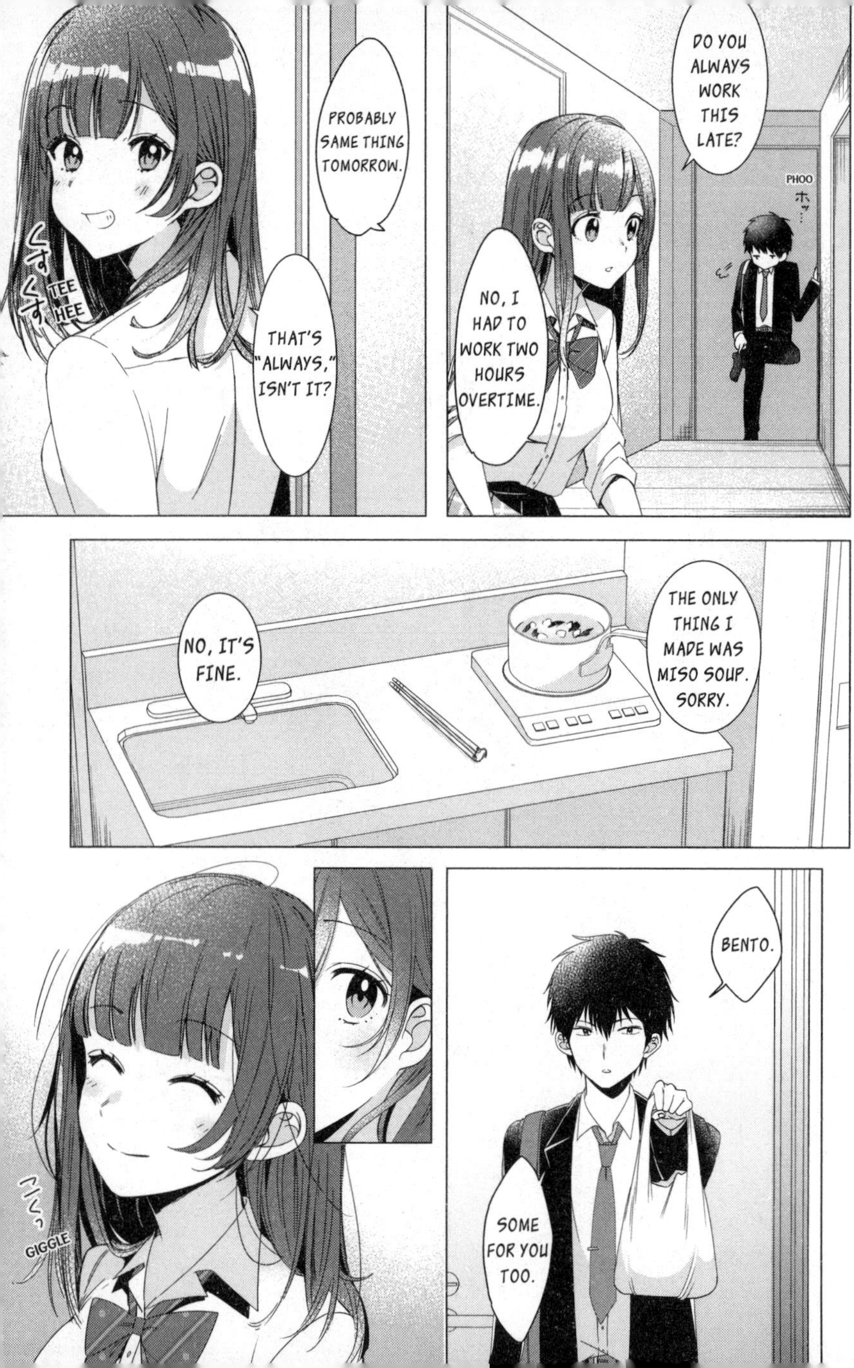
DO YOU ALWAYS WORK THIS LATE?
PHOO
ホッ…
NO, I HAD TO WORK TWO HOURS OVERTIME.
PROBABLY SAME THING TOMORROW.
THAT'S "ALWAYS," ISN'T IT?
くすくす
TEE HEE
THE ONLY THING I MADE WAS MISO SOUP. SORRY.
NO, IT'S FINE.
BENTO.
SOME FOR YOU TOO.
こくっ
GIGGLE

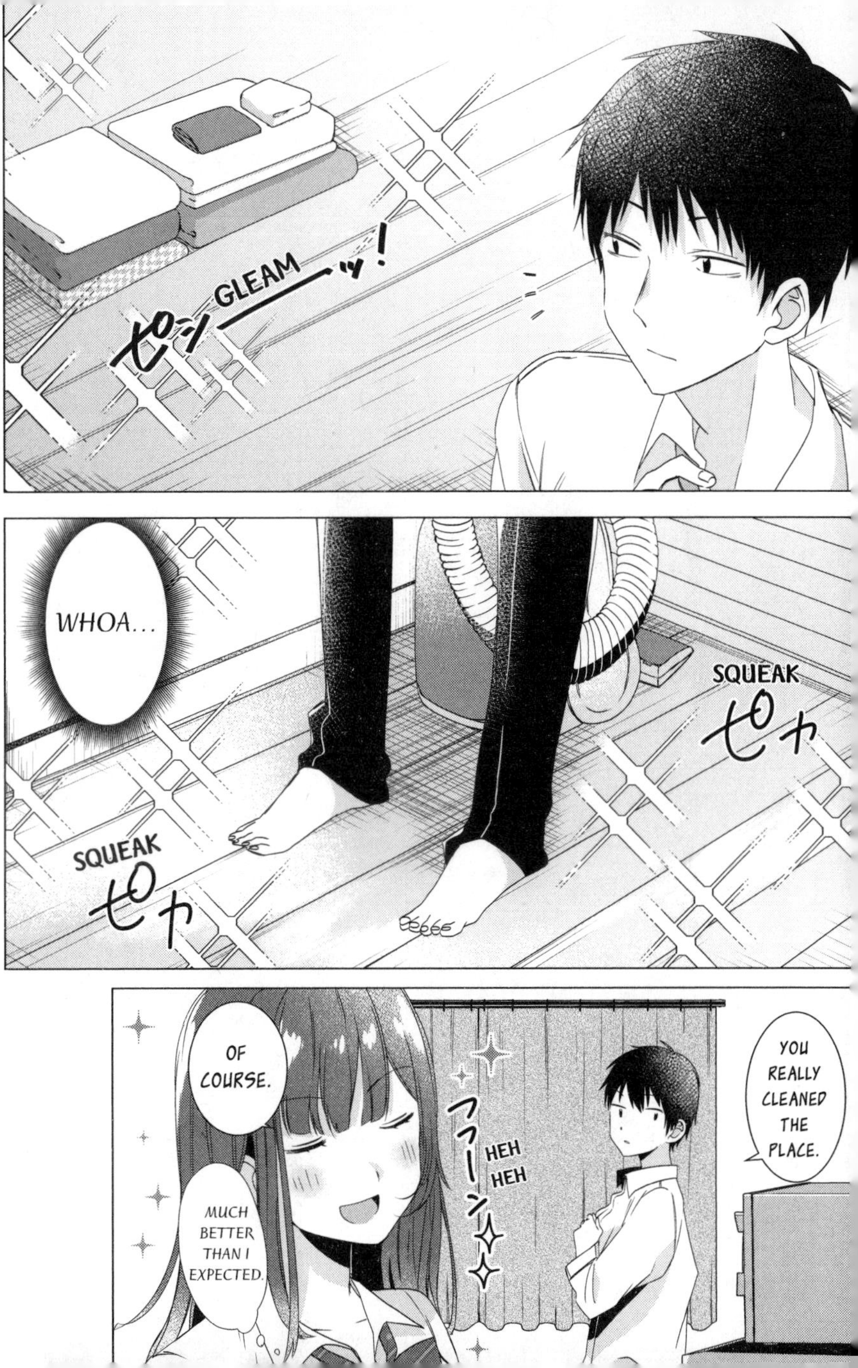
GLEAM
SQUEAK
WHOA...
SQUEAK
YOU REALLY CLEANED THE PLACE.
HEH HEH
OF COURSE.
MUCH BETTER THAN I EXPECTED.

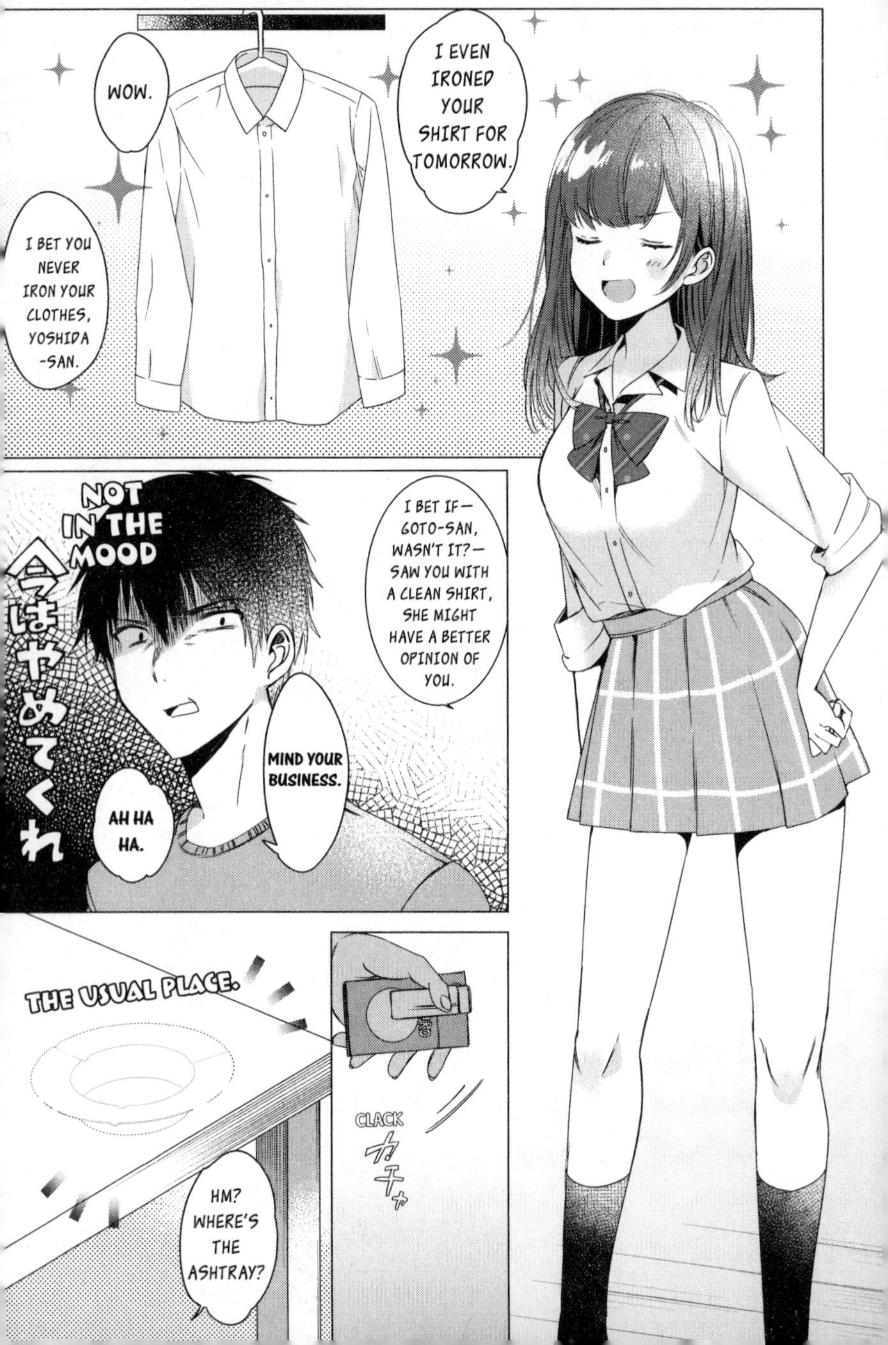
I EVEN IRONED YOUR SHIRT FOR TOMORROW.
WOW.
I BET YOU NEVER IRON YOUR CLOTHES, YOSHIDA-SAN.
I BET IF—GOTO-SAN, WASN'T IT?—SAW YOU WITH A CLEAN SHIRT, SHE MIGHT HAVE A BETTER OPINION OF YOU.
NOT IN THE MOOD
今はやめてくれ
MIND YOUR BUSINESS.
AH HA HA.
CLACK
カチャ
THE USUAL PLACE.
HM? WHERE'S THE ASHTRAY?

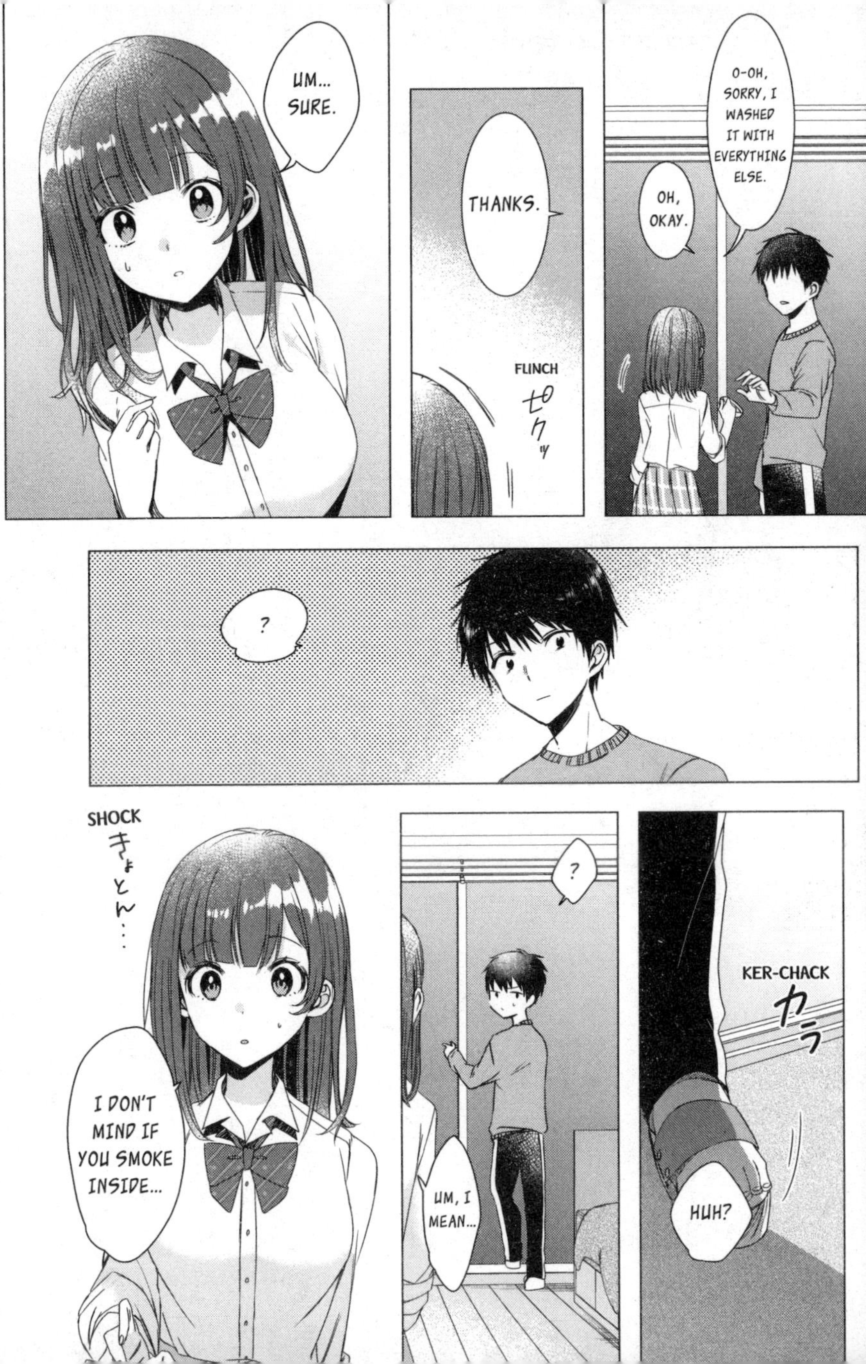
O-OH, SORRY, I WASHED IT WITH EVERYTHING ELSE.
OH, OKAY.
THANKS.
FLINCH
ピクッ
UM... SURE.
?
KER-CHACK
カラ
HUH?
?
UM, I MEAN...
SHOCK
きょとん…
I DON'T MIND IF YOU SMOKE INSIDE...

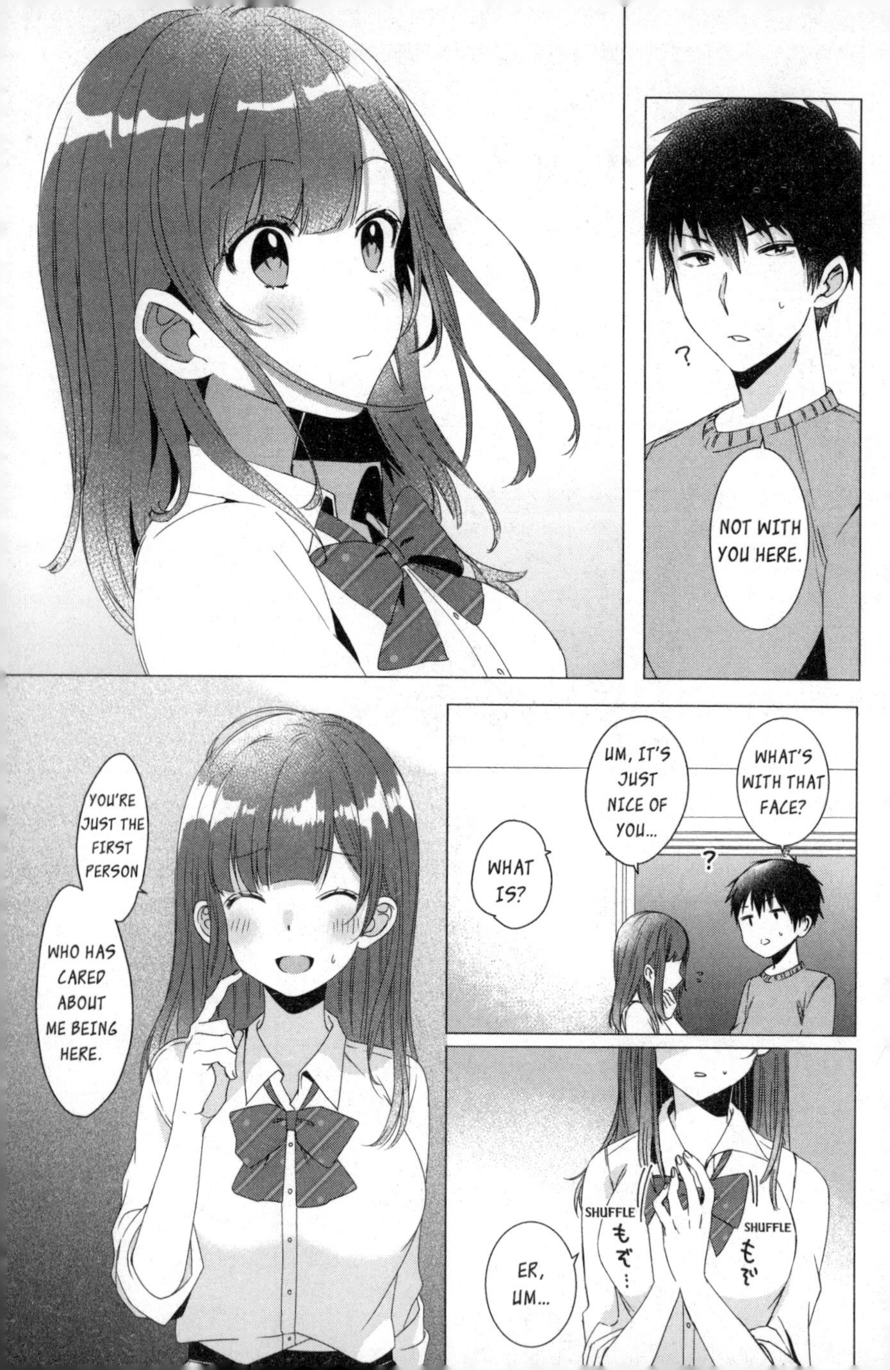
?
NOT WITH YOU HERE.
WHAT'S WITH THAT FACE?
UM, IT'S JUST NICE OF YOU...
?
WHAT IS?
SHUFFLE もぞ
SHUFFLE もぞ…
ER, UM...
YOU'RE JUST THE FIRST PERSON
WHO HAS CARED ABOUT ME BEING HERE.

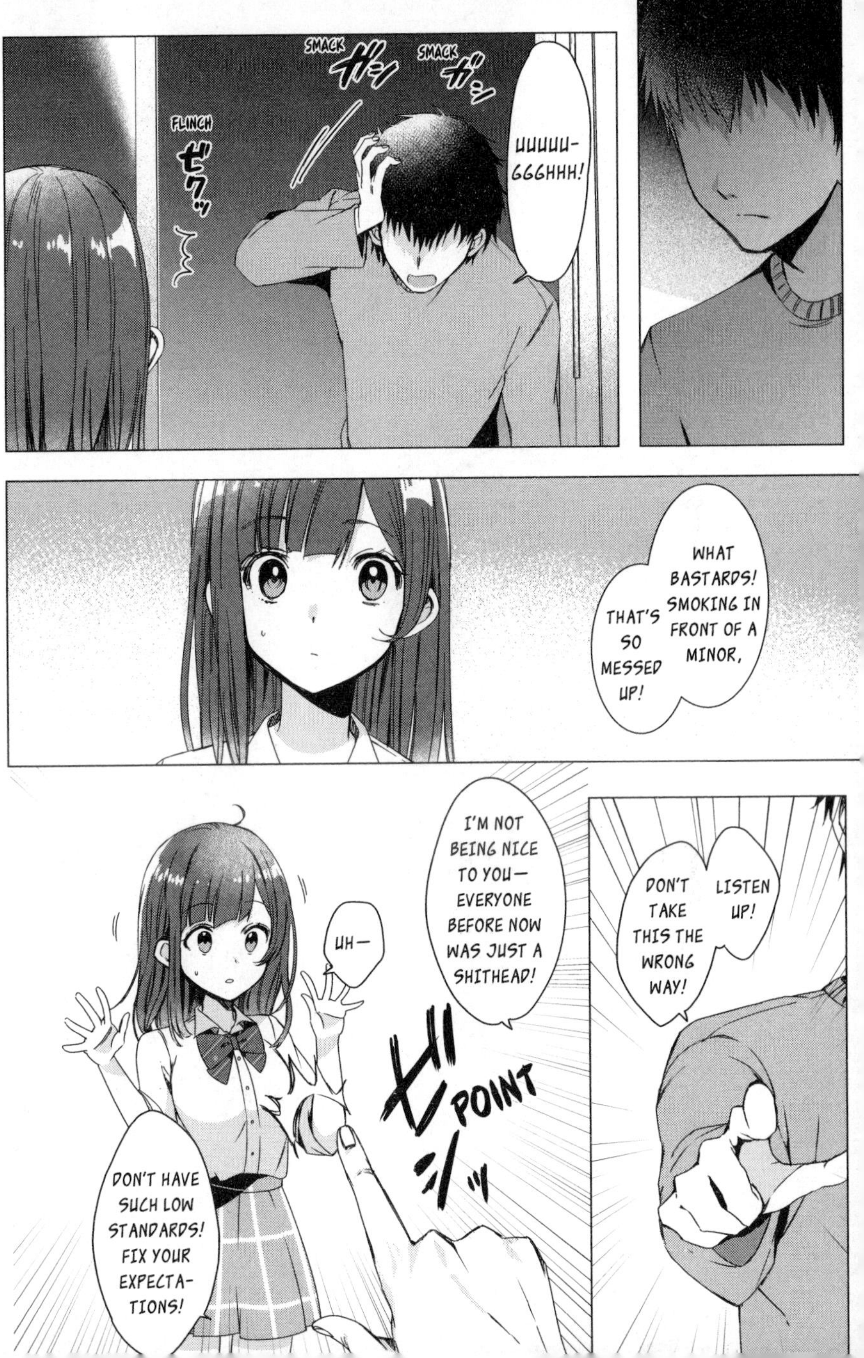
UUUUU-GGGHHH!
SMACK
SMACK
FLINCH
WHAT BASTARDS! SMOKING IN FRONT OF A MINOR,
THAT'S SO MESSED UP!
LISTEN UP!
DON'T TAKE THIS THE WRONG WAY!
I'M NOT BEING NICE TO YOU—EVERYONE BEFORE NOW WAS JUST A SHITHEAD!
UH—
POINT
DON'T HAVE SUCH LOW STANDARDS! FIX YOUR EXPECTA-TIONS!

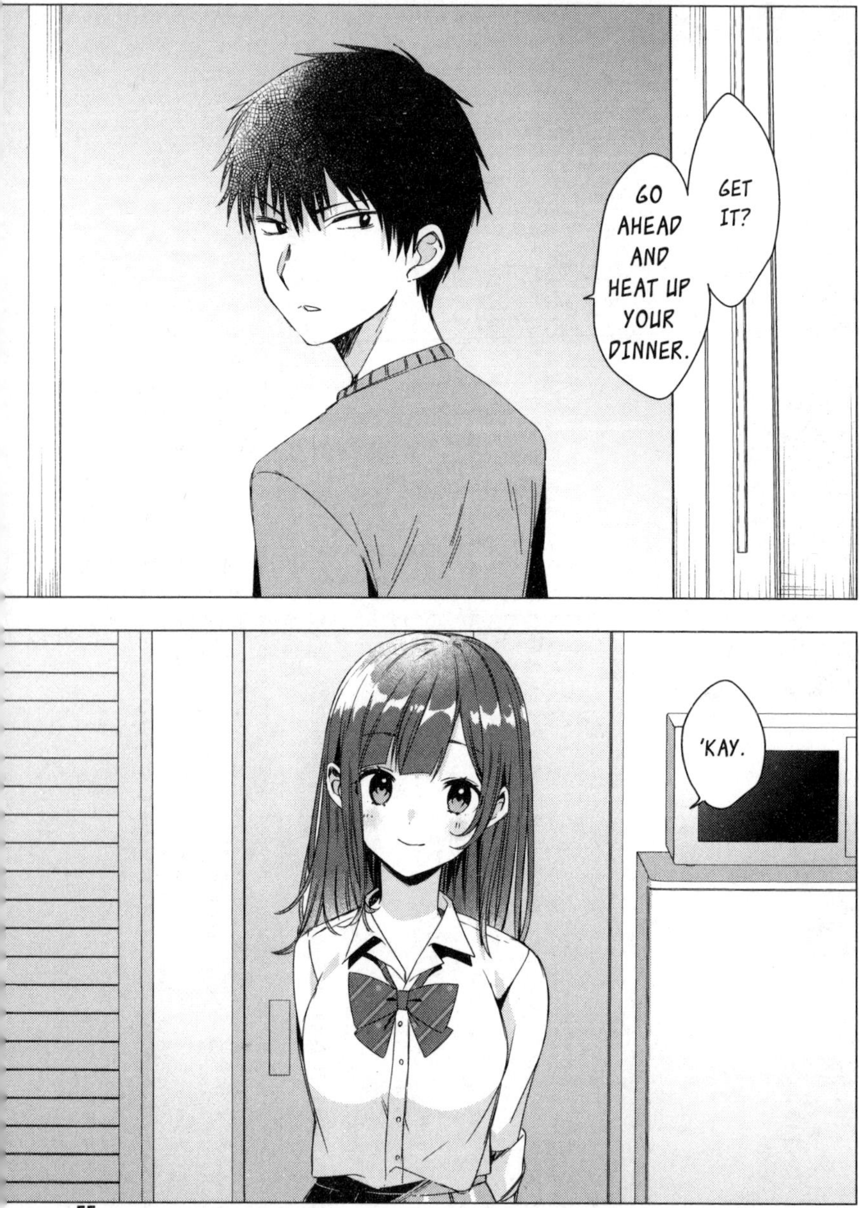
GET IT?
GO AHEAD AND HEAT UP YOUR DINNER.
'KAY.

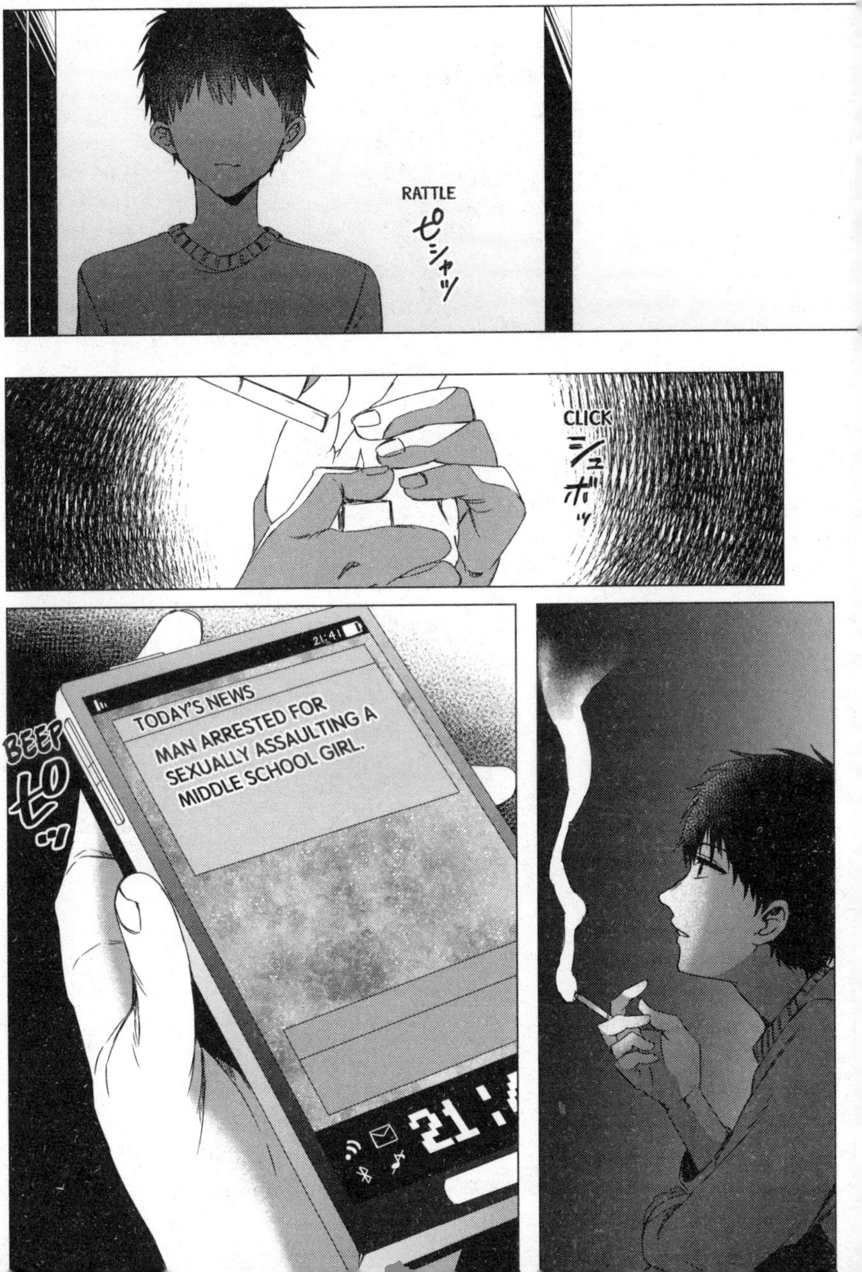
RATTLE
ピシャッ
CLICK
シュボッ
TODAY'S NEWS
MAN ARRESTED FOR SEXUALLY ASSAULTING A MIDDLE SCHOOL GIRL.
BEEP
ピロッ

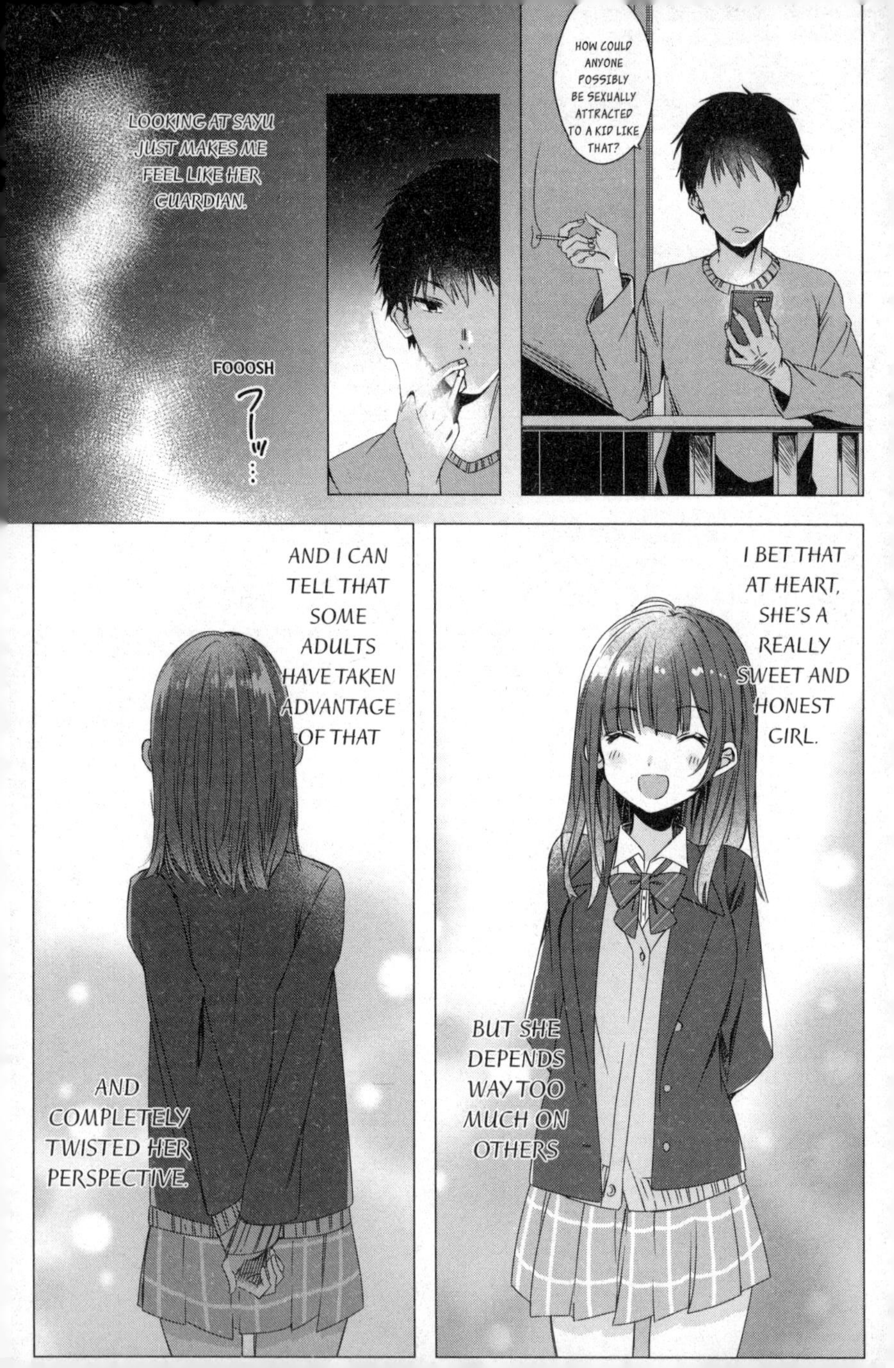
HOW COULD ANYONE POSSIBLY BE SEXUALLY ATTRACTED TO A KID LIKE THAT?
LOOKING AT SAYU JUST MAKES ME FEEL LIKE HER GUARDIAN.
FOOOSH
フーッ…
I BET THAT AT HEART, SHE'S A REALLY SWEET AND HONEST GIRL.
BUT SHE DEPENDS WAY TOO MUCH ON OTHERS
AND I CAN TELL THAT SOME ADULTS HAVE TAKEN ADVANTAGE OF THAT
AND COMPLETELY TWISTED HER PERSPECTIVE.

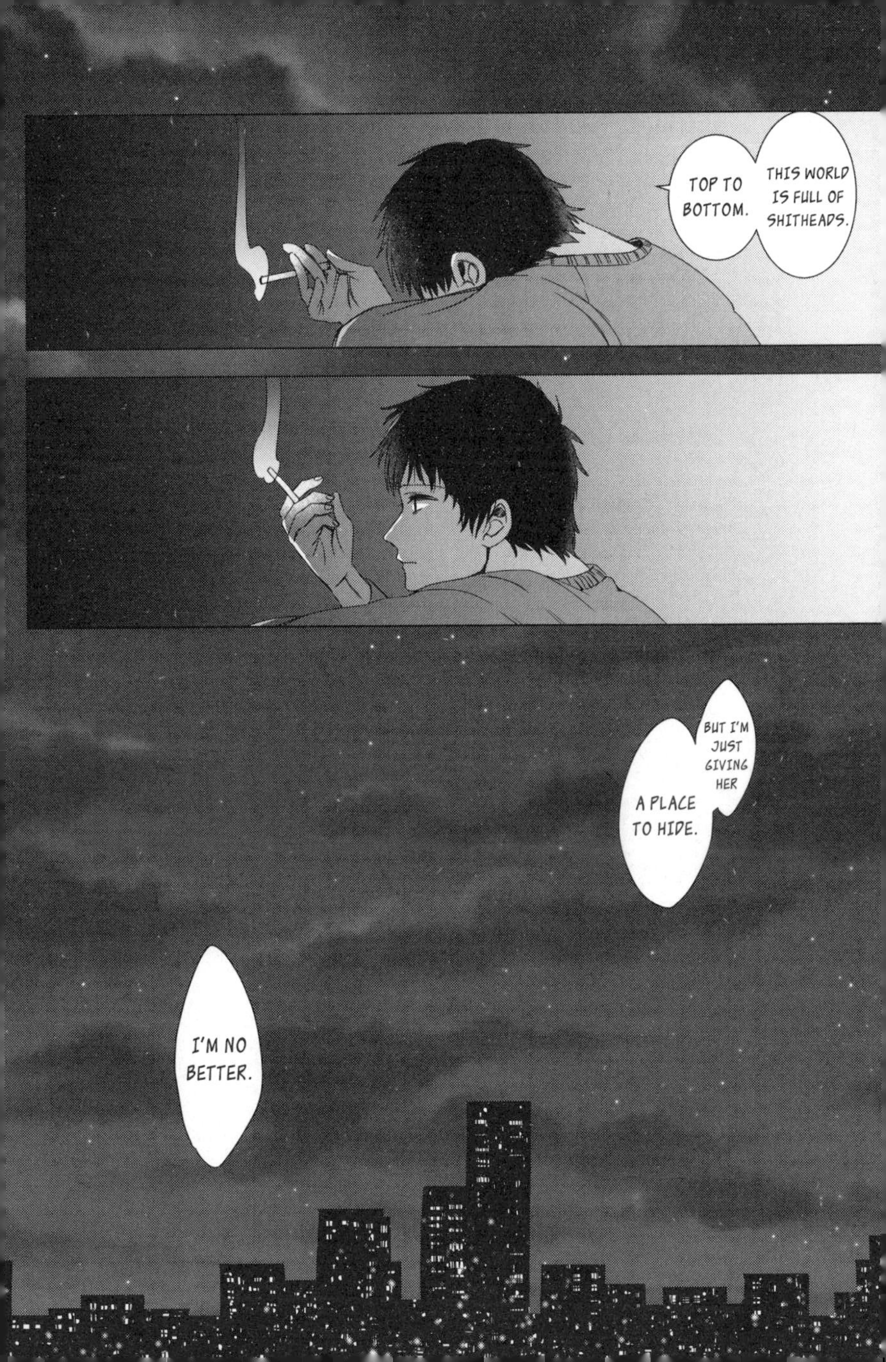
THIS WORLD IS FULL OF SHITHEADS.
TOP TO BOTTOM.
BUT I'M JUST GIVING HER
A PLACE TO HIDE.
I'M NO BETTER.

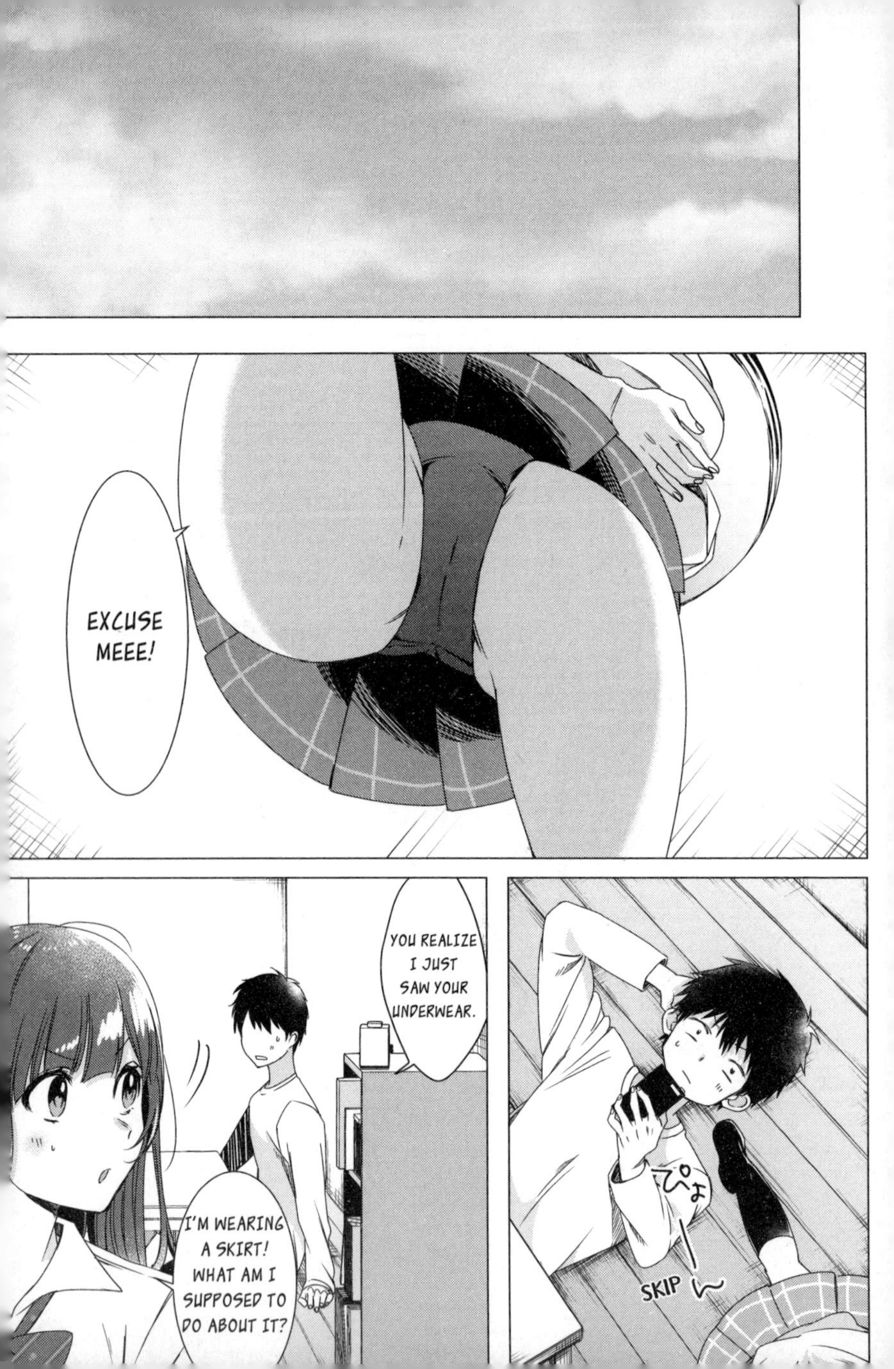
EXCUSE MEEE!
ぴょーん
SKIP
YOU REALIZE I JUST SAW YOUR UNDERWEAR.
I'M WEARING A SKIRT! WHAT AM I SUPPOSED TO DO ABOUT IT?

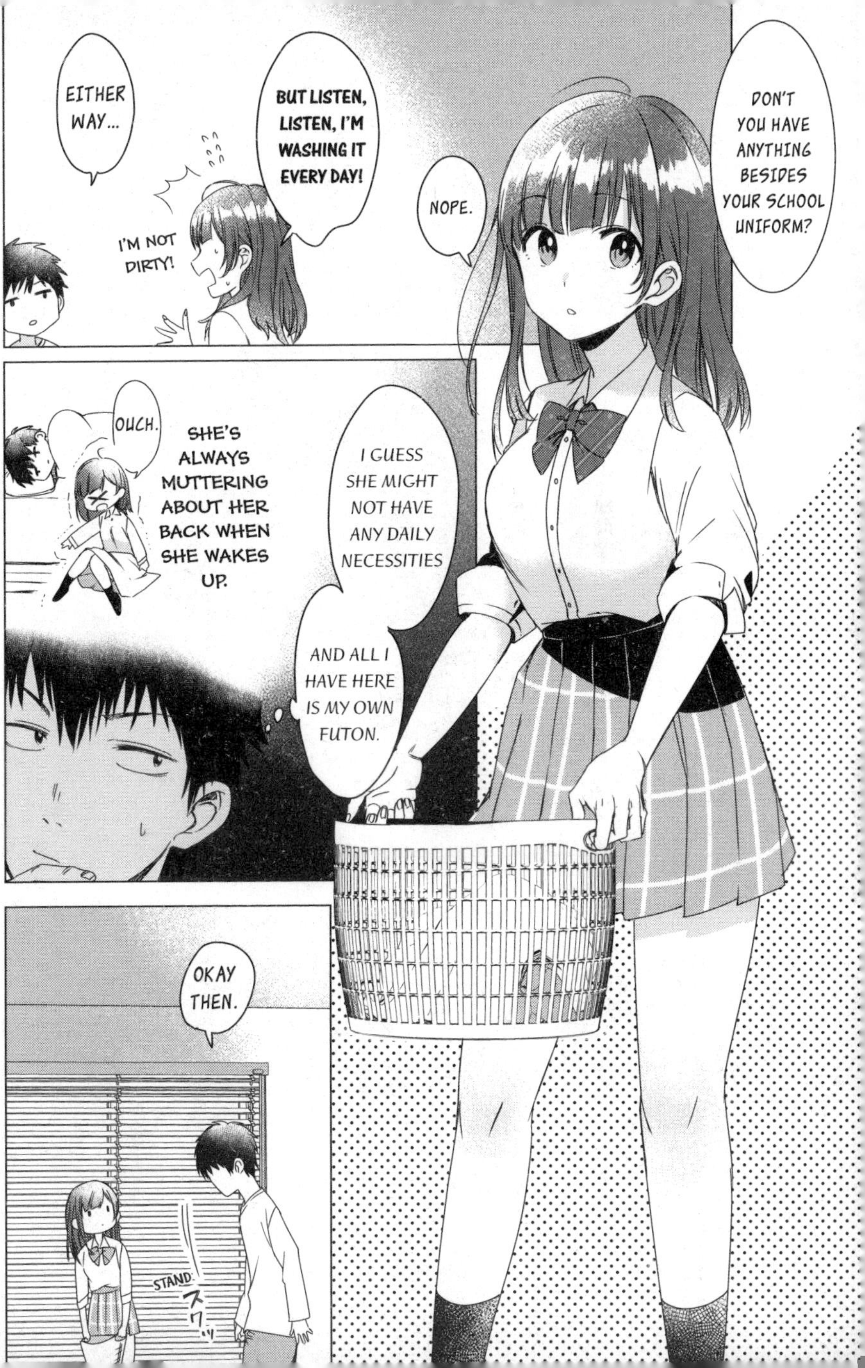
DON'T YOU HAVE ANYTHING BESIDES YOUR SCHOOL UNIFORM?
NOPE.
BUT LISTEN, LISTEN, I'M WASHING IT EVERY DAY!
I'M NOT DIRTY!
EITHER WAY...
OUCH.
SHE'S ALWAYS MUTTERING ABOUT HER BACK WHEN SHE WAKES UP.
I GUESS SHE MIGHT NOT HAVE ANY DAILY NECESSITIES
AND ALL I HAVE HERE IS MY OWN FUTON.
OKAY THEN.
STAND
スク

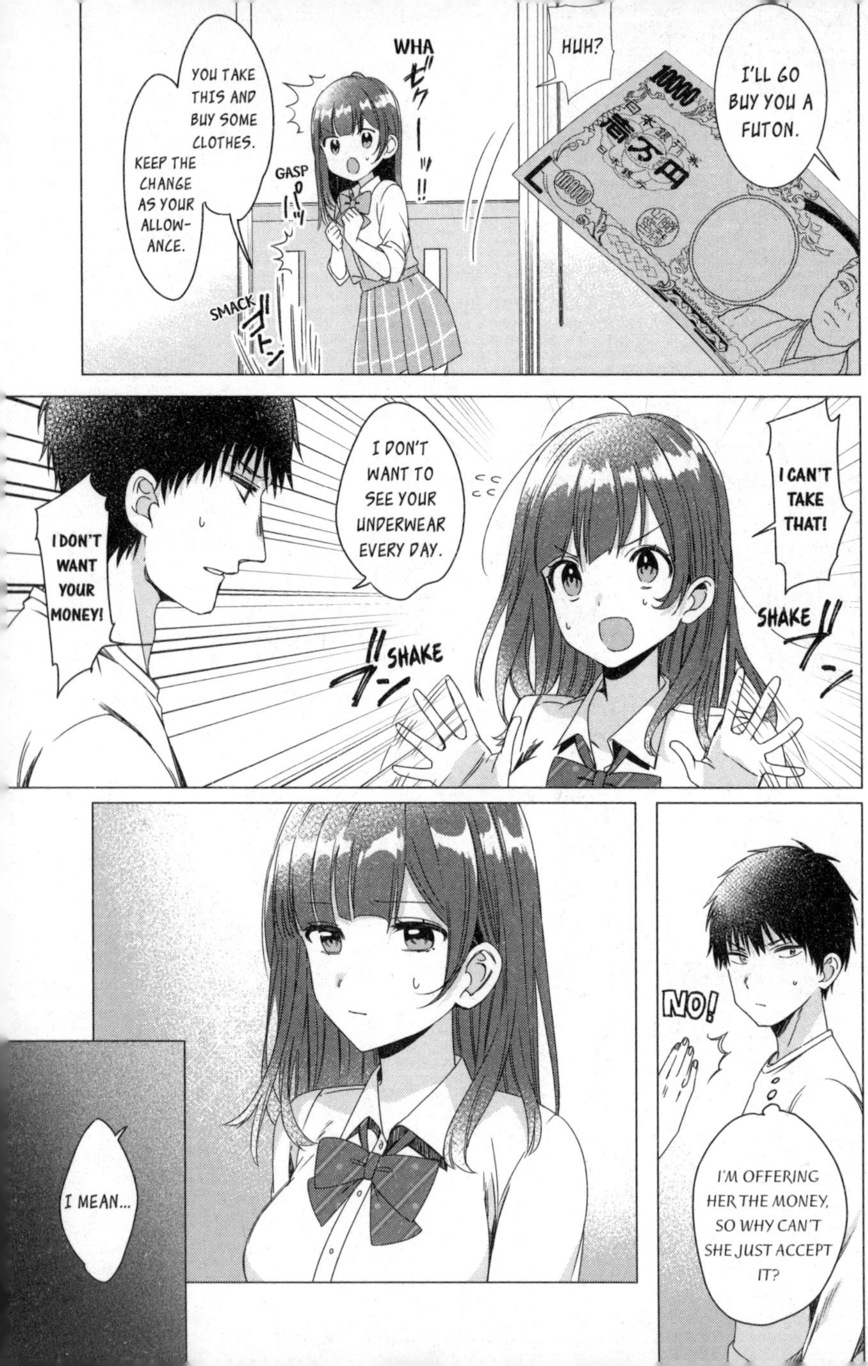
I'LL GO BUY YOU A FUTON.
HUH?
WHA
YOU TAKE THIS AND BUY SOME CLOTHES. KEEP THE CHANGE AS YOUR ALLOW-ANCE.
GASP
SMACK
I CAN'T TAKE THAT!
SHAKE
I DON'T WANT TO SEE YOUR UNDERWEAR EVERY DAY.
SHAKE
I DON'T WANT YOUR MONEY!
NO!
I'M OFFERING HER THE MONEY, SO WHY CAN'T SHE JUST ACCEPT IT?
I MEAN...

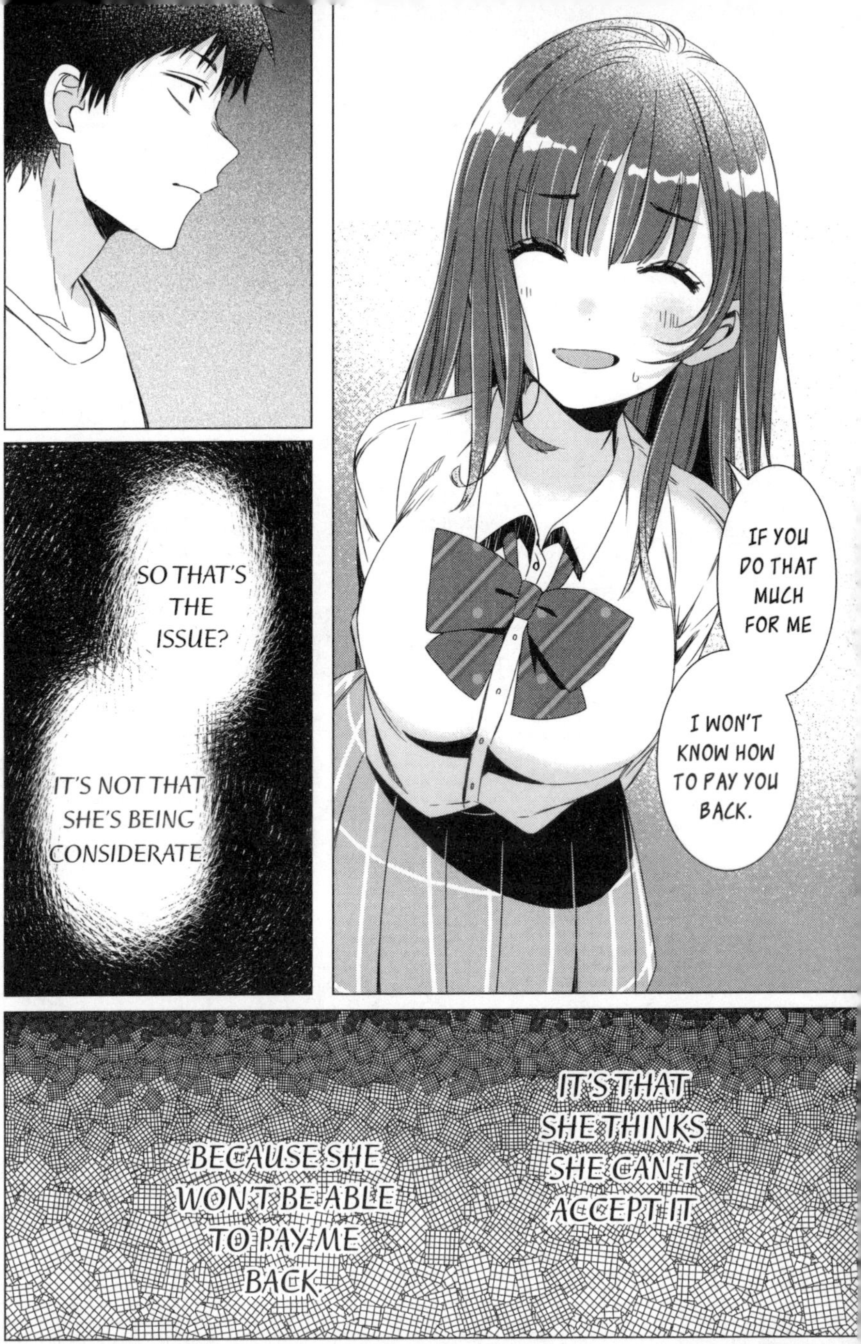
IF YOU DO THAT MUCH FOR ME
I WON'T KNOW HOW TO PAY YOU BACK.
SO THAT'S THE ISSUE?
IT'S NOT THAT SHE'S BEING CONSIDERATE
IT'S THAT SHE THINKS SHE CAN'T ACCEPT IT
BECAUSE SHE WON'T BE ABLE TO PAY ME BACK.

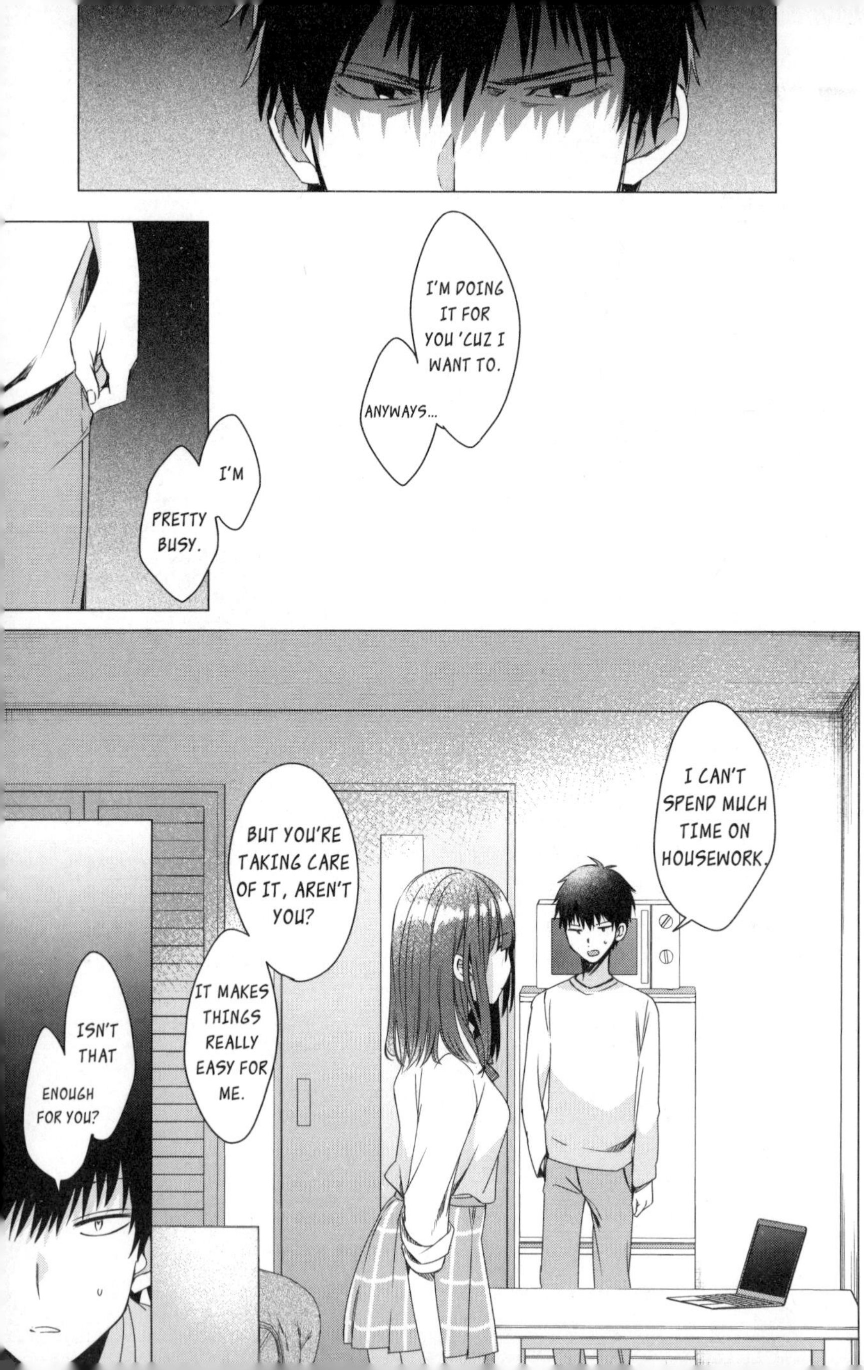
I'M DOING IT FOR YOU 'CUZ I WANT TO.
ANYWAYS...
I'M PRETTY BUSY.
I CAN'T SPEND MUCH TIME ON HOUSEWORK.
BUT YOU'RE TAKING CARE OF IT, AREN'T YOU?
IT MAKES THINGS REALLY EASY FOR ME.
ISN'T THAT ENOUGH FOR YOU?

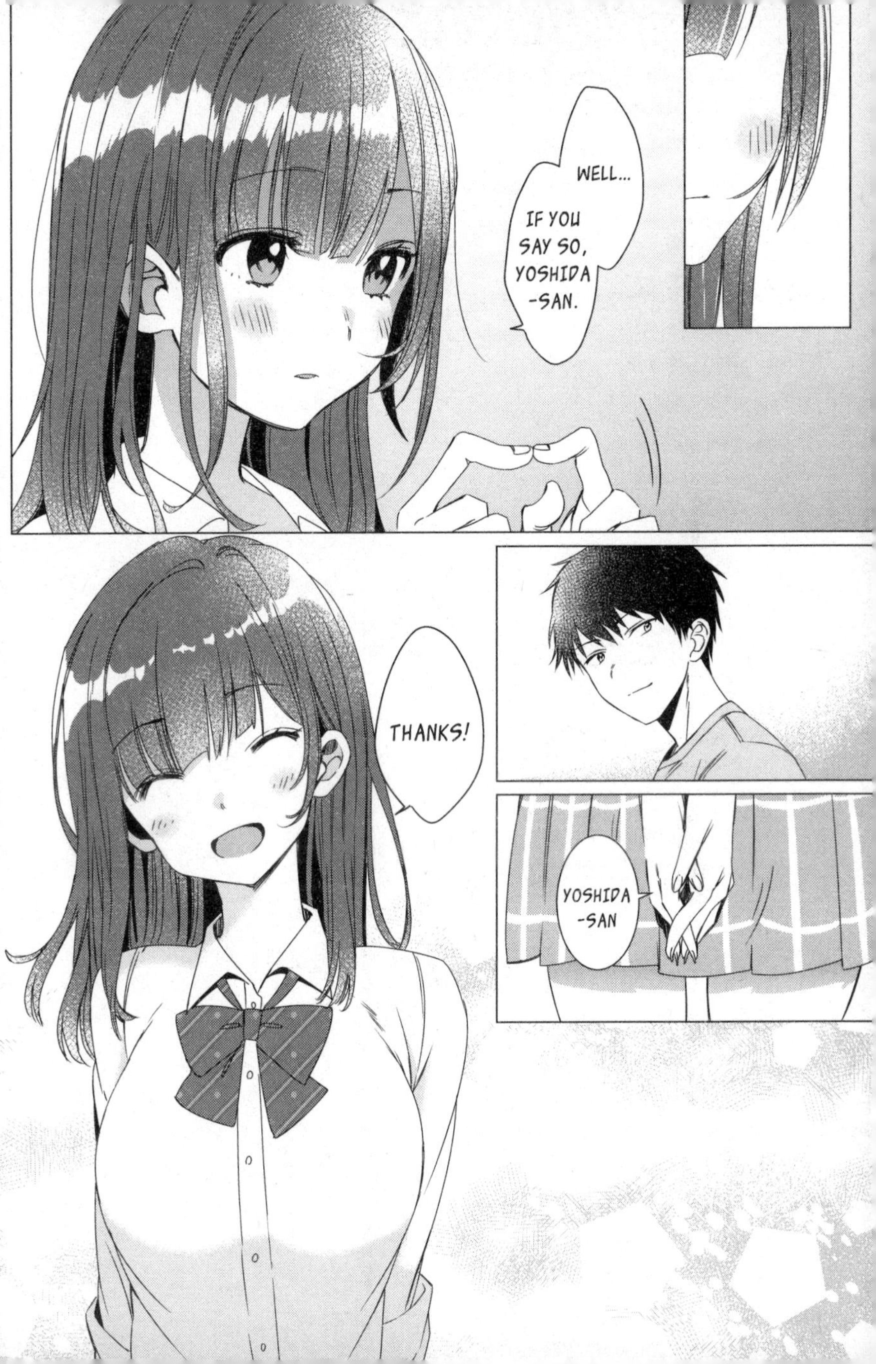
WELL...
IF YOU SAY SO, YOSHIDA-SAN.
YOSHIDA-SAN
THANKS!

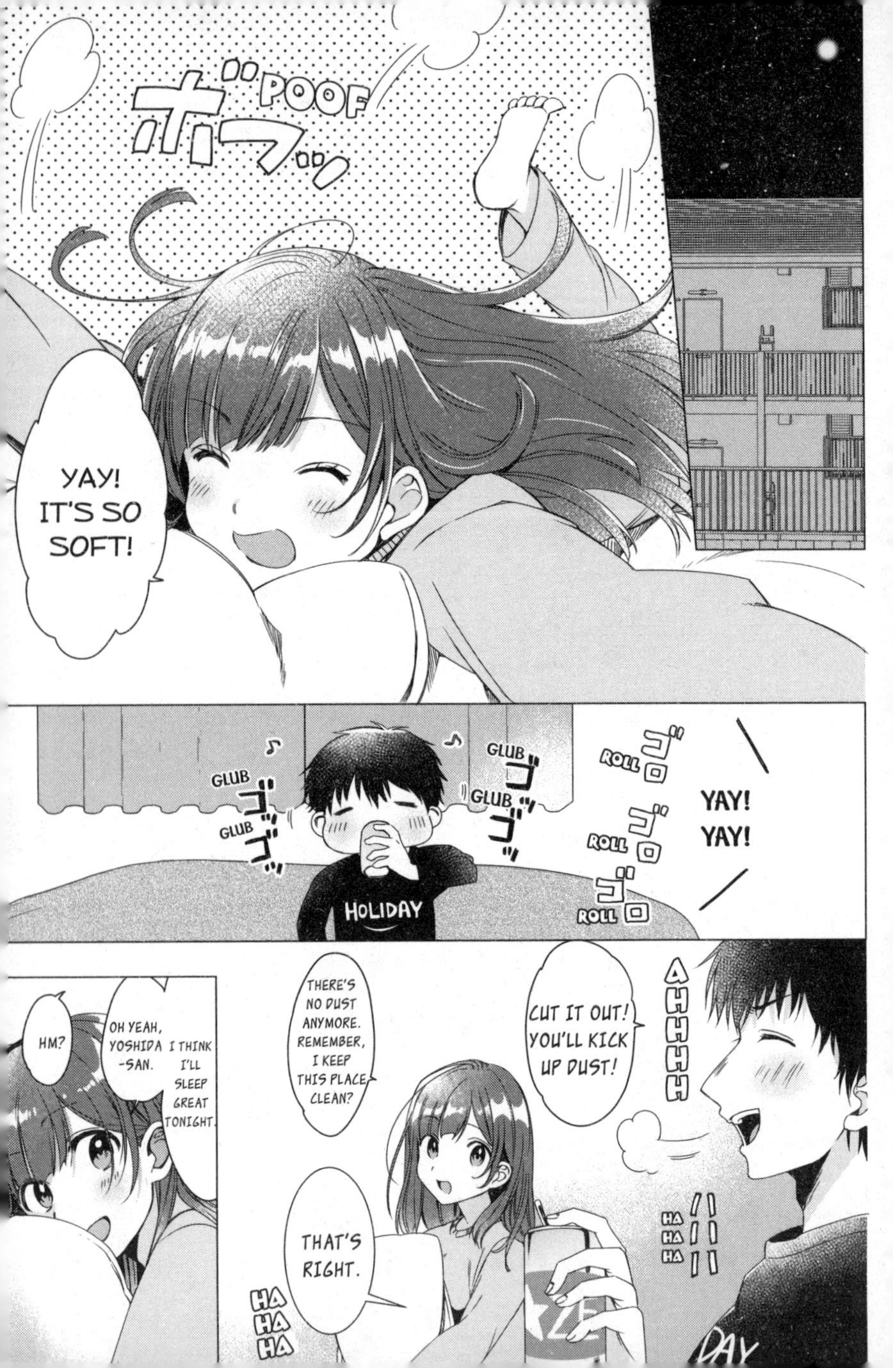
POOF
YAY! IT'S SO SOFT!
YAY! YAY!
ROLL
ROLL
ROLL
GLUB
GLUB
GLUB
HOLIDAY
AHHHHHH
CUT IT OUT! YOU'LL KICK UP DUST!
THERE'S NO DUST ANYMORE. REMEMBER, I KEEP THIS PLACE CLEAN?
HA HA HA
THAT'S RIGHT.
HA HA HA
OH YEAH, YOSHIDA-SAN.
I THINK I'LL SLEEP GREAT TONIGHT.
HM?

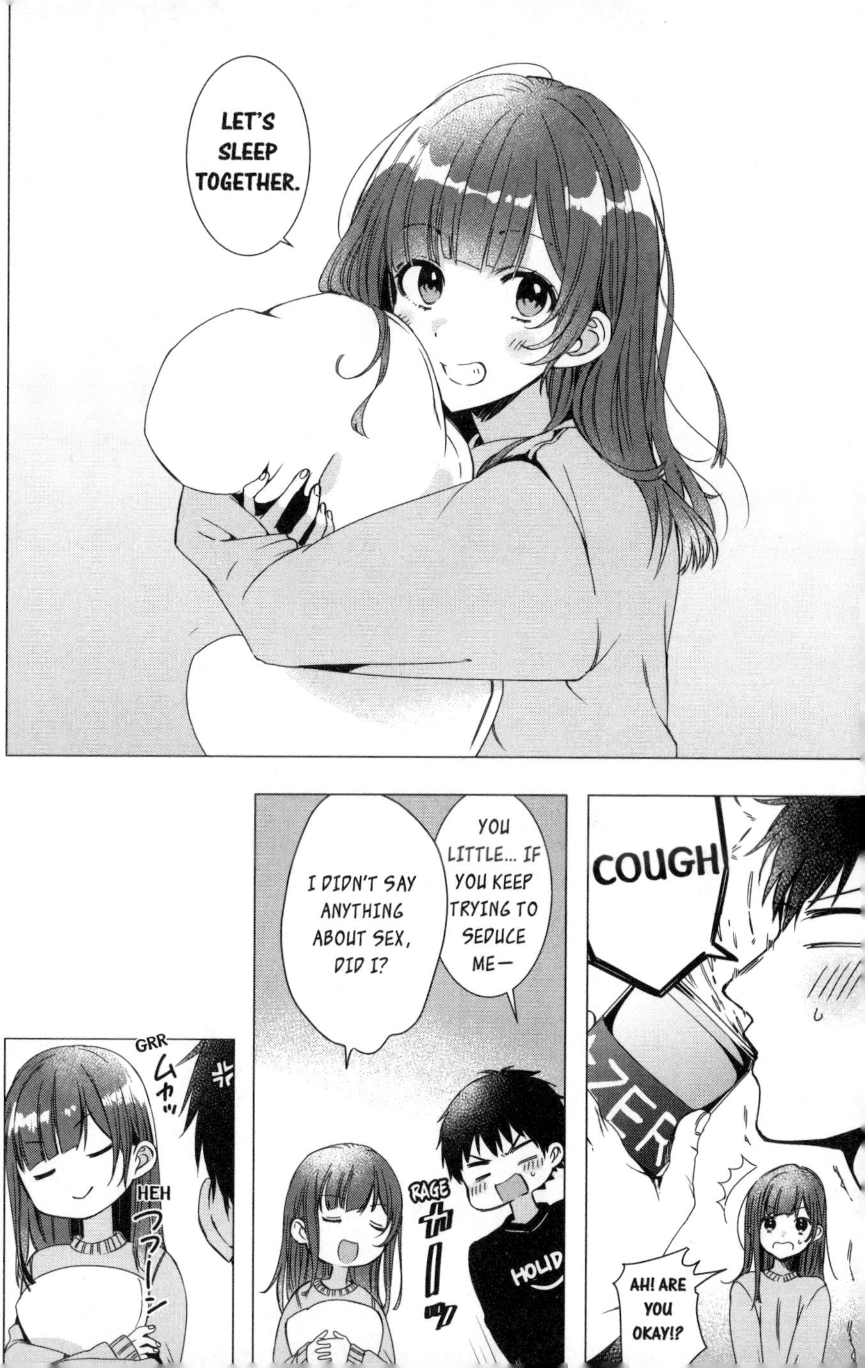
LET'S SLEEP TOGETHER.
COUGH
AH! ARE YOU OKAY!?
YOU LITTLE... IF YOU KEEP TRYING TO SEDUCE ME—
I DIDN'T SAY ANYTHING ABOUT SEX, DID I?
RAGE
カーーッ
GRR
ムカッ
HEH

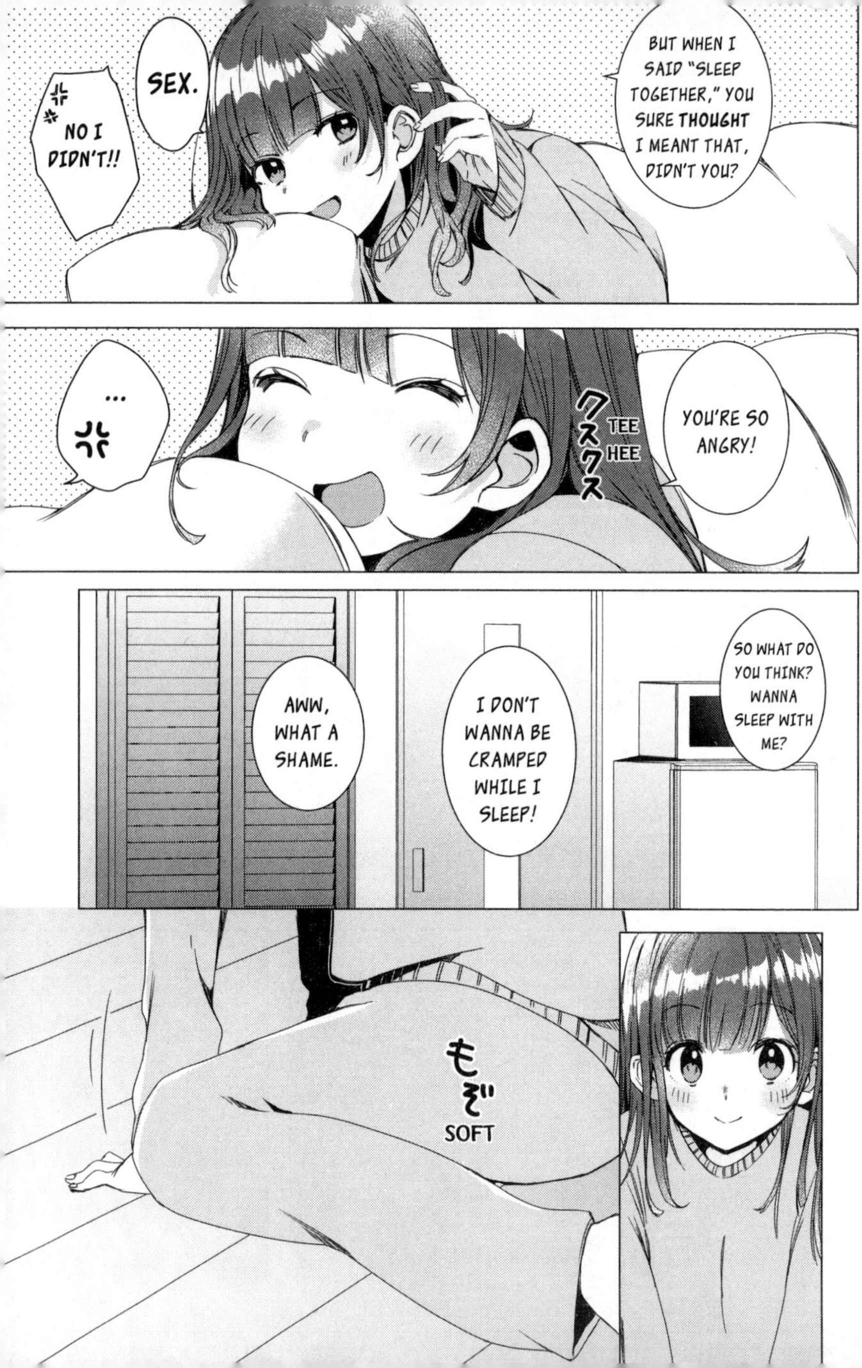
BUT WHEN I SAID "SLEEP TOGETHER," YOU SURE THOUGHT I MEANT THAT, DIDN'T YOU?
SEX.
NO I DIDN'T!!
YOU'RE SO ANGRY!
クスクス TEE HEE
...
SO WHAT DO YOU THINK? WANNA SLEEP WITH ME?
I DON'T WANNA BE CRAMPED WHILE I SLEEP!
AWW, WHAT A SHAME.
もぞ SOFT

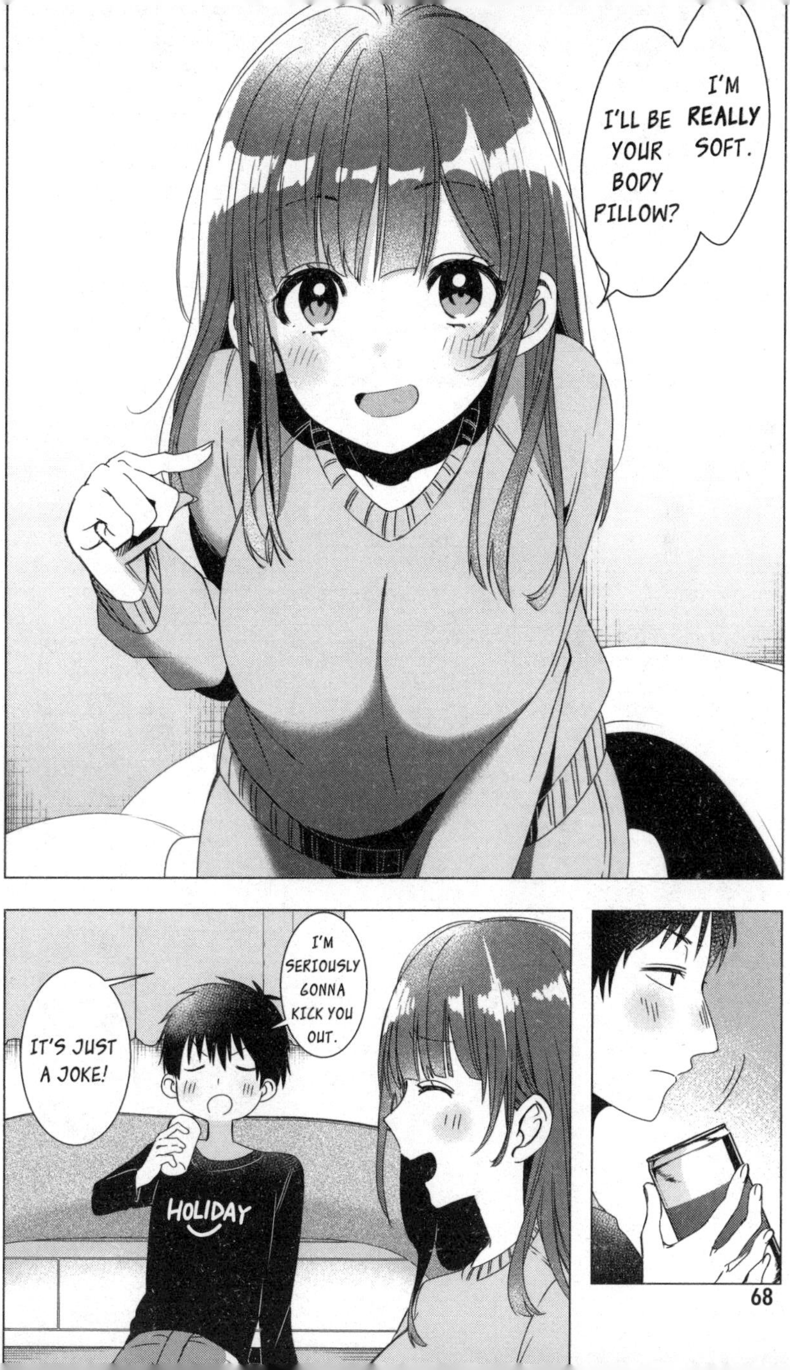
I'M REALLY SOFT.
I'LL BE YOUR BODY PILLOW?
I'M SERIOUSLY GONNA KICK YOU OUT.
IT'S JUST A JOKE!
HOLIDAY

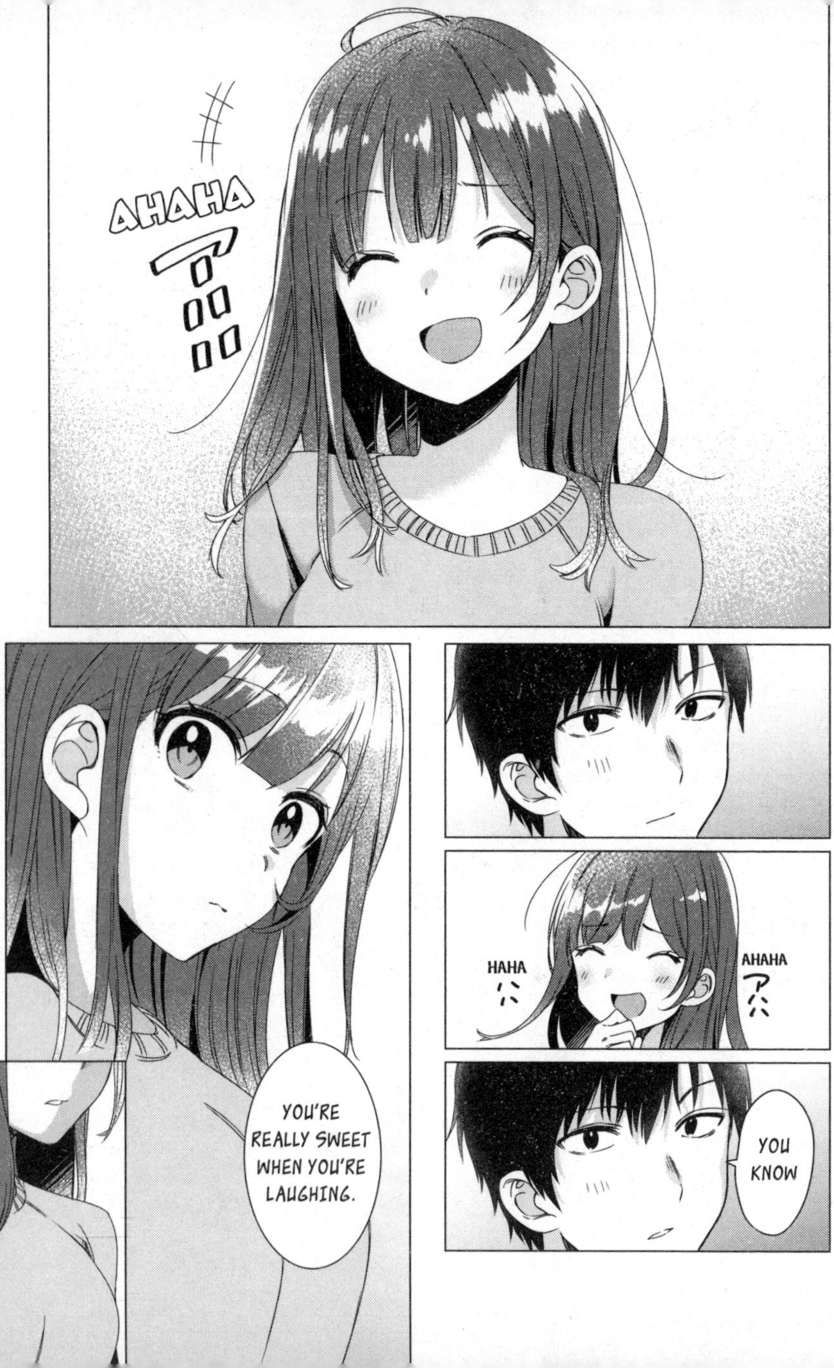
AHAHA
AHAHA
HAHA
YOU KNOW
YOU'RE REALLY SWEET WHEN YOU'RE LAUGHING.

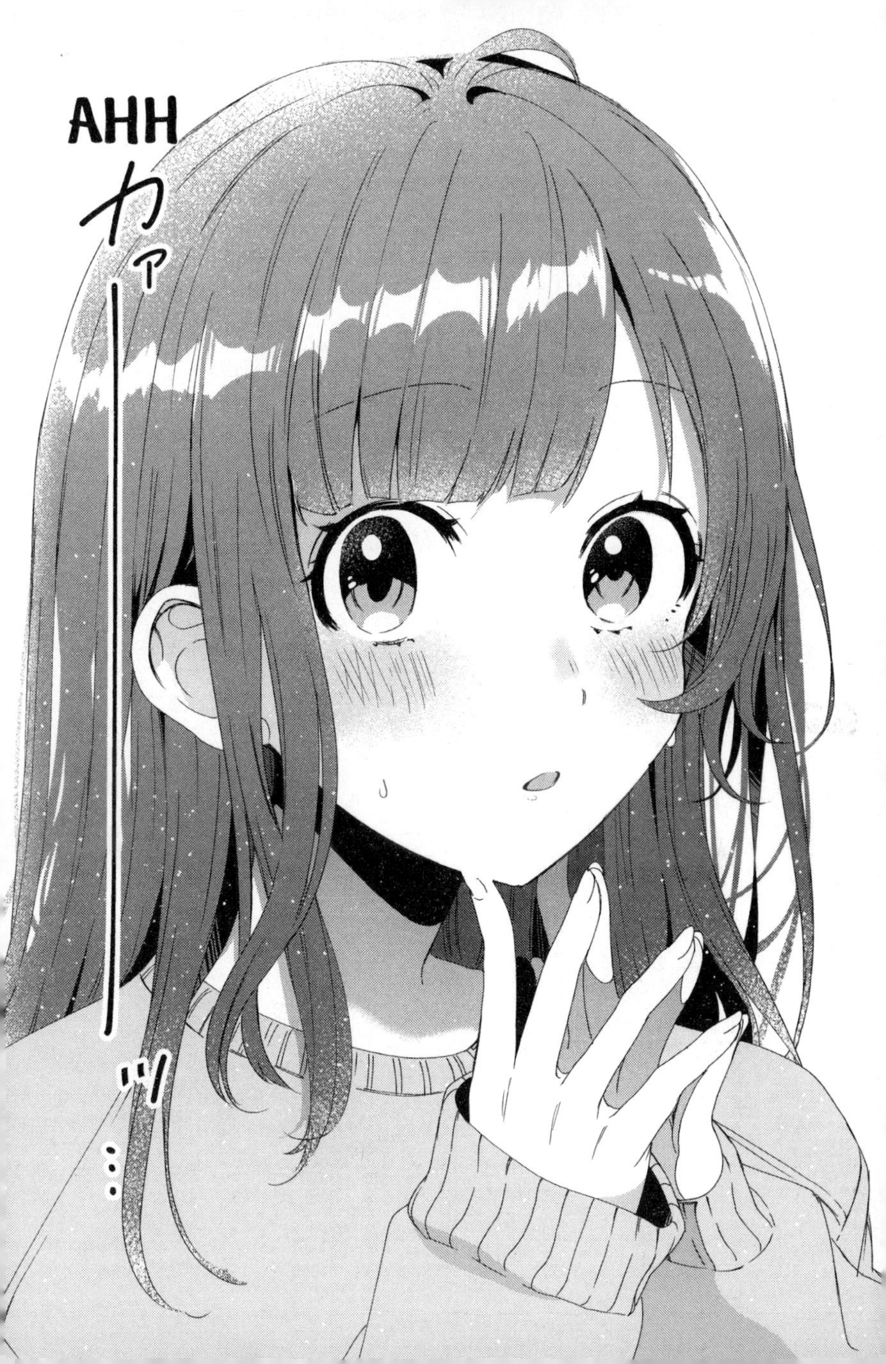
AHH
カァーッ…

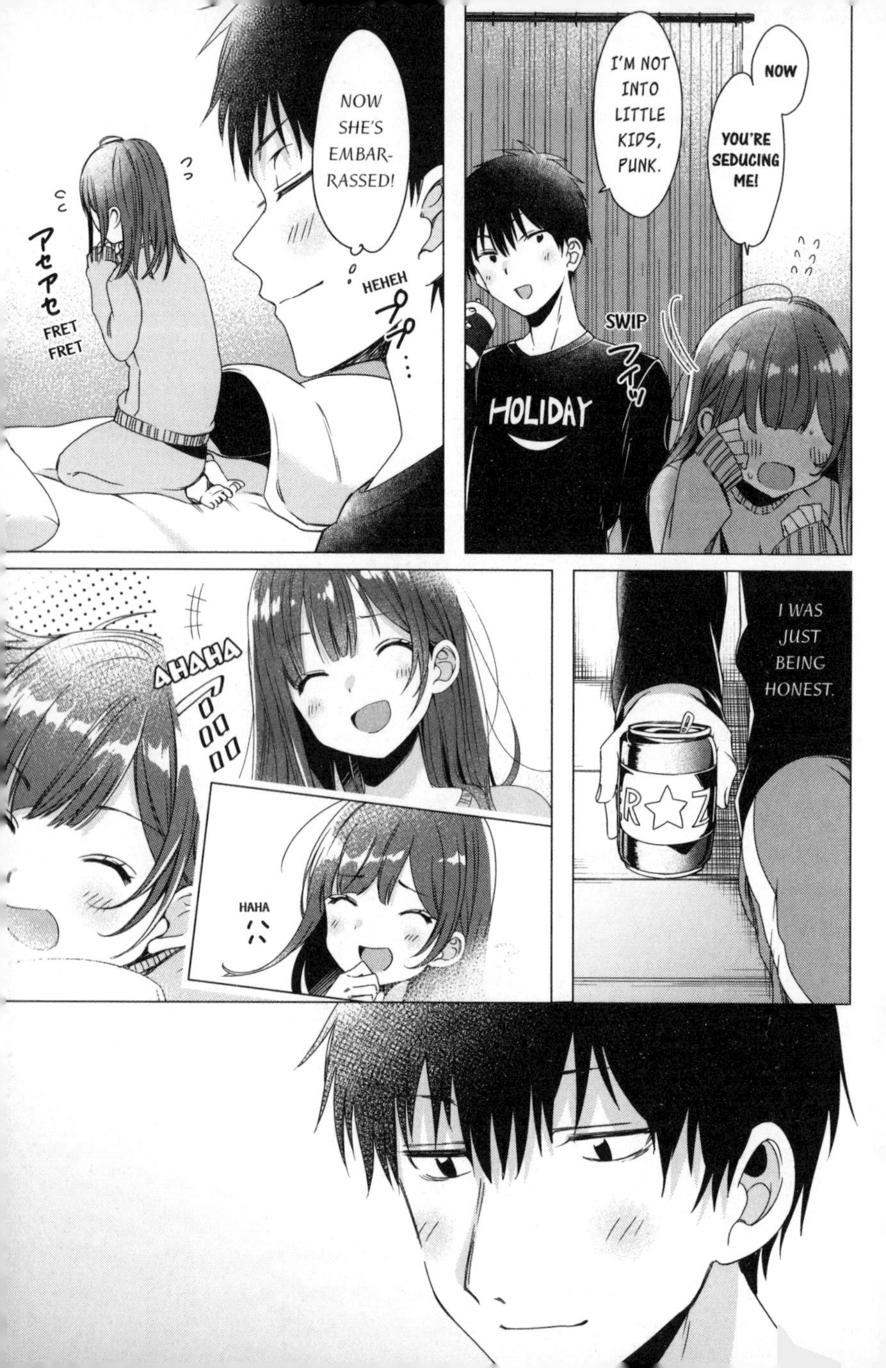

NOW YOU'RE SEDUCING ME!
I'M NOT INTO LITTLE KIDS, PUNK.
SWIP
フィッ
NOW SHE'S EMBARRASSED!
HEHEH
アセアセ
FRET FRET
I WAS JUST BEING HONEST.
AHAHA
HAHA

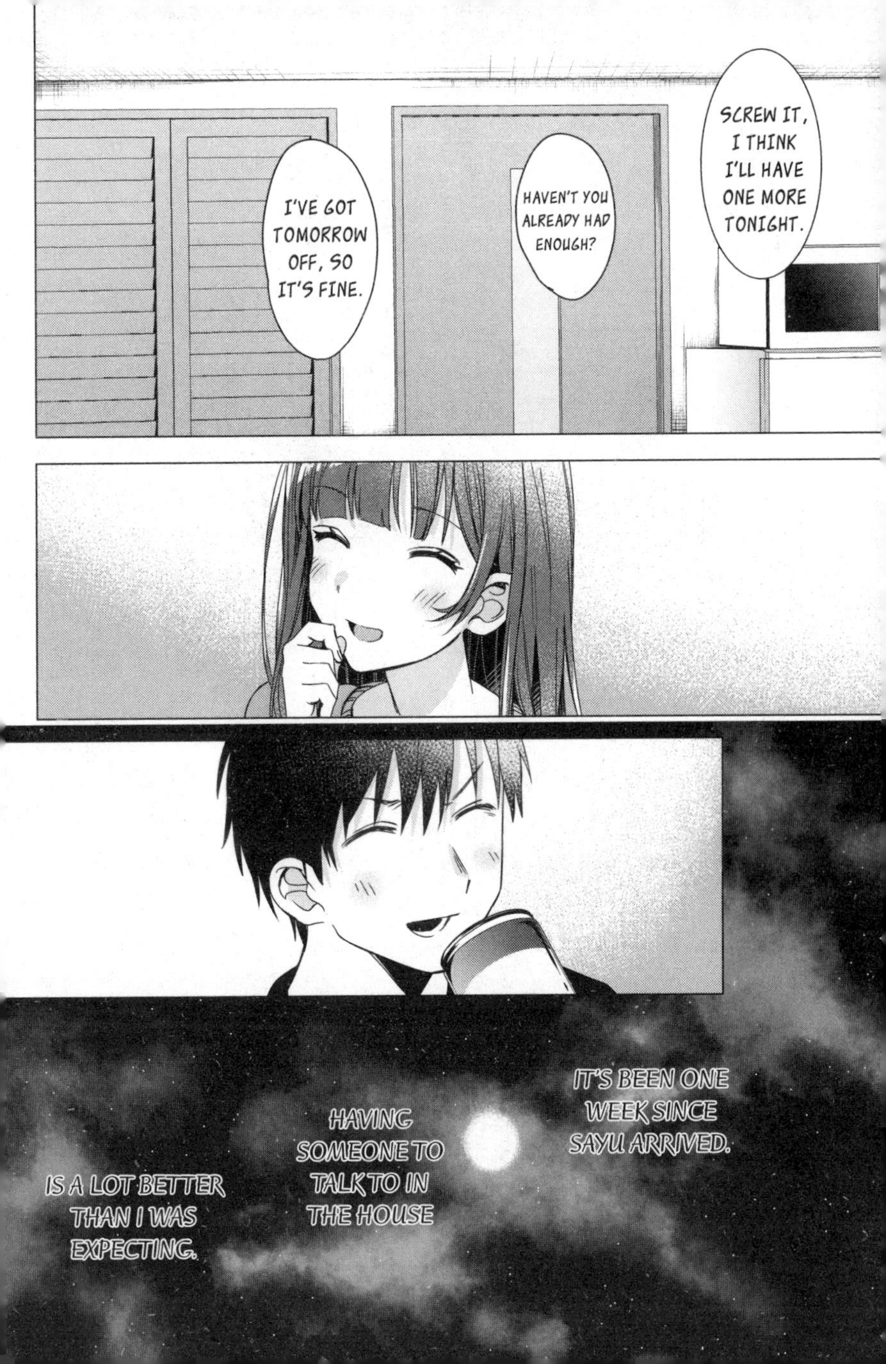
SCREW IT, I THINK I'LL HAVE ONE MORE TONIGHT.
HAVEN'T YOU ALREADY HAD ENOUGH?
I'VE GOT TOMORROW OFF, SO IT'S FINE.
IT'S BEEN ONE WEEK SINCE SAYU ARRIVED.
HAVING SOMEONE TO TALK TO IN THE HOUSE
IS A LOT BETTER THAN I WAS EXPECTING.

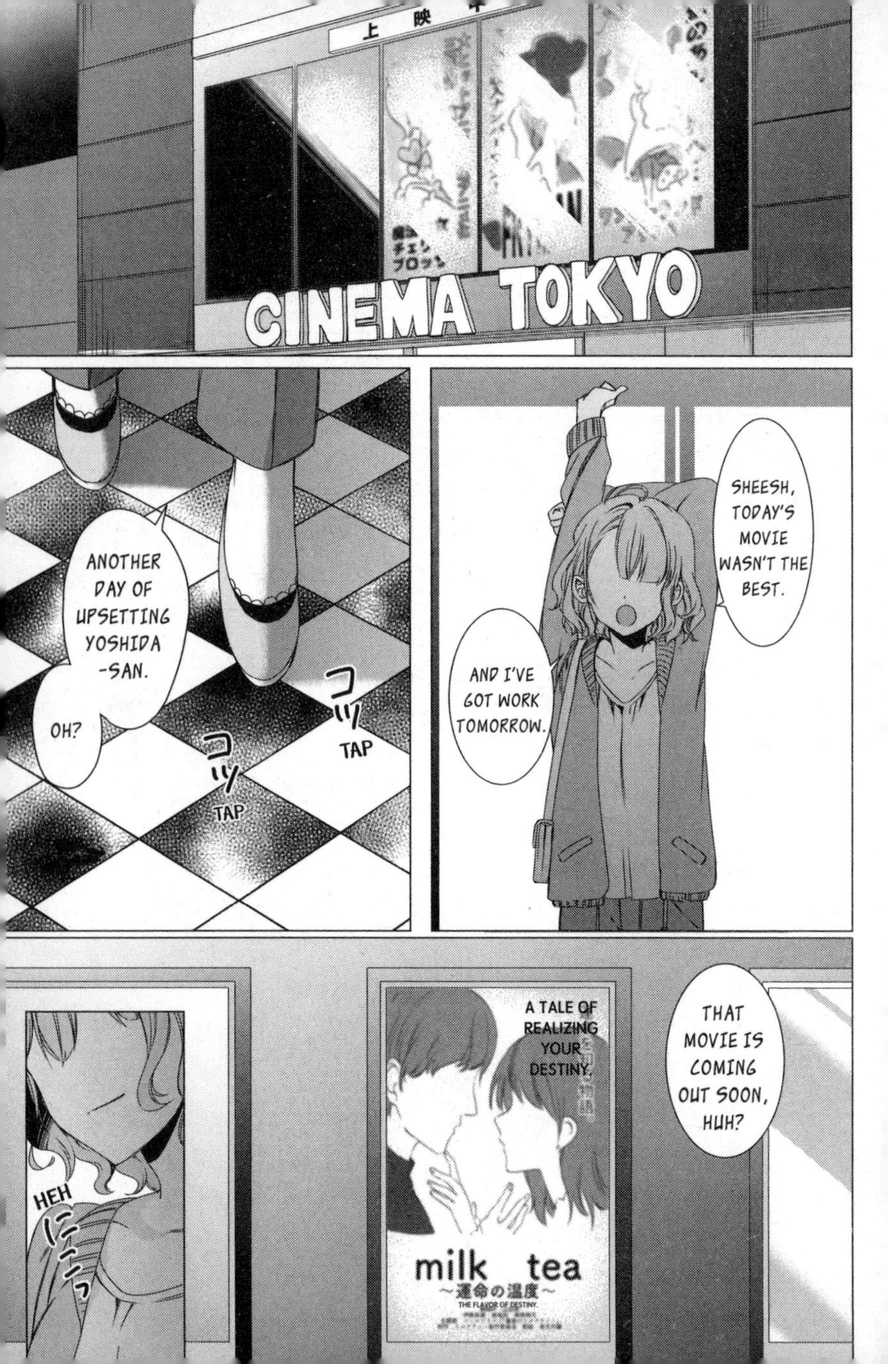
CINEMA TOKYO
SHEESH, TODAY'S MOVIE WASN'T THE BEST.
AND I'VE GOT WORK TOMORROW.
ANOTHER DAY OF UPSETTING YOSHIDA-SAN.
OH?
コツ
TAP
コツ
TAP
THAT MOVIE IS COMING OUT SOON, HUH?
A TALE OF REALIZING YOUR DESTINY.
milk tea
〜運命の温度〜
THE FLAVOR OF DESTINY.
HEH
にこっ

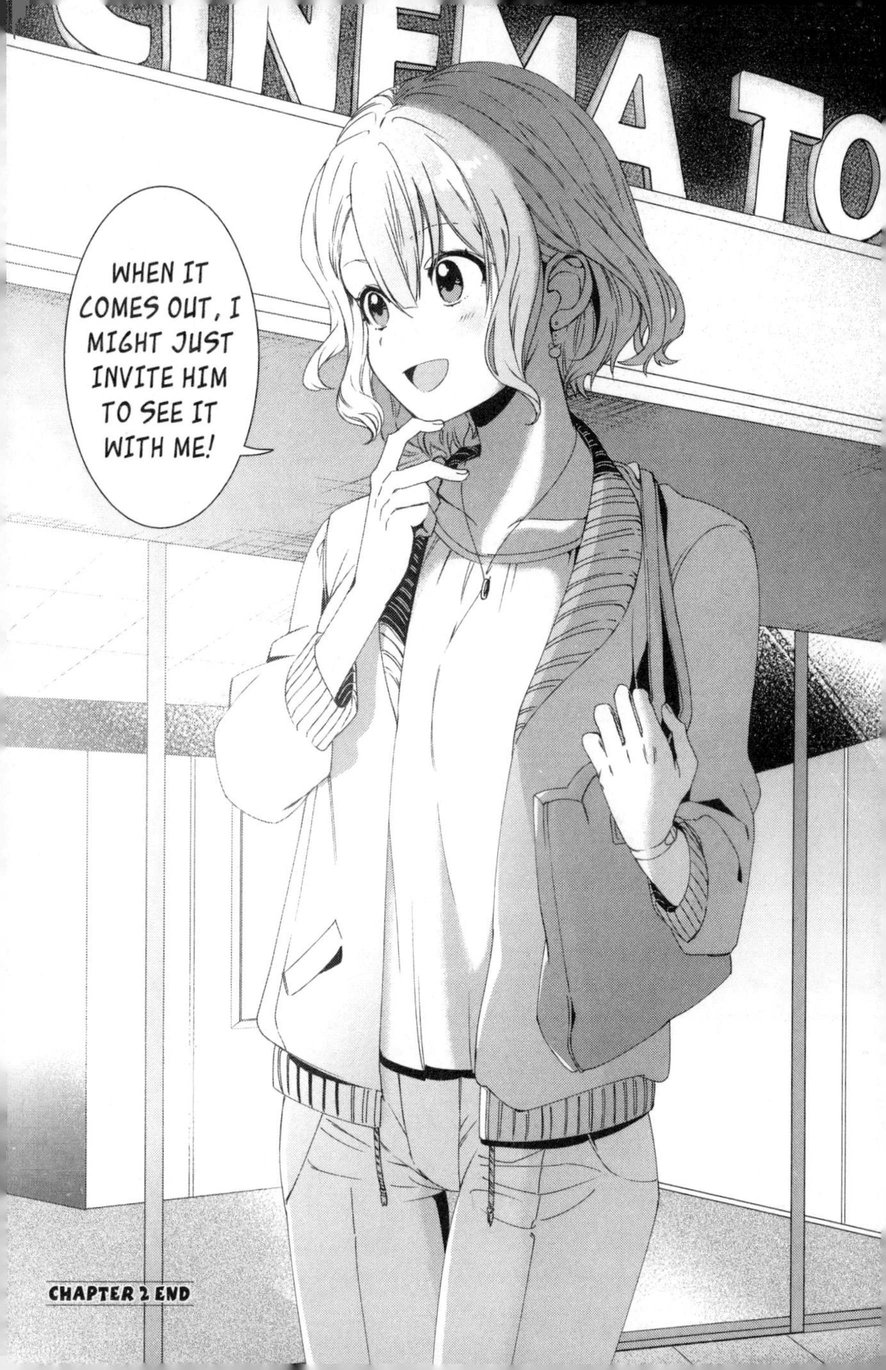
CINEMA TO
WHEN IT COMES OUT, I MIGHT JUST INVITE HIM TO SEE IT WITH ME!
CHAPTER 2 END

[CHAPTER 3]

WORK AND A COLLEAGUE

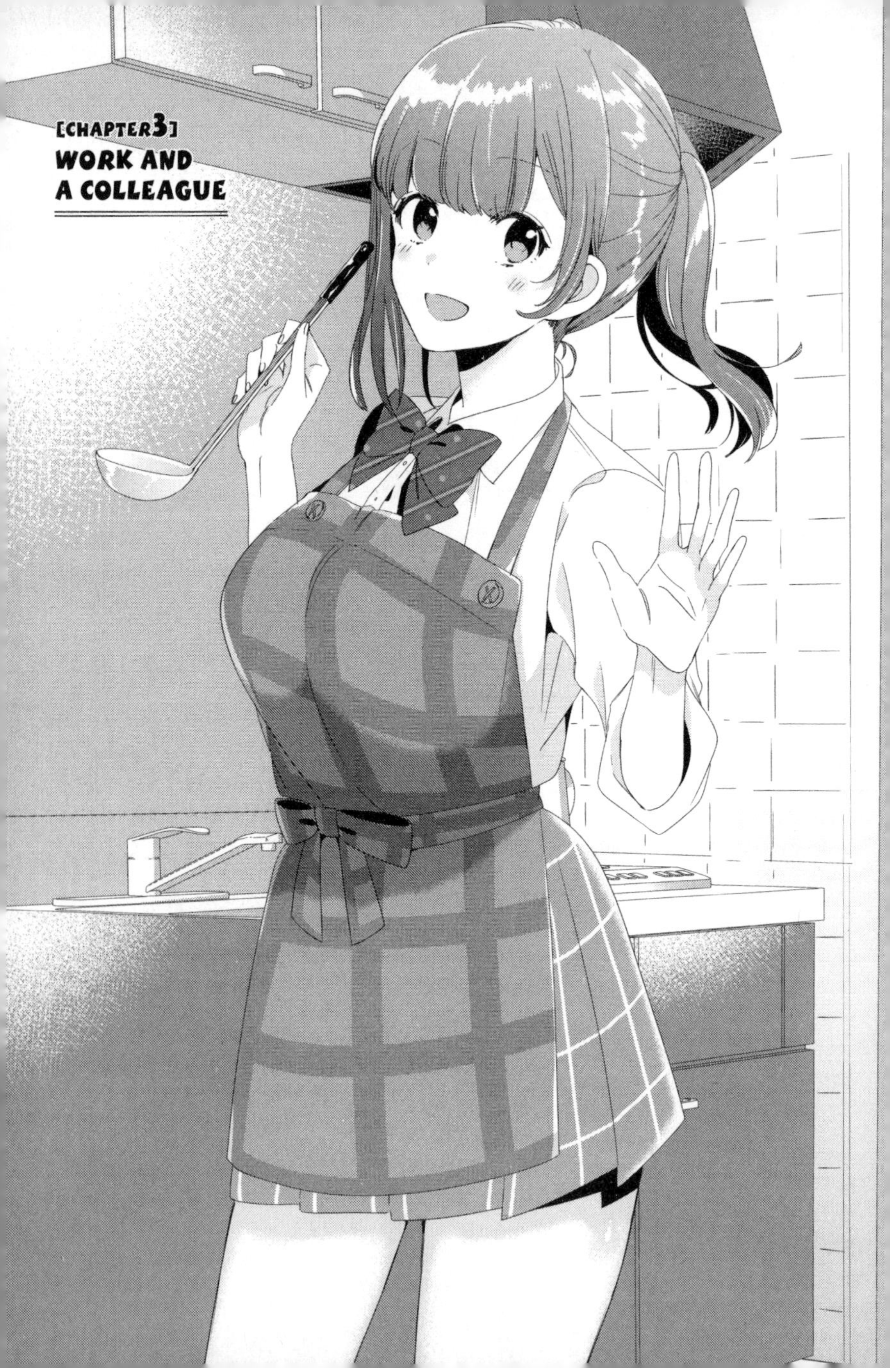

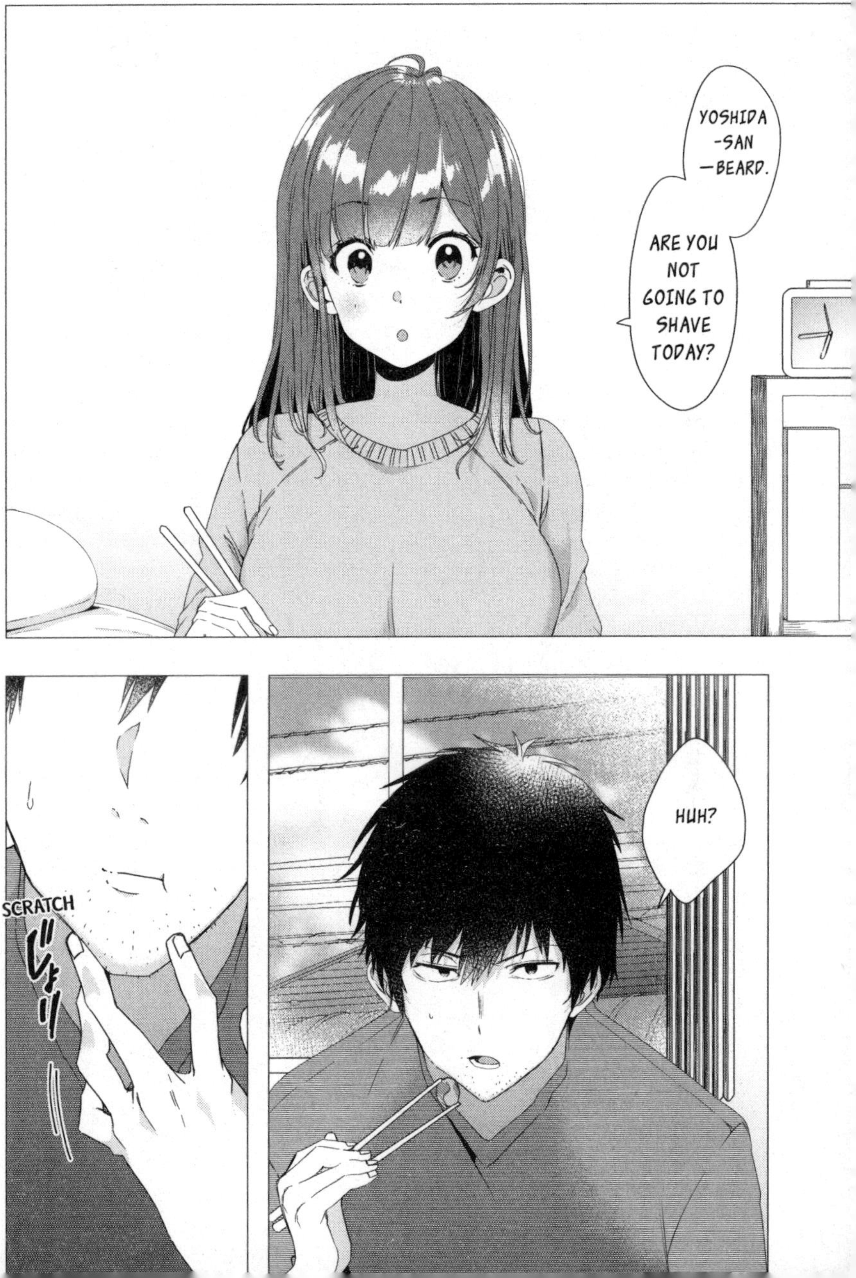
YOSHIDA-SAN—BEARD.
ARE YOU NOT GOING TO SHAVE TODAY?
HUH?
SCRATCH

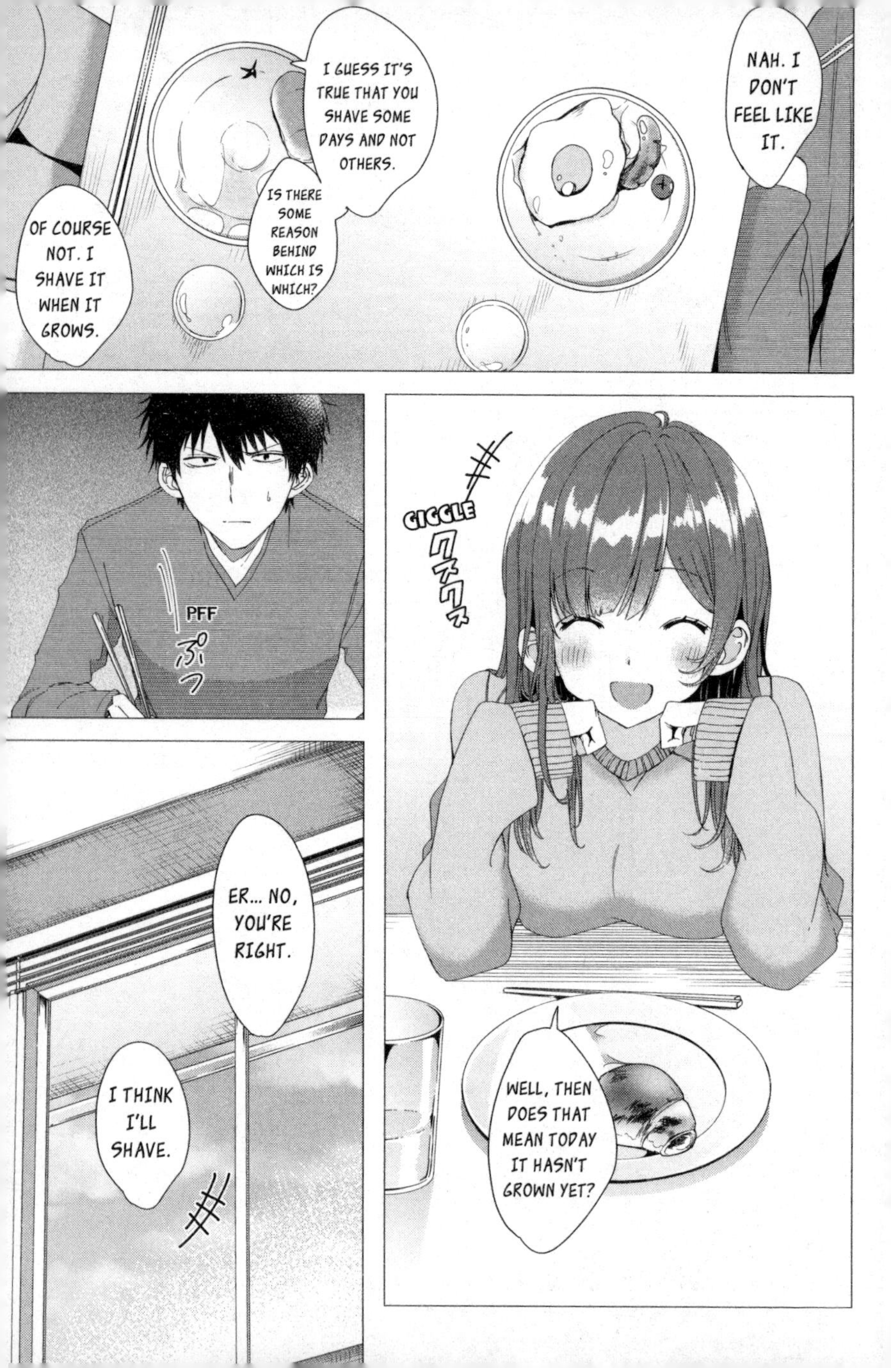
NAH. I DON'T FEEL LIKE IT.
I GUESS IT'S TRUE THAT YOU SHAVE SOME DAYS AND NOT OTHERS.
IS THERE SOME REASON BEHIND WHICH IS WHICH?
OF COURSE NOT. I SHAVE IT WHEN IT GROWS.
GIGGLE
クスクス
WELL, THEN DOES THAT MEAN TODAY IT HASN'T GROWN YET?
PFF
ぷっ
ER... NO, YOU'RE RIGHT.
I THINK I'LL SHAVE.

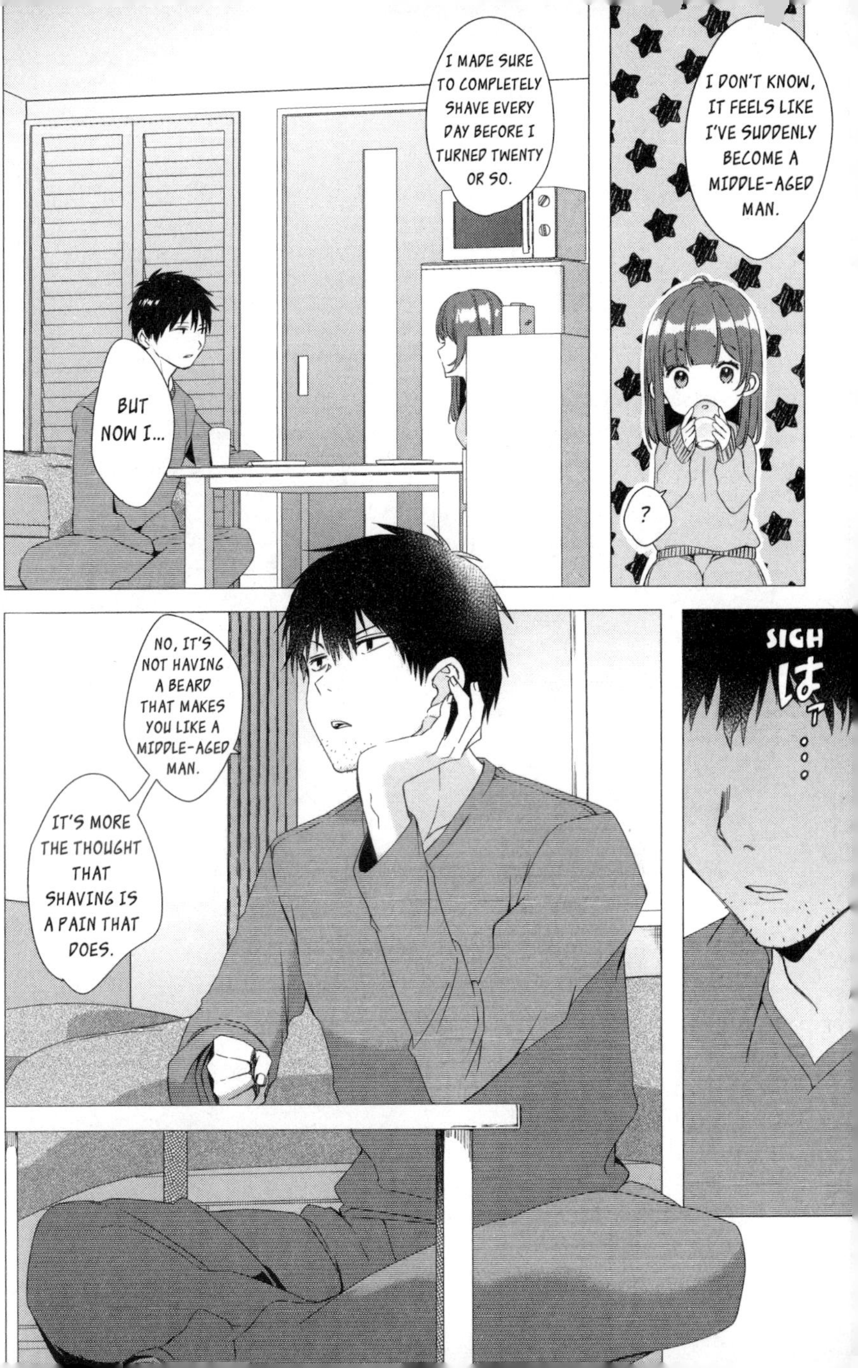
I DON'T KNOW, IT FEELS LIKE I'VE SUDDENLY BECOME A MIDDLE-AGED MAN.
?
I MADE SURE TO COMPLETELY SHAVE EVERY DAY BEFORE I TURNED TWENTY OR SO.
BUT NOW I...
SIGH
はァ…
NO, IT'S NOT HAVING A BEARD THAT MAKES YOU LIKE A MIDDLE-AGED MAN.
IT'S MORE THE THOUGHT THAT SHAVING IS A PAIN THAT DOES.

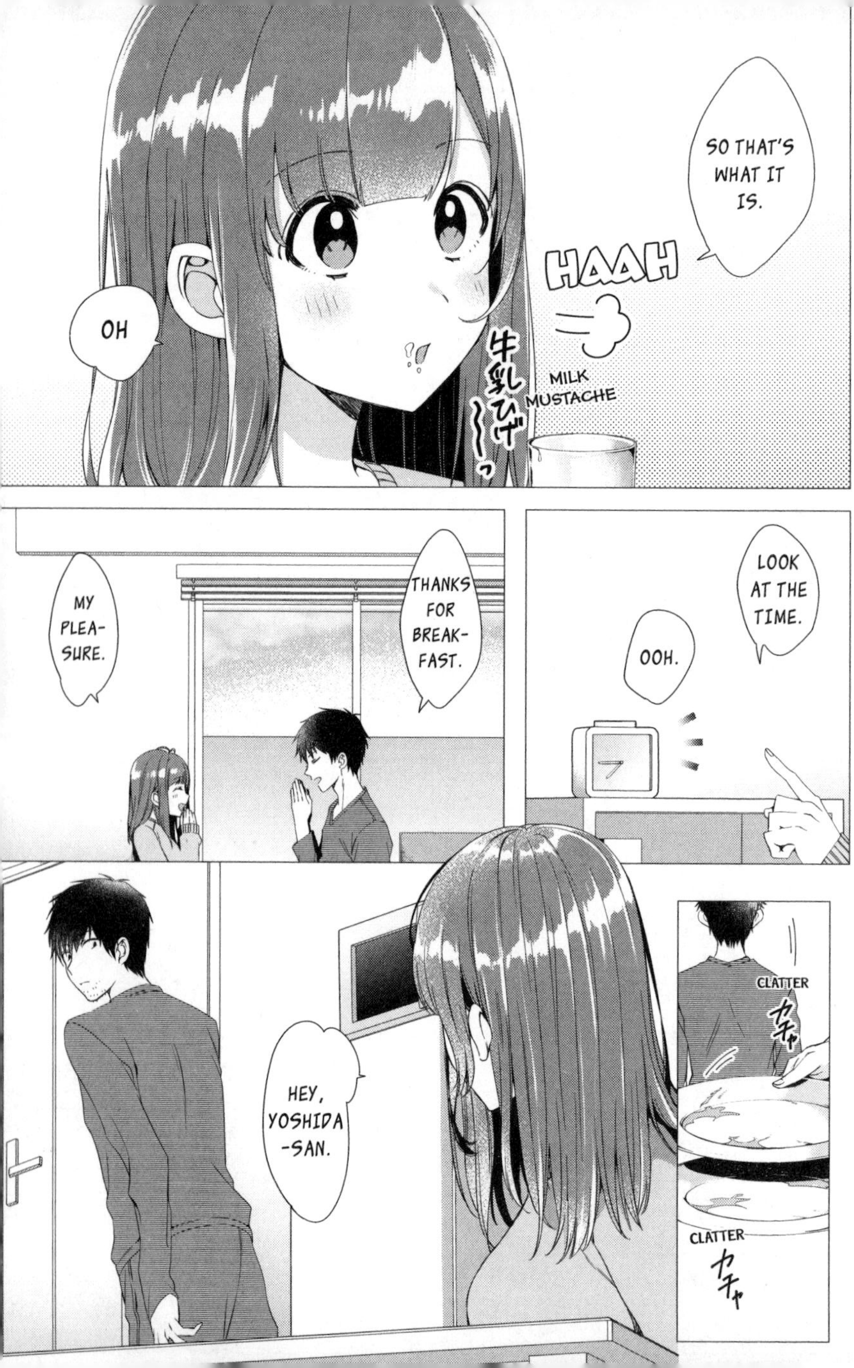

SO THAT'S WHAT IT IS.
HAAH
牛乳ひげ〜〜っ
MILK MUSTACHE
OH
LOOK AT THE TIME.
OOH.
THANKS FOR BREAK-FAST.
MY PLEA-SURE.
CLATTER
カチャ
CLATTER
カチャ
HEY, YOSHIDA-SAN.

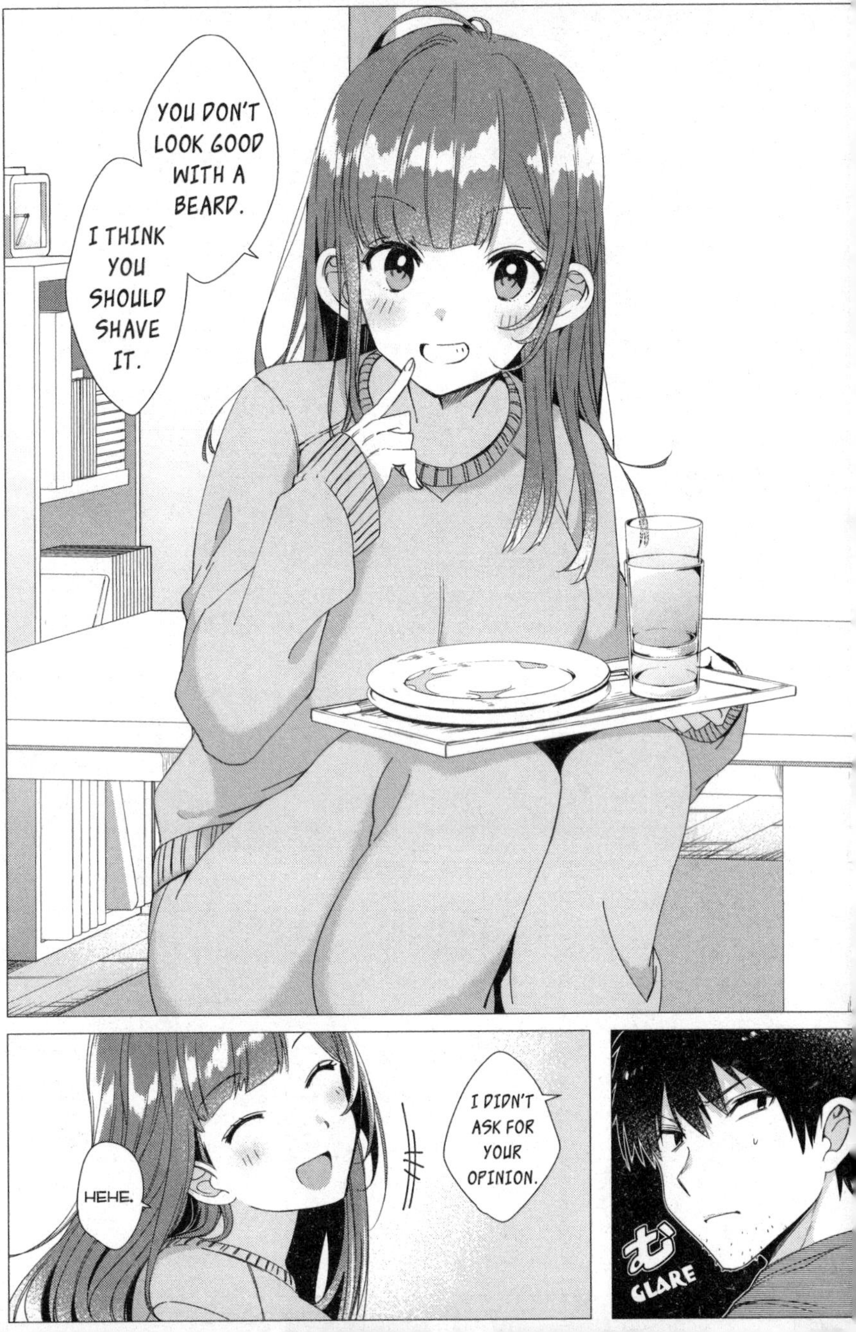
YOU DON'T LOOK GOOD WITH A BEARD.
I THINK YOU SHOULD SHAVE IT.
む
GLARE
I DIDN'T ASK FOR YOUR OPINION.
HEHE.

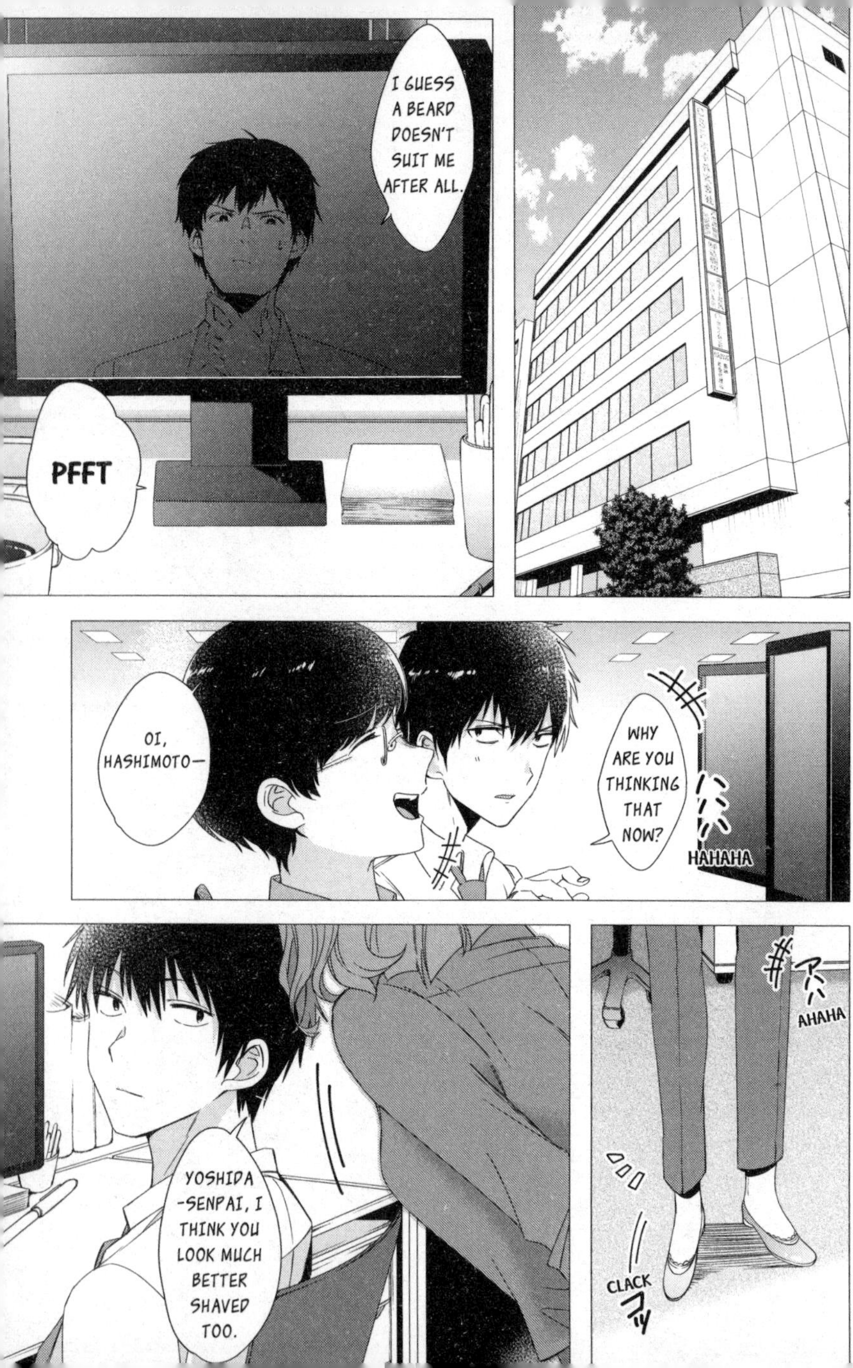
I GUESS A BEARD DOESN'T SUIT ME AFTER ALL.
PFFT
WHY ARE YOU THINKING THAT NOW?
HAHAHA
OI, HASHIMOTO—
AHAHA
CLACK
YOSHIDA-SENPAI, I THINK YOU LOOK MUCH BETTER SHAVED TOO.

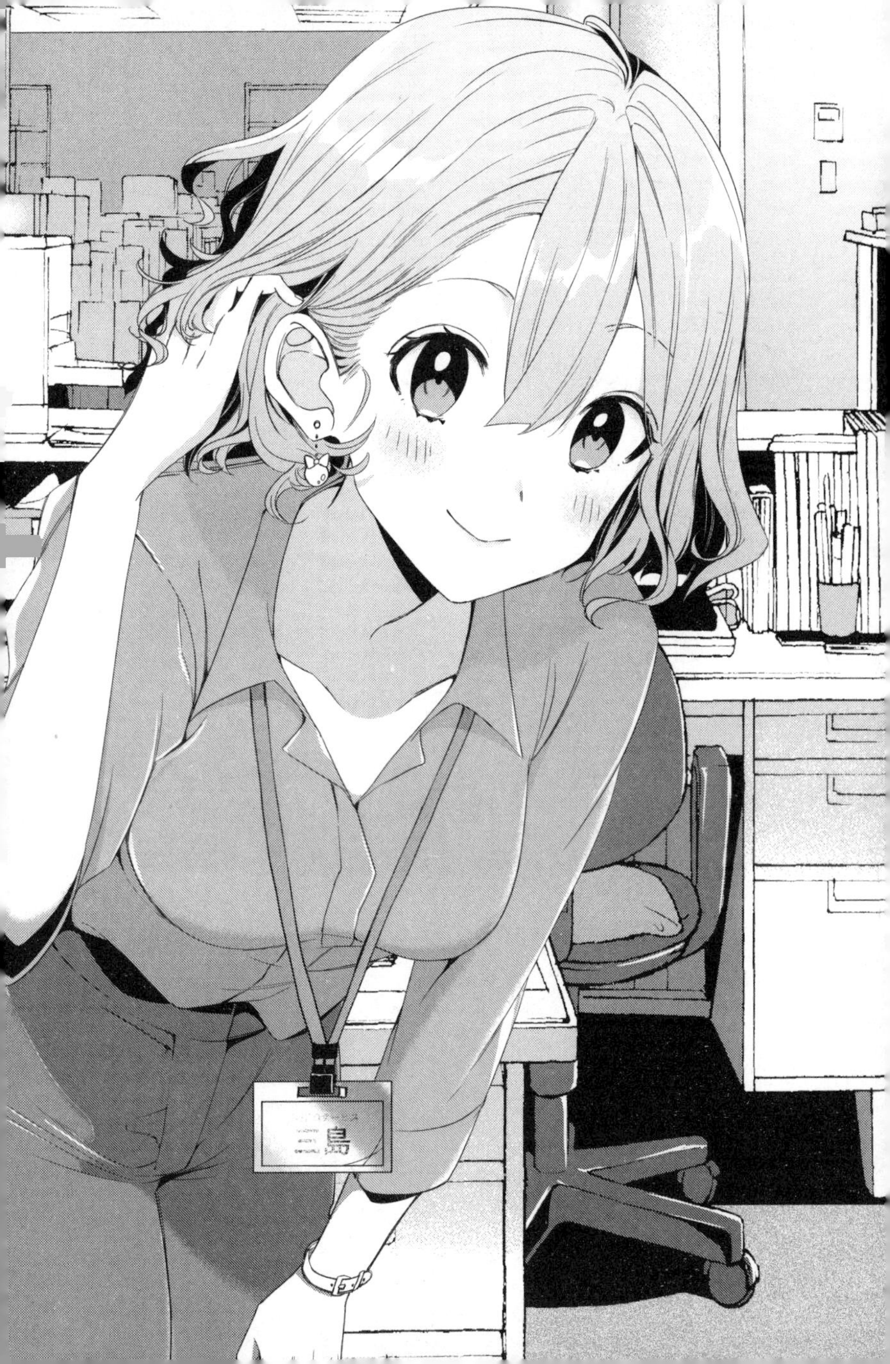
島

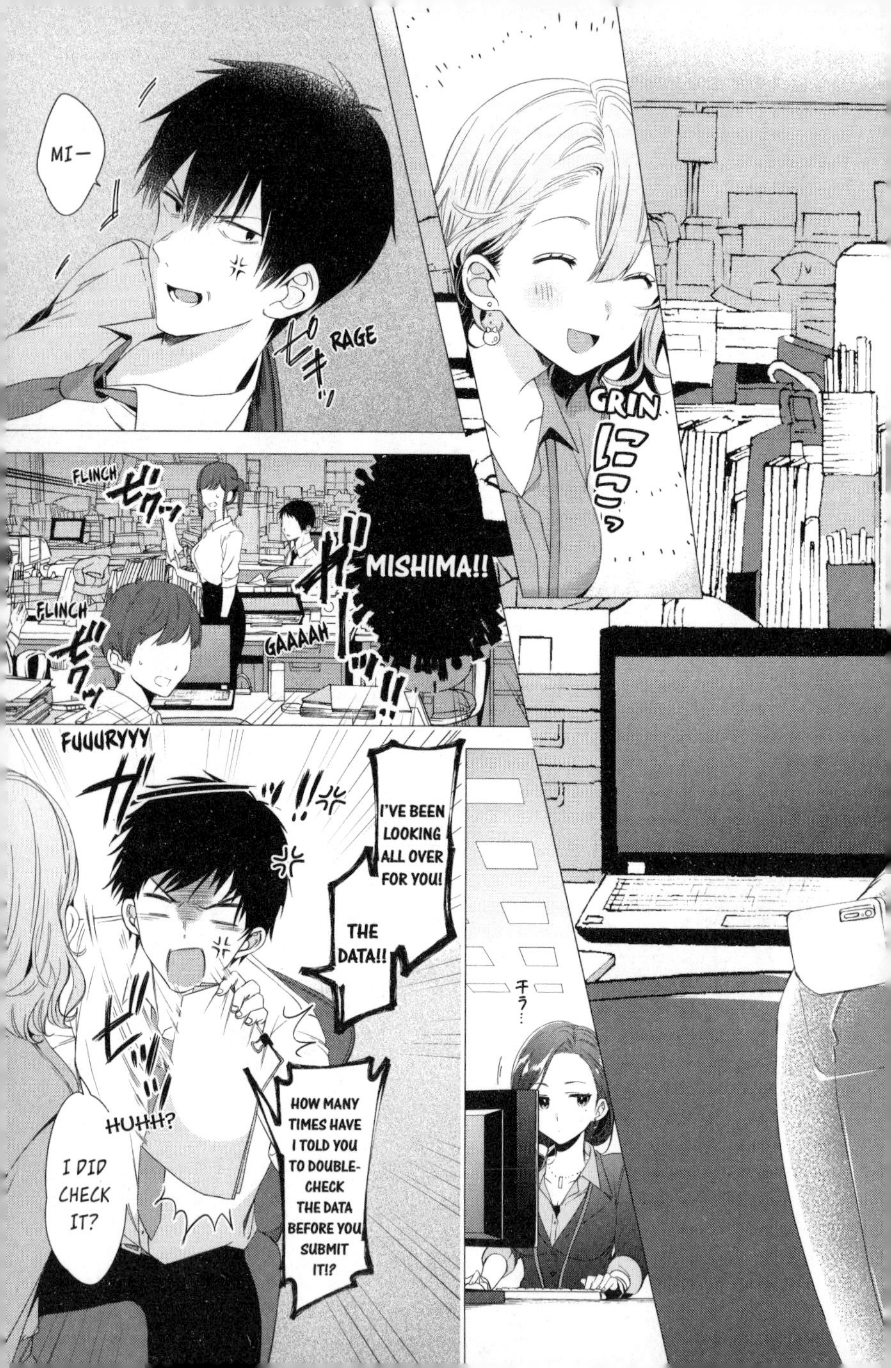
GRIN
にこっ
MI—
RAGE
ピキッ
MISHIMA!!
ガーッ!!
FLINCH
ビクッ
GAAAAH
FLINCH
ビクッ
チラ…
FUUURYYY
ガーッ!!
I'VE BEEN LOOKING ALL OVER FOR YOU!
THE DATA!!
HOW MANY TIMES HAVE I TOLD YOU TO DOUBLE-CHECK THE DATA BEFORE YOU SUBMIT IT!?
HUHH?
I DID CHECK IT?

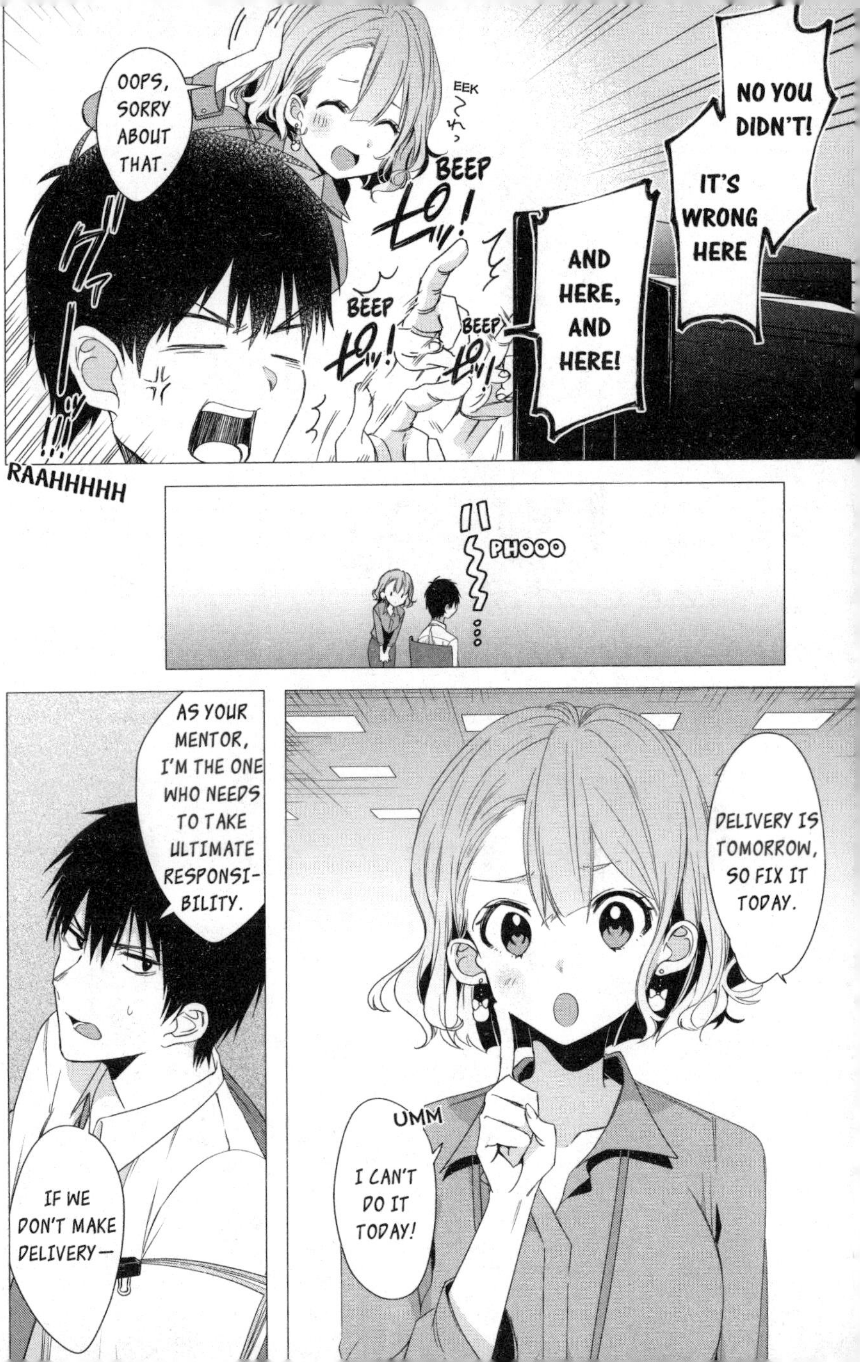
NO YOU DIDN'T!
IT'S WRONG HERE
AND HERE, AND HERE!
BEEP
BEEP
BEEP
EEK
OOPS, SORRY ABOUT THAT.
RAAHHHHH
PHOOO
DELIVERY IS TOMORROW, SO FIX IT TODAY.
UMM
I CAN'T DO IT TODAY!
AS YOUR MENTOR, I'M THE ONE WHO NEEDS TO TAKE ULTIMATE RESPONSI-BILITY.
IF WE DON'T MAKE DELIVERY—

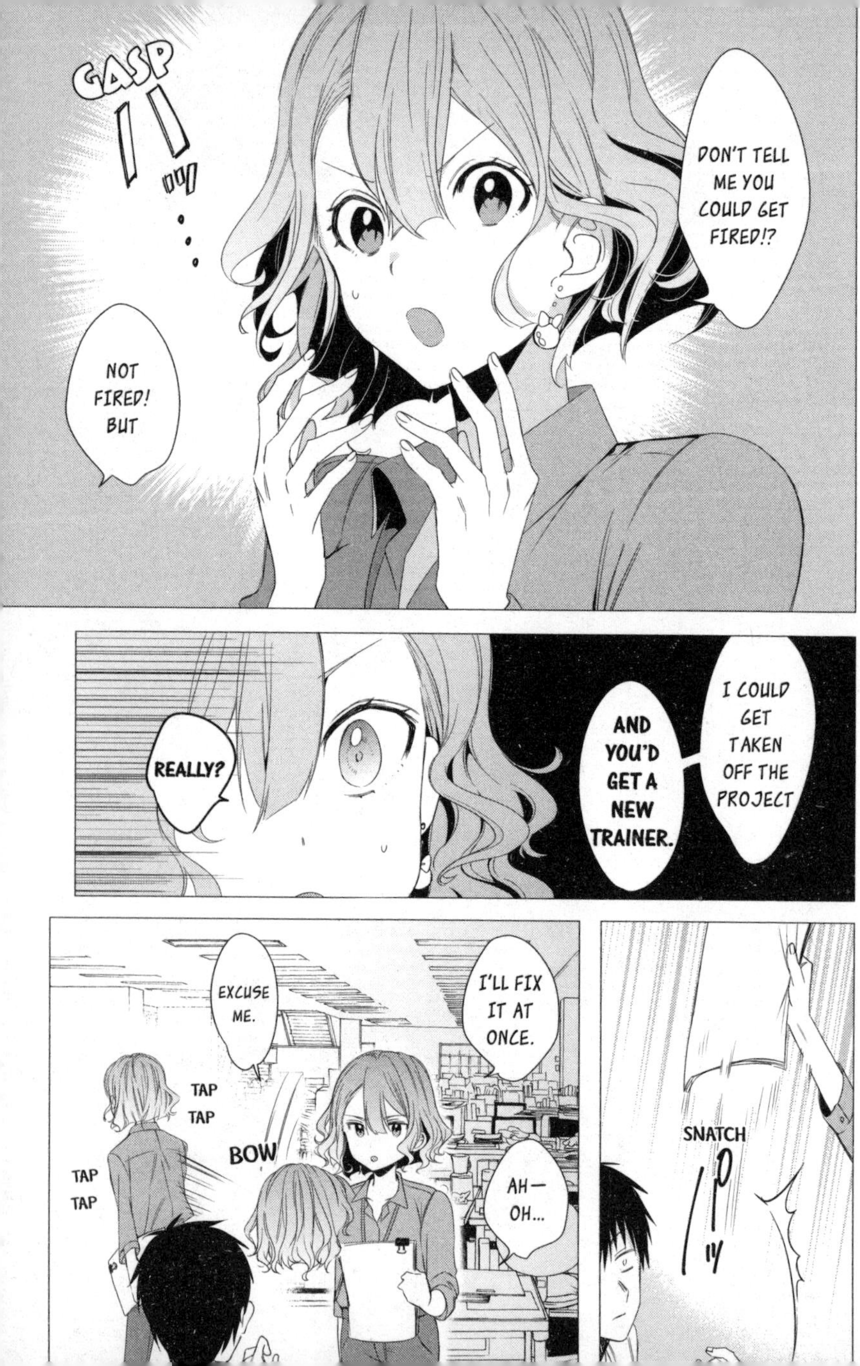
DON'T TELL ME YOU COULD GET FIRED!?
GASP
NOT FIRED! BUT
I COULD GET TAKEN OFF THE PROJECT
AND YOU'D GET A NEW TRAINER.
REALLY?
SNATCH
I'LL FIX IT AT ONCE.
EXCUSE ME.
TAP TAP
BOW
AH— OH...
TAP TAP

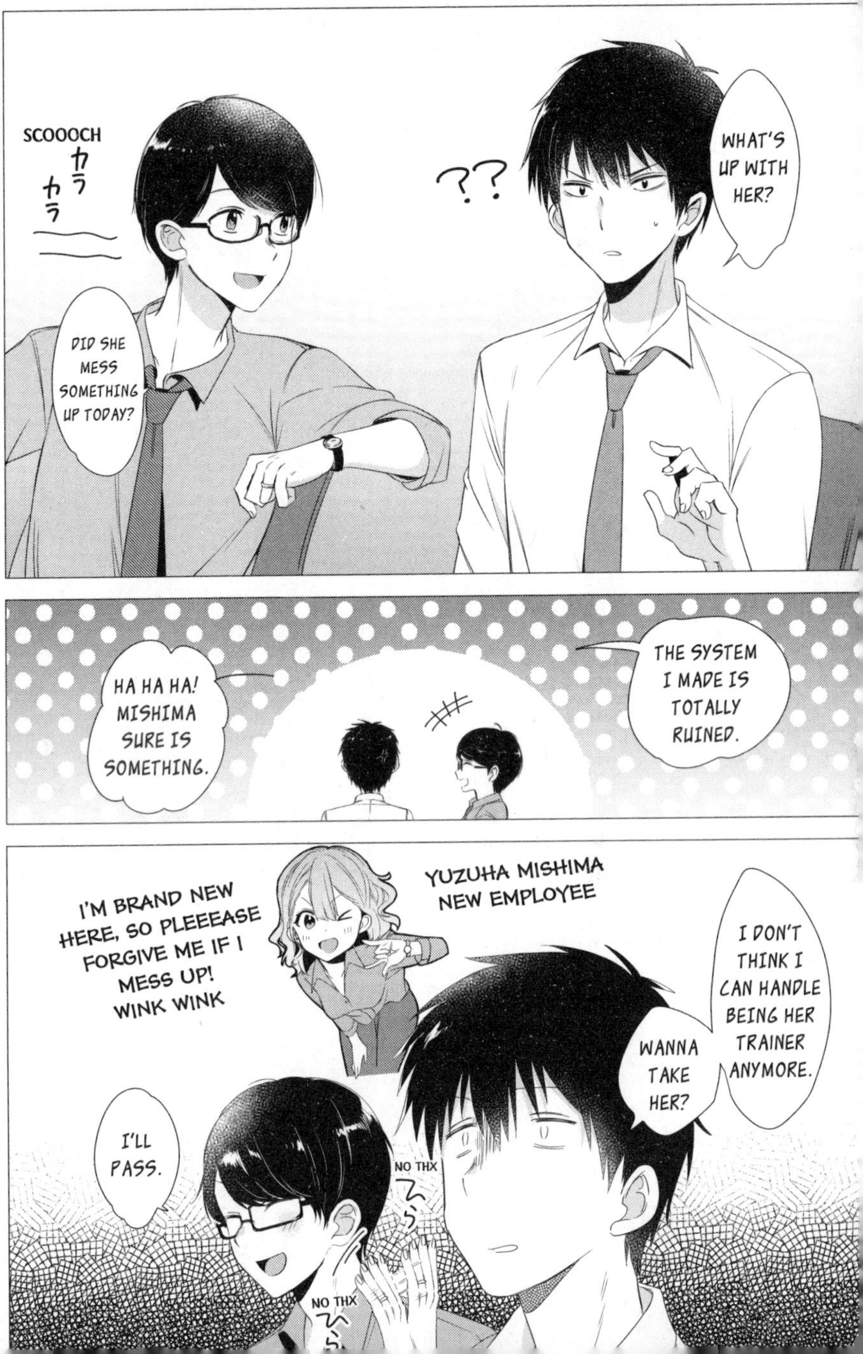
WHAT'S UP WITH HER?
??
SCOOOCH
カラカラ
DID SHE MESS SOMETHING UP TODAY?
THE SYSTEM I MADE IS TOTALLY RUINED.
HA HA HA! MISHIMA SURE IS SOMETHING.
I DON'T THINK I CAN HANDLE BEING HER TRAINER ANYMORE.
WANNA TAKE HER?
YUZUHA MISHIMA NEW EMPLOYEE
I'M BRAND NEW HERE, SO PLEEEASE FORGIVE ME IF I MESS UP! WINK WINK
NO THX
ひら
I'LL PASS.
NO THX
ひら

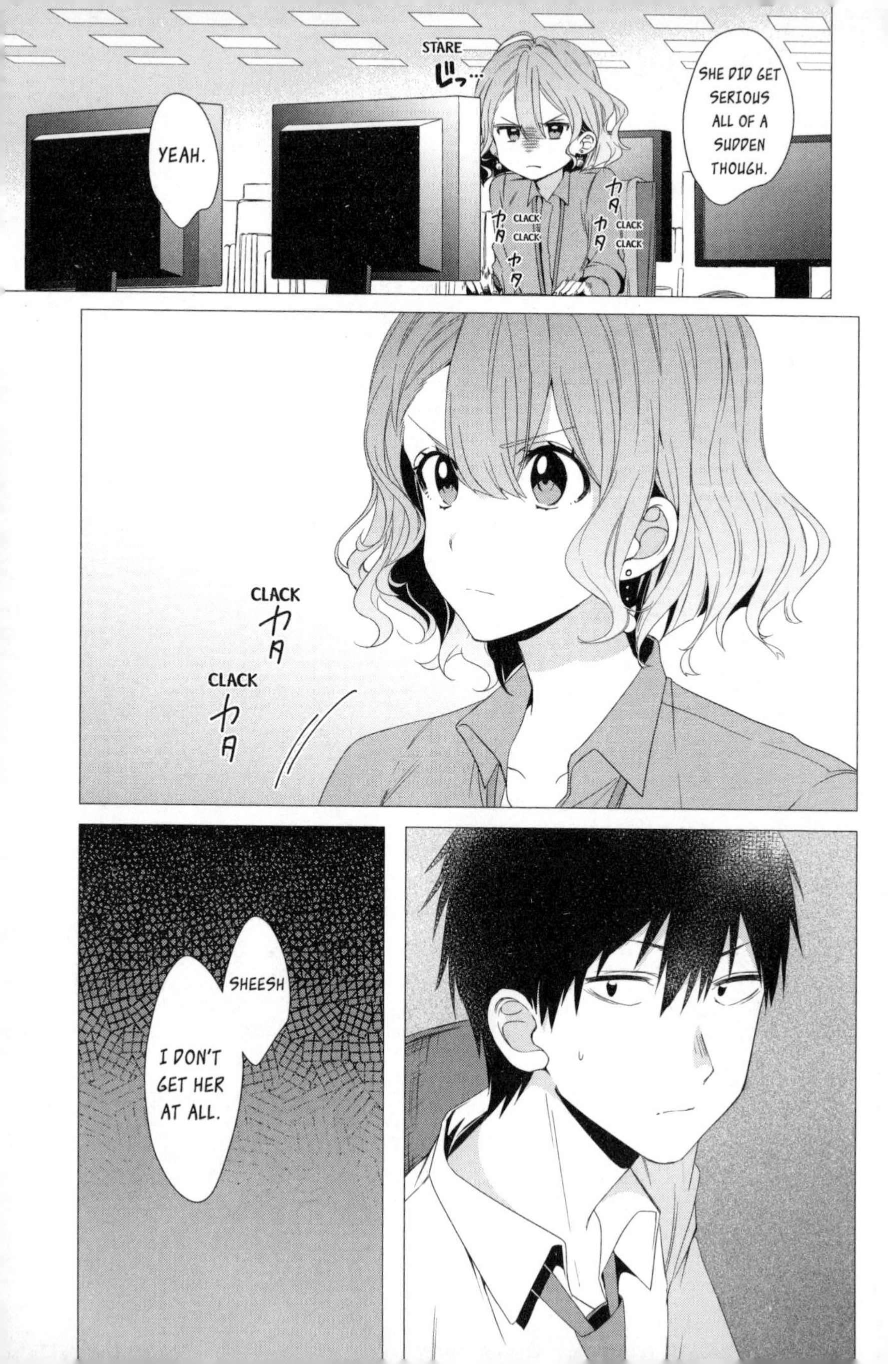
SHE DID GET SERIOUS ALL OF A SUDDEN THOUGH.
STARE
じっ…
CLACK CLACK
カタカタ
CLACK CLACK
カタカタ
カタ
YEAH.
CLACK
カタ
CLACK
カタ
SHEESH
I DON'T GET HER AT ALL.

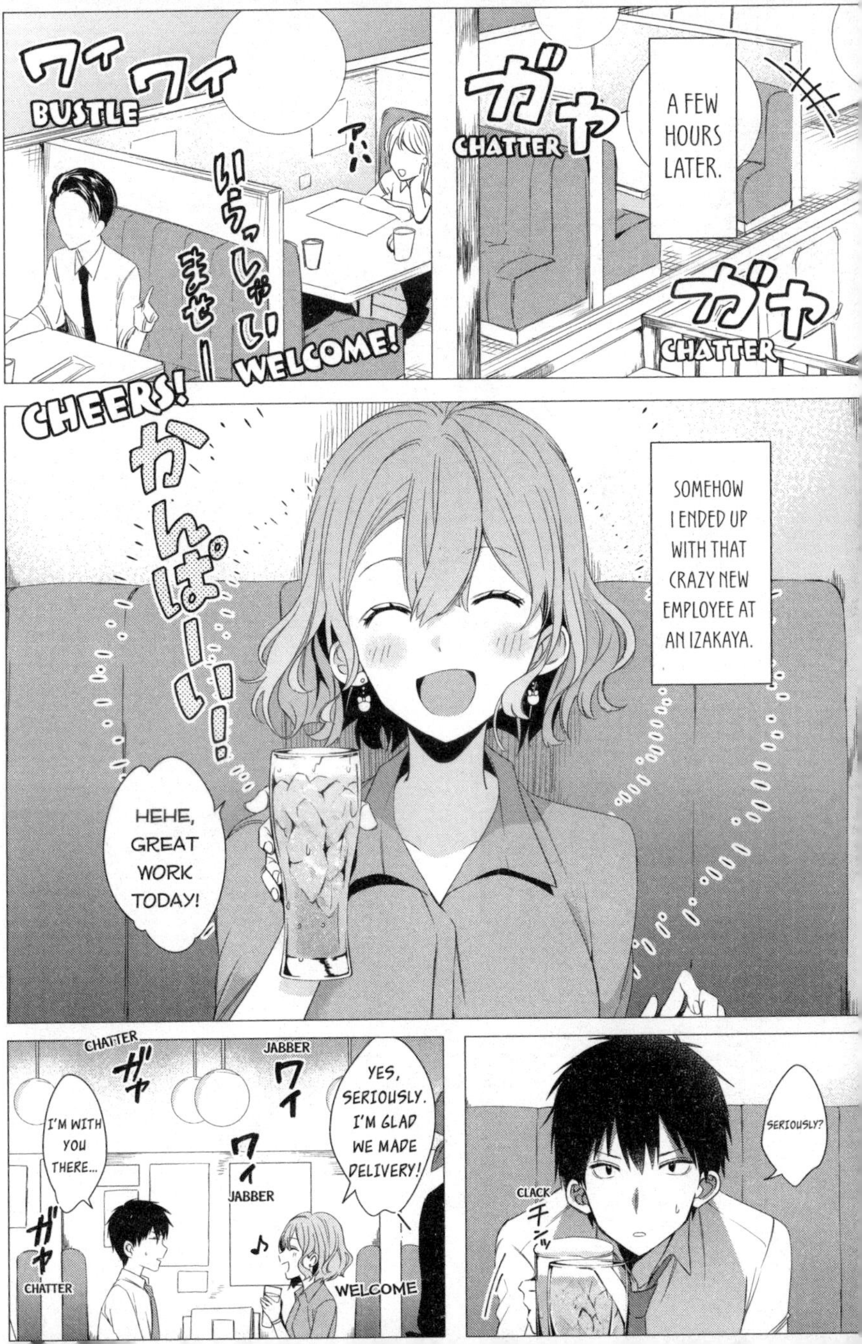

ガヤ
CHATTER
A FEW HOURS LATER.
ガヤ
CHATTER
ワイ ワイ
BUSTLE
いらっしゃいませー
WELCOME!
CHEERS!
かんぱーい!!
SOMEHOW I ENDED UP WITH THAT CRAZY NEW EMPLOYEE AT AN IZAKAYA.
HEHE, GREAT WORK TODAY!
SERIOUSLY?
CLACK
チンッ
CHATTER
ガヤ
JABBER
ワイ
YES, SERIOUSLY. I'M GLAD WE MADE DELIVERY!
ワイ
JABBER
I'M WITH YOU THERE...
ガヤ
CHATTER
WELCOME

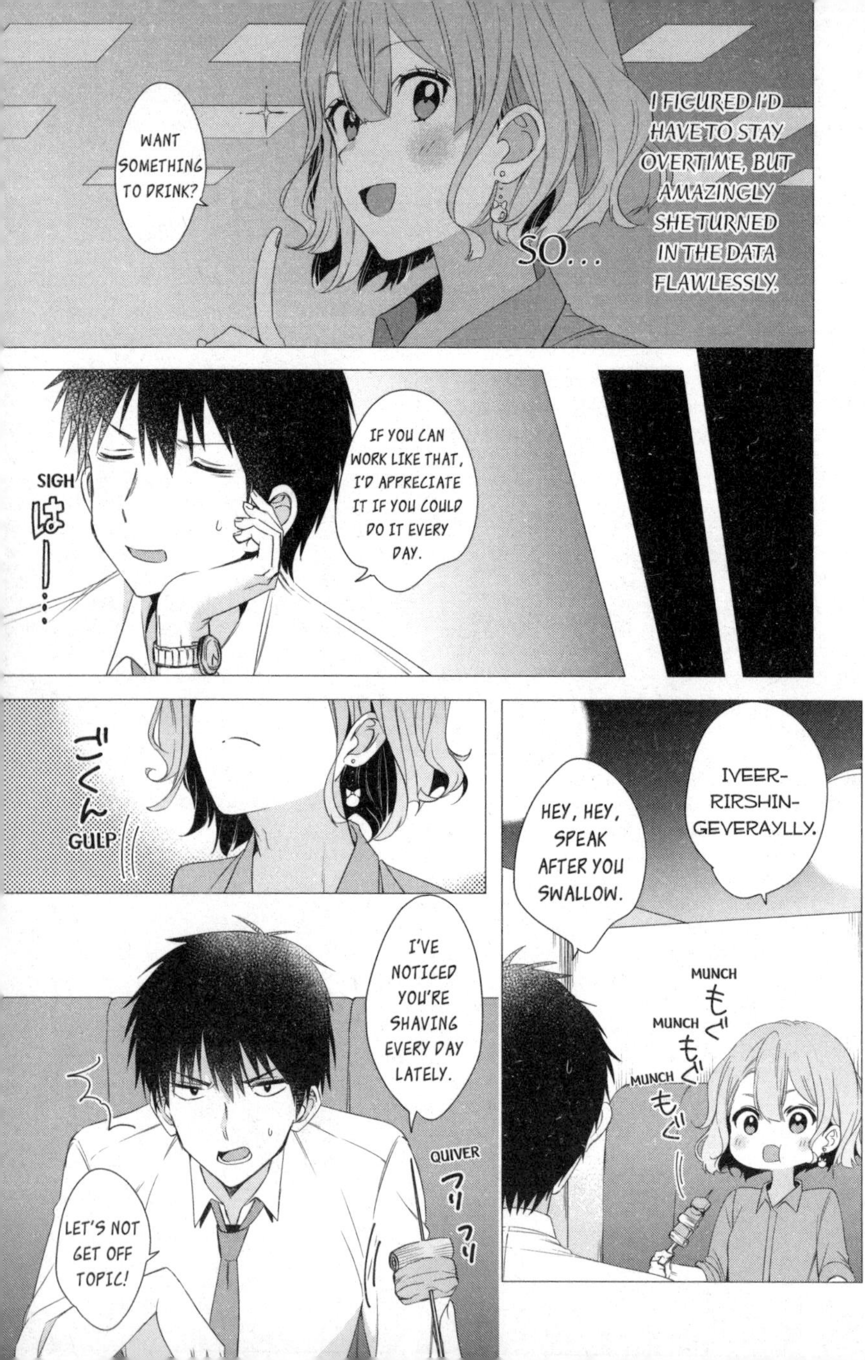
I FIGURED I'D HAVE TO STAY OVERTIME, BUT AMAZINGLY SHE TURNED IN THE DATA FLAWLESSLY.
SO...
WANT SOMETHING TO DRINK?
IF YOU CAN WORK LIKE THAT, I'D APPRECIATE IT IF YOU COULD DO IT EVERY DAY.
SIGH
はー…
IVEER-RIRSHIN-GEVERAYLLY.
HEY, HEY, SPEAK AFTER YOU SWALLOW.
MUNCH
もぐ
MUNCH
もぐ
MUNCH
もぐー
ごくん
GULP
I'VE NOTICED YOU'RE SHAVING EVERY DAY LATELY.
QUIVER
フリフリ
LET'S NOT GET OFF TOPIC!

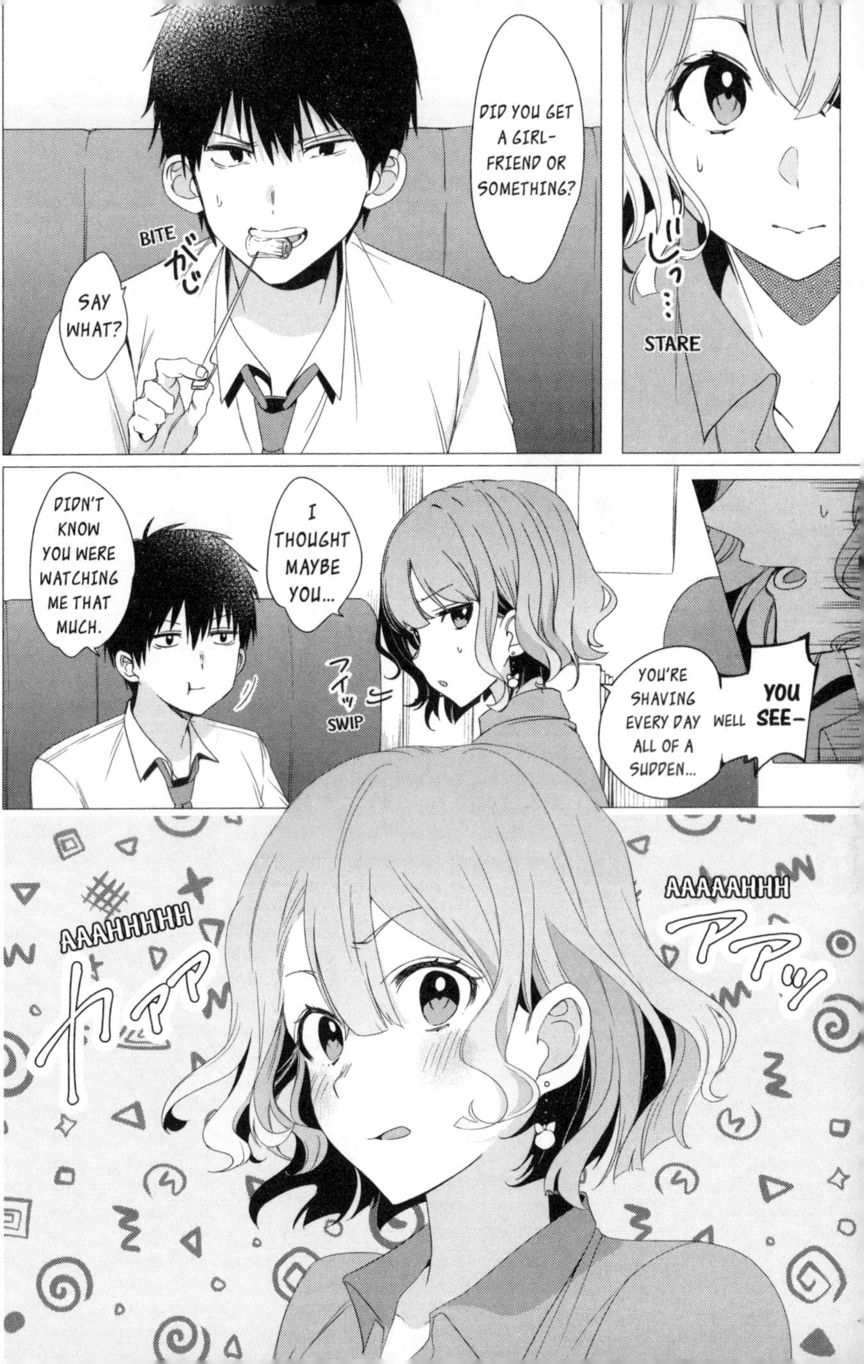

STARE
DID YOU GET A GIRL-FRIEND OR SOMETHING?
BITE
SAY WHAT?
WELL YOU SEE—
YOU'RE SHAVING EVERY DAY ALL OF A SUDDEN...
I THOUGHT MAYBE YOU...
SWIP
DIDN'T KNOW YOU WERE WATCHING ME THAT MUCH.
AAAAAHHH
AAAHHHHH

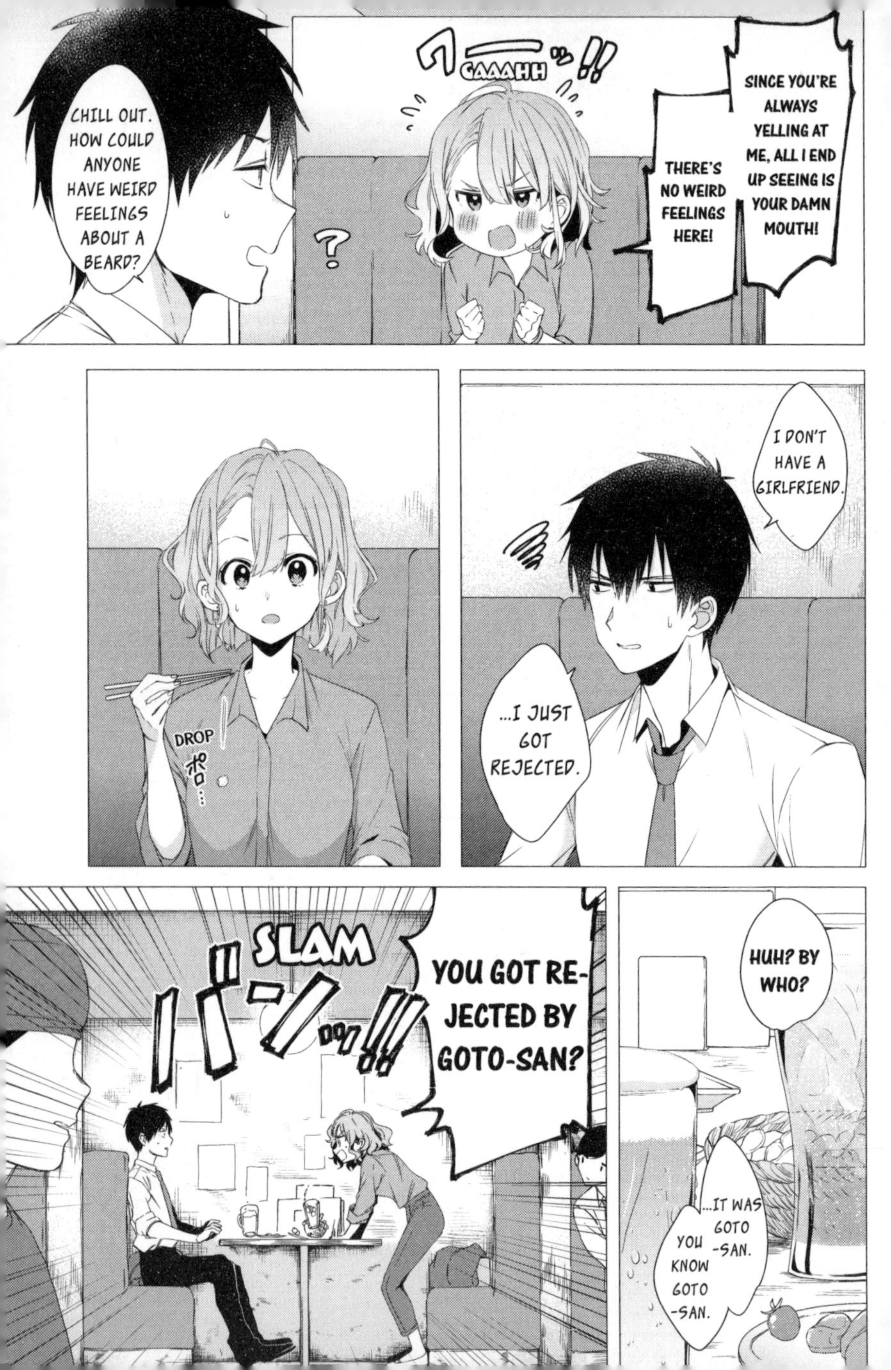
SINCE YOU'RE ALWAYS YELLING AT ME, ALL I END UP SEEING IS YOUR DAMN MOUTH!
THERE'S NO WEIRD FEELINGS HERE!
ア——ッ!!
GAAAHH
?
CHILL OUT. HOW COULD ANYONE HAVE WEIRD FEELINGS ABOUT A BEARD?
I DON'T HAVE A GIRLFRIEND.
...I JUST GOT REJECTED.
DROP
ポロ…
HUH? BY WHO?
...IT WAS GOTO-SAN.
YOU KNOW GOTO-SAN.
YOU GOT RE-JECTED BY GOTO-SAN?
SLAM
バーン!!

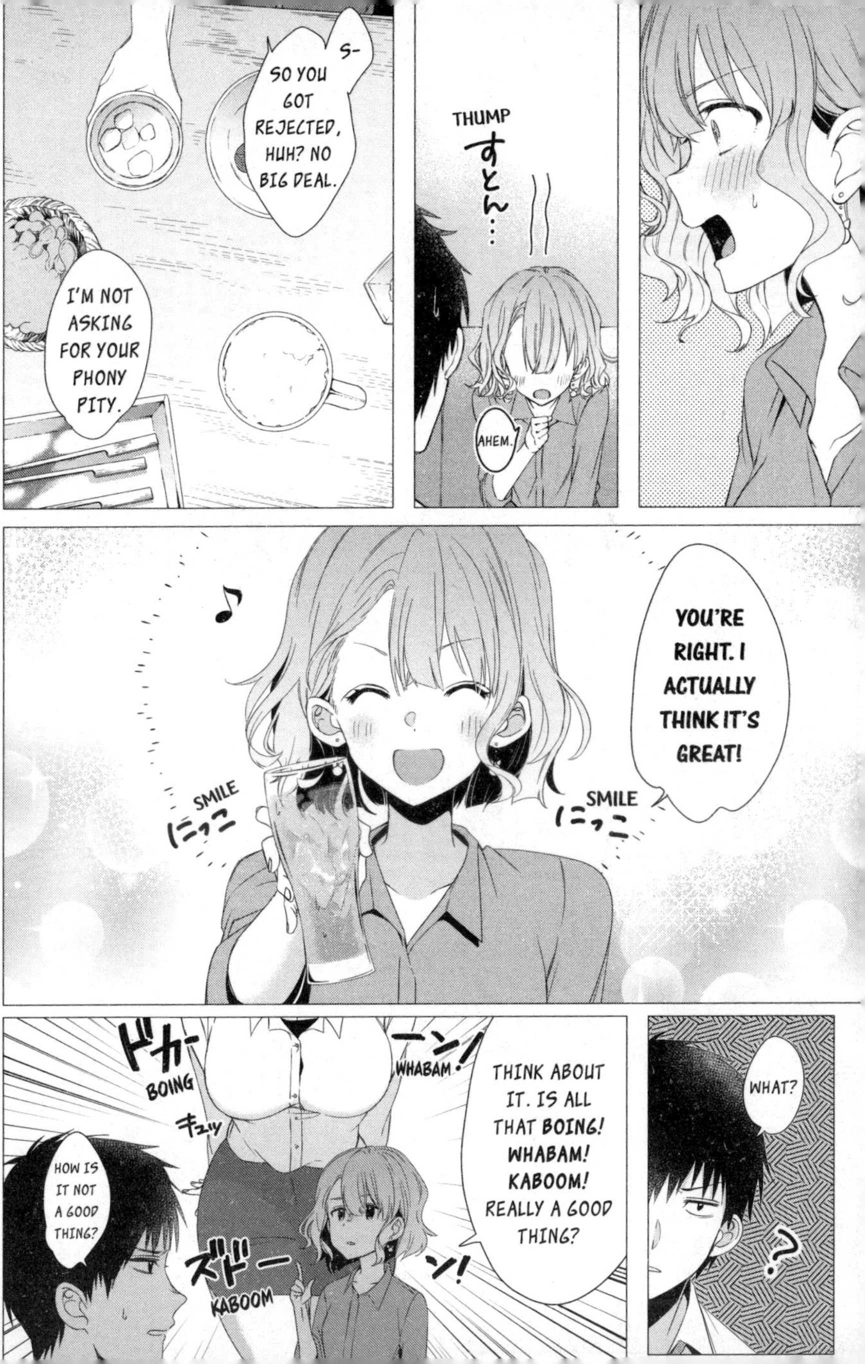
THUMP
すとん…
AHEM.
S-
SO YOU GOT REJECTED, HUH? NO BIG DEAL.
I'M NOT ASKING FOR YOUR PHONY PITY.
YOU'RE RIGHT. I ACTUALLY THINK IT'S GREAT!
SMILE
にっこ
SMILE
にっこ
♪
WHAT?
?
ドカーーン!
WHABAM
THINK ABOUT IT. IS ALL THAT BOING! WHABAM! KABOOM! REALLY A GOOD THING?
BOING
キュッ
HOW IS IT NOT A GOOD THING?
ズドーン!
KABOOM

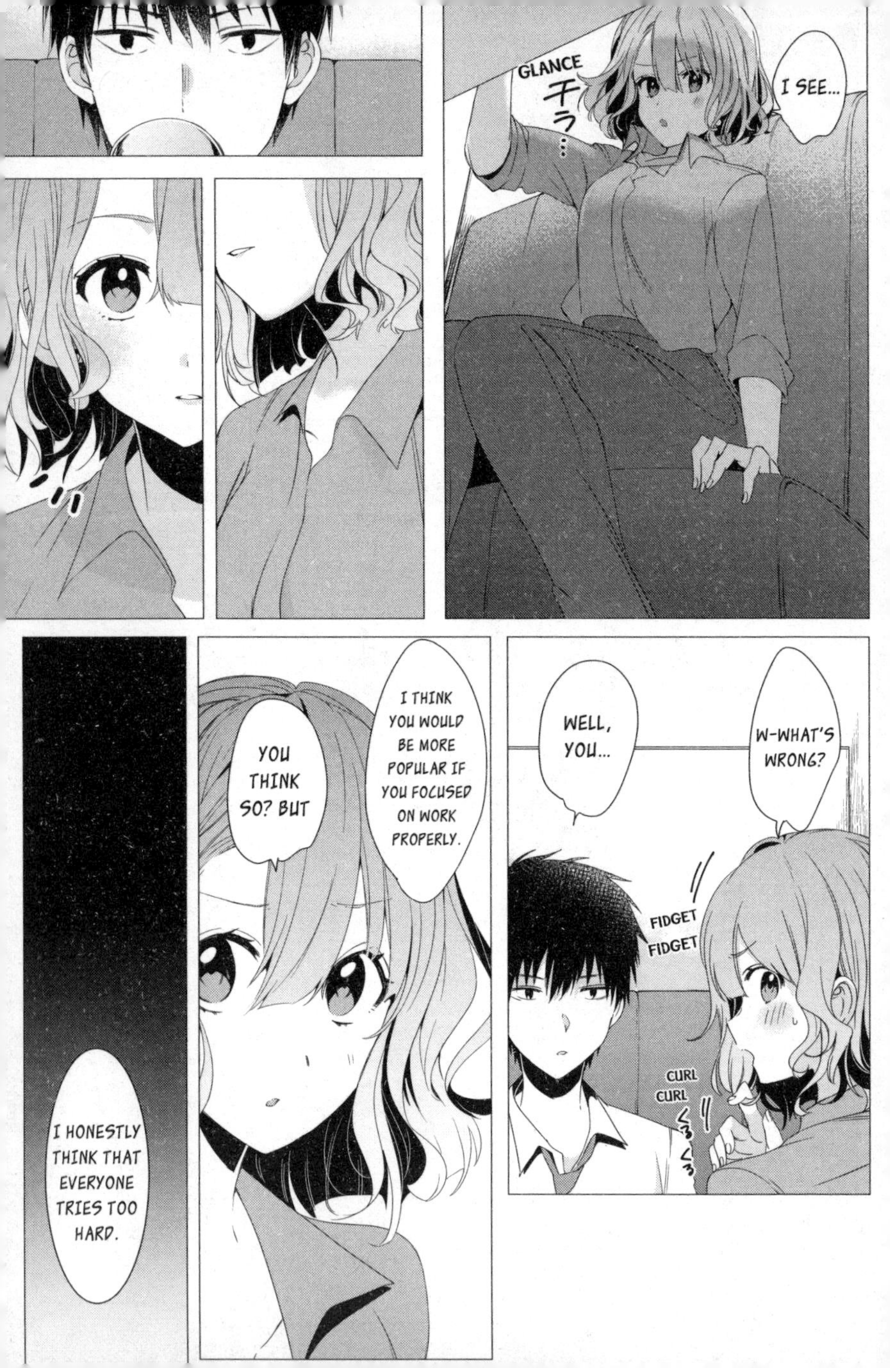
GLANCE
チラ…
I SEE...
W-WHAT'S WRONG?
WELL, YOU...
FIDGET FIDGET
CURL CURL
くるくる
I THINK YOU WOULD BE MORE POPULAR IF YOU FOCUSED ON WORK PROPERLY.
YOU THINK SO? BUT
I HONESTLY THINK THAT EVERYONE TRIES TOO HARD.

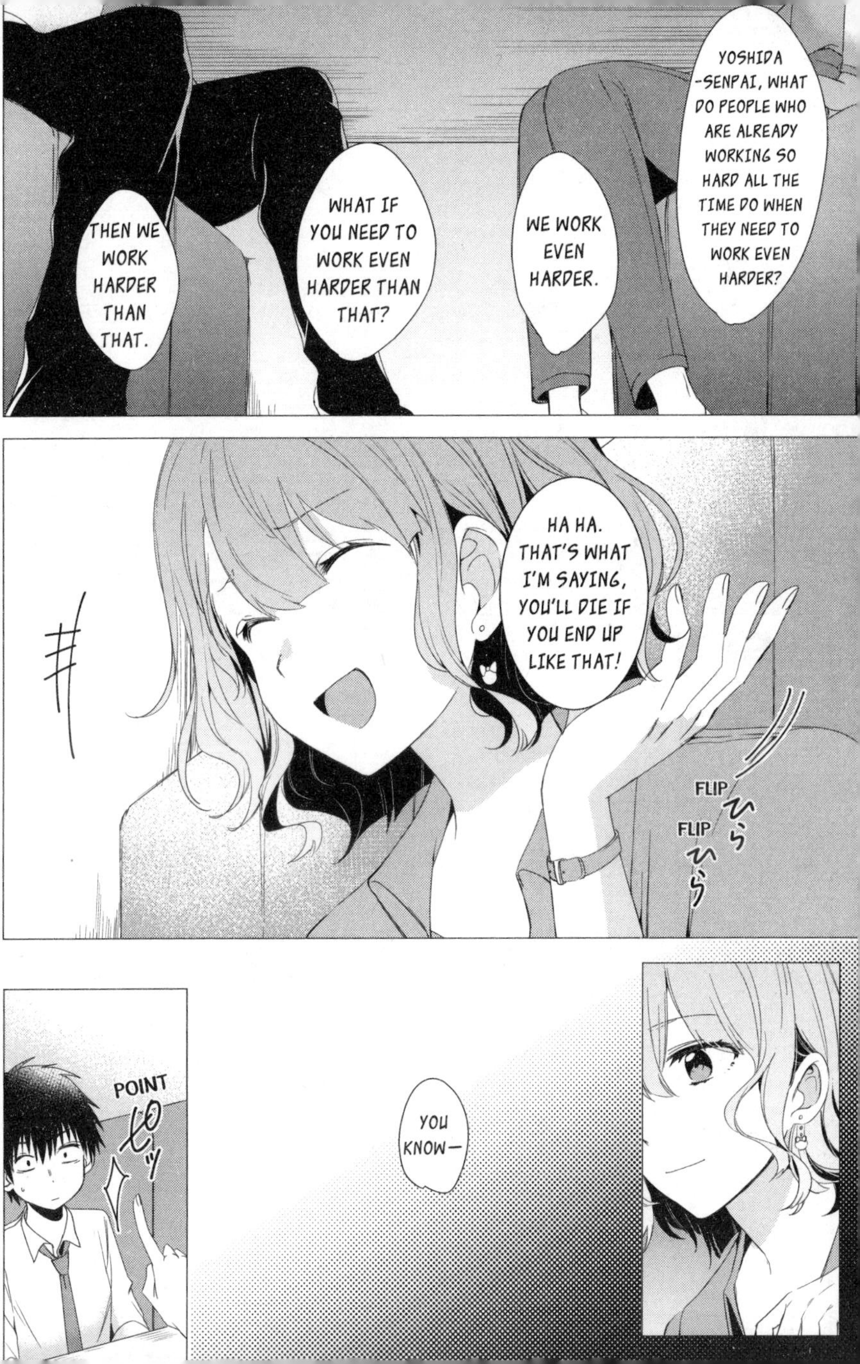
YOSHIDA-SENPAI, WHAT DO PEOPLE WHO ARE ALREADY WORKING SO HARD ALL THE TIME DO WHEN THEY NEED TO WORK EVEN HARDER?
WE WORK EVEN HARDER.
WHAT IF YOU NEED TO WORK EVEN HARDER THAN THAT?
THEN WE WORK HARDER THAN THAT.
HA HA. THAT'S WHAT I'M SAYING, YOU'LL DIE IF YOU END UP LIKE THAT!
FLIP ひら
FLIP ひら
YOU KNOW—
POINT ピッ

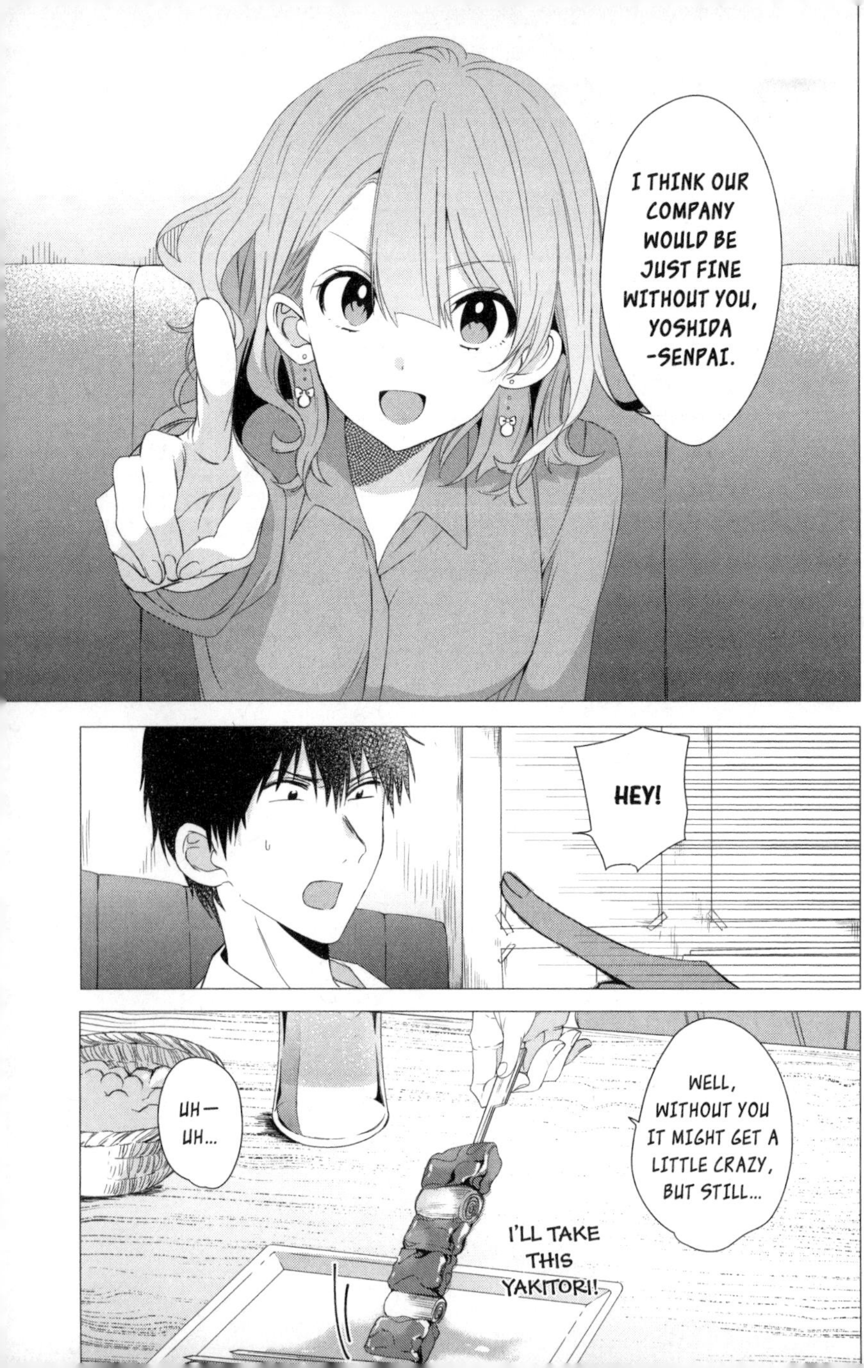
I THINK OUR COMPANY WOULD BE JUST FINE WITHOUT YOU, YOSHIDA -SENPAI.
HEY!
WELL, WITHOUT YOU IT MIGHT GET A LITTLE CRAZY, BUT STILL...
I'LL TAKE THIS YAKITORI!
UH— UH...

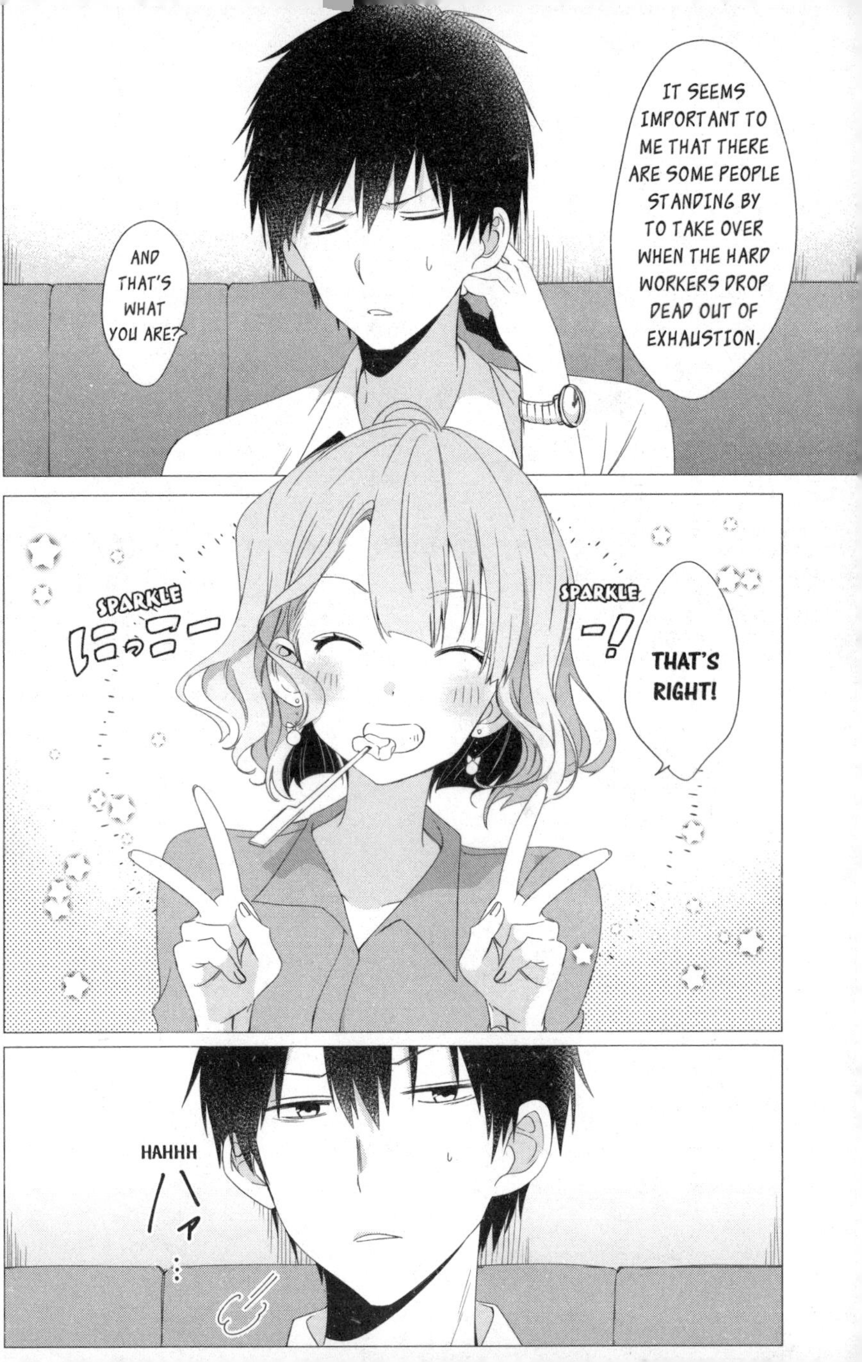
IT SEEMS IMPORTANT TO ME THAT THERE ARE SOME PEOPLE STANDING BY TO TAKE OVER WHEN THE HARD WORKERS DROP DEAD OUT OF EXHAUSTION.
AND THAT'S WHAT YOU ARE?
SPARKLE
THAT'S RIGHT!
SPARKLE
にっこーー!
HAHHH
ハァ…

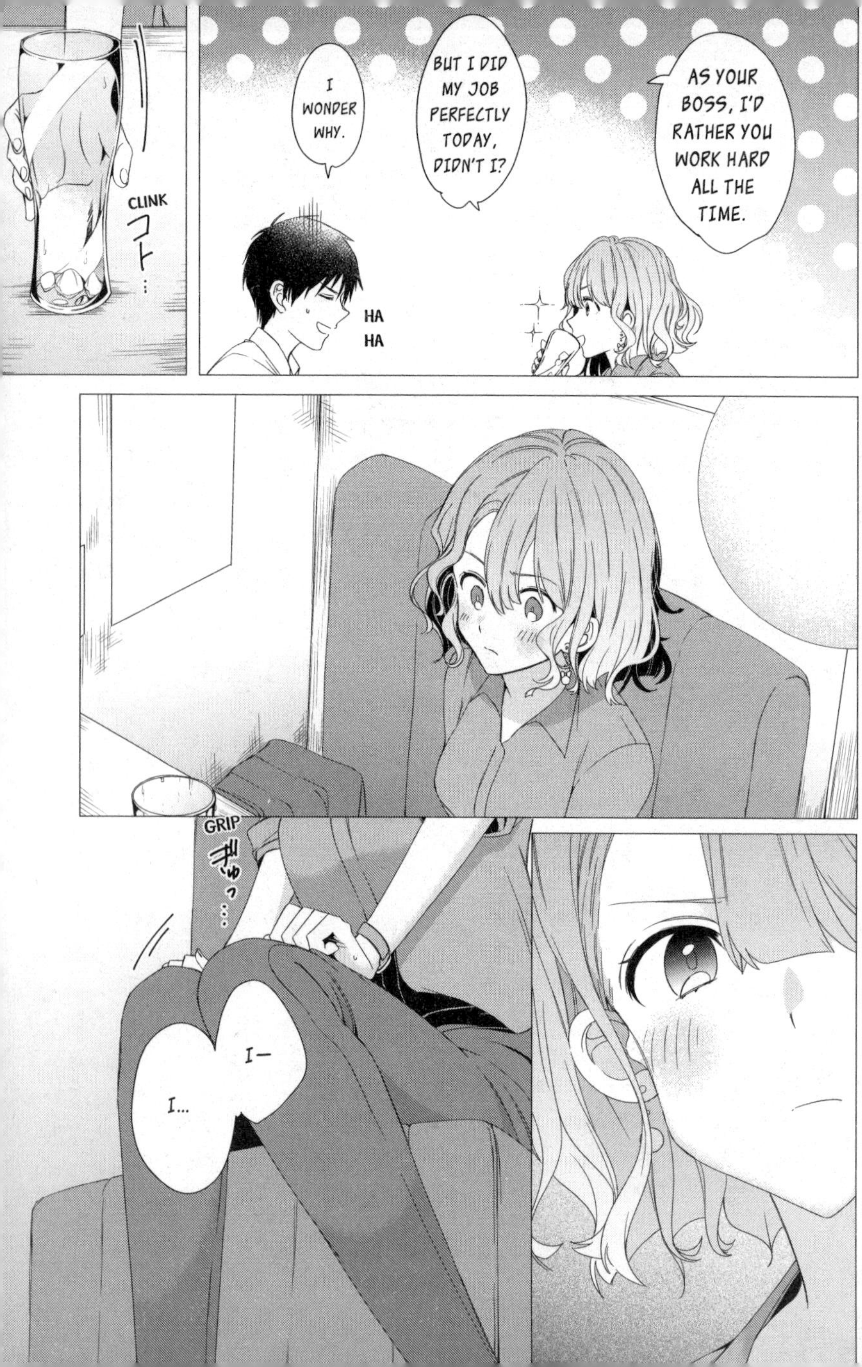
AS YOUR BOSS, I'D RATHER YOU WORK HARD ALL THE TIME.
BUT I DID MY JOB PERFECTLY TODAY, DIDN'T I?
I WONDER WHY.
HA HA
CLINK
コト…
GRIP
ギュッ…
I— I...

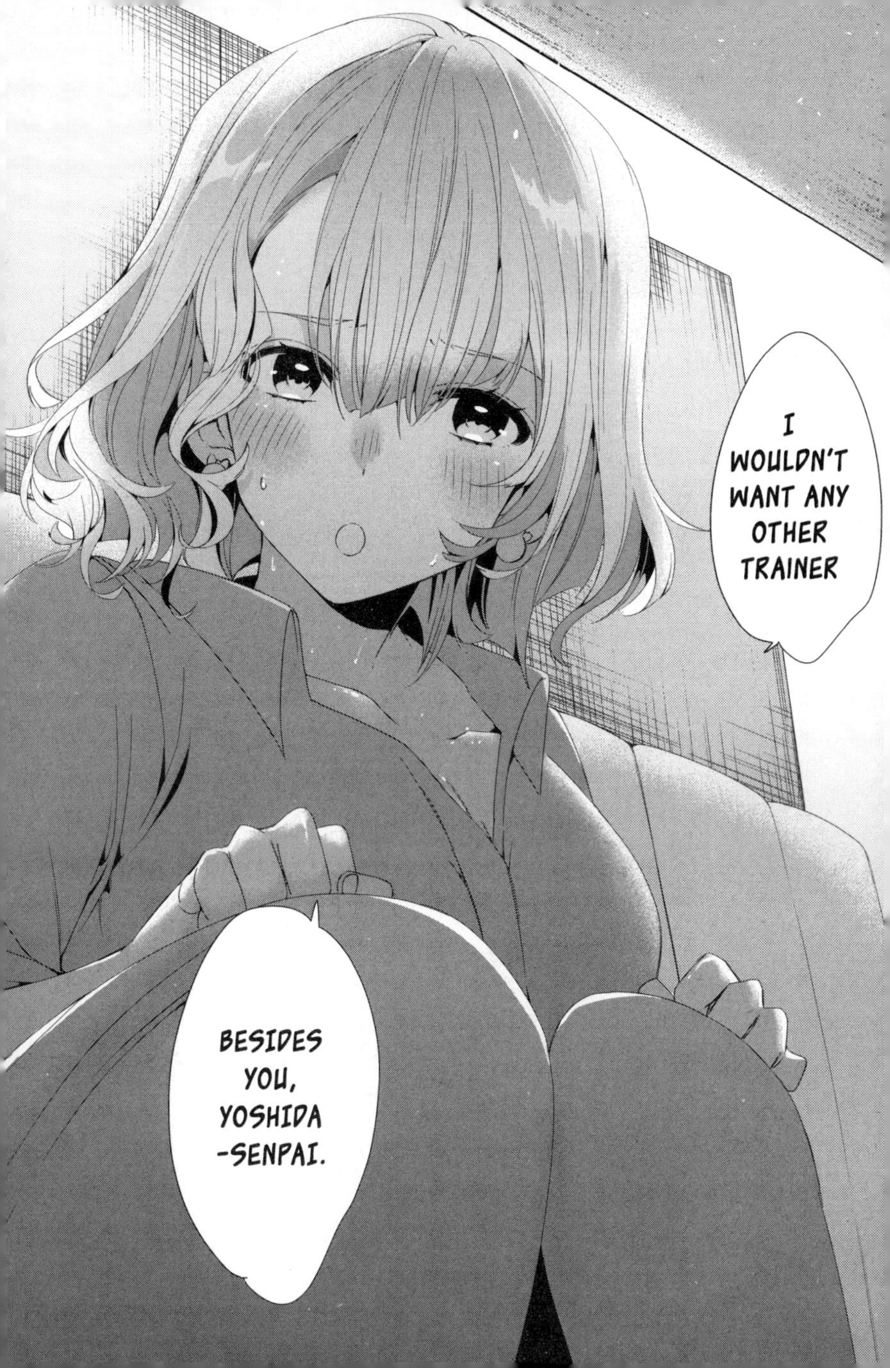
I WOULDN'T WANT ANY OTHER TRAINER
BESIDES YOU, YOSHIDA-SENPAI.

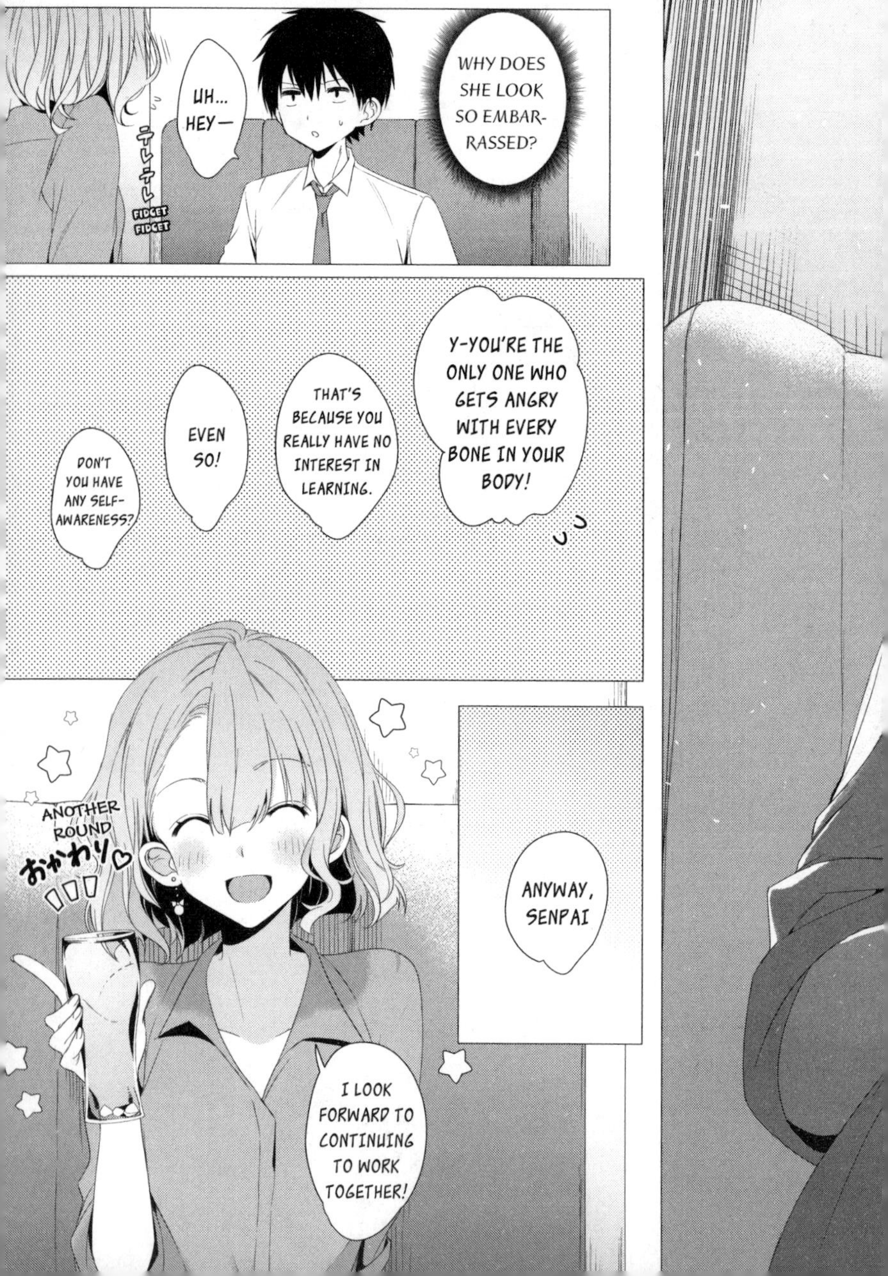
WHY DOES SHE LOOK SO EMBARRASSED?
UH... HEY—
テレテレ
FIDGET FIDGET
Y-YOU'RE THE ONLY ONE WHO GETS ANGRY WITH EVERY BONE IN YOUR BODY!
THAT'S BECAUSE YOU REALLY HAVE NO INTEREST IN LEARNING.
EVEN SO!
DON'T YOU HAVE ANY SELF-AWARENESS?
ANYWAY, SENPAI
I LOOK FORWARD TO CONTINUING TO WORK TOGETHER!
ANOTHER ROUND
おかわり♡

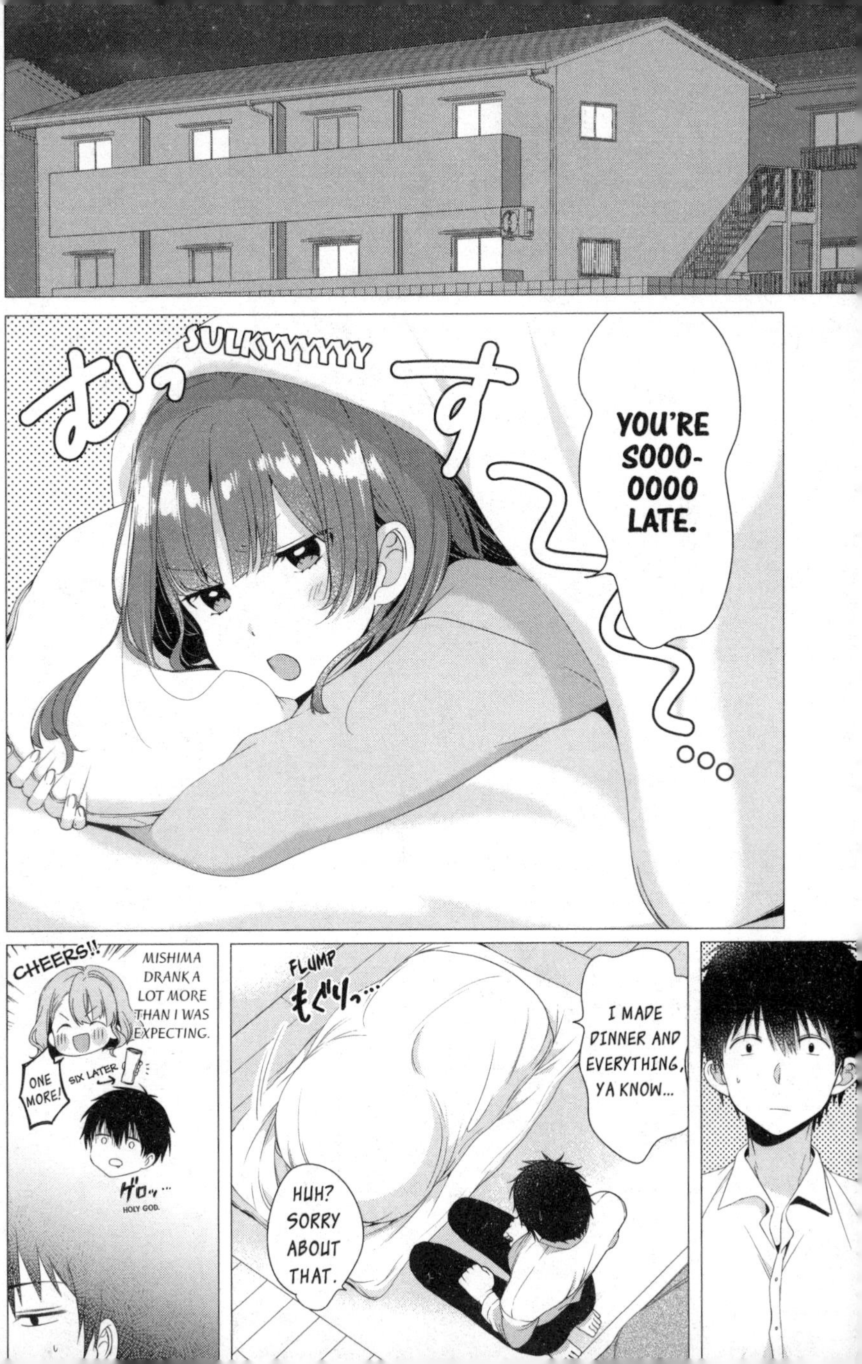
SULKYYYYYY
YOU'RE SOOO-OOOO LATE.
FLUMP
もぐりっ…
I MADE DINNER AND EVERYTHING, YA KNOW...
HUH? SORRY ABOUT THAT.
MISHIMA DRANK A LOT MORE THAN I WAS EXPECTING.
CHEERS!!
ONE MORE!
SIX LATER
ゲロッ…
HOLY GOD.

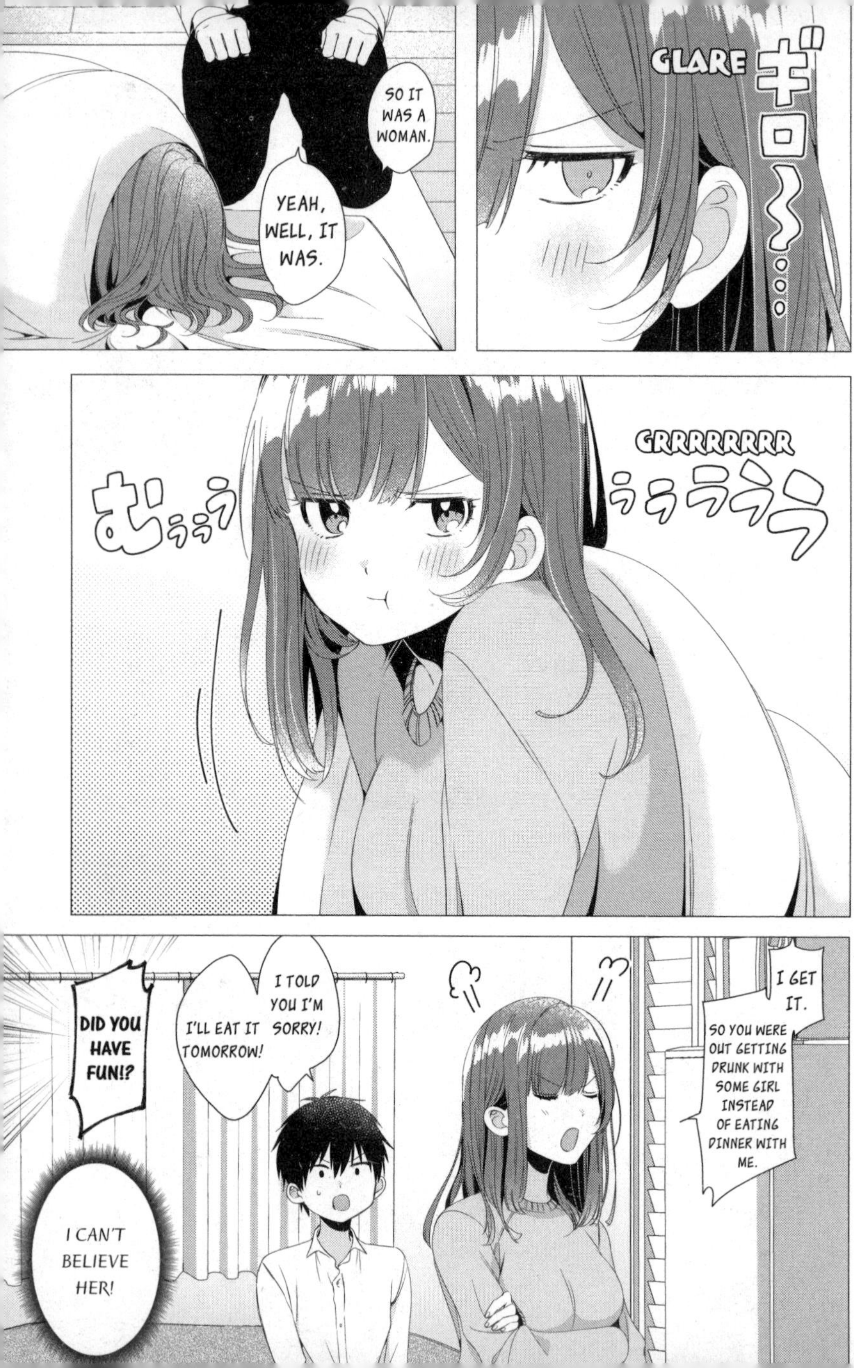
GLARE
ギロ～
SO IT WAS A WOMAN.
YEAH, WELL, IT WAS.
GRRRRRRRR
I GET IT.
SO YOU WERE OUT GETTING DRUNK WITH SOME GIRL INSTEAD OF EATING DINNER WITH ME.
I TOLD YOU I'M SORRY!
I'LL EAT IT TOMORROW!
DID YOU HAVE FUN!?
I CAN'T BELIEVE HER!

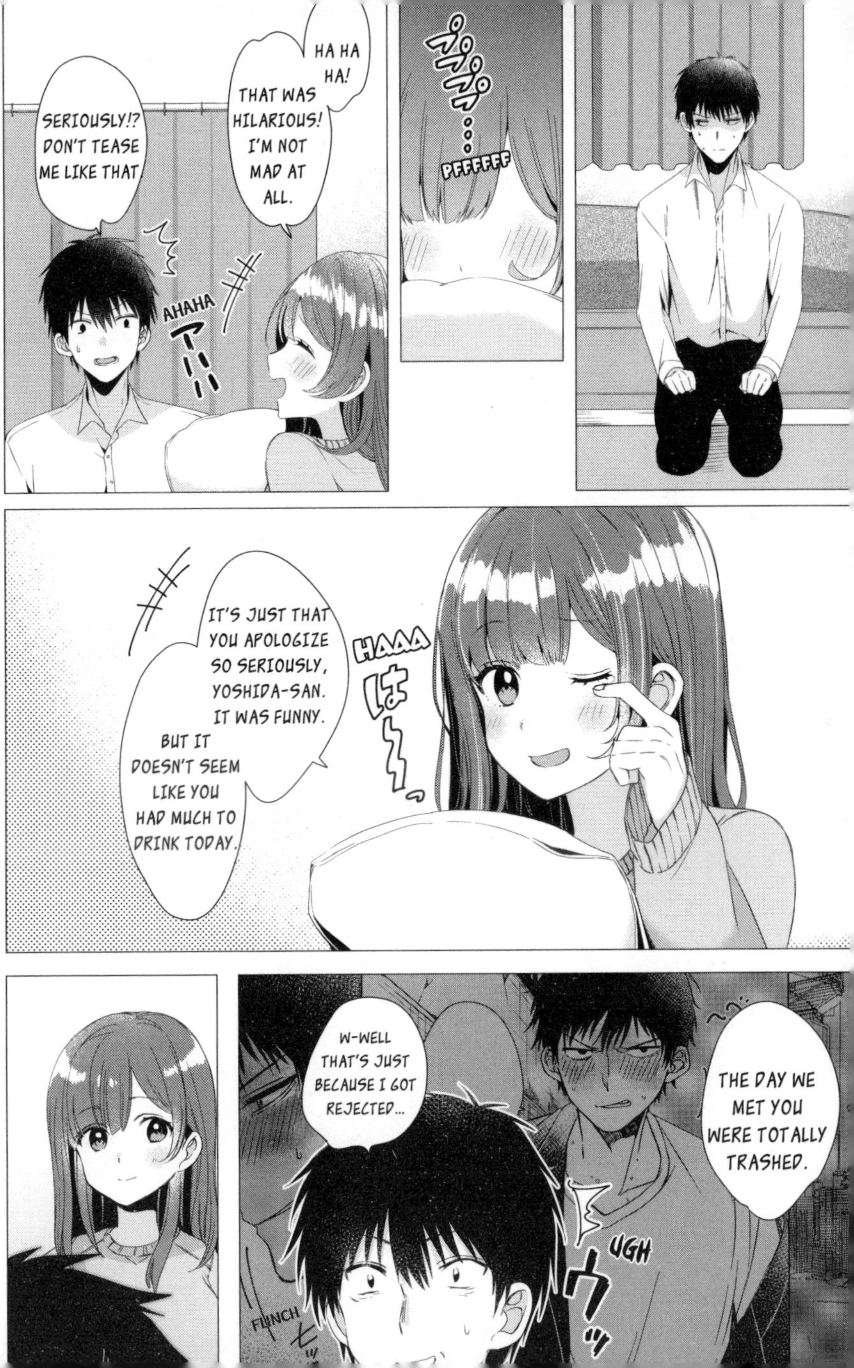

PFFFFFF
HA HA HA!
THAT WAS HILARIOUS! I'M NOT MAD AT ALL.
AHAHA
SERIOUSLY!? DON'T TEASE ME LIKE THAT.
HAAA
IT'S JUST THAT YOU APOLOGIZE SO SERIOUSLY, YOSHIDA-SAN. IT WAS FUNNY.
BUT IT DOESN'T SEEM LIKE YOU HAD MUCH TO DRINK TODAY.
THE DAY WE MET YOU WERE TOTALLY TRASHED.
UGH
W-WELL THAT'S JUST BECAUSE I GOT REJECTED...
FLINCH

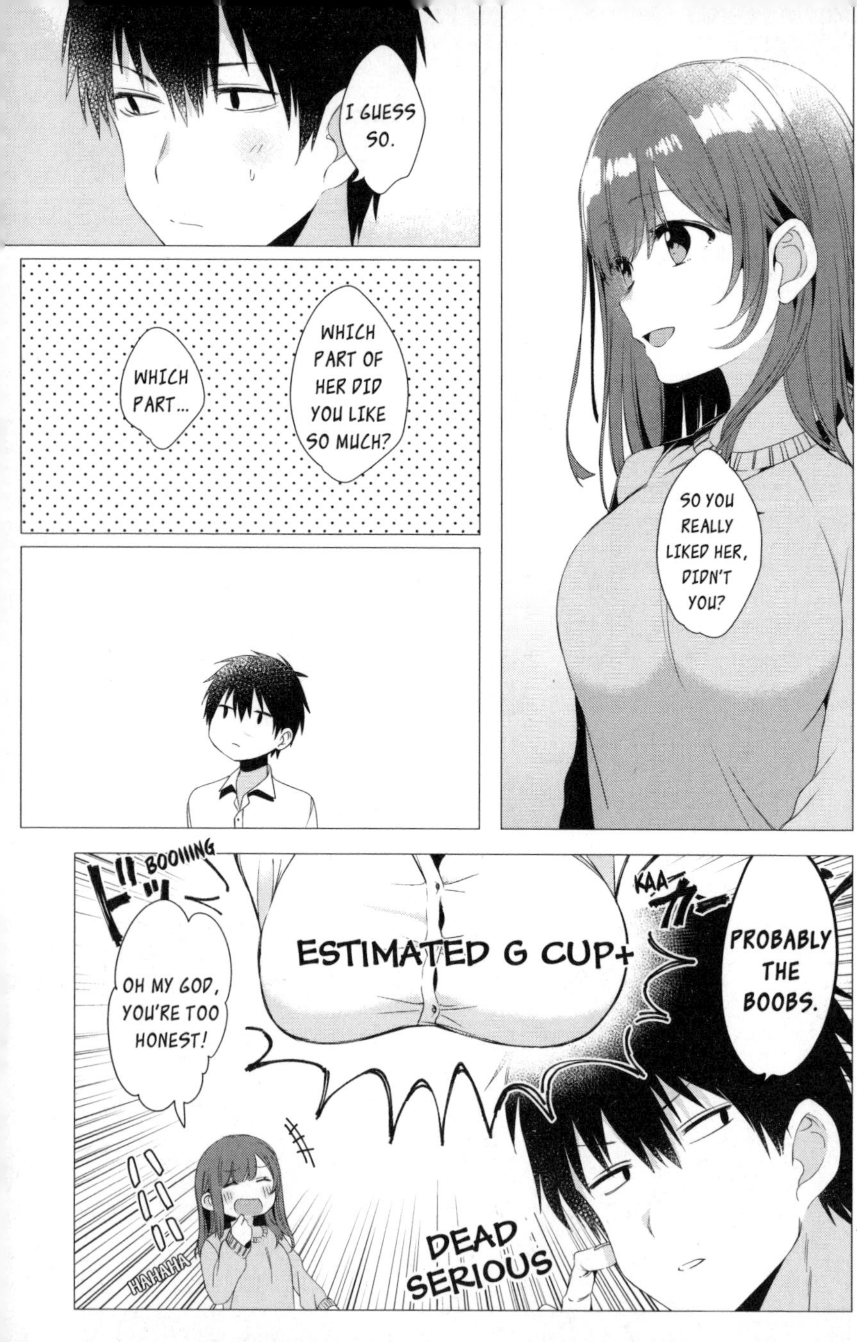
SO YOU REALLY LIKED HER, DIDN'T YOU?
I GUESS SO.
WHICH PART OF HER DID YOU LIKE SO MUCH?
WHICH PART...
KAA
PROBABLY THE BOOBS.
ESTIMATED G CUP+
BOOIIING
OH MY GOD, YOU'RE TOO HONEST!
DEAD SERIOUS
HAHAHA

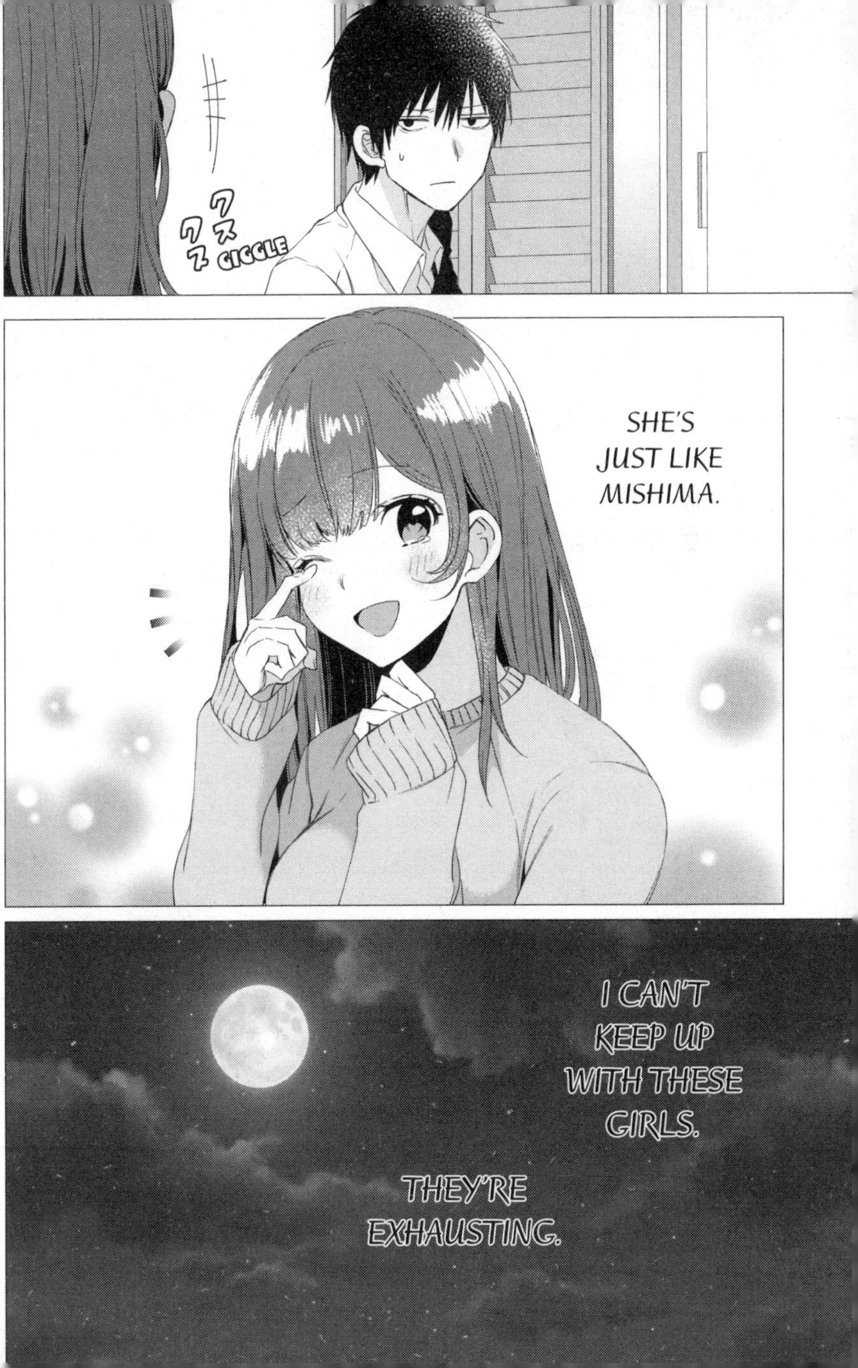
クスクス
GIGGLE
SHE'S JUST LIKE MISHIMA.
I CAN'T KEEP UP WITH THESE GIRLS.
THEY'RE EXHAUSTING.

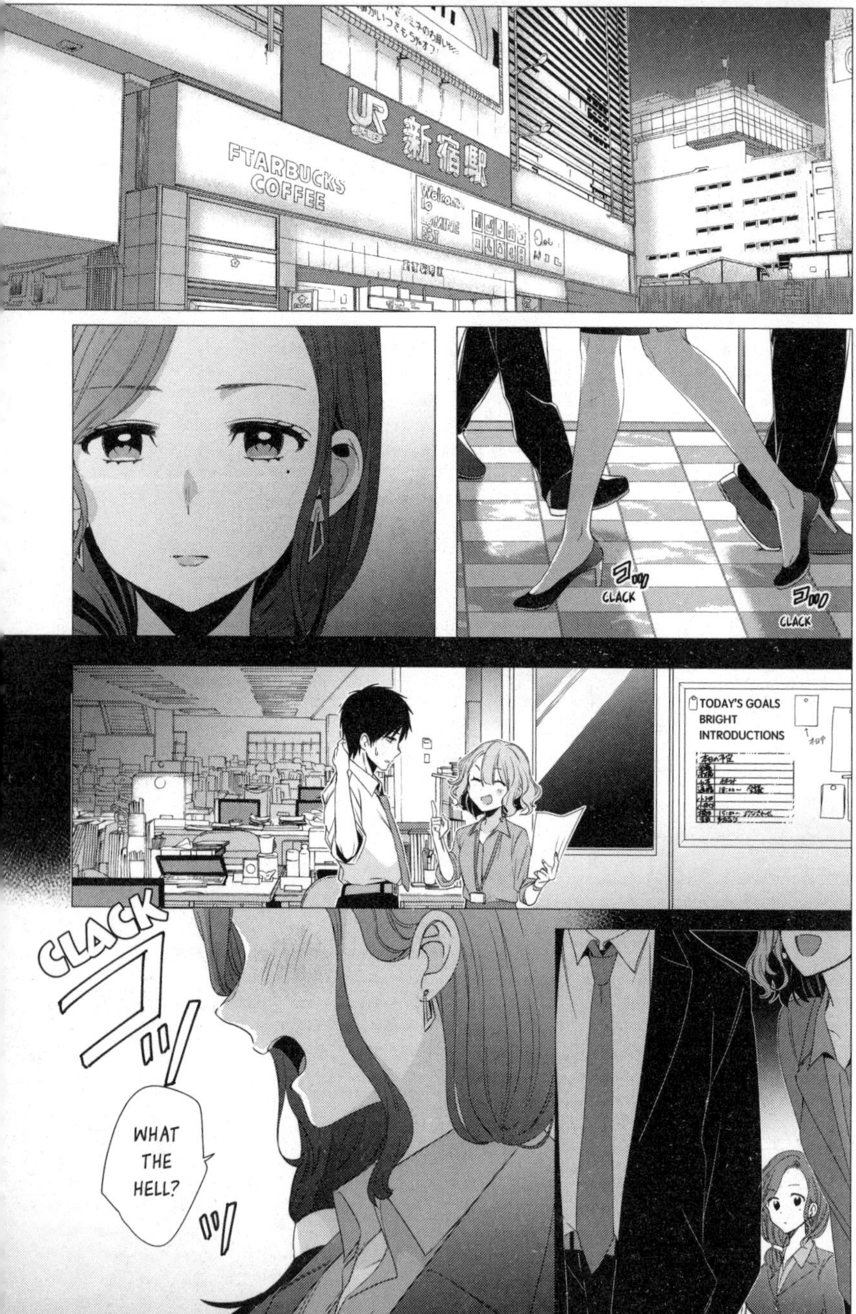
FTARBUCKS
COFFEE
新宿駅
Welcome to LUMINE EST
コッ
CLACK
コッ
CLACK
TODAY'S GOALS
BRIGHT
INTRODUCTIONS
本日の予定
CLACK
コッ
WHAT THE HELL?

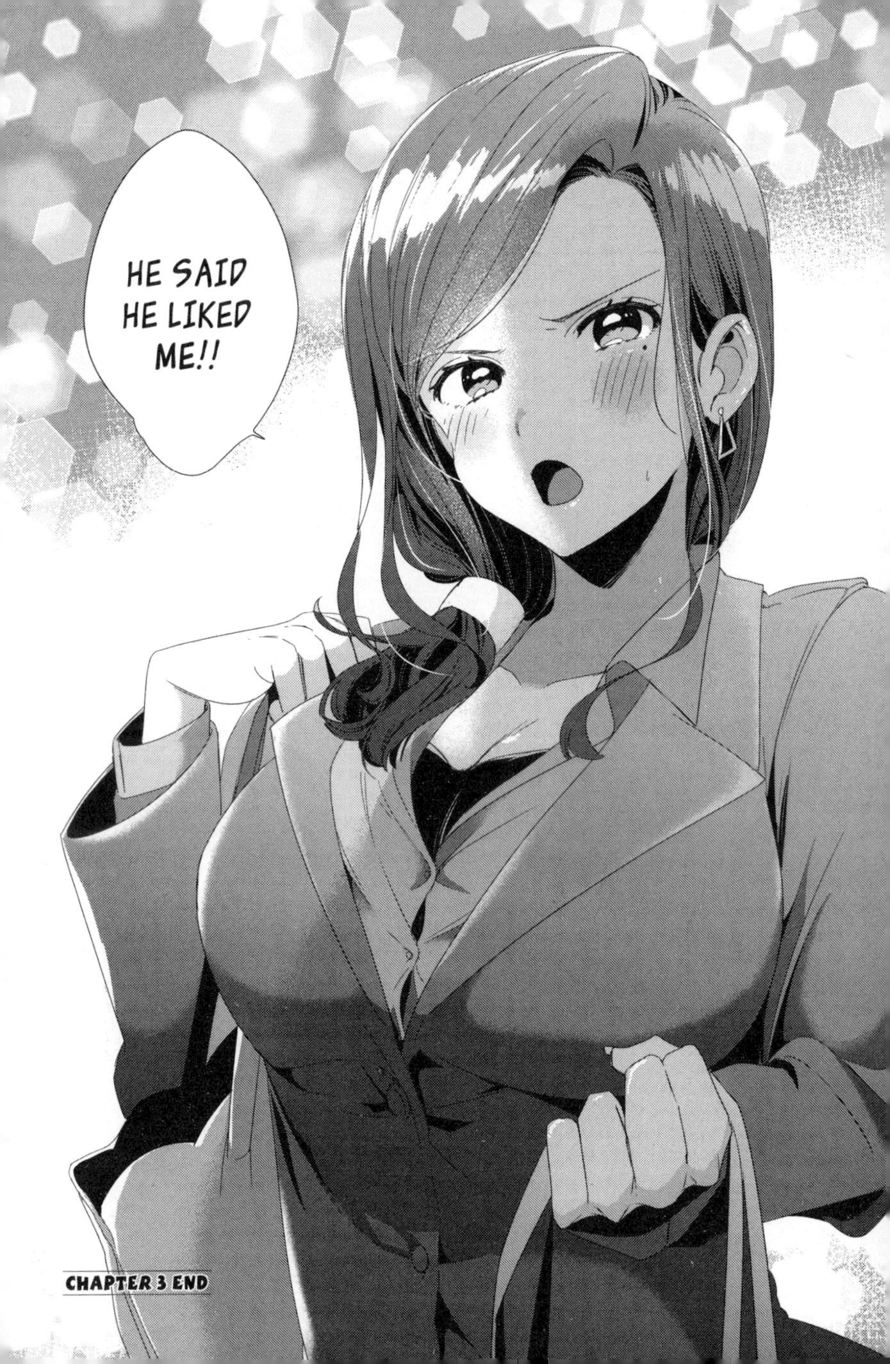
HE SAID HE LIKED ME!!
CHAPTER 3 END

[CHAPTER 4] A BARBECUE AND A SWEETHEART

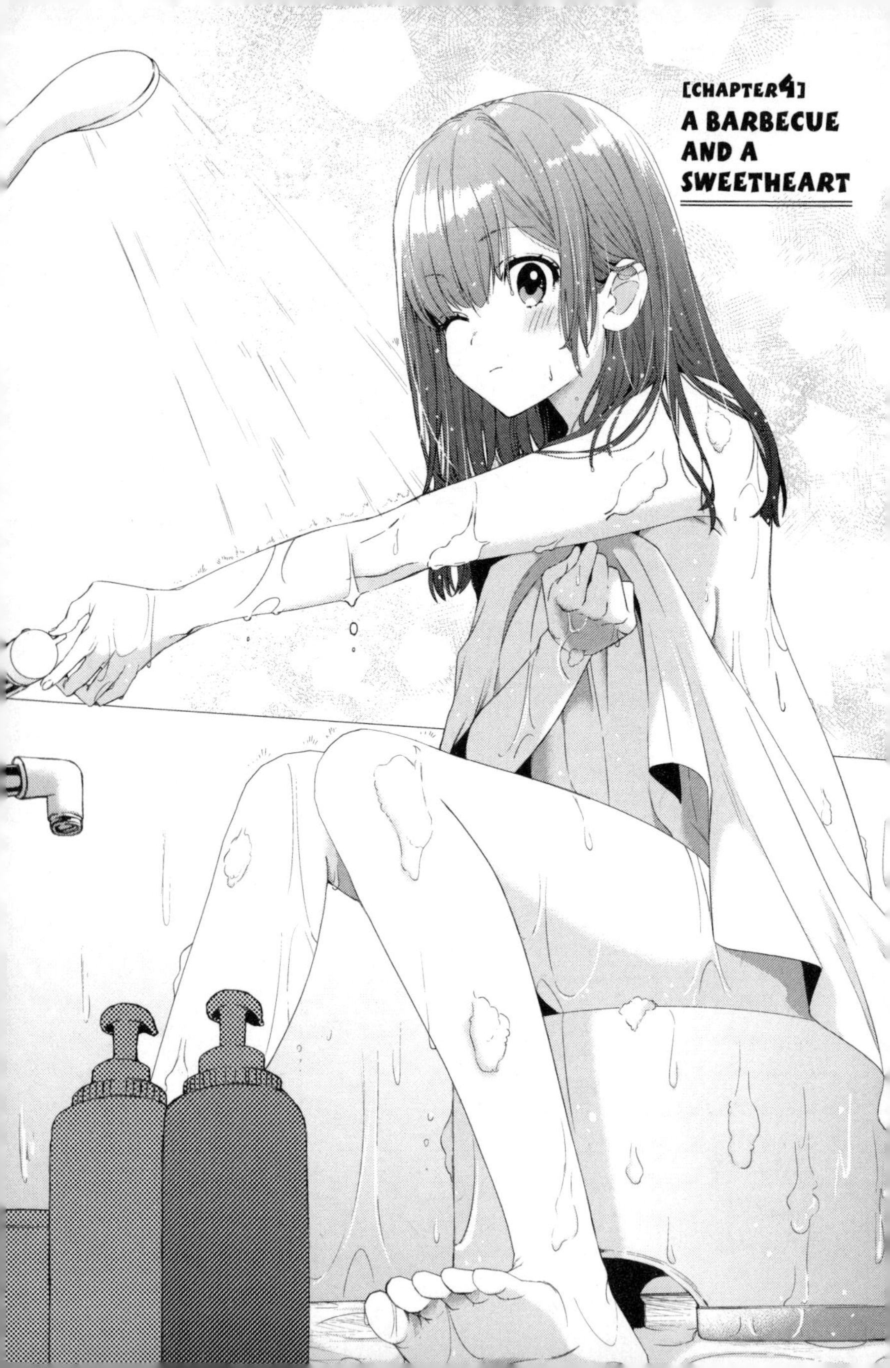

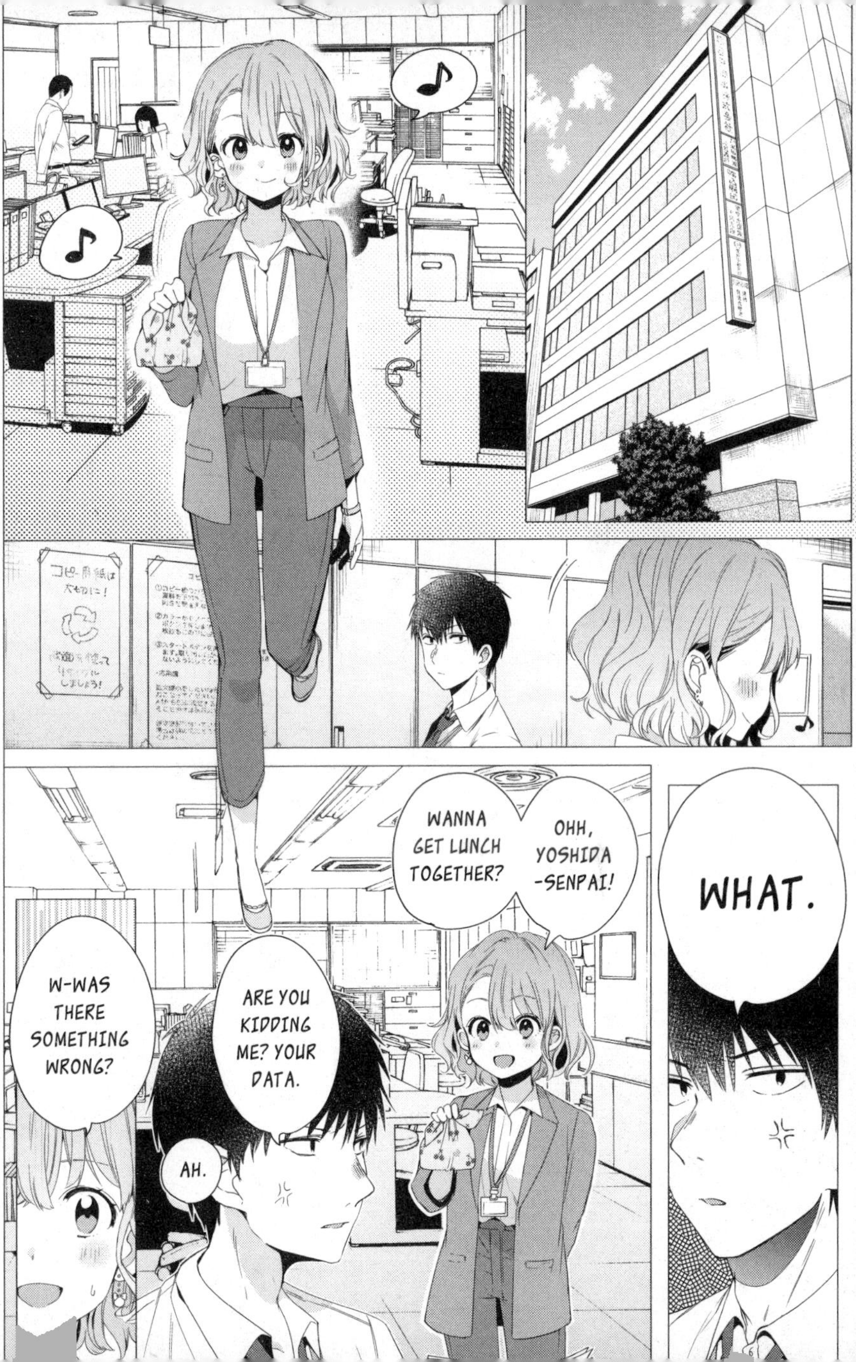
♪
♪
♪
WHAT.
OHH, YOSHIDA -SENPAI!
WANNA GET LUNCH TOGETHER?
ARE YOU KIDDING ME? YOUR DATA.
AH.
W-WAS THERE SOMETHING WRONG?

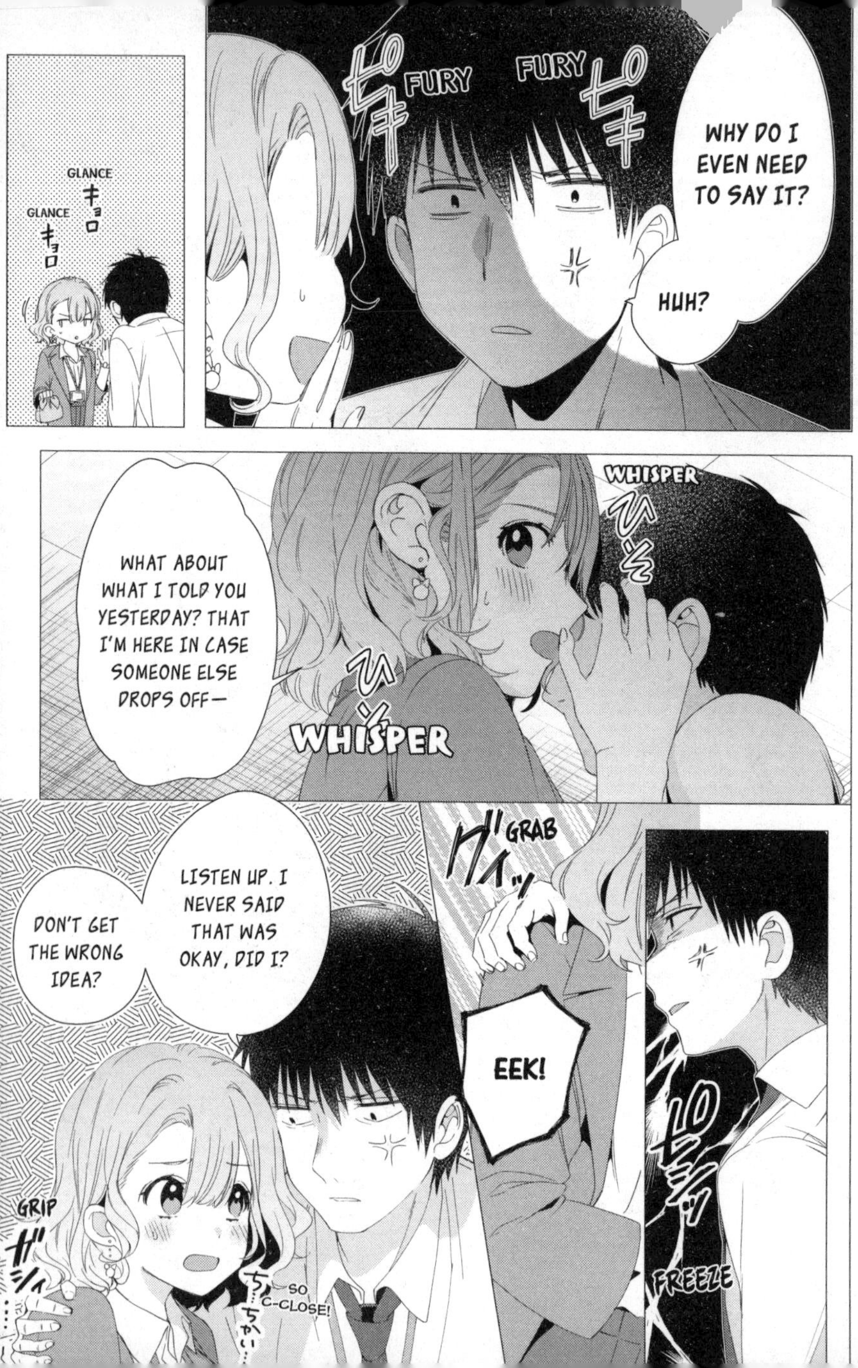
WHY DO I EVEN NEED TO SAY IT?
ピキ FURY
FURY ピキ
HUH?
GLANCE キョロ
GLANCE キョロ
WHISPER ひそ
WHAT ABOUT WHAT I TOLD YOU YESTERDAY? THAT I'M HERE IN CASE SOMEONE ELSE DROPS OFF—
ひそ WHISPER
FREEZE
GRAB
EEK!
LISTEN UP. I NEVER SAID THAT WAS OKAY, DID I?
DON'T GET THE WRONG IDEA?
SO C-CLOSE!
ち…ちかい…
GRIP
ガシィ

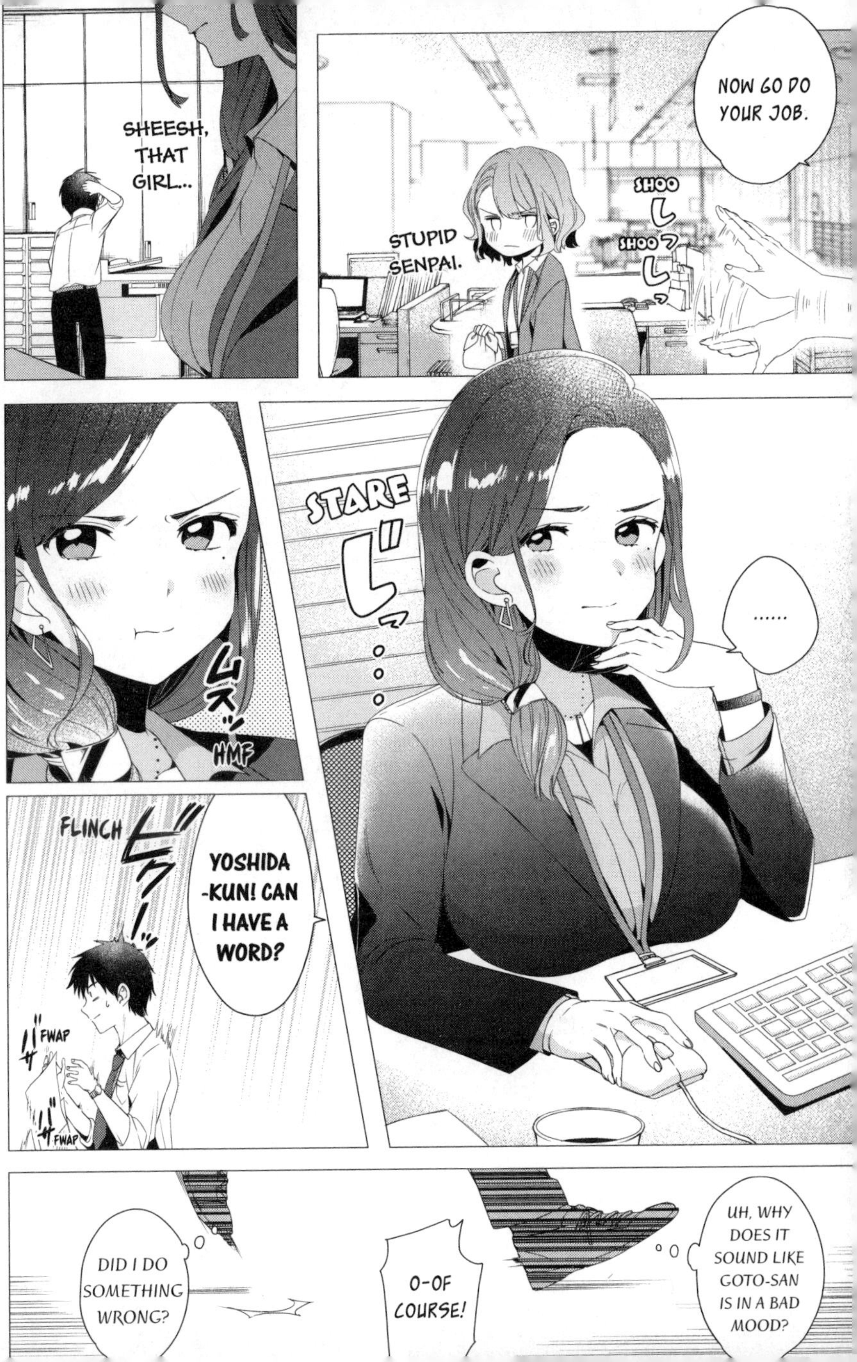
NOW GO DO YOUR JOB.
SHOO
SHOO
STUPID SENPAI.
SHEESH, THAT GIRL...
STARE
......
HMF
FLINCH
YOSHIDA-KUN! CAN I HAVE A WORD?
FWAP
FWAP
UH, WHY DOES IT SOUND LIKE GOTO-SAN IS IN A BAD MOOD?
O-OF COURSE!
DID I DO SOMETHING WRONG?

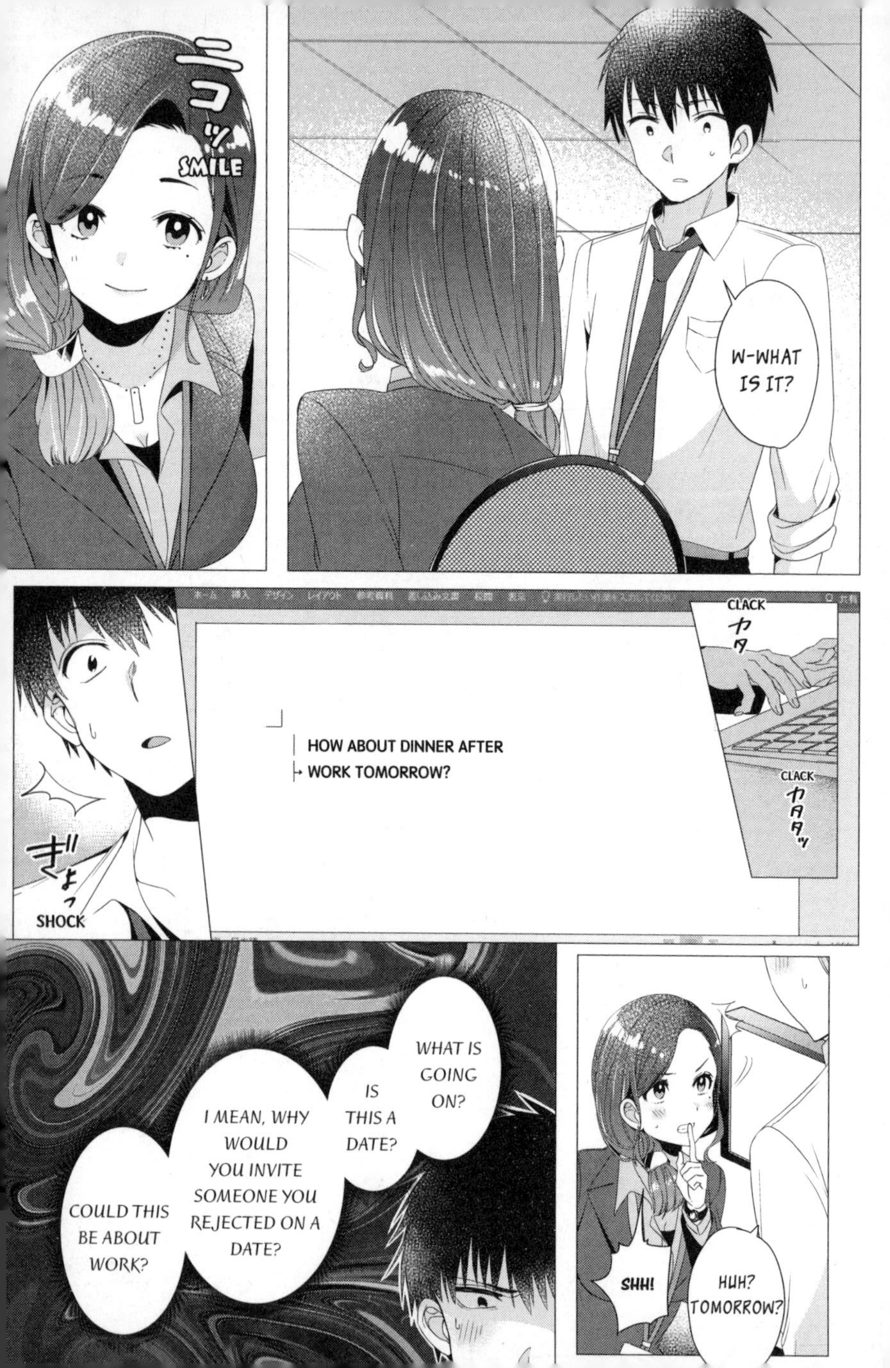
W-WHAT IS IT?
ニコッ
SMILE
CLACK
カタ
CLACK
カタタッ
HOW ABOUT DINNER AFTER
WORK TOMORROW?
ぎょっ
SHOCK
HUH? TOMORROW?
SHH!
WHAT IS GOING ON?
IS THIS A DATE?
I MEAN, WHY WOULD YOU INVITE SOMEONE YOU REJECTED ON A DATE?
COULD THIS BE ABOUT WORK?

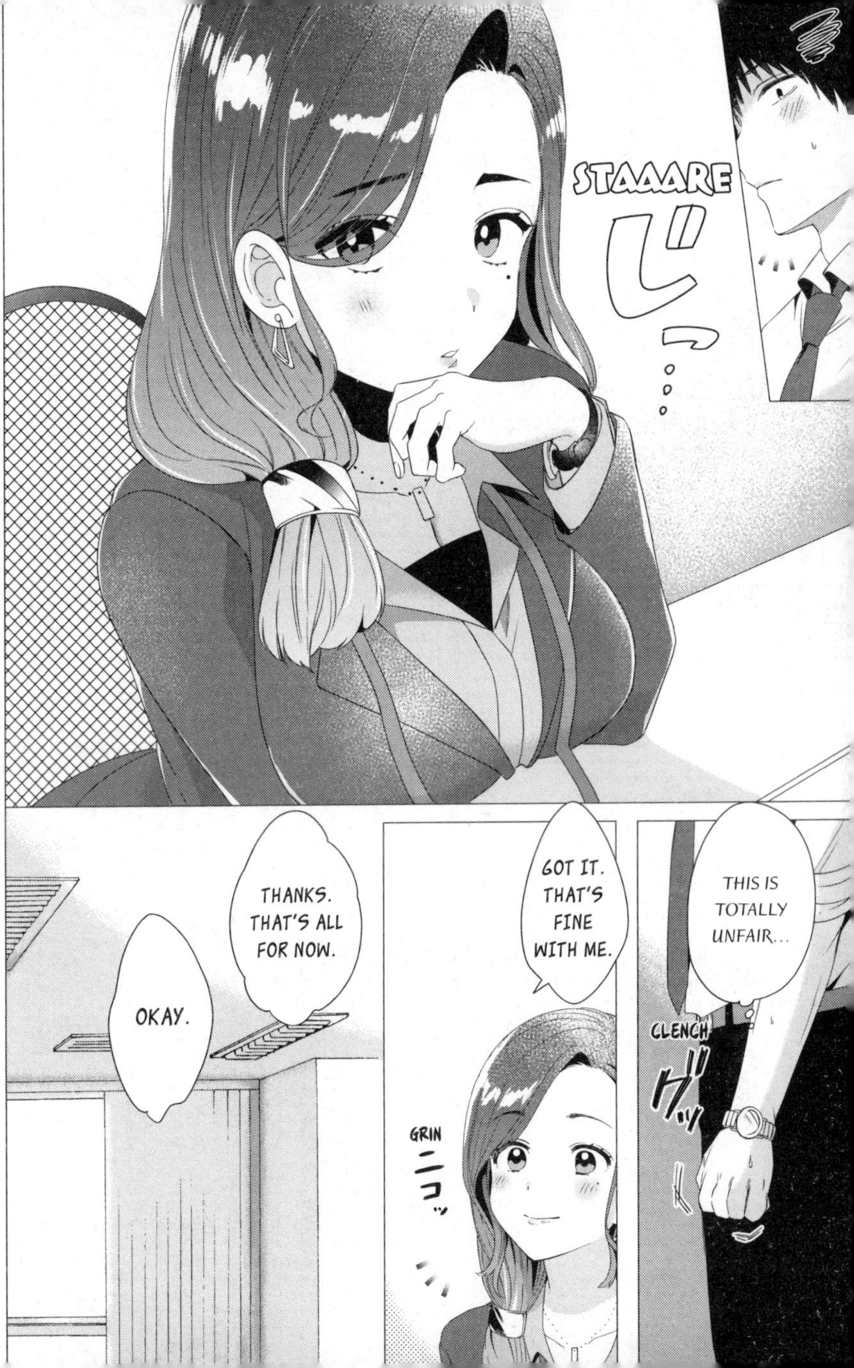
STAAARE
じっ
THIS IS TOTALLY UNFAIR...
CLENCH
GOT IT. THAT'S FINE WITH ME.
GRIN
ニコッ
THANKS. THAT'S ALL FOR NOW.
OKAY.

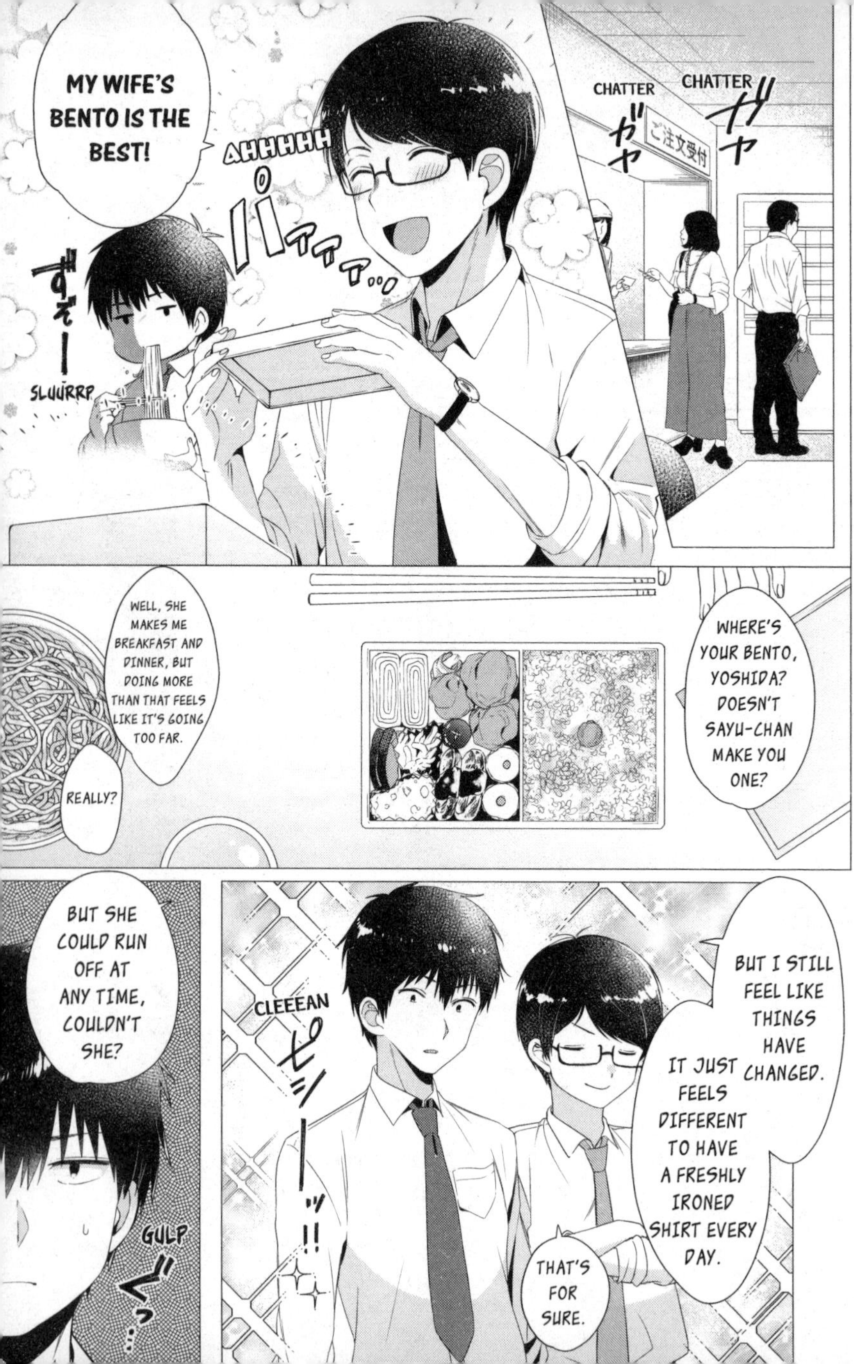
CHATTER
CHATTER
ガヤガヤ
ご注文受付
AHHHHH
パァァァ…
MY WIFE'S BENTO IS THE BEST!
ずぞー
SLUURRP
WHERE'S YOUR BENTO, YOSHIDA? DOESN'T SAYU-CHAN MAKE YOU ONE?
WELL, SHE MAKES ME BREAKFAST AND DINNER, BUT DOING MORE THAN THAT FEELS LIKE IT'S GOING TOO FAR.
REALLY?
BUT I STILL FEEL LIKE THINGS HAVE CHANGED.
IT JUST FEELS DIFFERENT TO HAVE A FRESHLY IRONED SHIRT EVERY DAY.
THAT'S FOR SURE.
CLEEEAN
ピシーッ!!
BUT SHE COULD RUN OFF AT ANY TIME, COULDN'T SHE?
GULP
ぐっ…

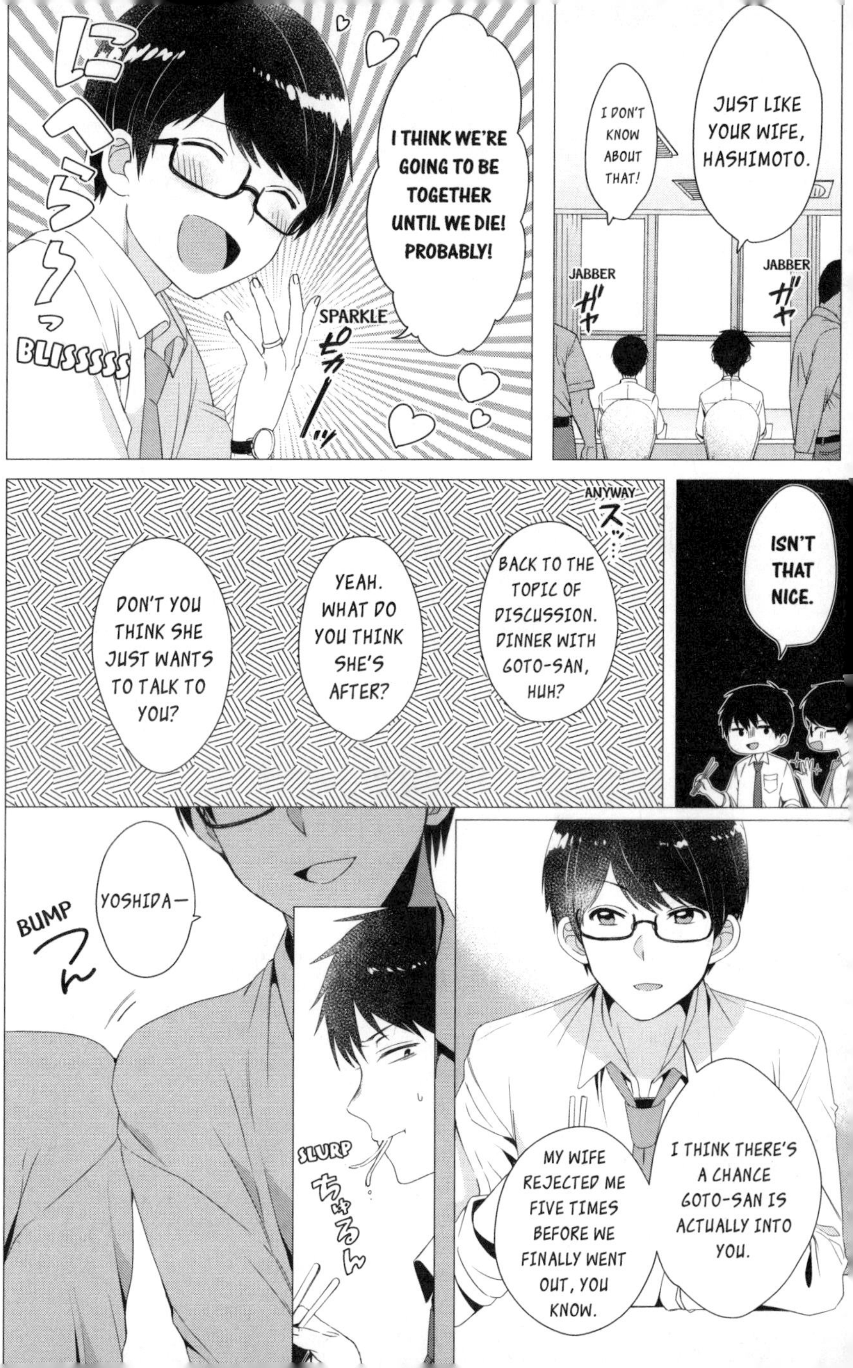
JABBER
ガヤ
JABBER
ガヤ
JUST LIKE YOUR WIFE, HASHIMOTO.
I DON'T KNOW ABOUT THAT!
I THINK WE'RE GOING TO BE TOGETHER UNTIL WE DIE! PROBABLY!
SPARKLE
BLISSSSSS
ISN'T THAT NICE.
ANYWAY
スッ
BACK TO THE TOPIC OF DISCUSSION. DINNER WITH GOTO-SAN, HUH?
YEAH. WHAT DO YOU THINK SHE'S AFTER?
DON'T YOU THINK SHE JUST WANTS TO TALK TO YOU?
I THINK THERE'S A CHANCE GOTO-SAN IS ACTUALLY INTO YOU.
MY WIFE REJECTED ME FIVE TIMES BEFORE WE FINALLY WENT OUT, YOU KNOW.
SLURP
ちゅるん
YOSHIDA—
BUMP
つん

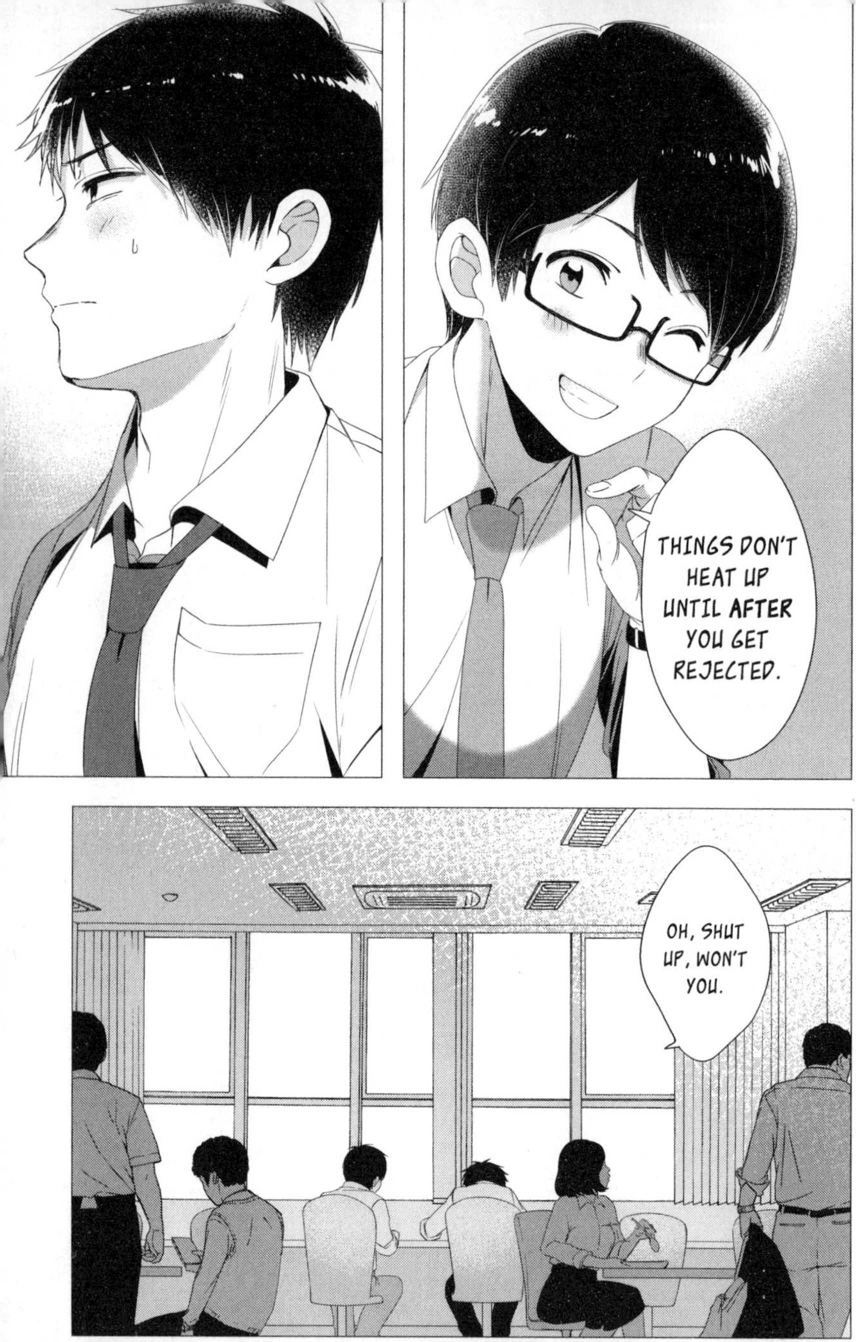
THINGS DON'T HEAT UP UNTIL **AFTER** YOU GET REJECTED.
OH, SHUT UP, WON'T YOU.

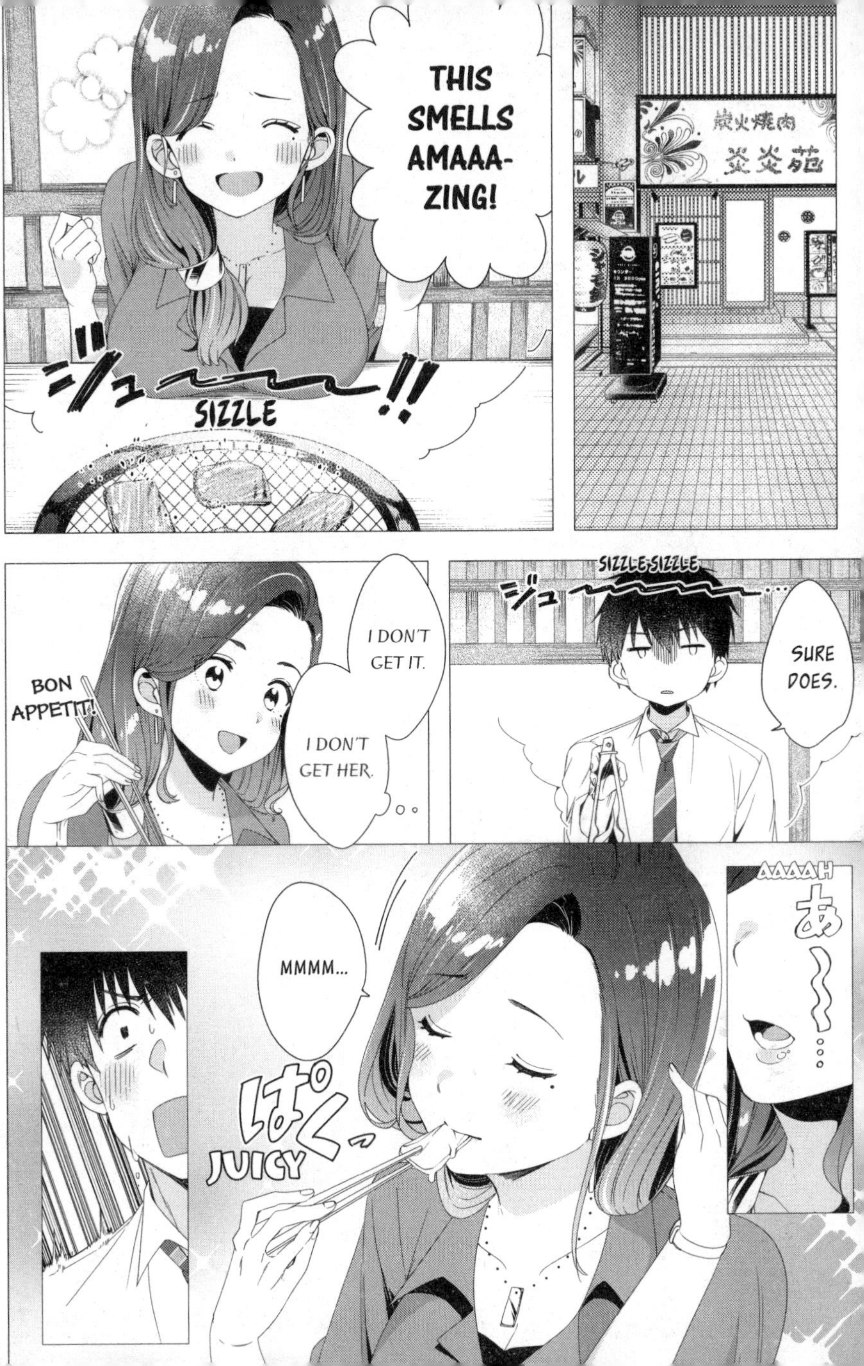
炭火焼肉
炎炎苑
THIS SMELLS AMAAA-ZING!
ジュ〜〜〜!!
SIZZLE
ジュ〜〜…
SIZZLE SIZZLE
SURE DOES.
I DON'T GET IT.
I DON'T GET HER.
BON APPETIT!
AAAAH
あ〜〜…
MMMM...
ぱく
JUICY

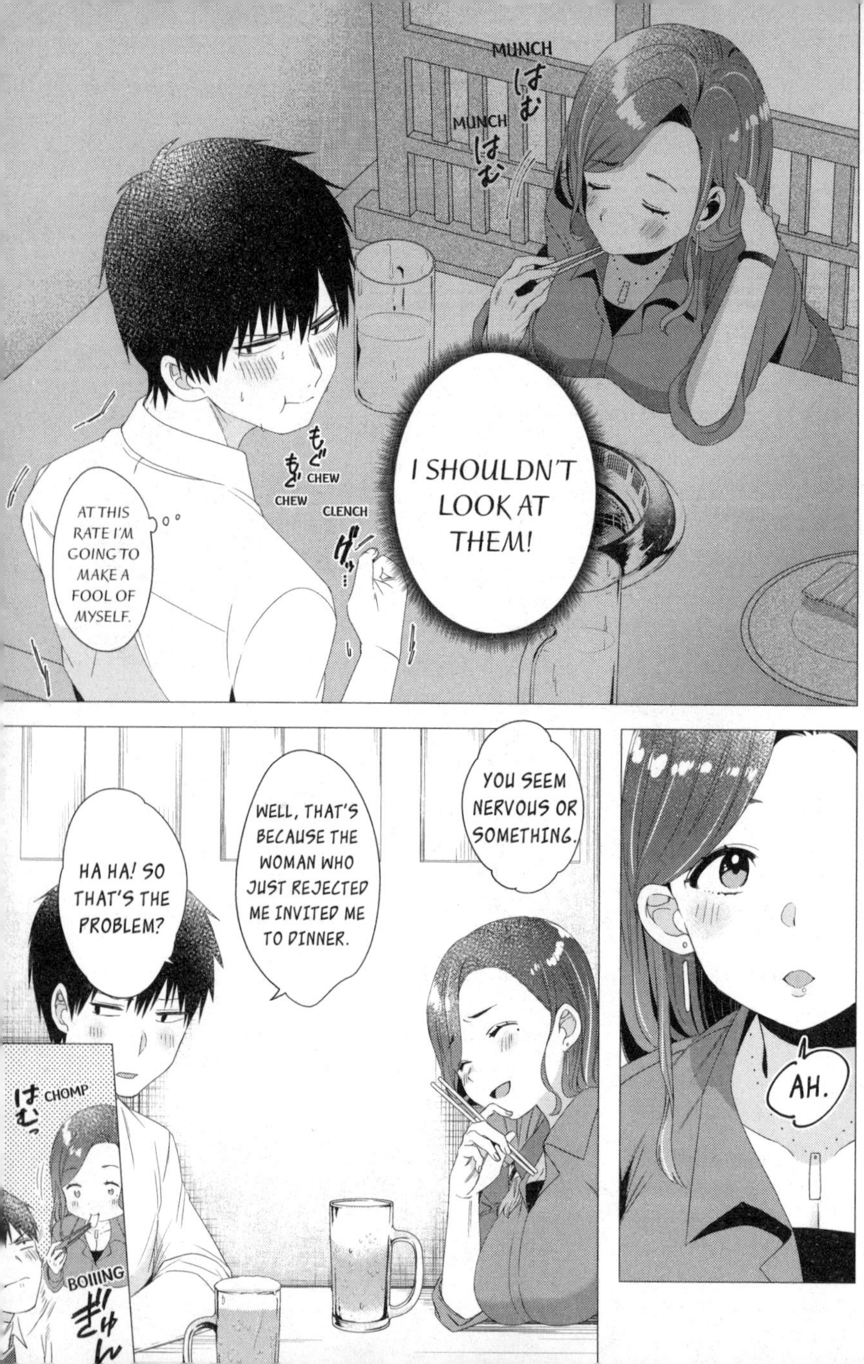
MUNCH
はむ
MUNCH
はむ
I SHOULDN'T LOOK AT THEM!
CLENCH
ギュッ
もぐもぐ
CHEW
CHEW
AT THIS RATE I'M GOING TO MAKE A FOOL OF MYSELF.
AH.
YOU SEEM NERVOUS OR SOMETHING.
WELL, THAT'S BECAUSE THE WOMAN WHO JUST REJECTED ME INVITED ME TO DINNER.
HA HA! SO THAT'S THE PROBLEM?
はむっ
CHOMP
BOIIING
ぎゅん

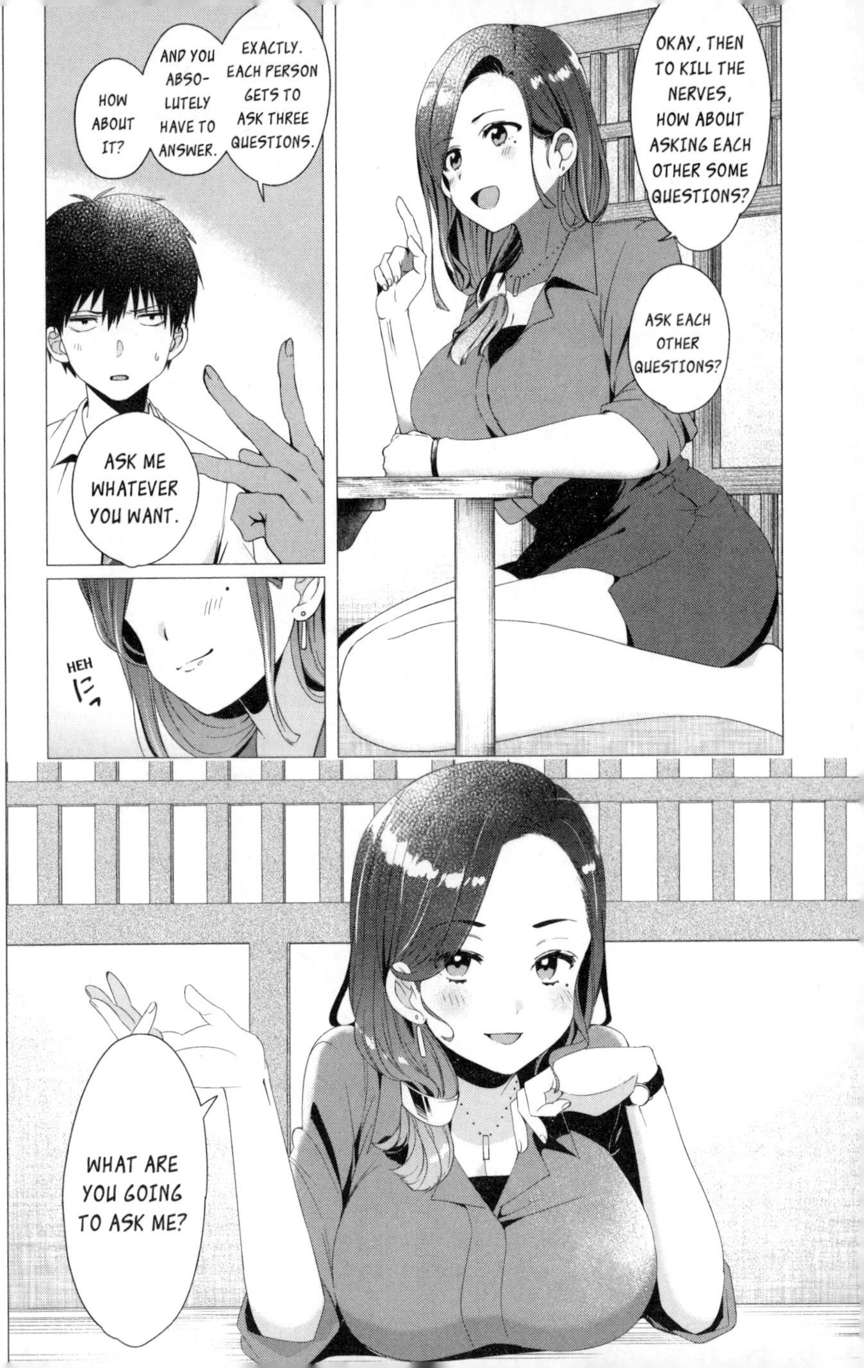
OKAY, THEN TO KILL THE NERVES, HOW ABOUT ASKING EACH OTHER SOME QUESTIONS?
ASK EACH OTHER QUESTIONS?
EXACTLY. EACH PERSON GETS TO ASK THREE QUESTIONS.
AND YOU ABSO-LUTELY HAVE TO ANSWER.
HOW ABOUT IT?
ASK ME WHATEVER YOU WANT.
HEH
WHAT ARE YOU GOING TO ASK ME?

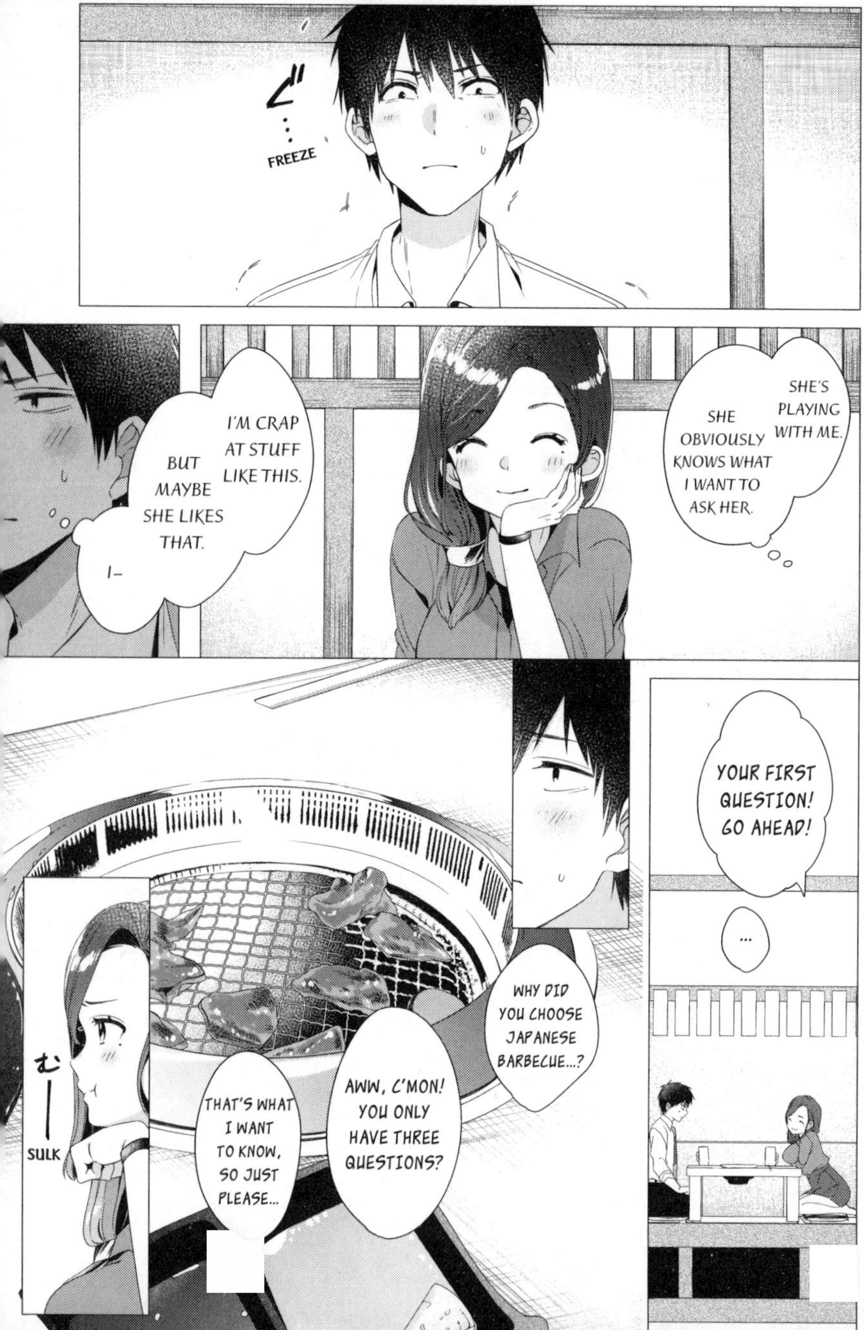
FREEZE
SHE'S PLAYING WITH ME.
SHE OBVIOUSLY KNOWS WHAT I WANT TO ASK HER.
I'M CRAP AT STUFF LIKE THIS.
BUT MAYBE SHE LIKES THAT.
I–
YOUR FIRST QUESTION! GO AHEAD!
...
WHY DID YOU CHOOSE JAPANESE BARBECUE...?
AWW, C'MON! YOU ONLY HAVE THREE QUESTIONS?
THAT'S WHAT I WANT TO KNOW, SO JUST PLEASE...
むー
SULK

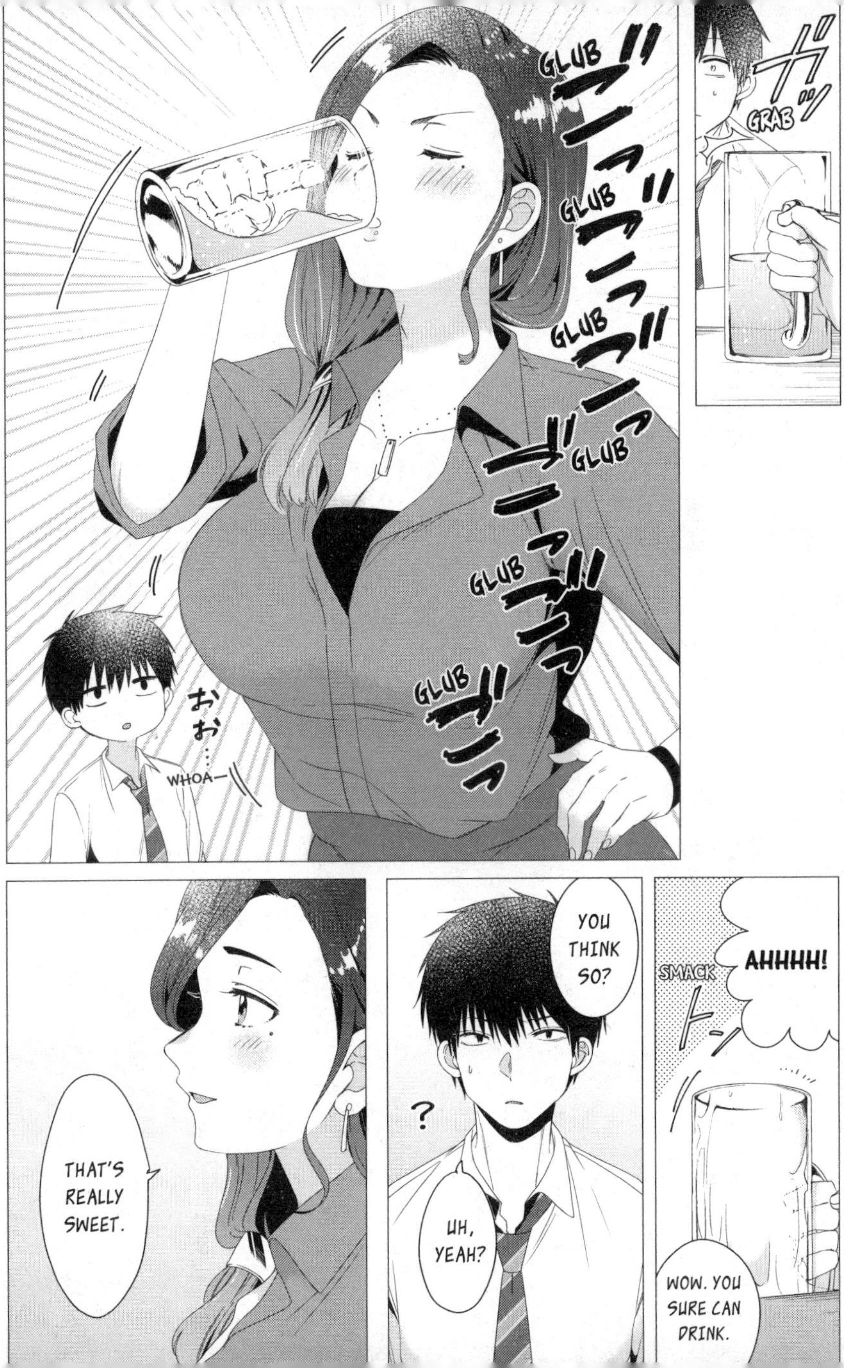
GRAB
GLUB
GLUB
GLUB
GLUB
GLUB
GLUB
おお…
WHOA—
SMACK
AHHHH!
WOW. YOU SURE CAN DRINK.
YOU THINK SO?
?
UH, YEAH?
THAT'S REALLY SWEET.

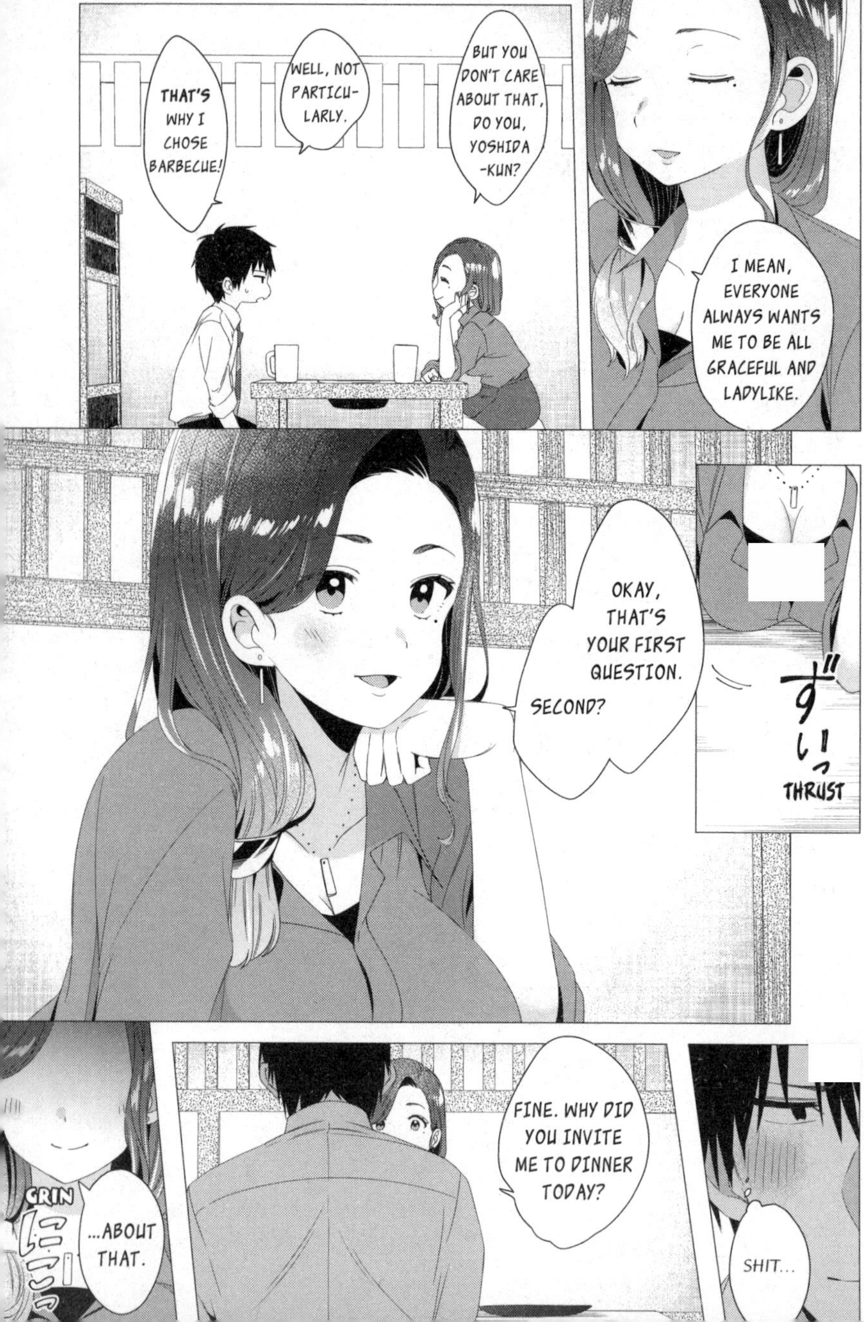

I MEAN, EVERYONE ALWAYS WANTS ME TO BE ALL GRACEFUL AND LADYLIKE.
BUT YOU DON'T CARE ABOUT THAT, DO YOU, YOSHIDA-KUN?
WELL, NOT PARTICU-LARLY.
THAT'S WHY I CHOSE BARBECUE!
ずいっ
THRUST
OKAY, THAT'S YOUR FIRST QUESTION.
SECOND?
SHIT...
FINE. WHY DID YOU INVITE ME TO DINNER TODAY?
...ABOUT THAT.
GRIN

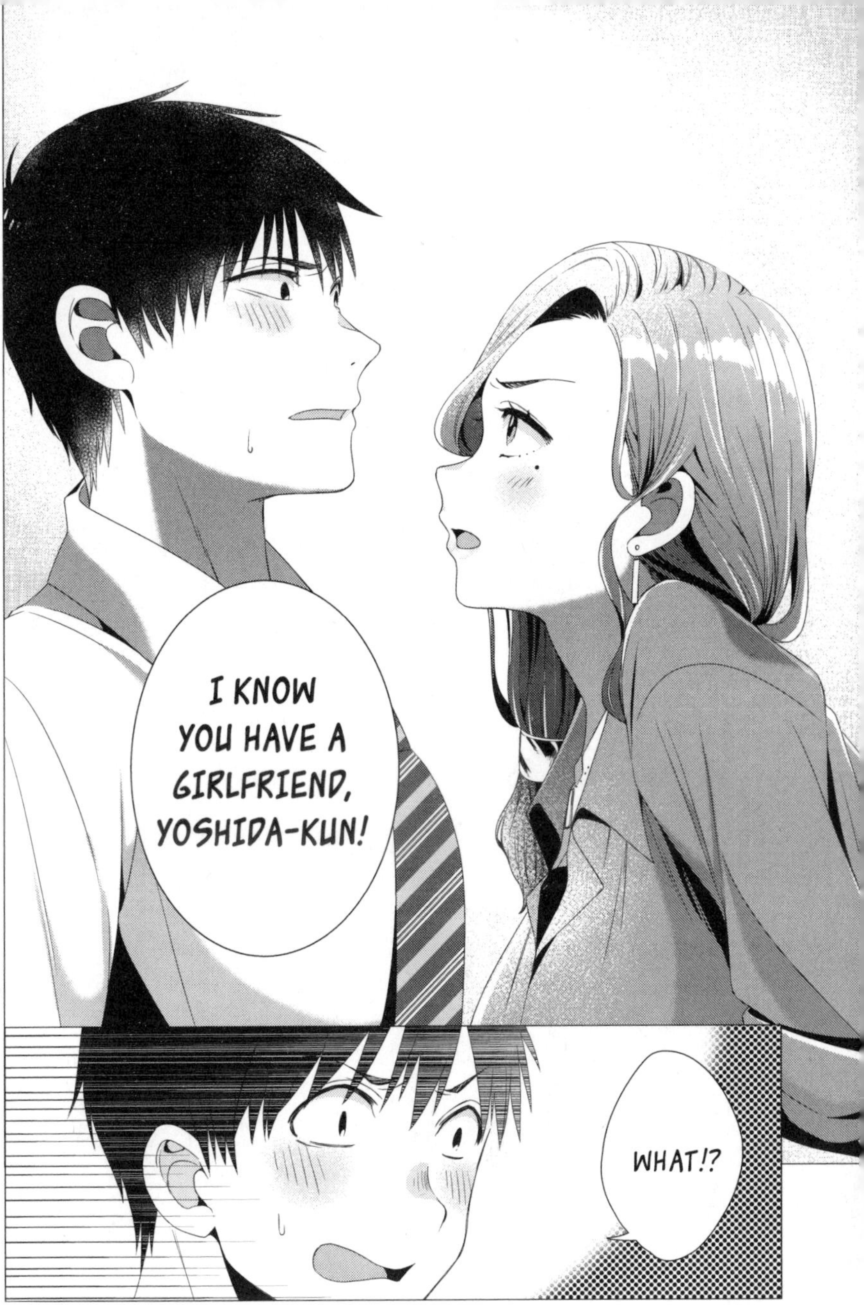
I KNOW YOU HAVE A GIRLFRIEND, YOSHIDA-KUN!
WHAT!?

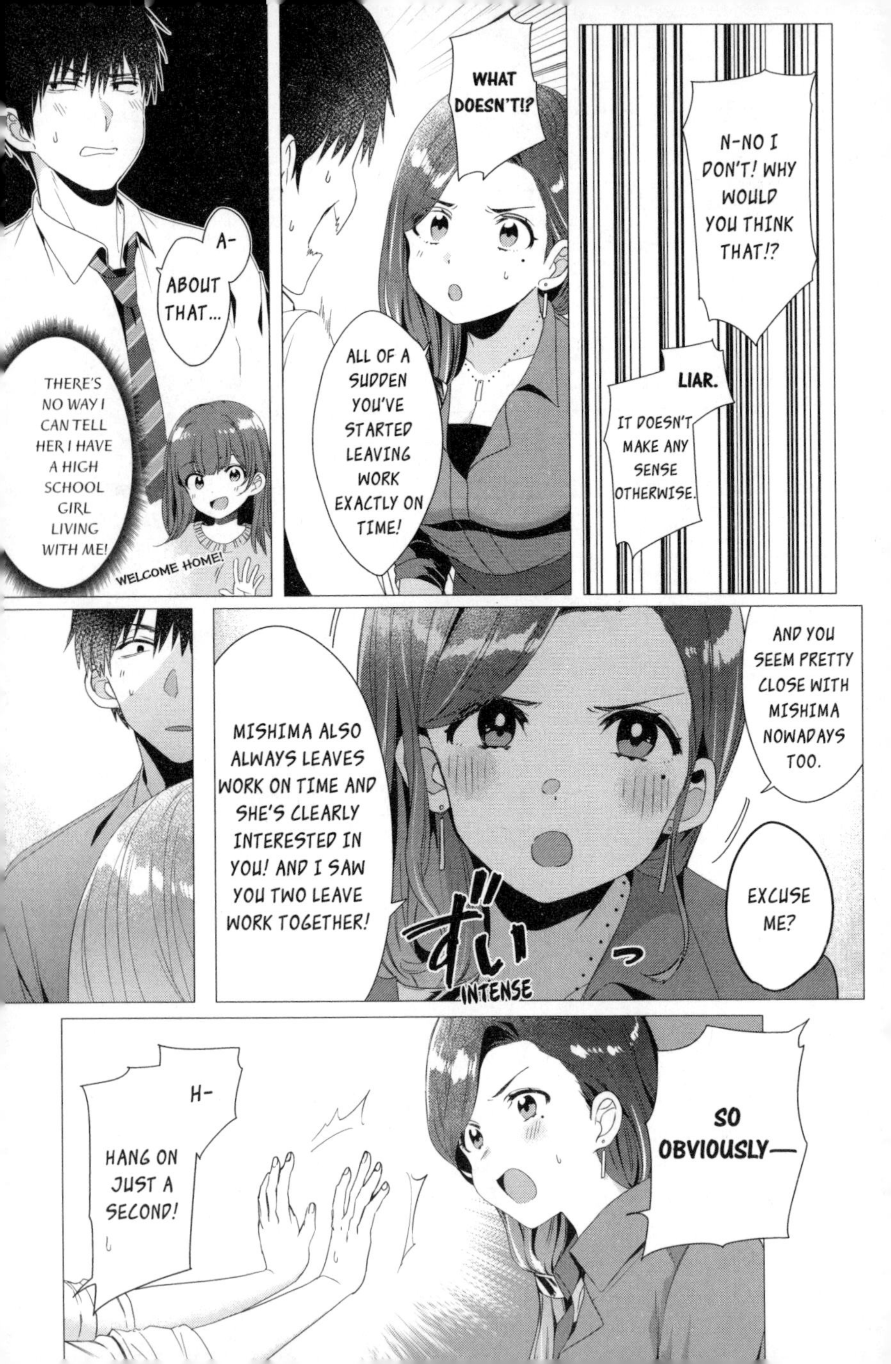
N-NO I DON'T! WHY WOULD YOU THINK THAT!?
LIAR.
IT DOESN'T MAKE ANY SENSE OTHERWISE.
WHAT DOESN'T!?
ALL OF A SUDDEN YOU'VE STARTED LEAVING WORK EXACTLY ON TIME!
A-
ABOUT THAT...
THERE'S NO WAY I CAN TELL HER I HAVE A HIGH SCHOOL GIRL LIVING WITH ME!
WELCOME HOME!
AND YOU SEEM PRETTY CLOSE WITH MISHIMA NOWADAYS TOO.
EXCUSE ME?
MISHIMA ALSO ALWAYS LEAVES WORK ON TIME AND SHE'S CLEARLY INTERESTED IN YOU! AND I SAW YOU TWO LEAVE WORK TOGETHER!
ずいっ
INTENSE
SO OBVIOUSLY—
H-
HANG ON JUST A SECOND!

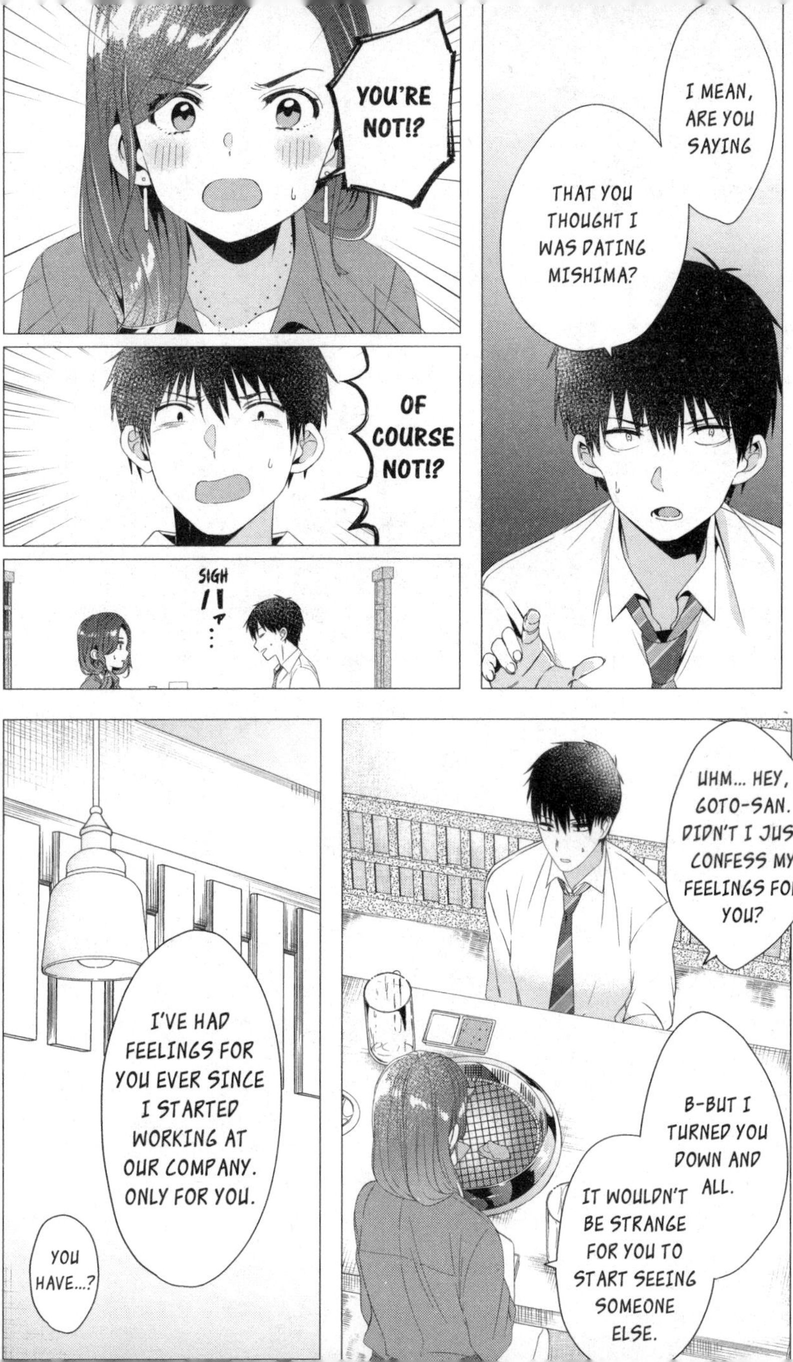
I MEAN, ARE YOU SAYING
THAT YOU THOUGHT I WAS DATING MISHIMA?
YOU'RE NOT!?
OF COURSE NOT!?
SIGH
ハァ…
UHM... HEY, GOTO-SAN. DIDN'T I JUST CONFESS MY FEELINGS FOR YOU?
B-BUT I TURNED YOU DOWN AND ALL.
IT WOULDN'T BE STRANGE FOR YOU TO START SEEING SOMEONE ELSE.
I'VE HAD FEELINGS FOR YOU EVER SINCE I STARTED WORKING AT OUR COMPANY. ONLY FOR YOU.
YOU HAVE...?

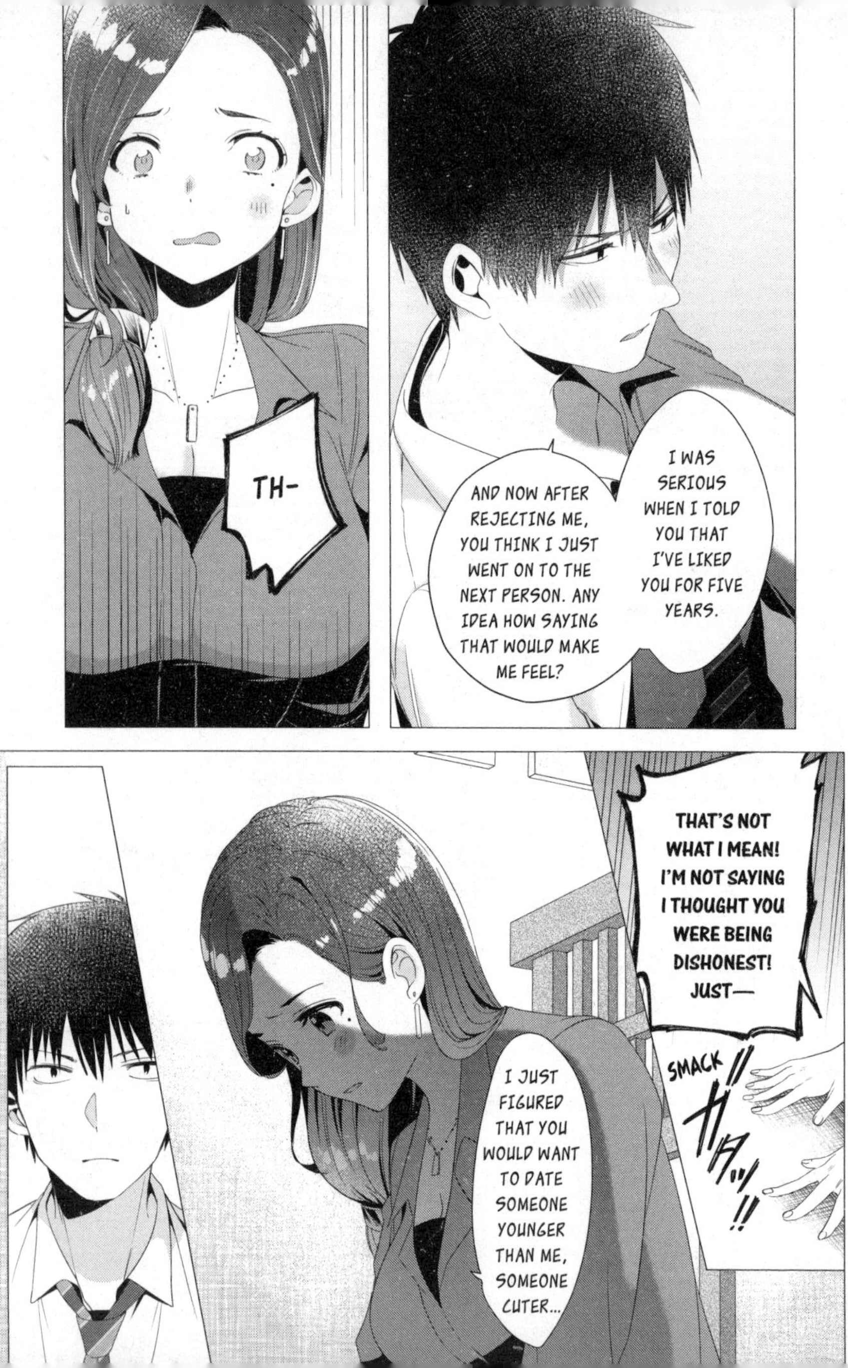
I WAS SERIOUS WHEN I TOLD YOU THAT I'VE LIKED YOU FOR FIVE YEARS.
AND NOW AFTER REJECTING ME, YOU THINK I JUST WENT ON TO THE NEXT PERSON. ANY IDEA HOW SAYING THAT WOULD MAKE ME FEEL?
TH-
THAT'S NOT WHAT I MEAN! I'M NOT SAYING I THOUGHT YOU WERE BEING DISHONEST! JUST—
SMACK
I JUST FIGURED THAT YOU WOULD WANT TO DATE SOMEONE YOUNGER THAN ME, SOMEONE CUTER...

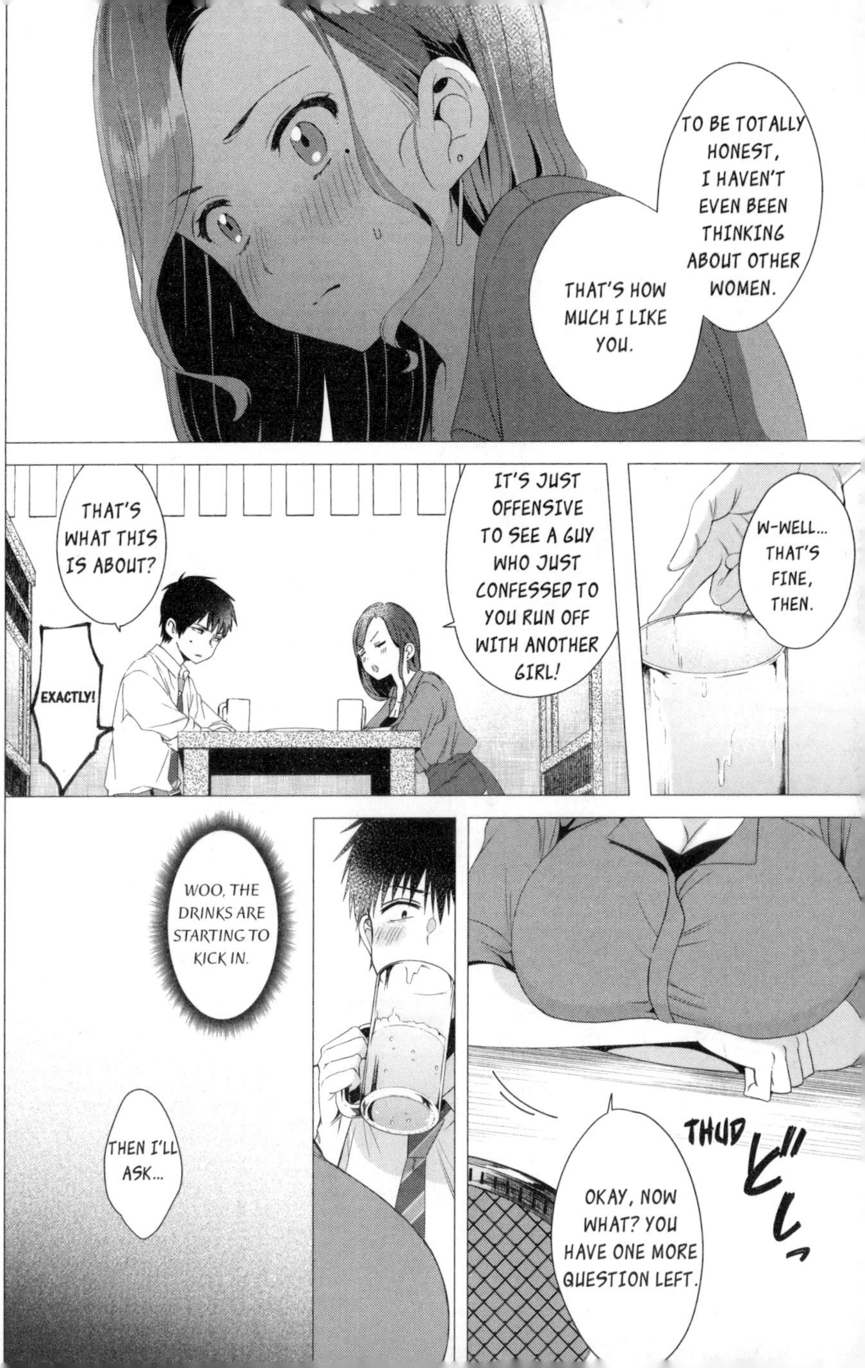
TO BE TOTALLY HONEST, I HAVEN'T EVEN BEEN THINKING ABOUT OTHER WOMEN.
THAT'S HOW MUCH I LIKE YOU.
W-WELL... THAT'S FINE, THEN.
IT'S JUST OFFENSIVE TO SEE A GUY WHO JUST CONFESSED TO YOU RUN OFF WITH ANOTHER GIRL!
THAT'S WHAT THIS IS ABOUT?
EXACTLY!
THUD
OKAY, NOW WHAT? YOU HAVE ONE MORE QUESTION LEFT.
WOO, THE DRINKS ARE STARTING TO KICK IN.
THEN I'LL ASK...

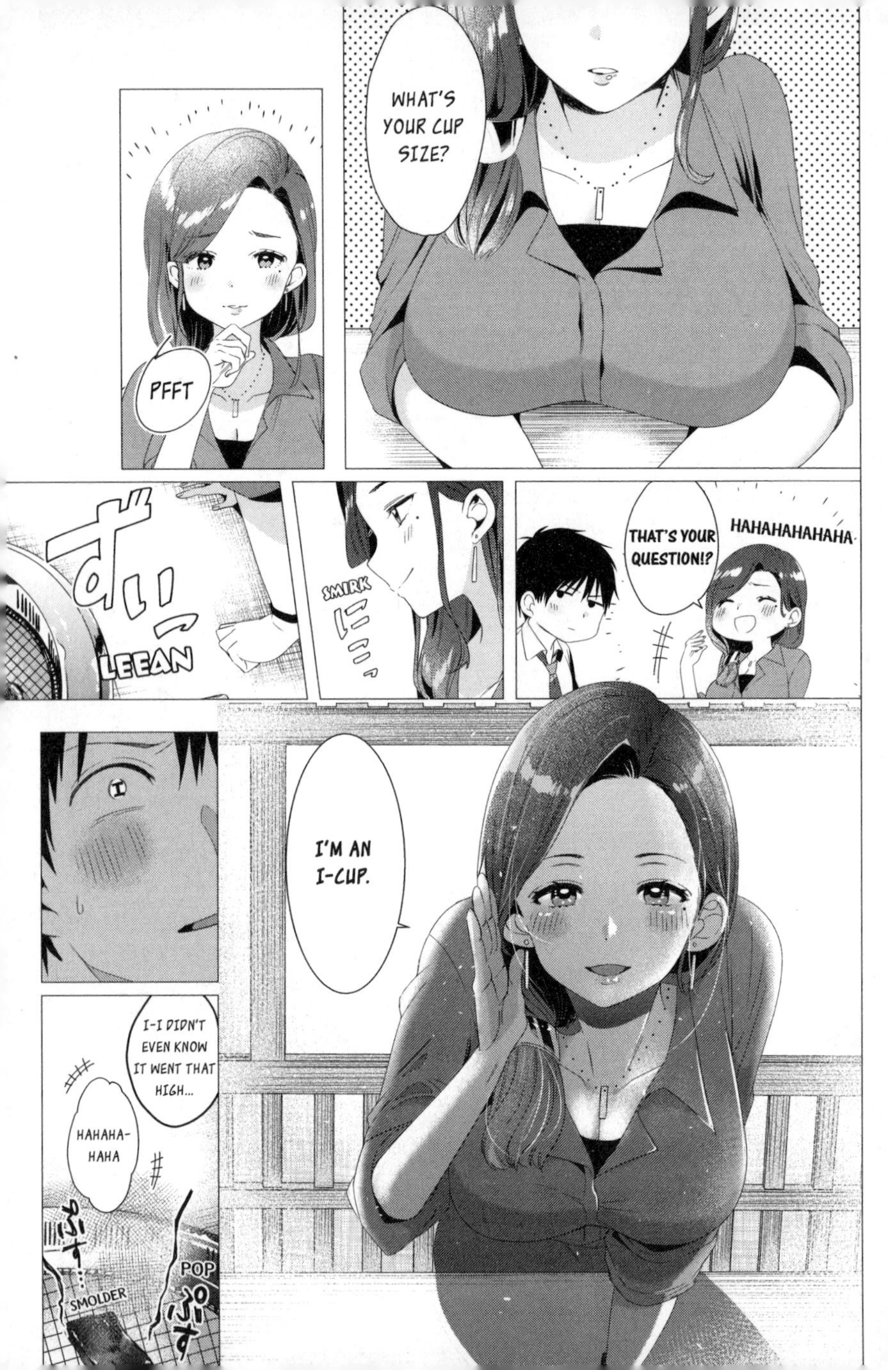

WHAT'S YOUR CUP SIZE?
PFFT
HAHAHAHAHAHA
THAT'S YOUR QUESTION!?
SMIRK
LEEAN
I'M AN I-CUP.
I
I-I DIDN'T EVEN KNOW IT WENT THAT HIGH...
HAHAHA-HAHA
POP
ぷす
ぷす…
SMOLDER

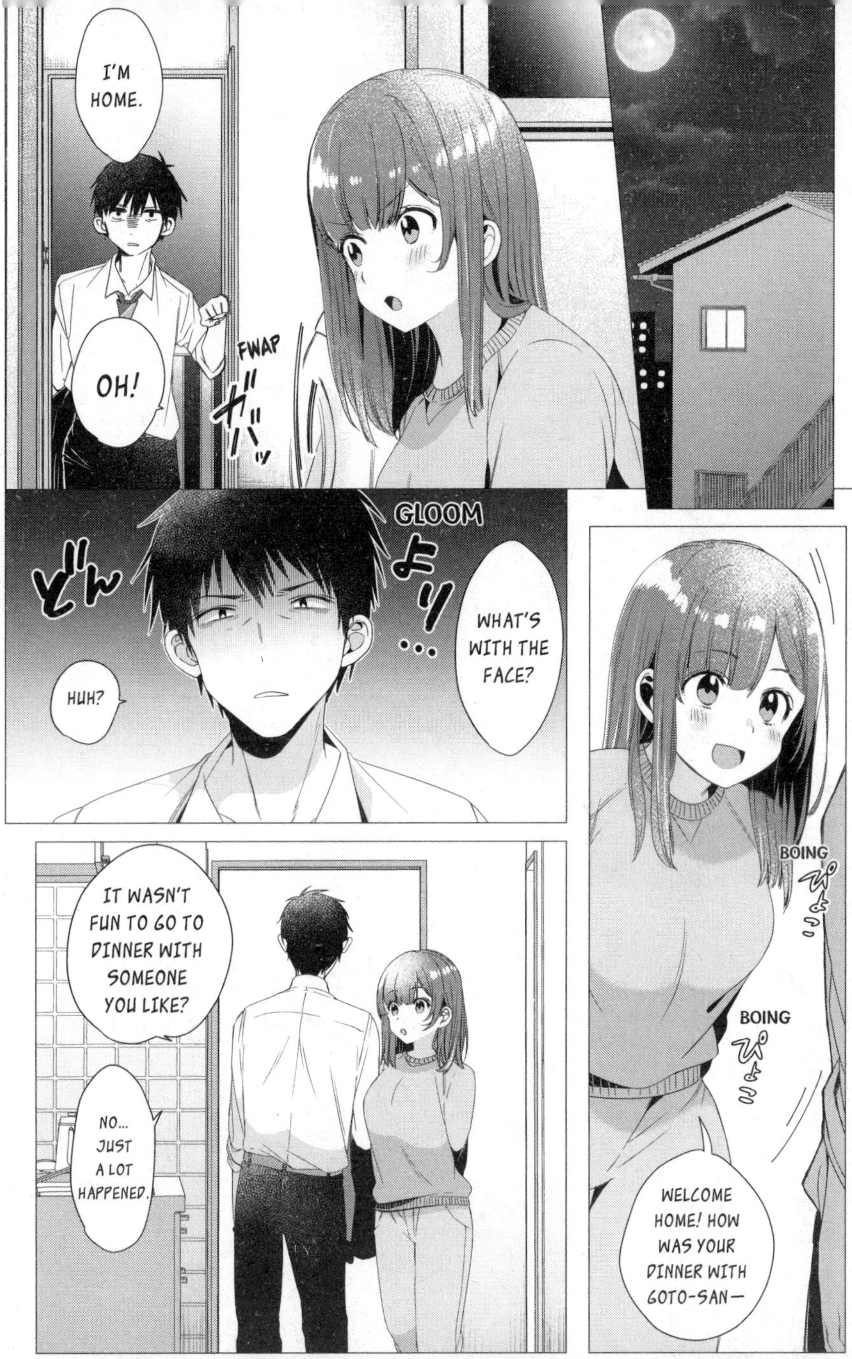
I'M HOME.
OH!
FWAP
BOING
BOING
WELCOME HOME! HOW WAS YOUR DINNER WITH GOTO-SAN—
GLOOM
WHAT'S WITH THE FACE?
HUH?
IT WASN'T FUN TO GO TO DINNER WITH SOMEONE YOU LIKE?
NO... JUST A LOT HAPPENED.

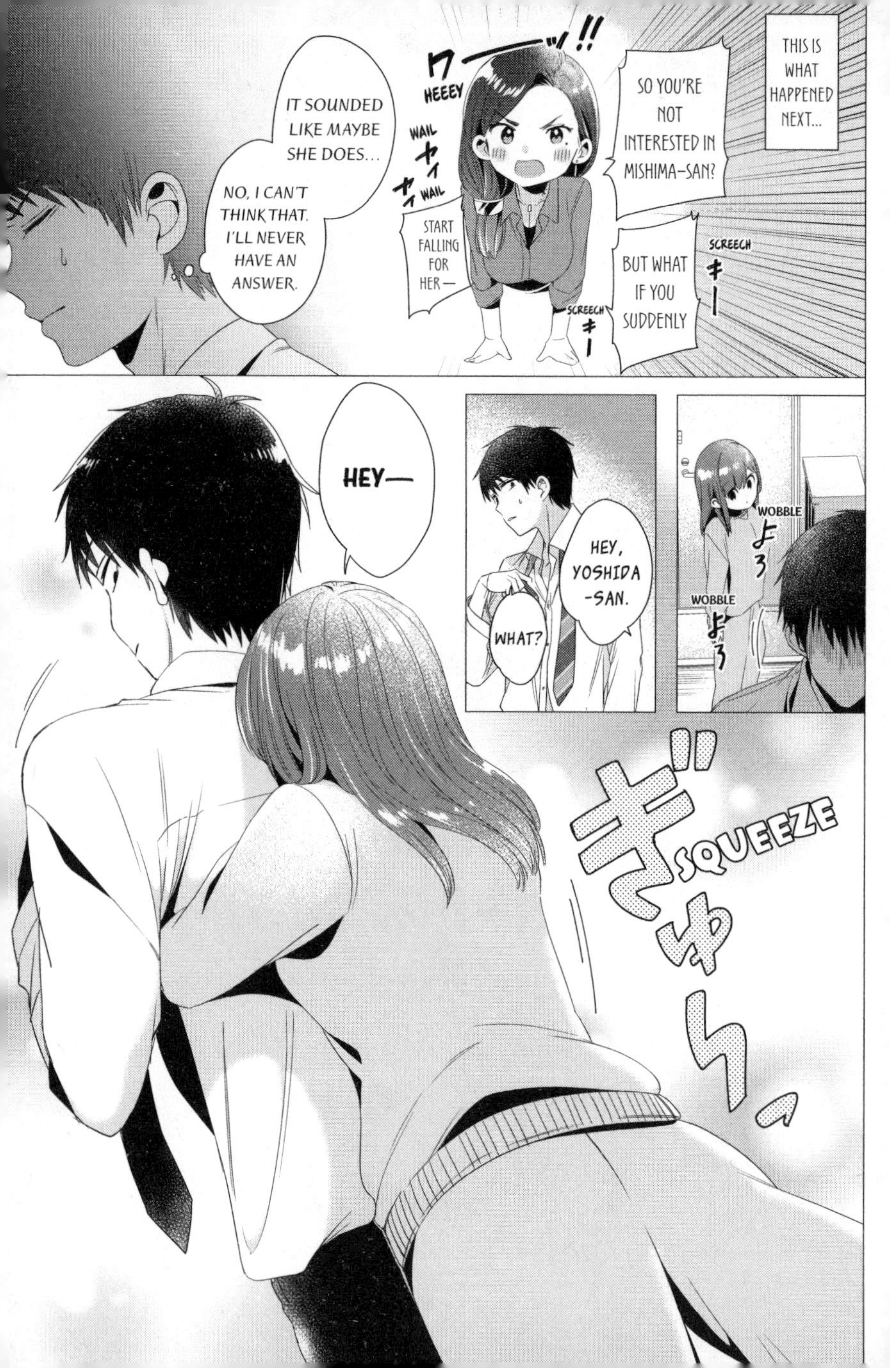
THIS IS WHAT HAPPENED NEXT...
SO YOU'RE NOT INTERESTED IN MISHIMA-SAN?
BUT WHAT IF YOU SUDDENLY
START FALLING FOR HER—
ワーーッ!!
HEEEY
WAIL
WAIL
SCREECH
SCREECH
IT SOUNDED LIKE MAYBE SHE DOES...
NO, I CAN'T THINK THAT. I'LL NEVER HAVE AN ANSWER.
WOBBLE
WOBBLE
HEY, YOSHIDA-SAN.
WHAT?
HEY—
SQUEEZE

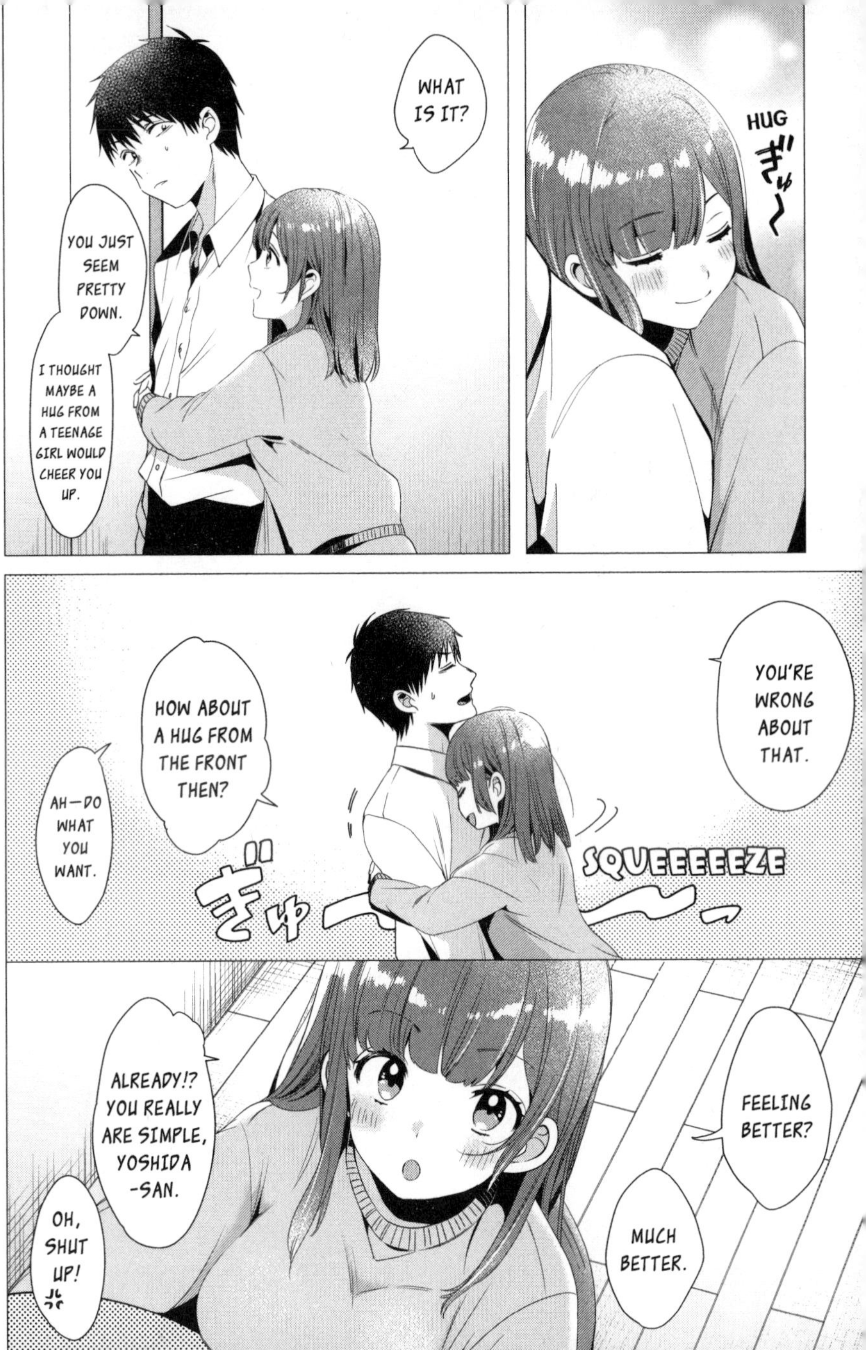
HUG
ぎゅ〜
WHAT IS IT?
YOU JUST SEEM PRETTY DOWN.
I THOUGHT MAYBE A HUG FROM A TEENAGE GIRL WOULD CHEER YOU UP.
YOU'RE WRONG ABOUT THAT.
SQUEEEEEEZE
HOW ABOUT A HUG FROM THE FRONT THEN?
AH—DO WHAT YOU WANT.
ぎゅ〜〜っ
FEELING BETTER?
MUCH BETTER.
ALREADY!? YOU REALLY ARE SIMPLE, YOSHIDA-SAN.
OH, SHUT UP!

PAT PAT

NOW IT'S TIME FOR YOUR BATH!

GO WASH YOURSELF AND SOAK IN THE HOT WATER, AND ALL YOUR WORRIES WILL MELT AWAY!

...GOOD IDEA.

DRIP

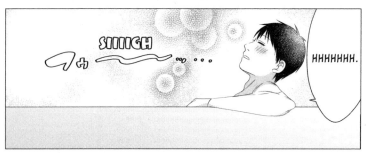

SIIIIGH

HHHHHHH.

SHE PREPARED THE BATH FOR ME EVEN THOUGH SHE DIDN'T KNOW WHAT TIME I'D GET BACK.

IT EVEN SMELLS LIKE CITRUS TODAY.

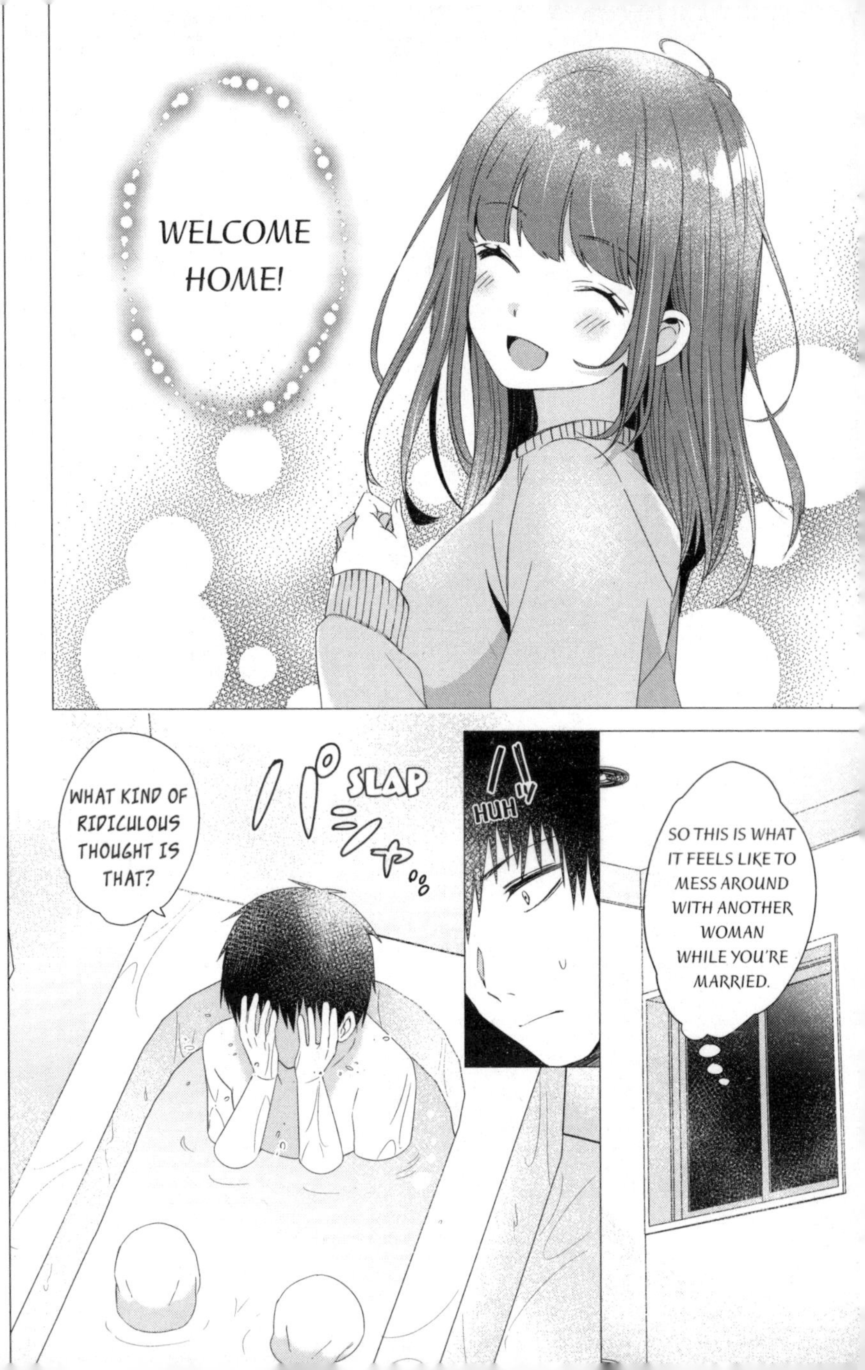
WELCOME HOME!
SO THIS IS WHAT IT FEELS LIKE TO MESS AROUND WITH ANOTHER WOMAN WHILE YOU'RE MARRIED.
HUH
SLAP
WHAT KIND OF RIDICULOUS THOUGHT IS THAT?

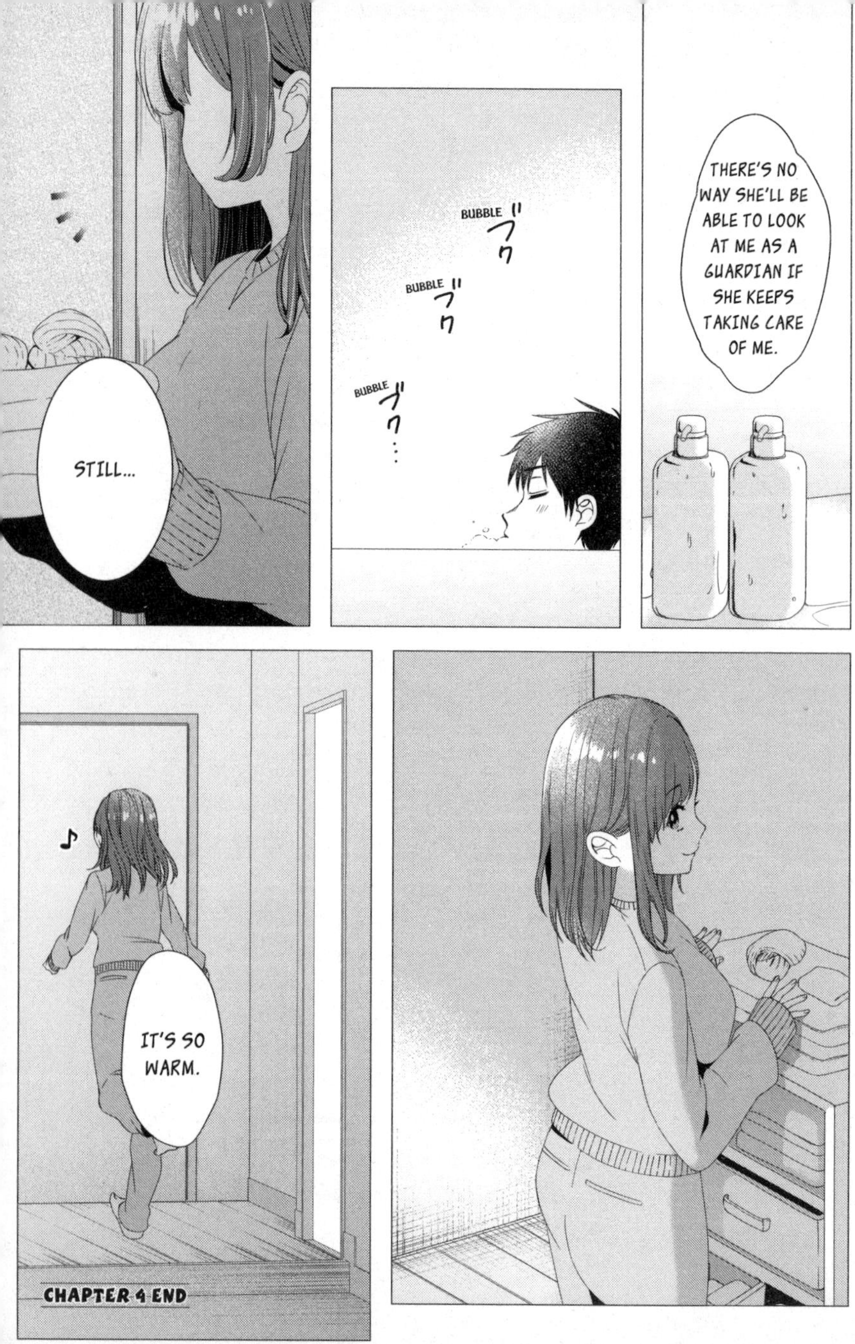
THERE'S NO WAY SHE'LL BE ABLE TO LOOK AT ME AS A GUARDIAN IF SHE KEEPS TAKING CARE OF ME.
BUBBLE ブク
BUBBLE ブク
BUBBLE ブク…
STILL...
♪
IT'S SO WARM.
CHAPTER 4 END

HIGEHIRO

After Being Rejected,
I Shaved and Took
in a High School Runaway

[CHAPTER 5]

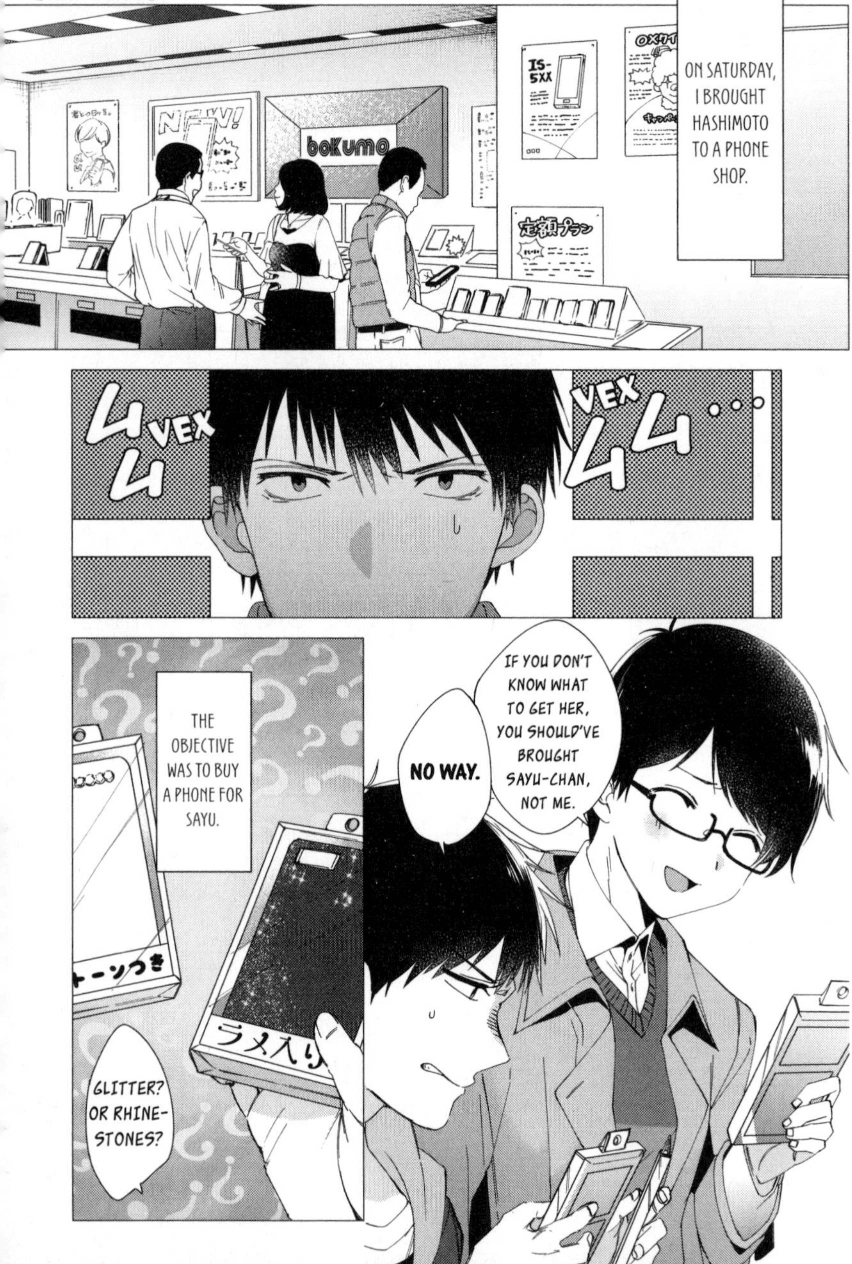

ON SATURDAY, I BROUGHT HASHIMOTO TO A PHONE SHOP.
定額プラン
IS-5XX
boKumo
NEW!
ムム VEX
ムム VEX
IF YOU DON'T KNOW WHAT TO GET HER, YOU SHOULD'VE BROUGHT SAYU-CHAN, NOT ME.
NO WAY.
THE OBJECTIVE WAS TO BUY A PHONE FOR SAYU.
ラメ入り
GLITTER? OR RHINE-STONES?

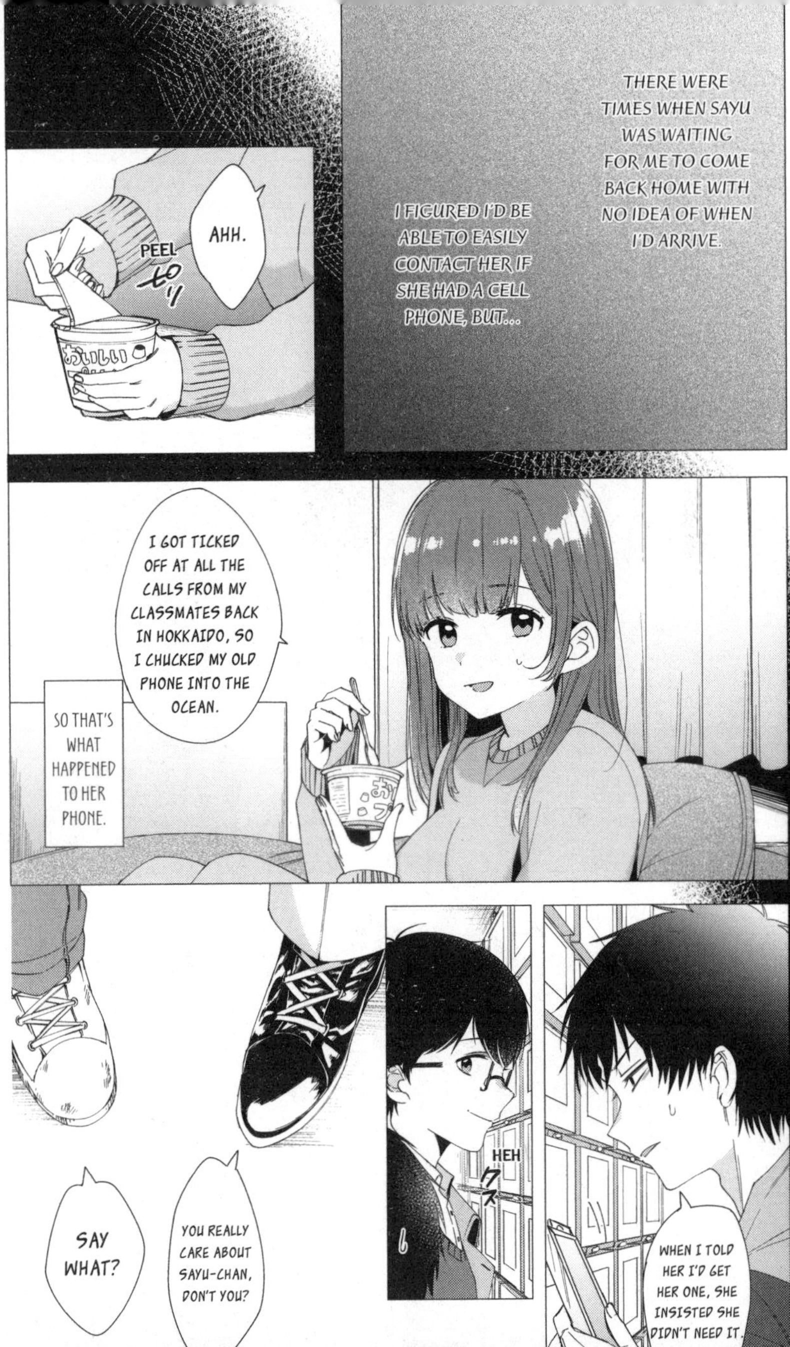

THERE WERE TIMES WHEN SAYU WAS WAITING FOR ME TO COME BACK HOME WITH NO IDEA OF WHEN I'D ARRIVE.
I FIGURED I'D BE ABLE TO EASILY CONTACT HER IF SHE HAD A CELL PHONE, BUT...
AHH.
PEEL
I GOT TICKED OFF AT ALL THE CALLS FROM MY CLASSMATES BACK IN HOKKAIDO, SO I CHUCKED MY OLD PHONE INTO THE OCEAN.
SO THAT'S WHAT HAPPENED TO HER PHONE.
WHEN I TOLD HER I'D GET HER ONE, SHE INSISTED SHE DIDN'T NEED IT.
HEH
YOU REALLY CARE ABOUT SAYU-CHAN, DON'T YOU?
SAY WHAT?

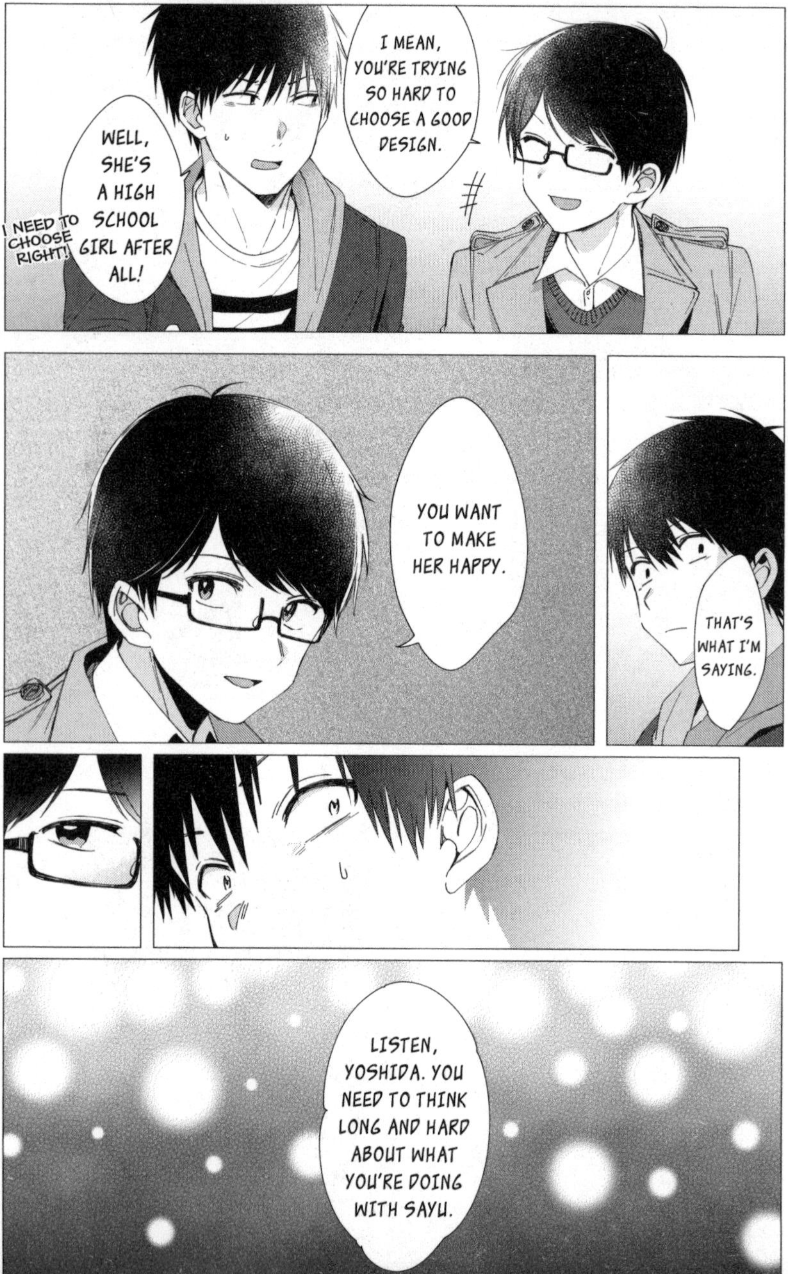
I MEAN, YOU'RE TRYING SO HARD TO CHOOSE A GOOD DESIGN.
WELL, SHE'S A HIGH SCHOOL GIRL AFTER ALL!
I NEED TO CHOOSE RIGHT!
THAT'S WHAT I'M SAYING.
YOU WANT TO MAKE HER HAPPY.
LISTEN, YOSHIDA. YOU NEED TO THINK LONG AND HARD ABOUT WHAT YOU'RE DOING WITH SAYU.

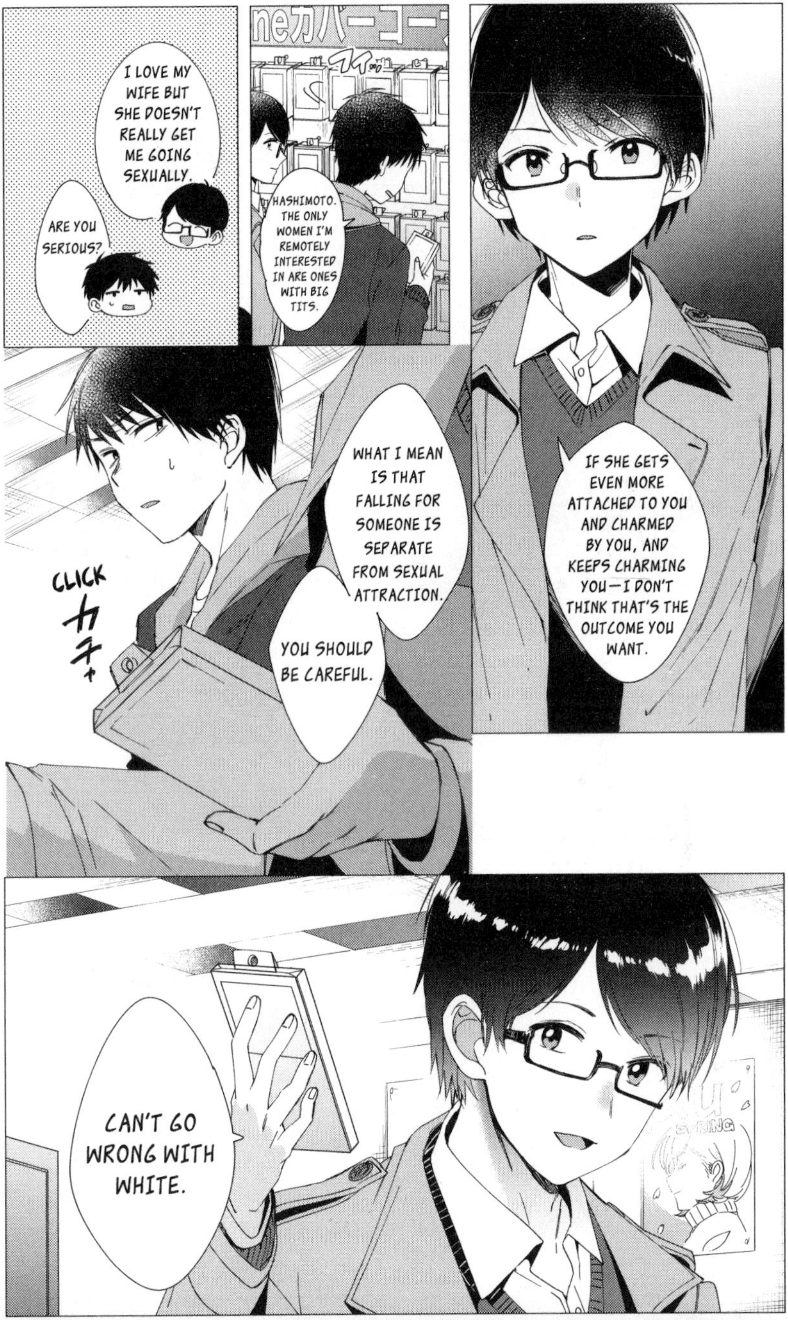
IF SHE GETS EVEN MORE ATTACHED TO YOU AND CHARMED BY YOU, AND KEEPS CHARMING YOU—I DON'T THINK THAT'S THE OUTCOME YOU WANT.
HASHIMOTO. THE ONLY WOMEN I'M REMOTELY INTERESTED IN ARE ONES WITH BIG TITS.
I LOVE MY WIFE BUT SHE DOESN'T REALLY GET ME GOING SEXUALLY.
ARE YOU SERIOUS?
WHAT I MEAN IS THAT FALLING FOR SOMEONE IS SEPARATE FROM SEXUAL ATTRACTION.
YOU SHOULD BE CAREFUL.
CLICK
カチャ
CAN'T GO WRONG WITH WHITE.

[CHAPTER 5]

FACIAL CLEANSER AND A DAY OFF

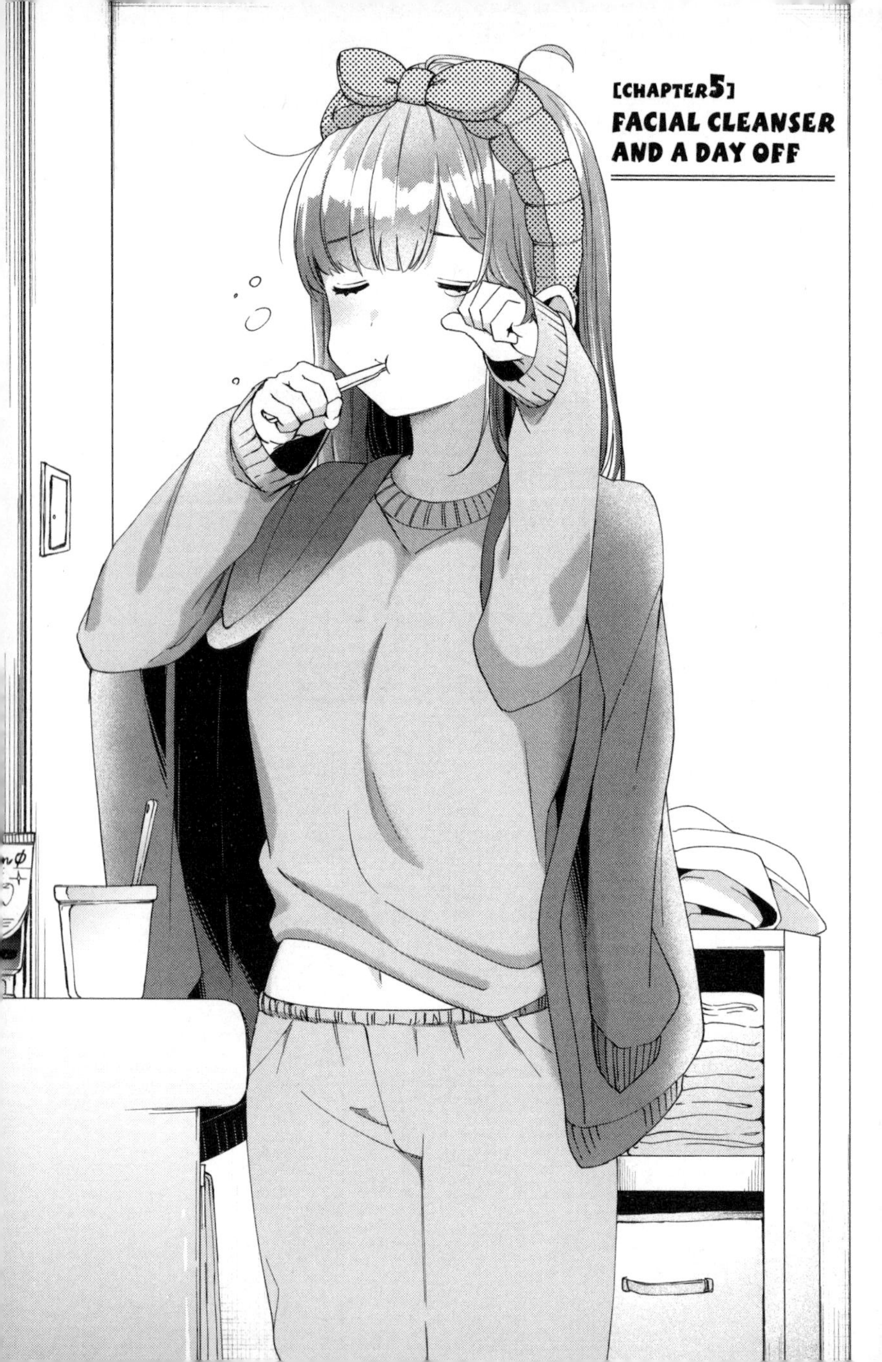

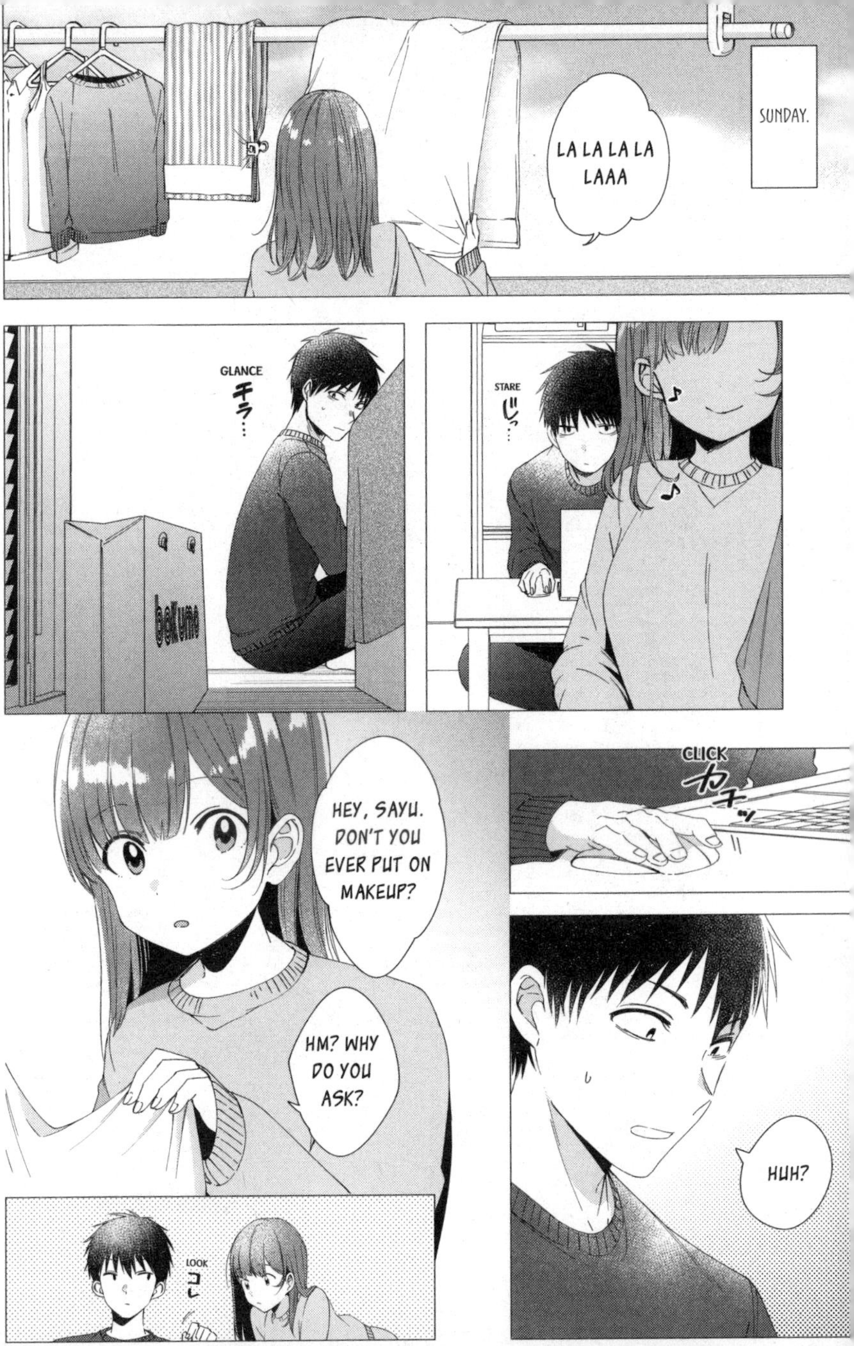
SUNDAY.
LA LA LA LA LAAA
STARE
じっ…
GLANCE
チラ…
CLICK
カチッ
HUH?
HEY, SAYU. DON'T YOU EVER PUT ON MAKEUP?
HM? WHY DO YOU ASK?
LOOK
コレ

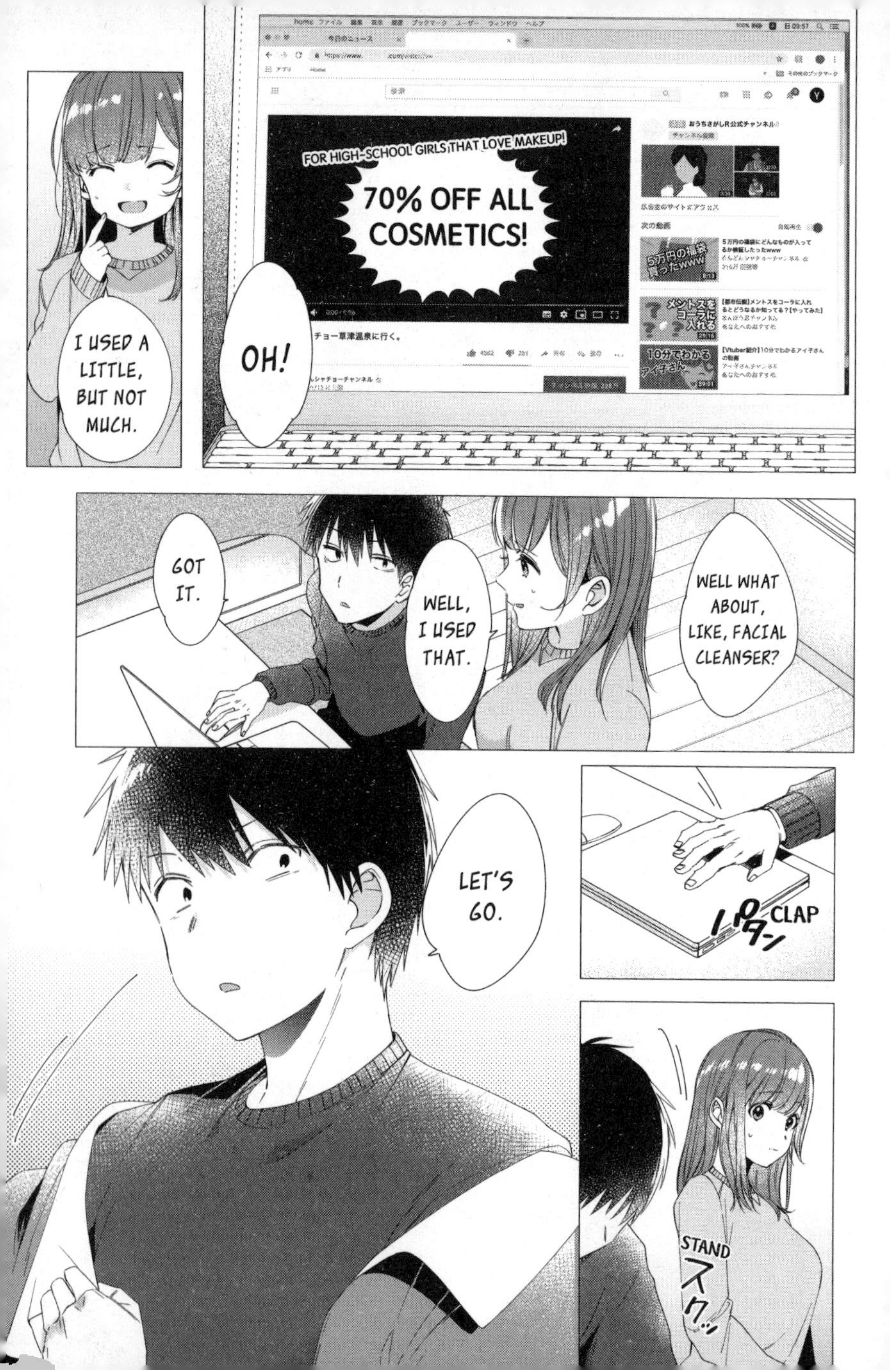
FOR HIGH-SCHOOL GIRLS THAT LOVE MAKEUP!
70% OFF ALL COSMETICS!
OH!
I USED A LITTLE, BUT NOT MUCH.
WELL WHAT ABOUT, LIKE, FACIAL CLEANSER?
WELL, I USED THAT.
GOT IT.
パタン CLAP
STAND スクッ
LET'S GO.

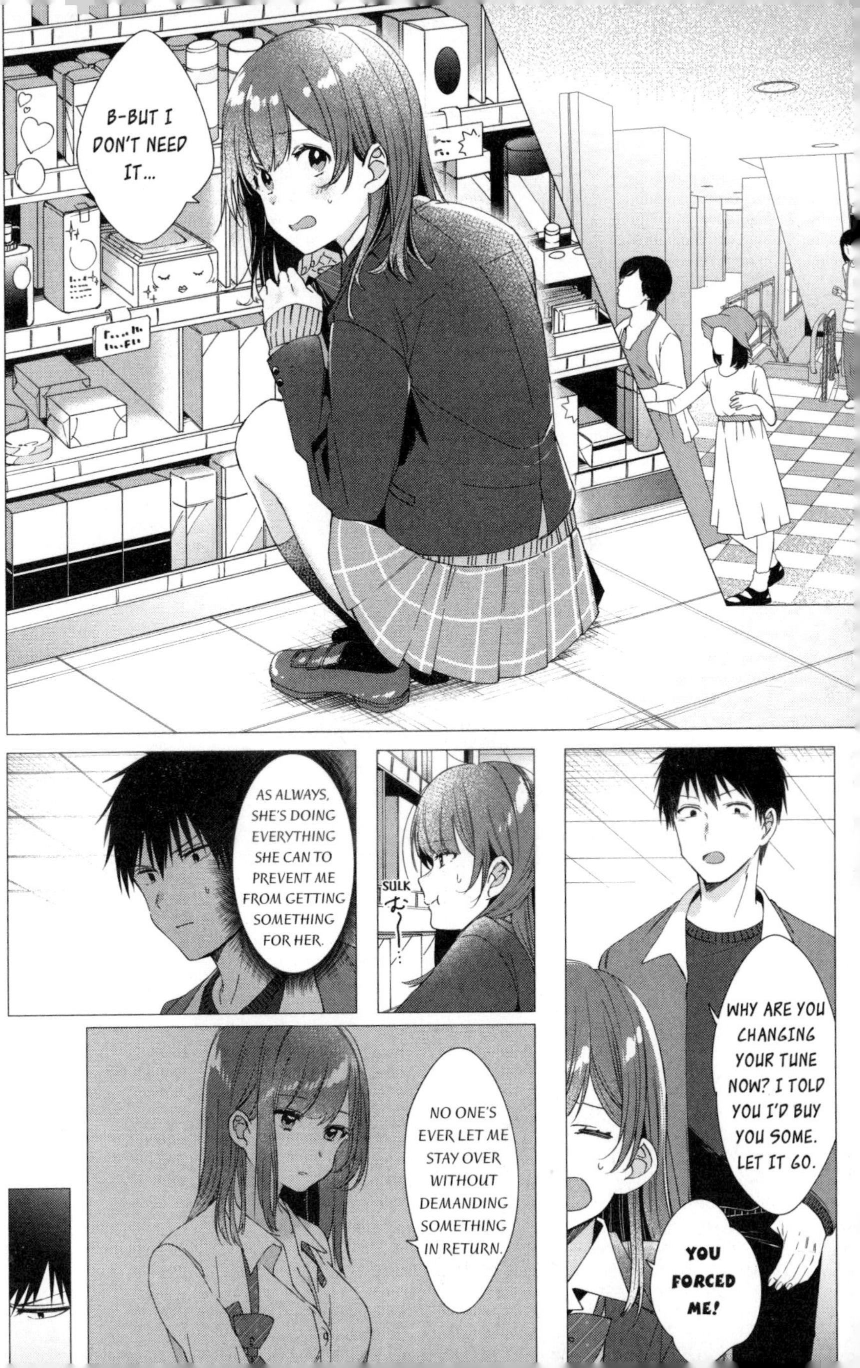
B-BUT I DON'T NEED IT...
WHY ARE YOU CHANGING YOUR TUNE NOW? I TOLD YOU I'D BUY YOU SOME. LET IT GO.
YOU FORCED ME!
SULK
むー…
AS ALWAYS, SHE'S DOING EVERYTHING SHE CAN TO PREVENT ME FROM GETTING SOMETHING FOR HER.
NO ONE'S EVER LET ME STAY OVER WITHOUT DEMANDING SOMETHING IN RETURN.

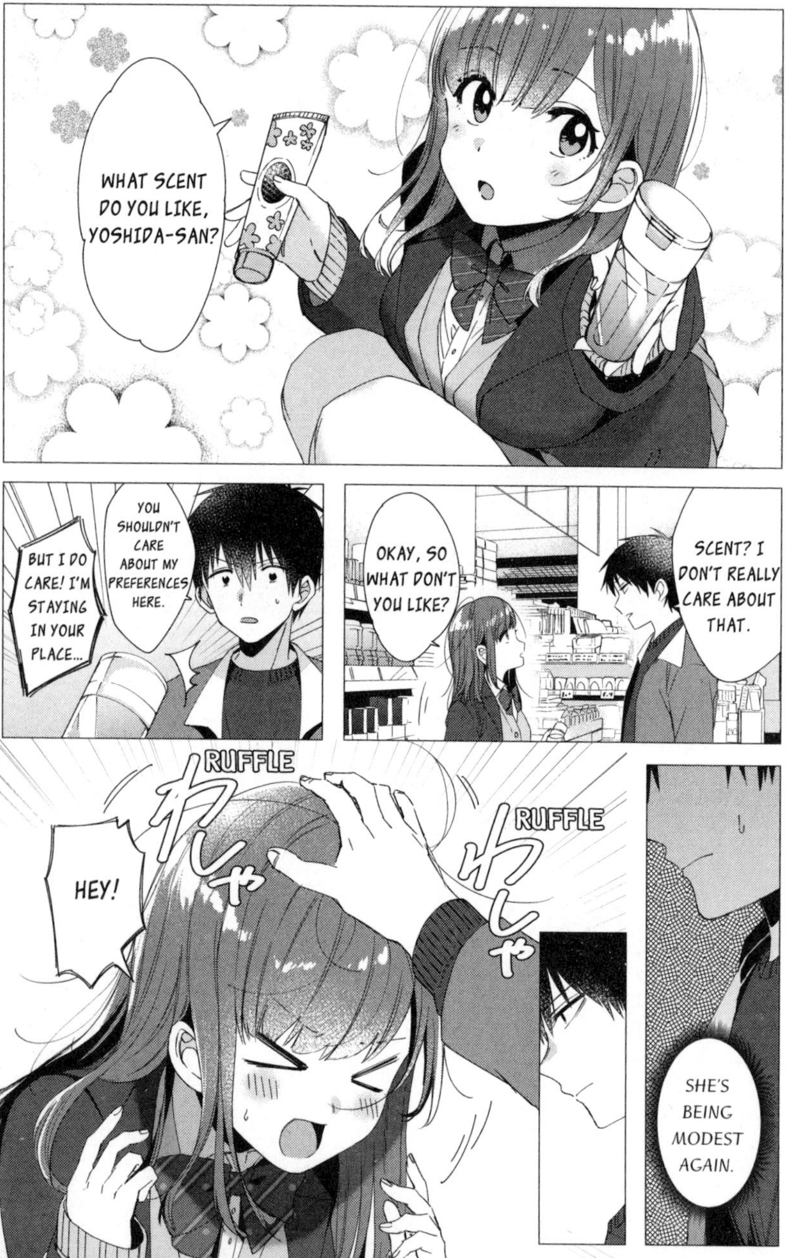
WHAT SCENT DO YOU LIKE, YOSHIDA-SAN?
SCENT? I DON'T REALLY CARE ABOUT THAT.
OKAY, SO WHAT DON'T YOU LIKE?
YOU SHOULDN'T CARE ABOUT MY PREFERENCES HERE.
BUT I DO CARE! I'M STAYING IN YOUR PLACE...
SHE'S BEING MODEST AGAIN.
わしゃ
RUFFLE
わしゃ
RUFFLE
HEY!

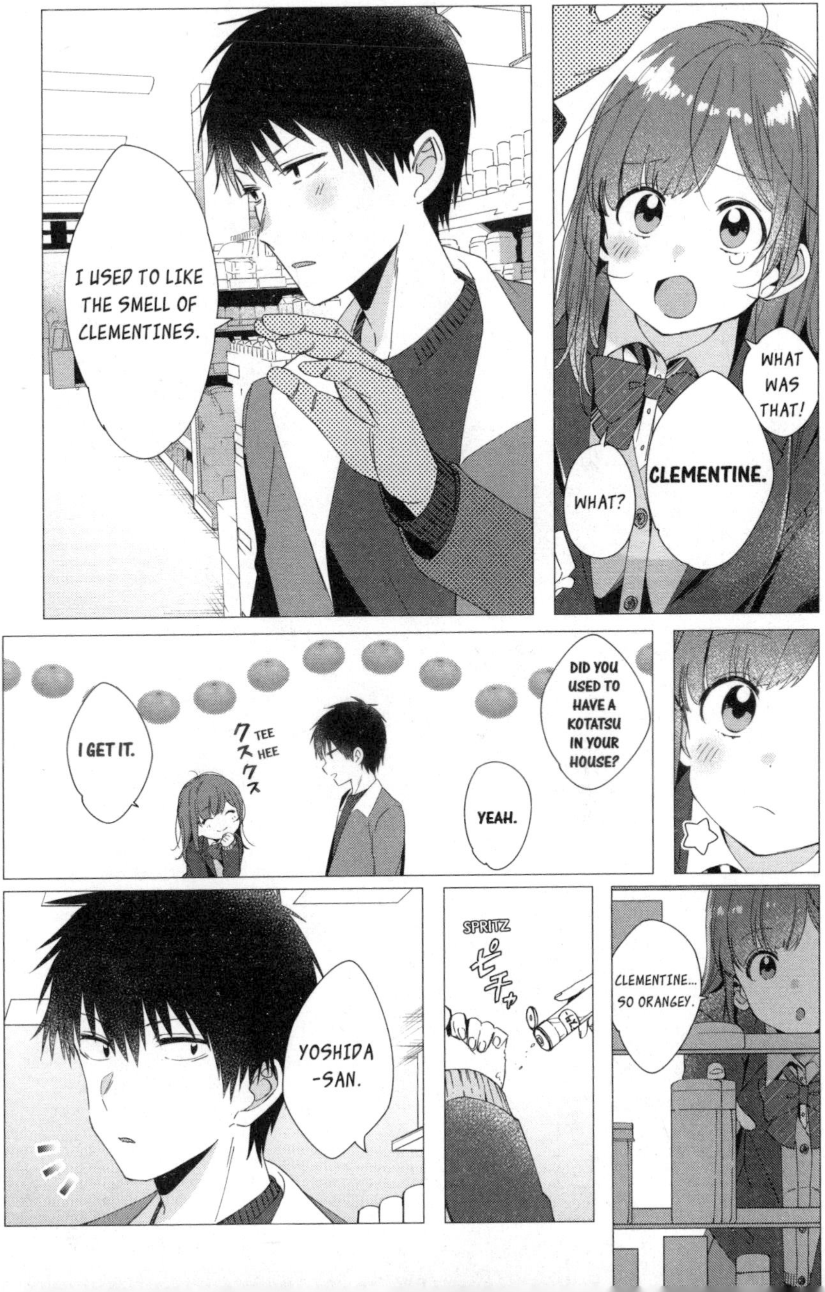
WHAT WAS THAT!
CLEMENTINE.
WHAT?
I USED TO LIKE THE SMELL OF CLEMENTINES.
DID YOU USED TO HAVE A KOTATSU IN YOUR HOUSE?
YEAH.
クスクス
TEE HEE
I GET IT.
CLEMENTINE... SO ORANGEY.
SPRITZ
ピチャ
YOSHIDA-SAN.

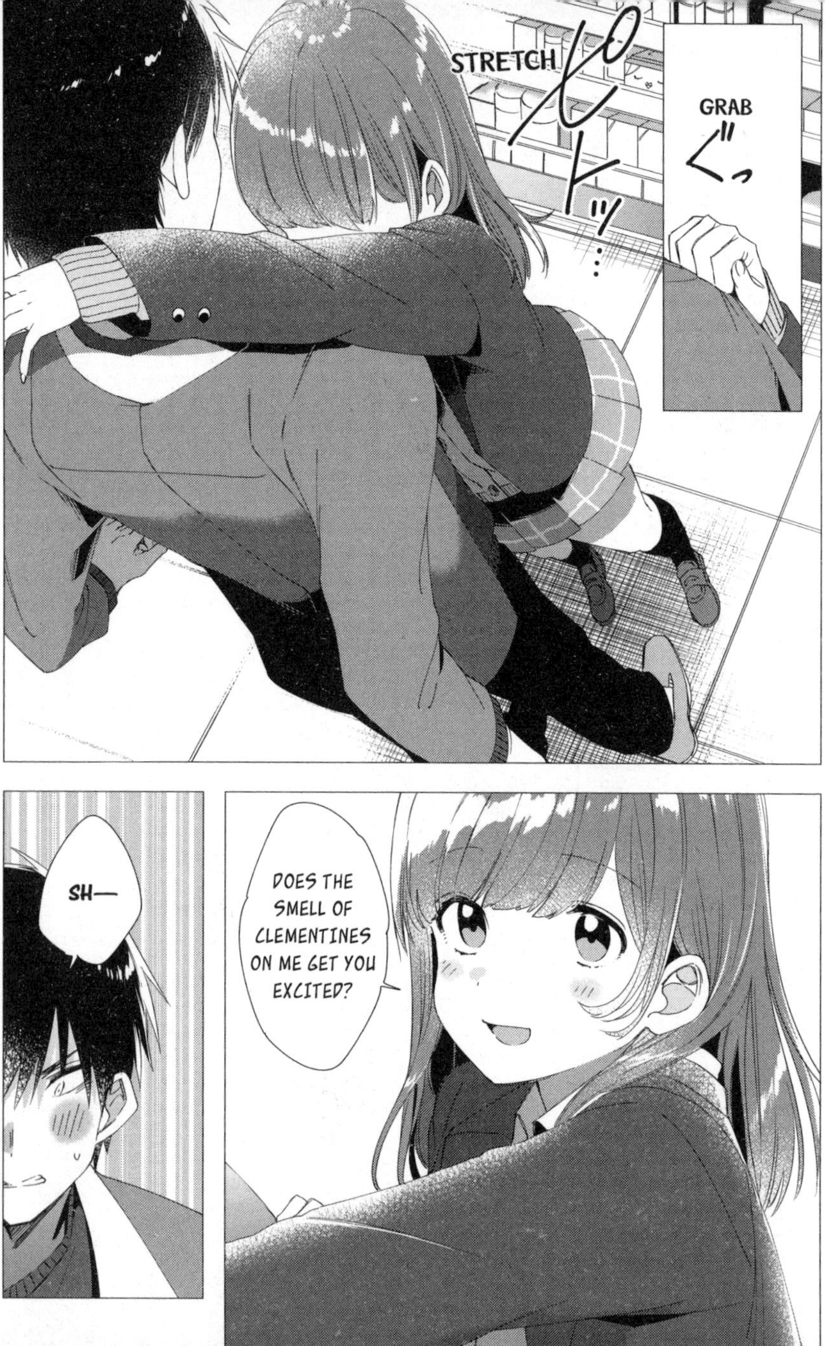
GRAB
ぐっ
STRETCH
ピトッ…
DOES THE SMELL OF CLEMENTINES ON ME GET YOU EXCITED?
SH—

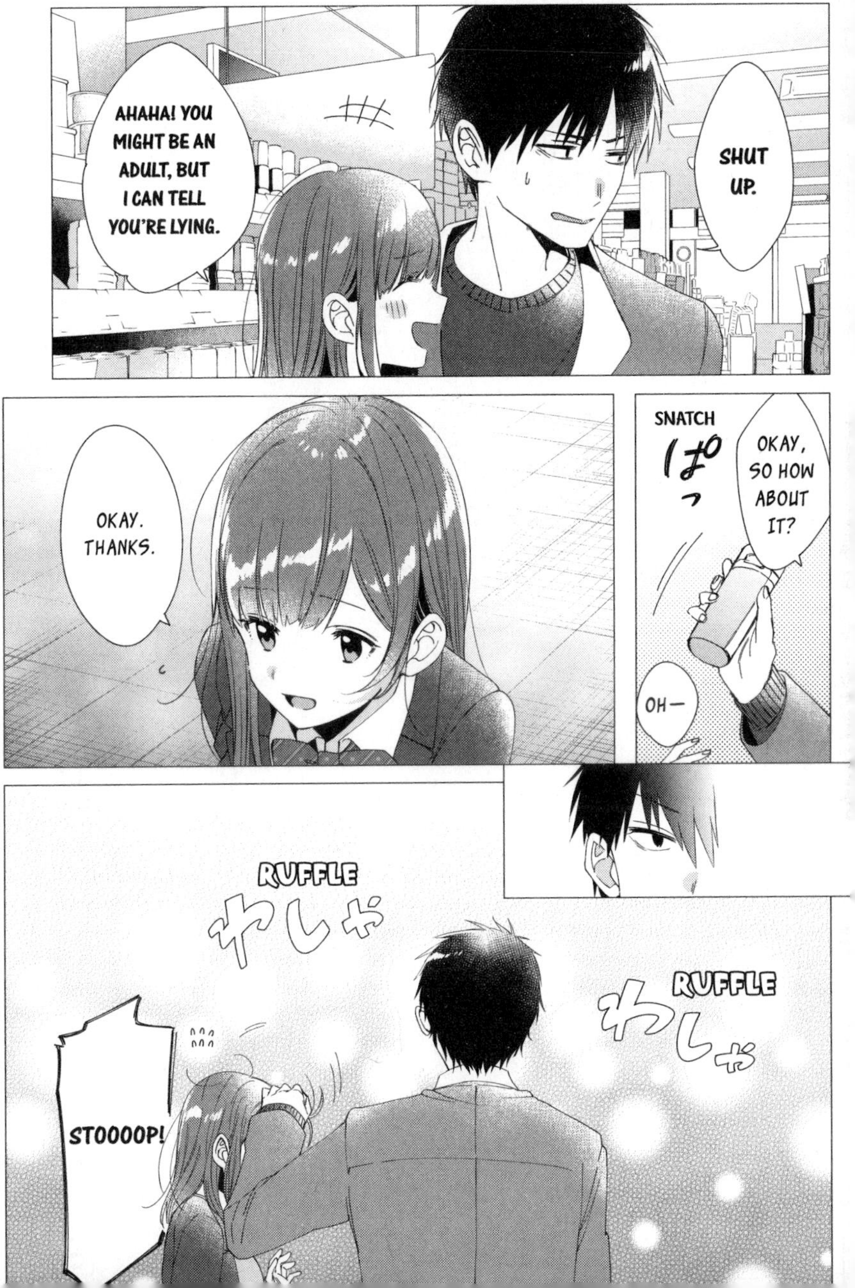
AHAHA! YOU MIGHT BE AN ADULT, BUT I CAN TELL YOU'RE LYING.
SHUT UP.
SNATCH
ぱっ
OKAY, SO HOW ABOUT IT?
OH—
OKAY. THANKS.
RUFFLE
わしゃ
RUFFLE
わしゃ
STOOOOP!

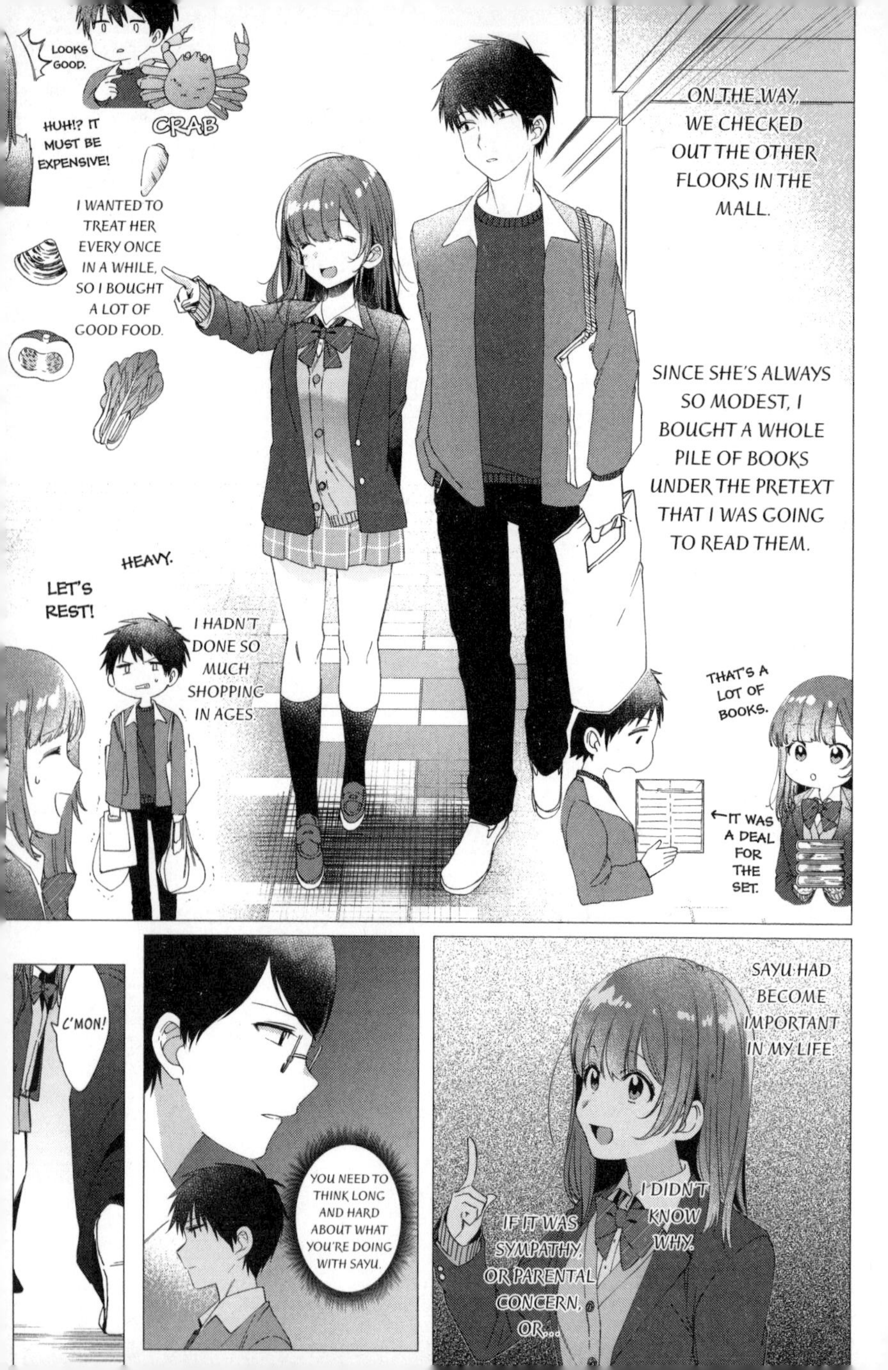
ON THE WAY, WE CHECKED OUT THE OTHER FLOORS IN THE MALL.
SINCE SHE'S ALWAYS SO MODEST, I BOUGHT A WHOLE PILE OF BOOKS UNDER THE PRETEXT THAT I WAS GOING TO READ THEM.
LOOKS GOOD.
CRAB
HUH!? IT MUST BE EXPENSIVE!
I WANTED TO TREAT HER EVERY ONCE IN A WHILE, SO I BOUGHT A LOT OF GOOD FOOD.
THAT'S A LOT OF BOOKS.
←IT WAS A DEAL FOR THE SET.
HEAVY.
LET'S REST!
I HADN'T DONE SO MUCH SHOPPING IN AGES.
SAYU HAD BECOME IMPORTANT IN MY LIFE.
I DIDN'T KNOW WHY.
IF IT WAS SYMPATHY, OR PARENTAL CONCERN, OR...
YOU NEED TO THINK LONG AND HARD ABOUT WHAT YOU'RE DOING WITH SAYU.
C'MON!

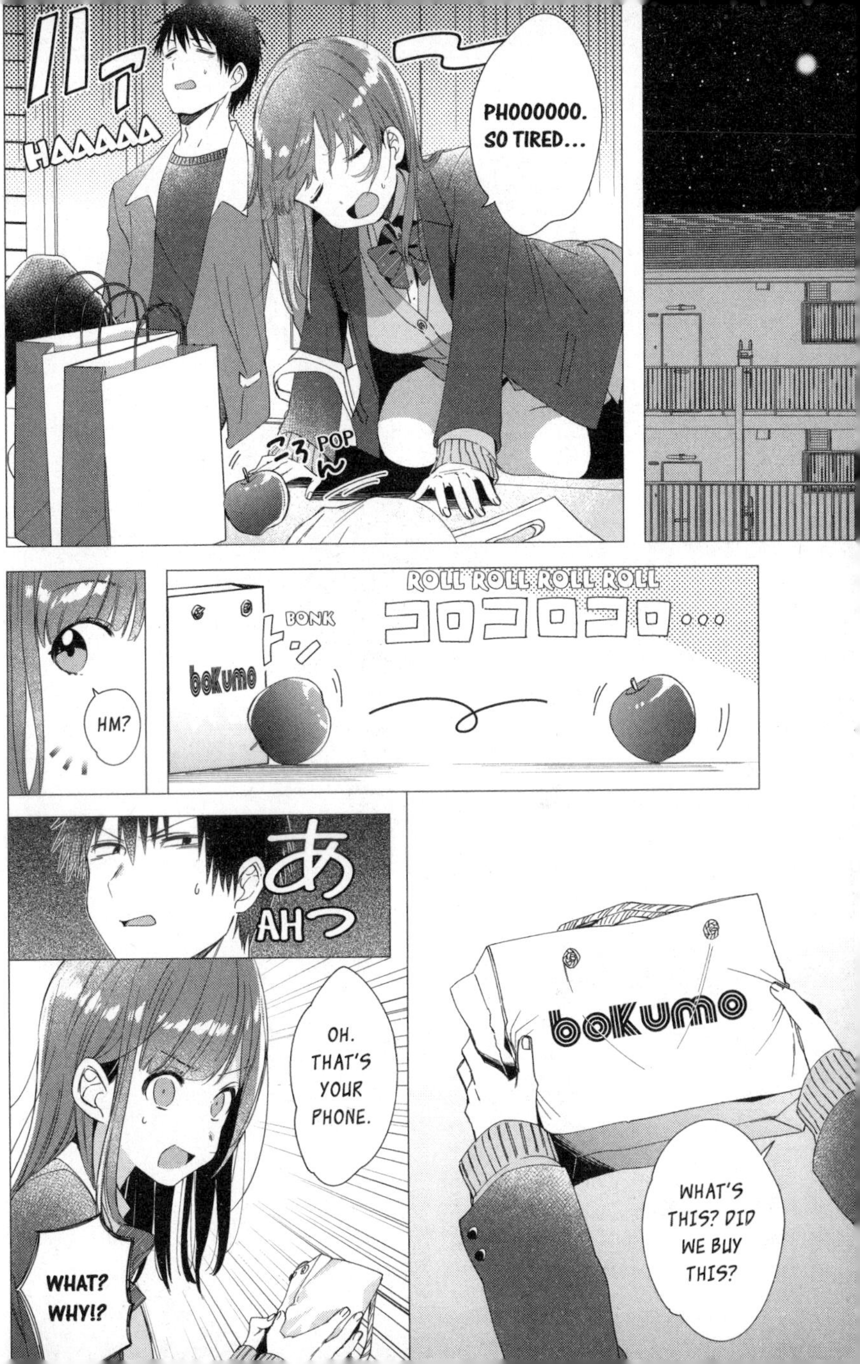

ハァ〜
HAAAAA
PHOOOOOO. SO TIRED...
ころん
POP
ROLL ROLL ROLL ROLL
コロコロコロ...
トン
BONK
boKumo
HM?
boKumo
WHAT'S THIS? DID WE BUY THIS?
あっ
AHっ
OH. THAT'S YOUR PHONE.
WHAT? WHY!?

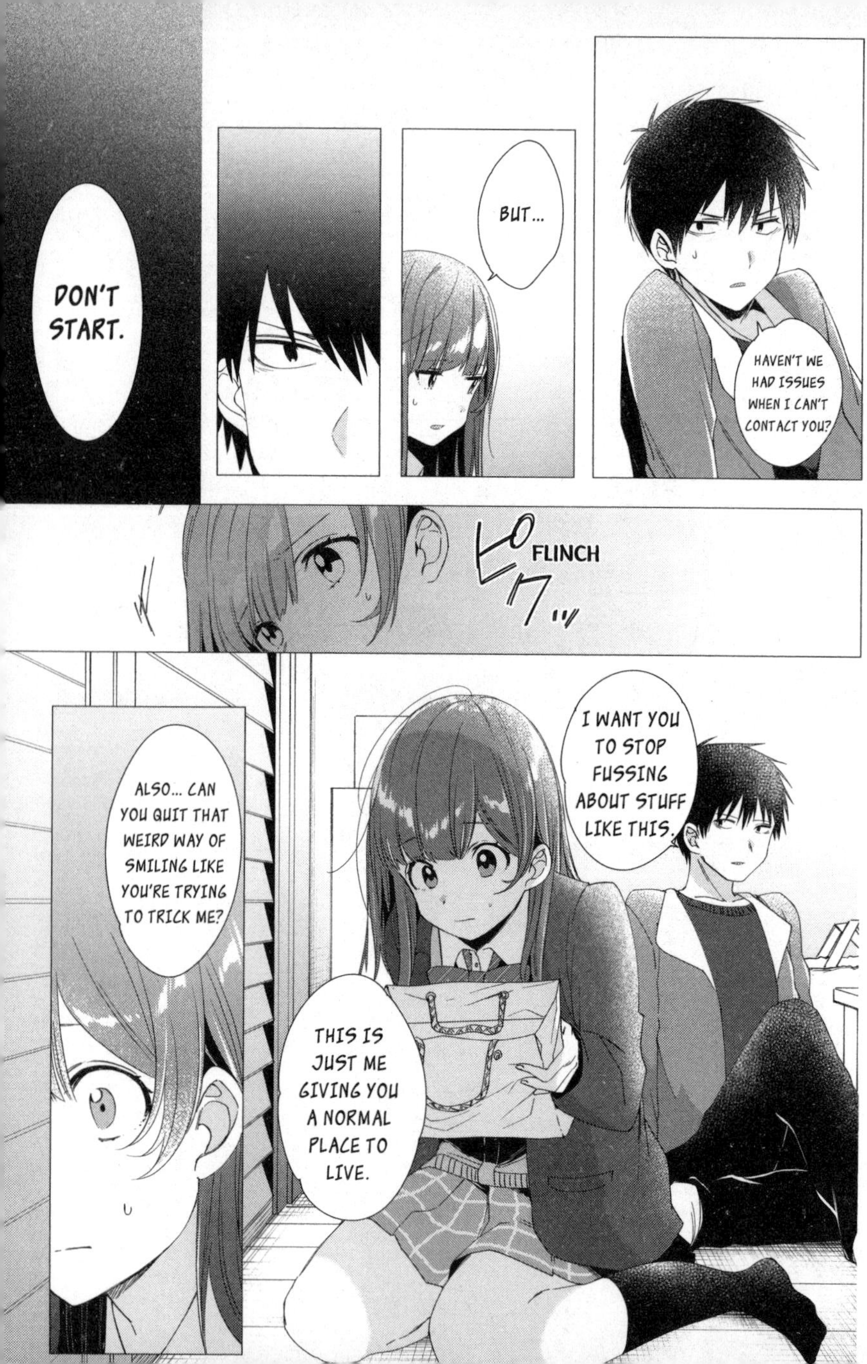
HAVEN'T WE HAD ISSUES WHEN I CAN'T CONTACT YOU?
BUT...
DON'T START.
ピクッ
FLINCH
I WANT YOU TO STOP FUSSING ABOUT STUFF LIKE THIS.
THIS IS JUST ME GIVING YOU A NORMAL PLACE TO LIVE.
ALSO... CAN YOU QUIT THAT WEIRD WAY OF SMILING LIKE YOU'RE TRYING TO TRICK ME?

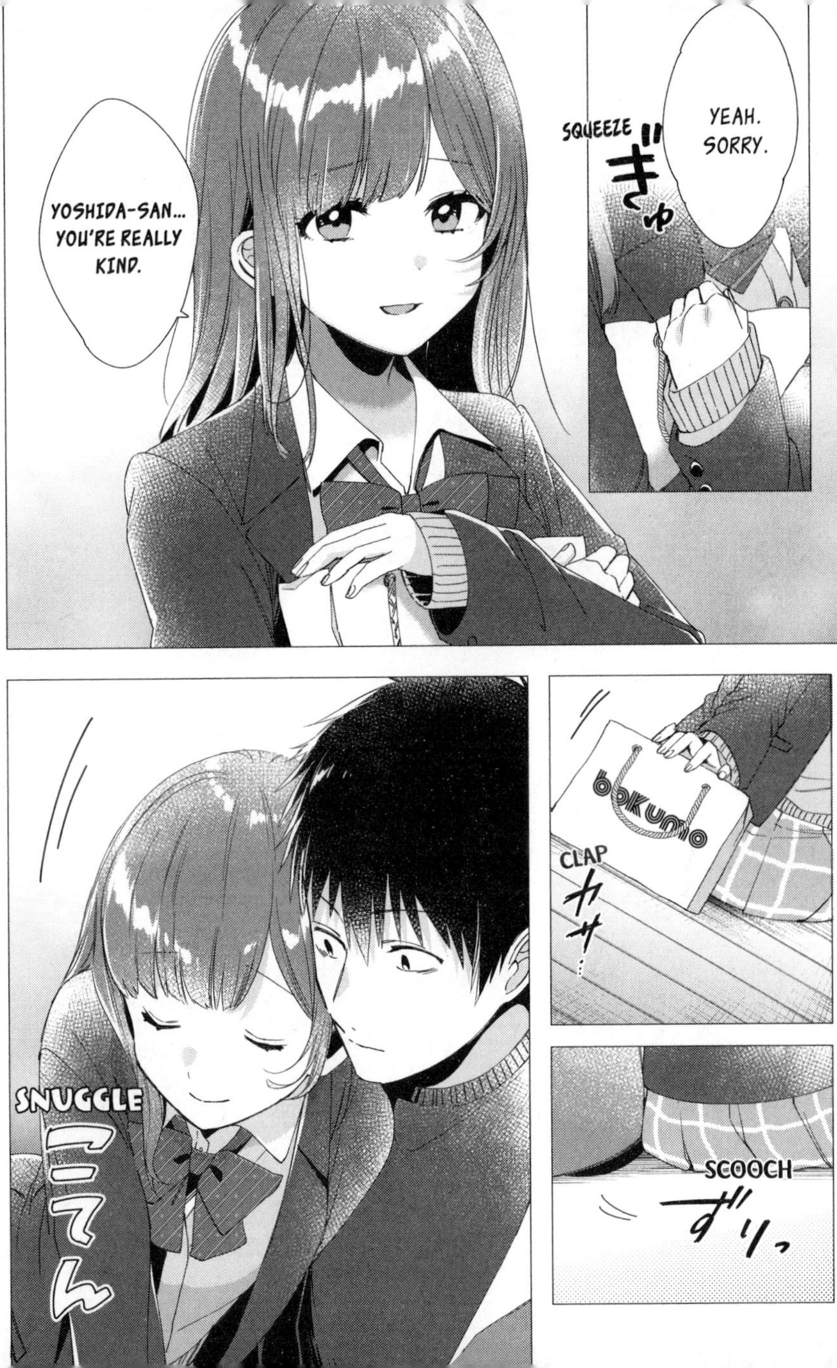
YEAH. SORRY.
SQUEEZE
ぎゅ
YOSHIDA-SAN... YOU'RE REALLY KIND.
CLAP
カサ…
SCOOCH
ずりっ
SNUGGLE
こてん

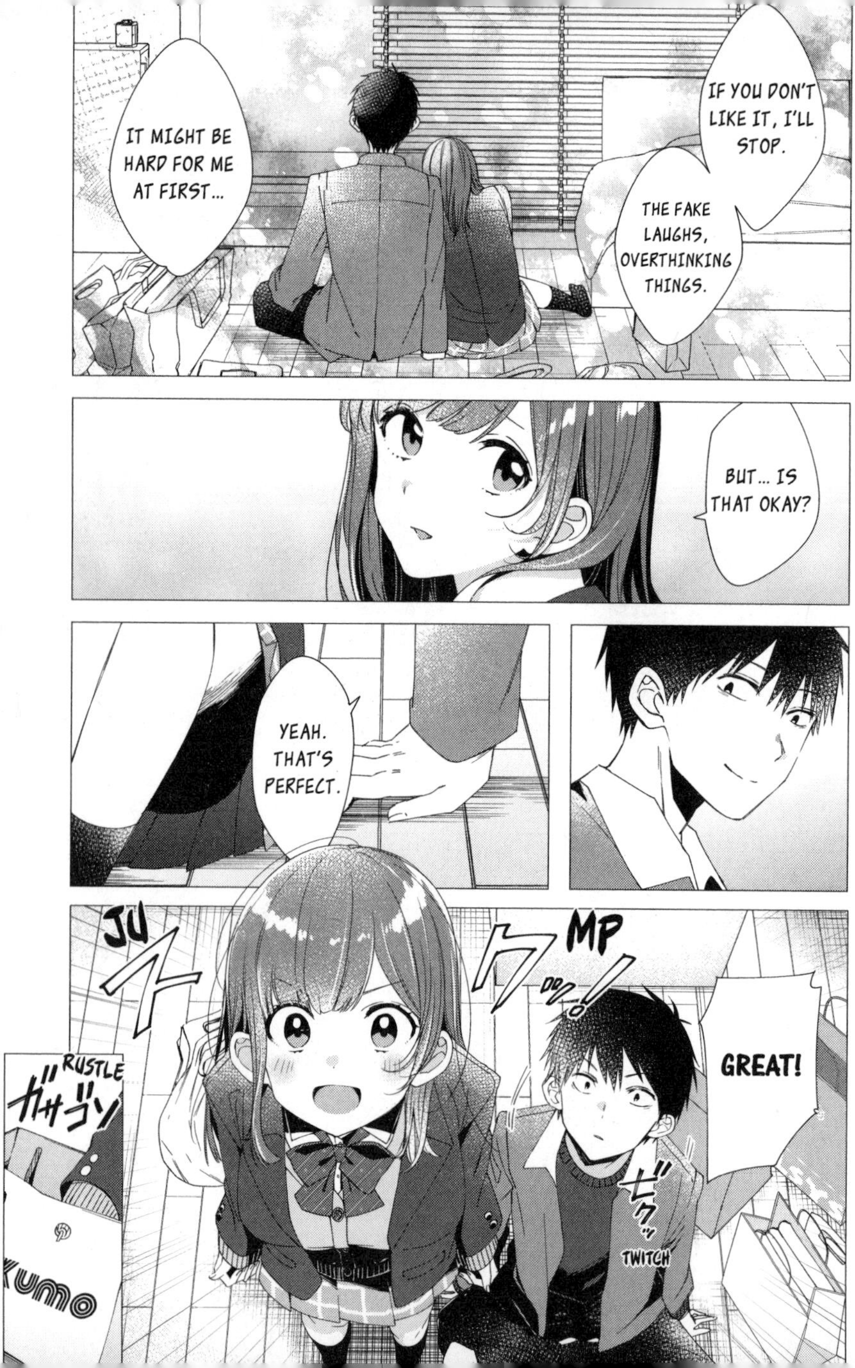
IF YOU DON'T LIKE IT, I'LL STOP.
THE FAKE LAUGHS, OVERTHINKING THINGS.
IT MIGHT BE HARD FOR ME AT FIRST...
BUT... IS THAT OKAY?
YEAH. THAT'S PERFECT.
GREAT!
JUMP
TWITCH
RUSTLE
ガサゴソ
KUMO

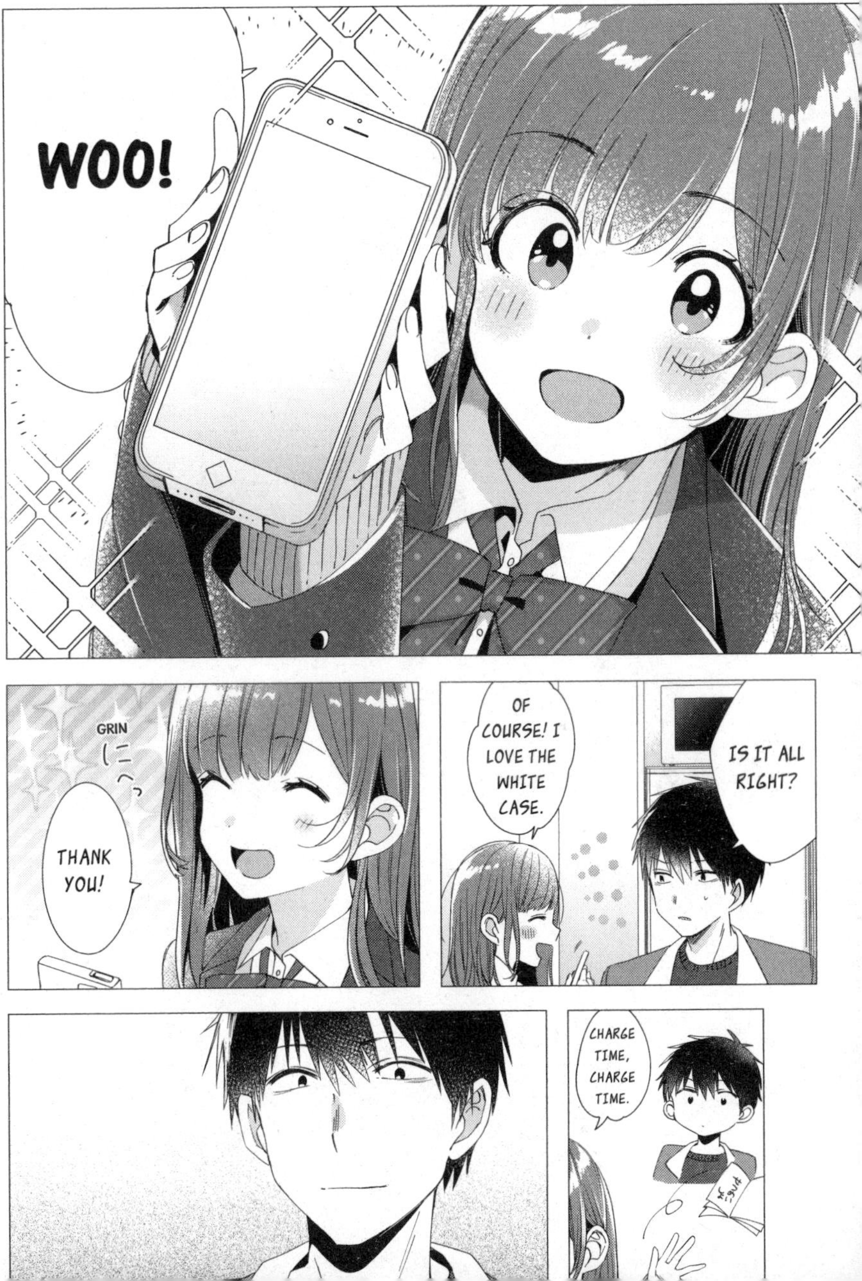
WOO!
IS IT ALL RIGHT?
OF COURSE! I LOVE THE WHITE CASE.
GRIN
THANK YOU!
CHARGE TIME, CHARGE TIME.

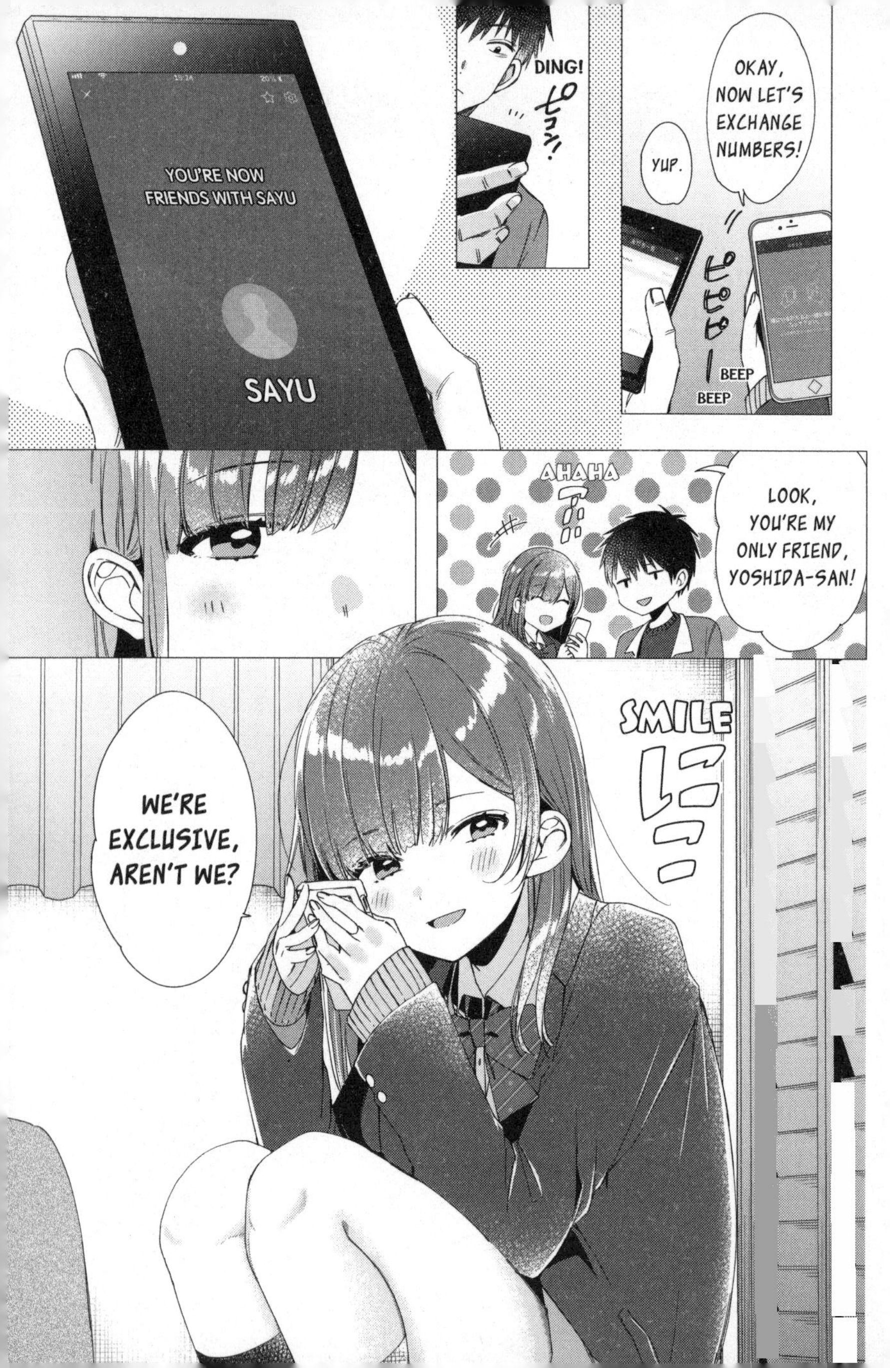
OKAY, NOW LET'S EXCHANGE NUMBERS!
YUP.
BEEP
BEEP
DING!
YOU'RE NOW FRIENDS WITH SAYU
SAYU
LOOK, YOU'RE MY ONLY FRIEND, YOSHIDA-SAN!
AHAHA
SMILE
WE'RE EXCLUSIVE, AREN'T WE?

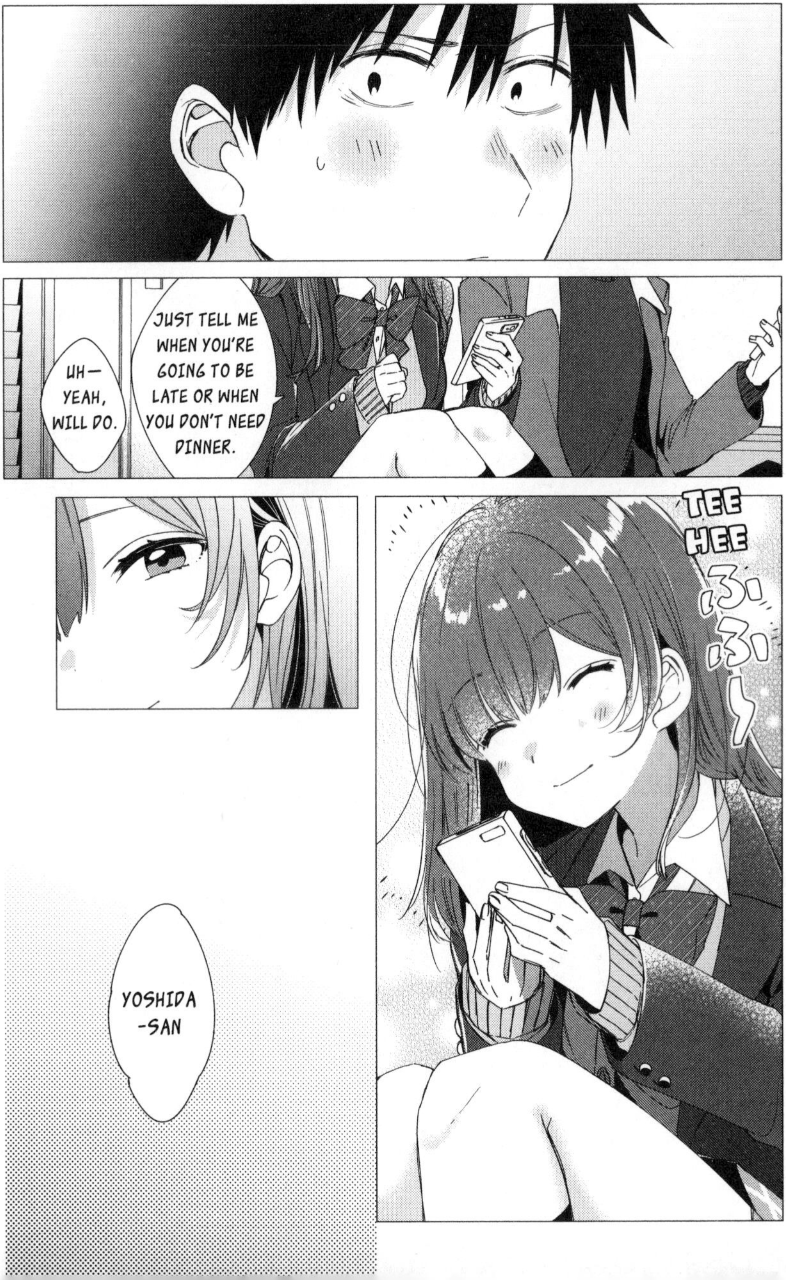
JUST TELL ME WHEN YOU'RE GOING TO BE LATE OR WHEN YOU DON'T NEED DINNER.
UH— YEAH, WILL DO.
TEE HEE
YOSHIDA -SAN

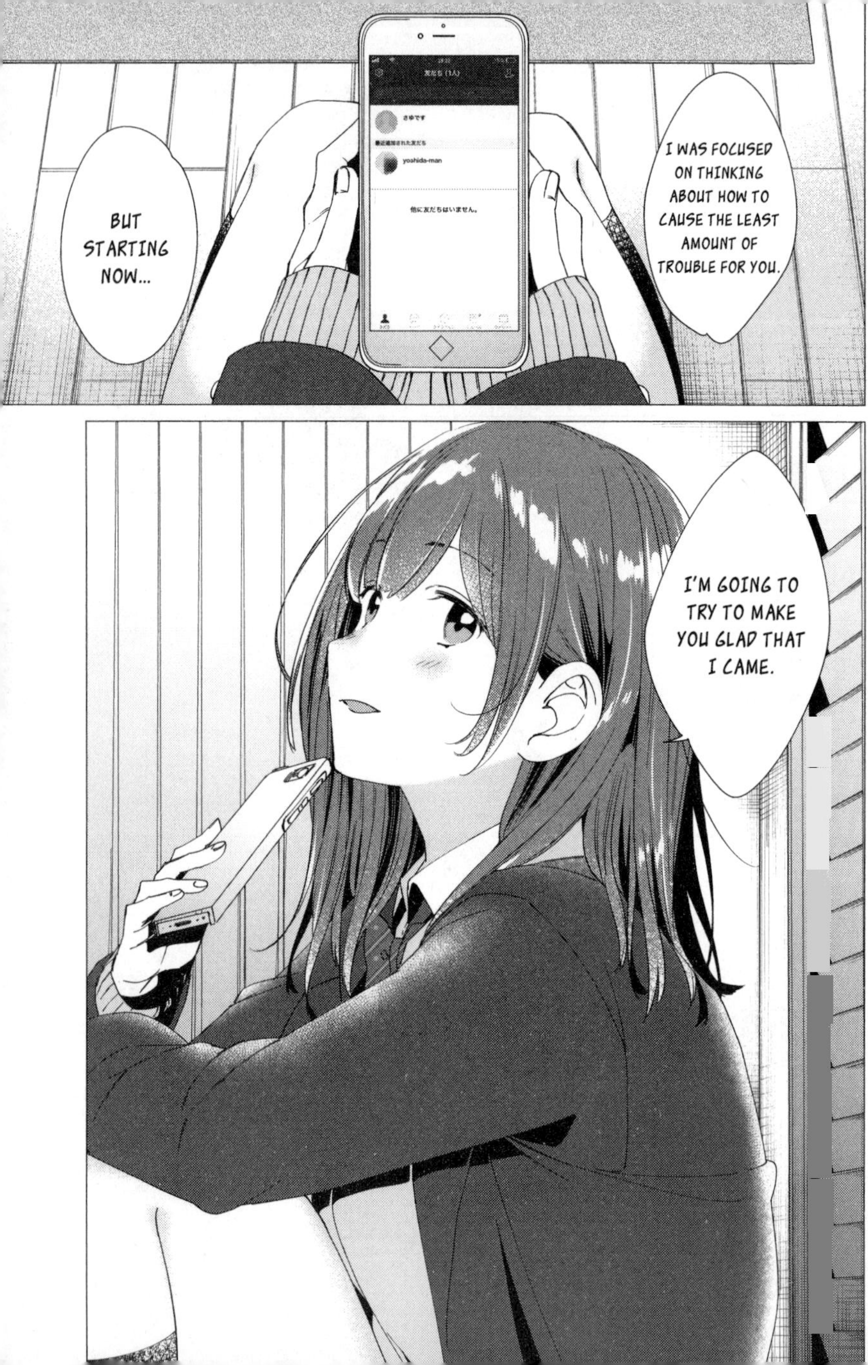
I WAS FOCUSED ON THINKING ABOUT HOW TO CAUSE THE LEAST AMOUNT OF TROUBLE FOR YOU.
BUT STARTING NOW...
I'M GOING TO TRY TO MAKE YOU GLAD THAT I CAME.

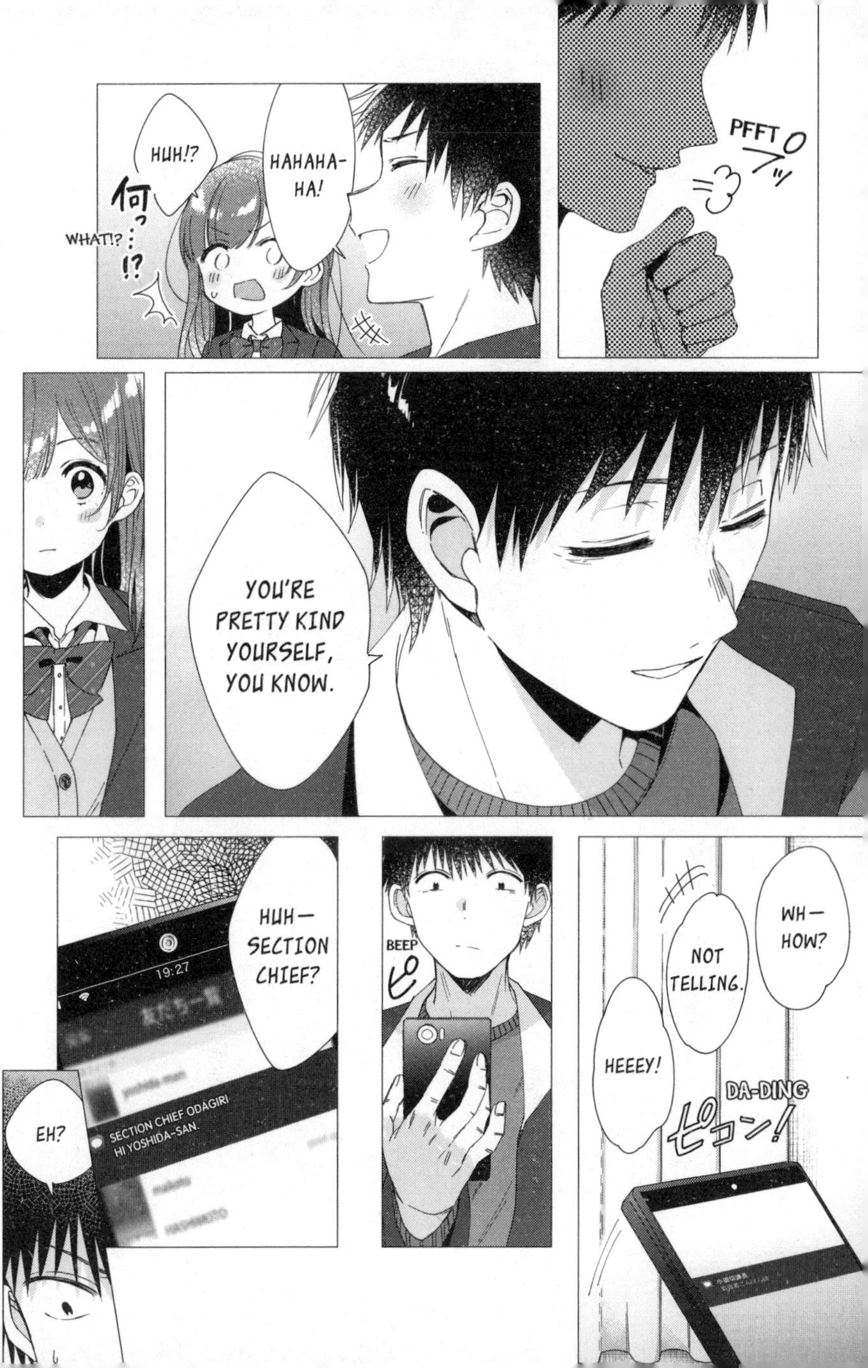
PFFT
プッ
HAHAHA-HA!
HUH!?
何っ…!?
WHAT!?
YOU'RE PRETTY KIND YOURSELF, YOU KNOW.
WH— HOW?
NOT TELLING.
HEEEY!
DA-DING
ピコン!
BEEP
ピ
HUH— SECTION CHIEF?
19:27
SECTION CHIEF ODAGIRI
HI YOSHIDA-SAN.
EH?

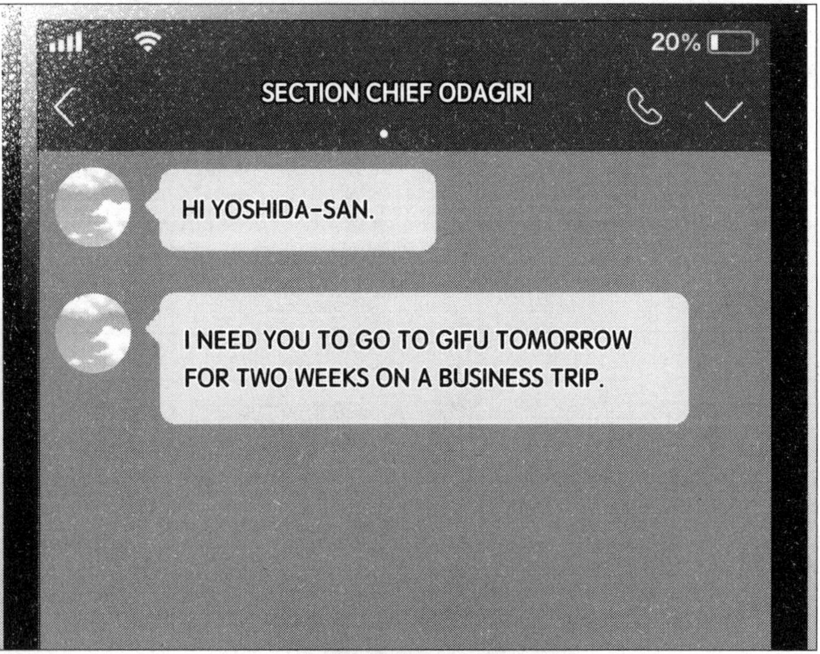
20%
SECTION CHIEF ODAGIRI
HI YOSHIDA-SAN.
I NEED YOU TO GO TO GIFU TOMORROW FOR TWO WEEKS ON A BUSINESS TRIP.
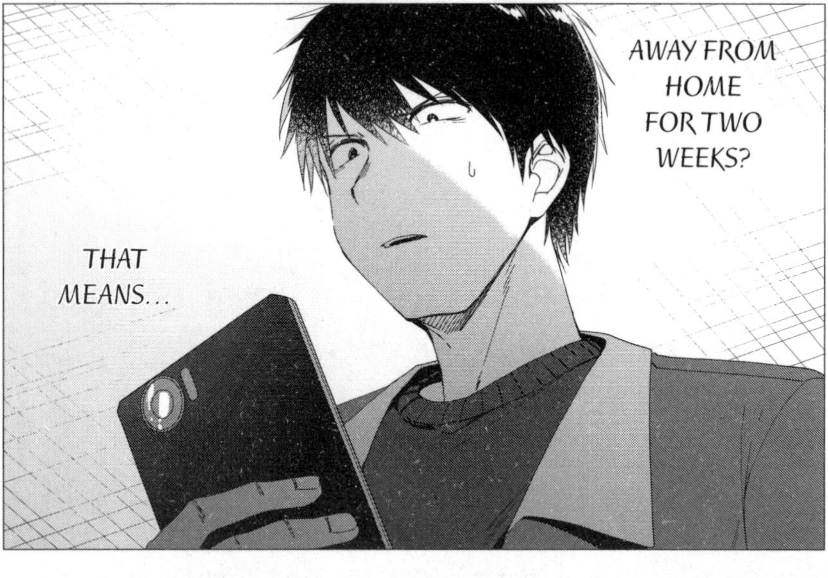
AWAY FROM HOME FOR TWO WEEKS?
THAT MEANS...

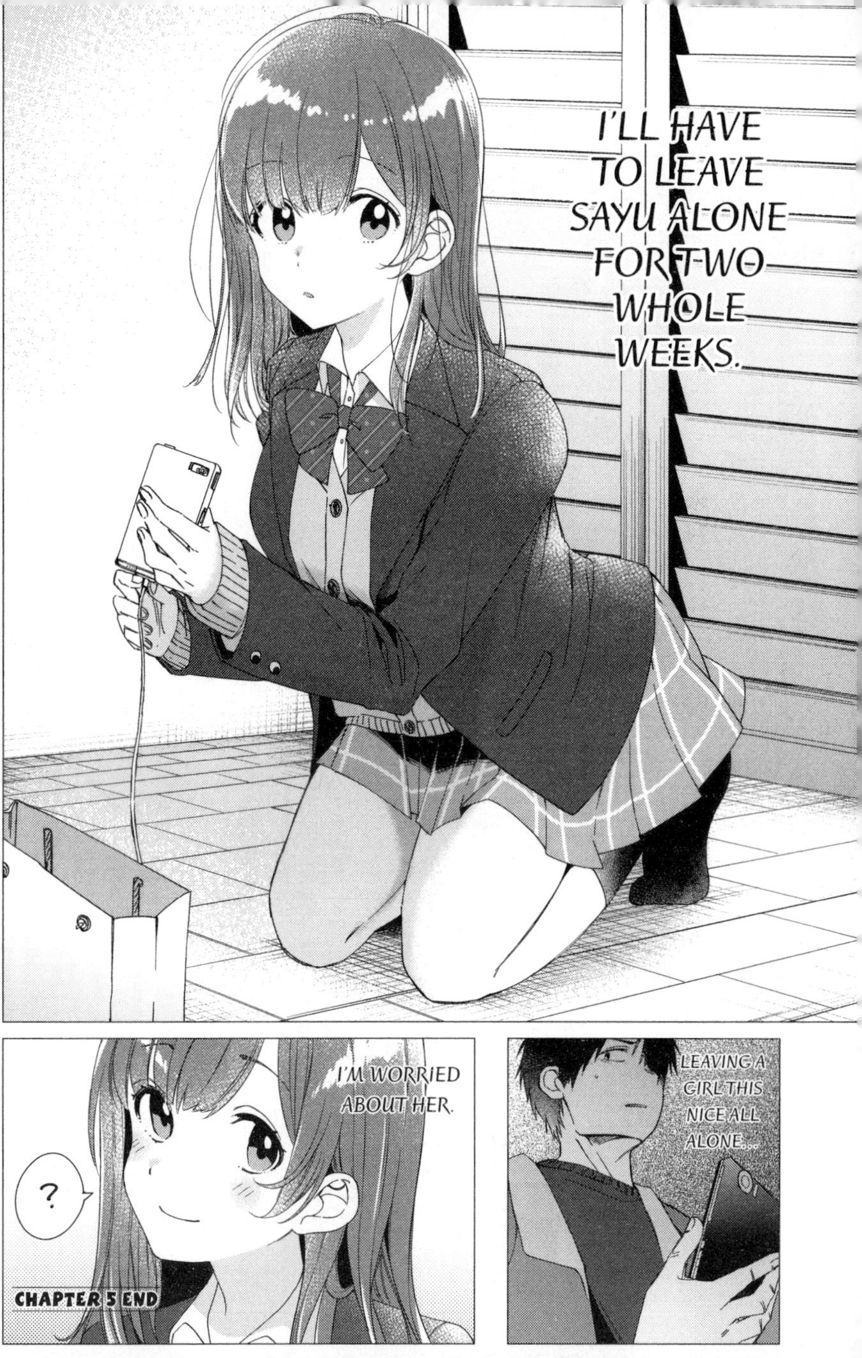
I'LL HAVE TO LEAVE SAYU ALONE FOR TWO WHOLE WEEKS.
LEAVING A GIRL THIS NICE ALL ALONE...
I'M WORRIED ABOUT HER.
?
CHAPTER 5 END

[CHAPTER 6] A MOVIE AND DESTINY

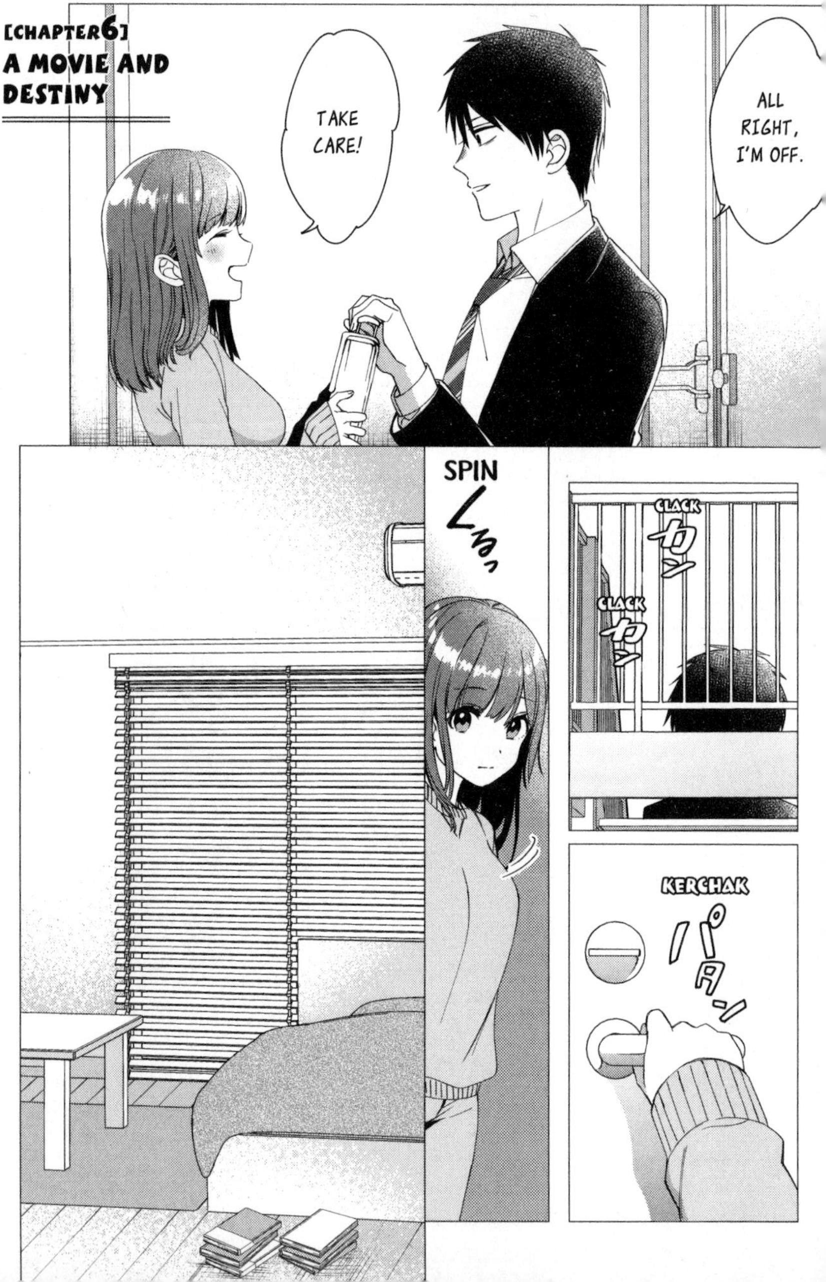
ALL RIGHT, I'M OFF.
TAKE CARE!
CLACK
カン
CLACK
カン
KERCHAK
パタン
SPIN
くるっ

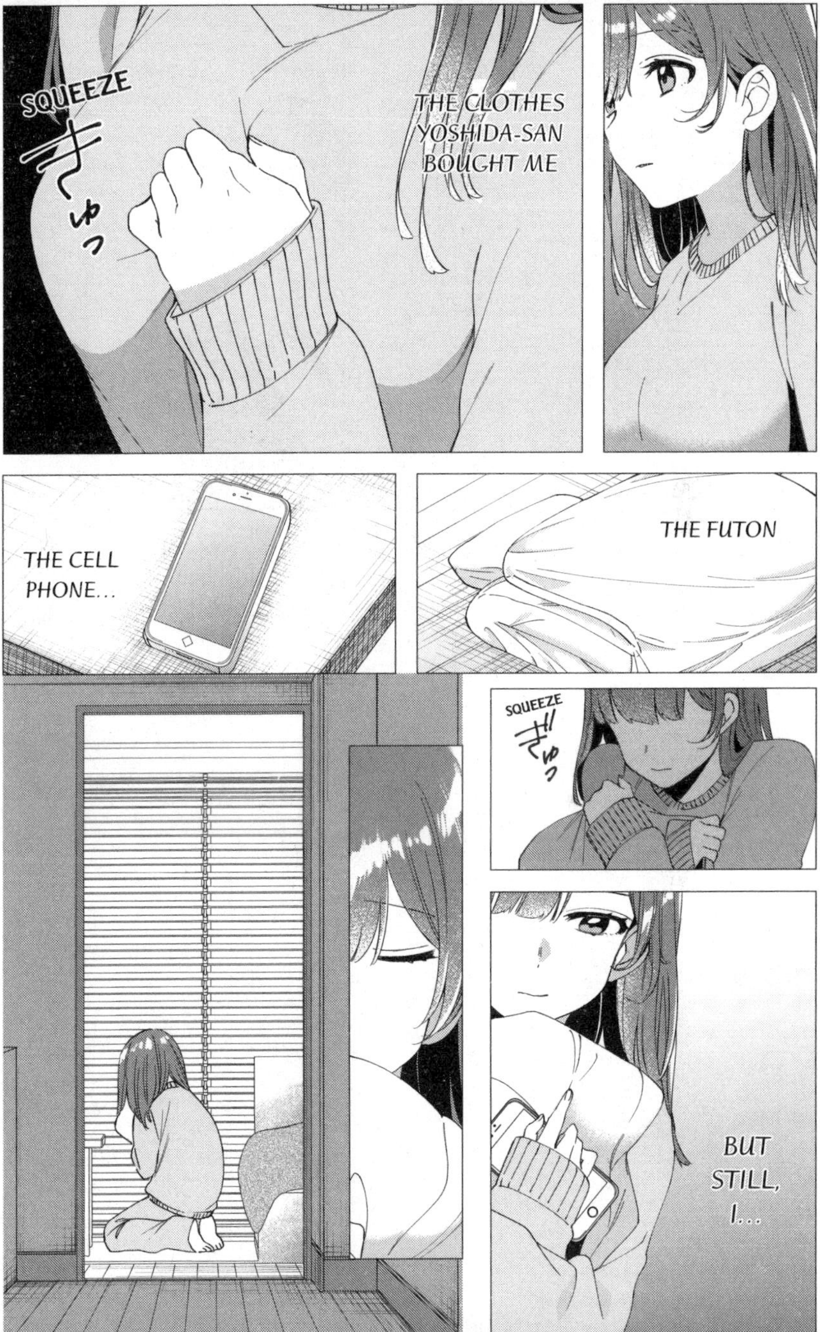
THE CLOTHES YOSHIDA-SAN BOUGHT ME
SQUEEZE
きゅっ
THE FUTON
THE CELL PHONE...
SQUEEZE
ぎゅっ
BUT STILL, I...

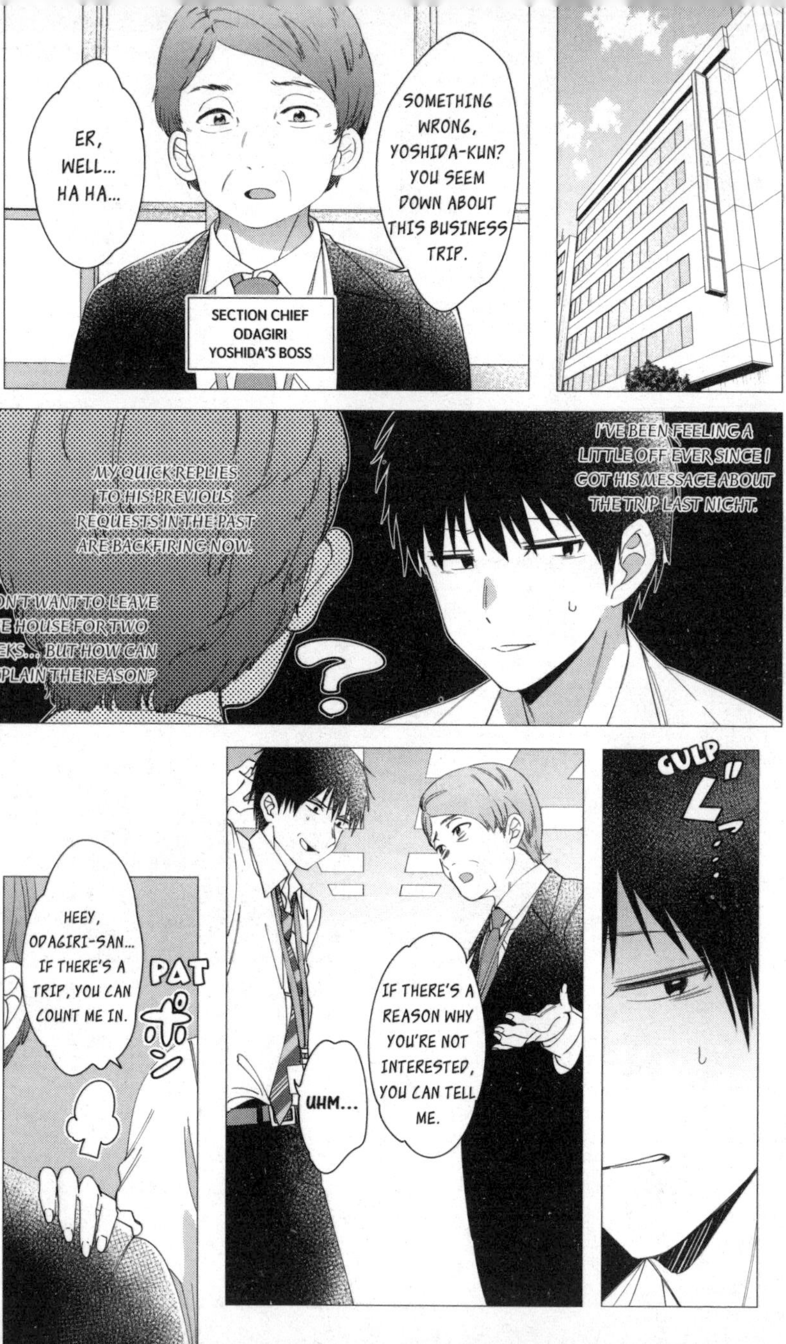
SOMETHING WRONG, YOSHIDA-KUN? YOU SEEM DOWN ABOUT THIS BUSINESS TRIP.
ER, WELL... HA HA...
SECTION CHIEF ODAGIRI YOSHIDA'S BOSS
I'VE BEEN FEELING A LITTLE OFF EVER SINCE I GOT HIS MESSAGE ABOUT THE TRIP LAST NIGHT.
MY QUICK REPLIES TO HIS PREVIOUS REQUESTS IN THE PAST ARE BACKFIRING NOW.
I DON'T WANT TO LEAVE THE HOUSE FOR TWO WEEKS... BUT HOW CAN I EXPLAIN THE REASON?
GULP
IF THERE'S A REASON WHY YOU'RE NOT INTERESTED, YOU CAN TELL ME.
UHM...
HEEY, ODAGIRI-SAN... IF THERE'S A TRIP, YOU CAN COUNT ME IN.
PAT

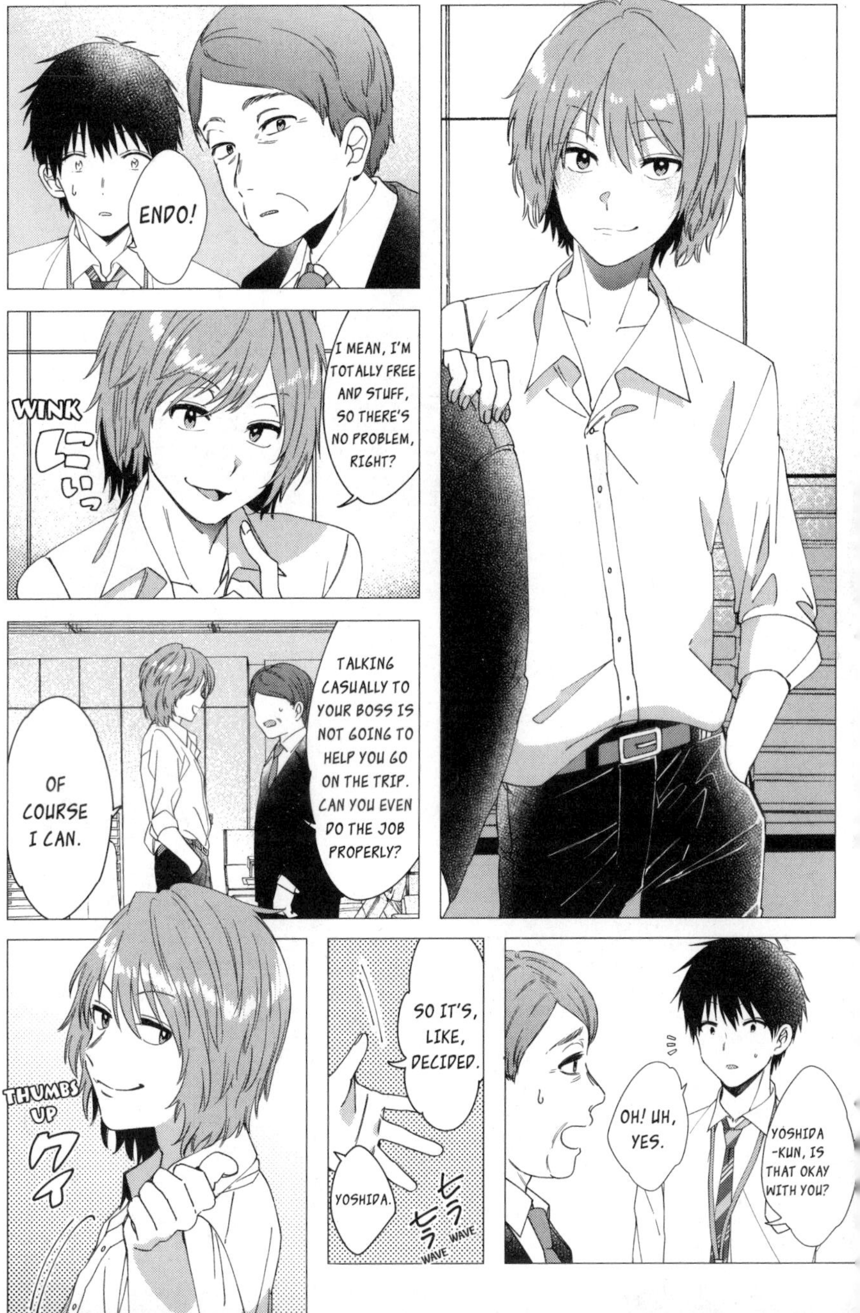
ENDO!
I MEAN, I'M TOTALLY FREE AND STUFF, SO THERE'S NO PROBLEM, RIGHT?
WINK
TALKING CASUALLY TO YOUR BOSS IS NOT GOING TO HELP YOU GO ON THE TRIP. CAN YOU EVEN DO THE JOB PROPERLY?
OF COURSE I CAN.
YOSHIDA-KUN, IS THAT OKAY WITH YOU?
OH! UH, YES.
SO IT'S, LIKE, DECIDED.
YOSHIDA.
WAVE WAVE
THUMBS UP

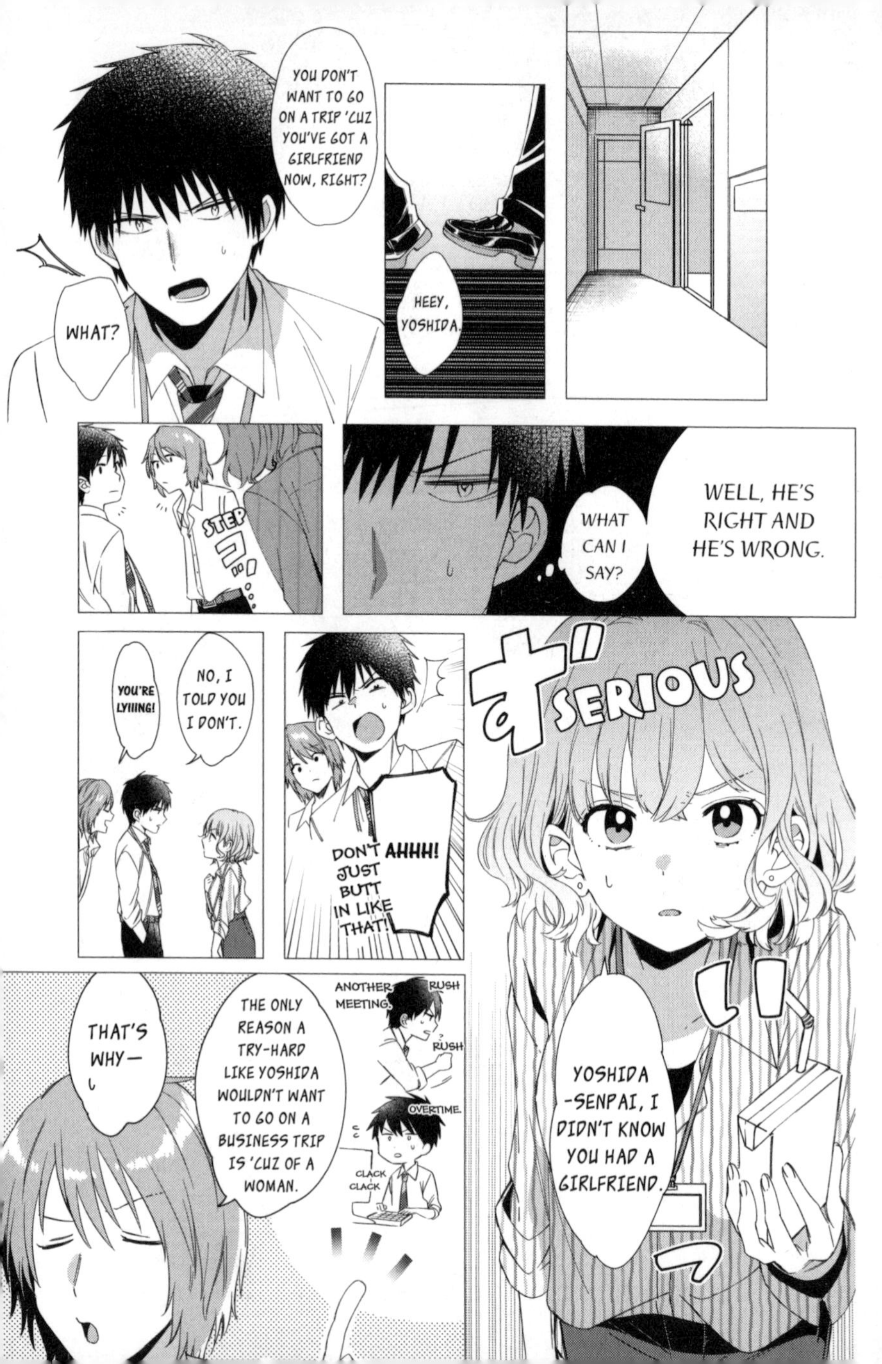
HEEY, YOSHIDA.
YOU DON'T WANT TO GO ON A TRIP 'CUZ YOU'VE GOT A GIRLFRIEND NOW, RIGHT?
WHAT?
WELL, HE'S RIGHT AND HE'S WRONG.
WHAT CAN I SAY?
STEP
SERIOUS
YOSHIDA-SENPAI, I DIDN'T KNOW YOU HAD A GIRLFRIEND.
AHHH!
DON'T JUST BUTT IN LIKE THAT!
NO, I TOLD YOU I DON'T.
YOU'RE LYIIING!
THE ONLY REASON A TRY-HARD LIKE YOSHIDA WOULDN'T WANT TO GO ON A BUSINESS TRIP IS 'CUZ OF A WOMAN.
RUSH
ANOTHER MEETING.
RUSH
OVERTIME.
CLACK CLACK
THAT'S WHY—

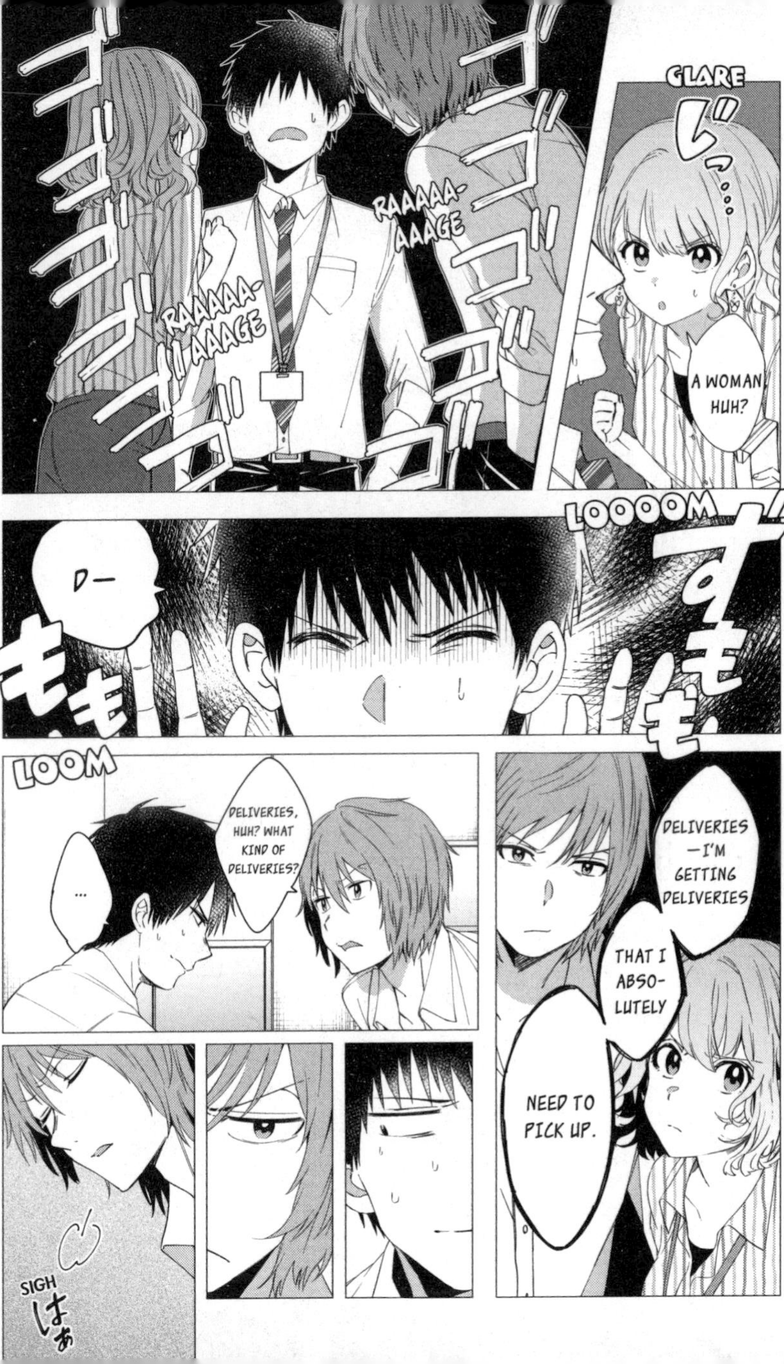
GLARE
A WOMAN HUH?
RAAAAA-AAAGE
RAAAAA-AAAGE
LOOOOM
D—
DELIVERIES—I'M GETTING DELIVERIES
THAT I ABSOLUTELY
NEED TO PICK UP.
LOOM
DELIVERIES, HUH? WHAT KIND OF DELIVERIES?
...
SIGH

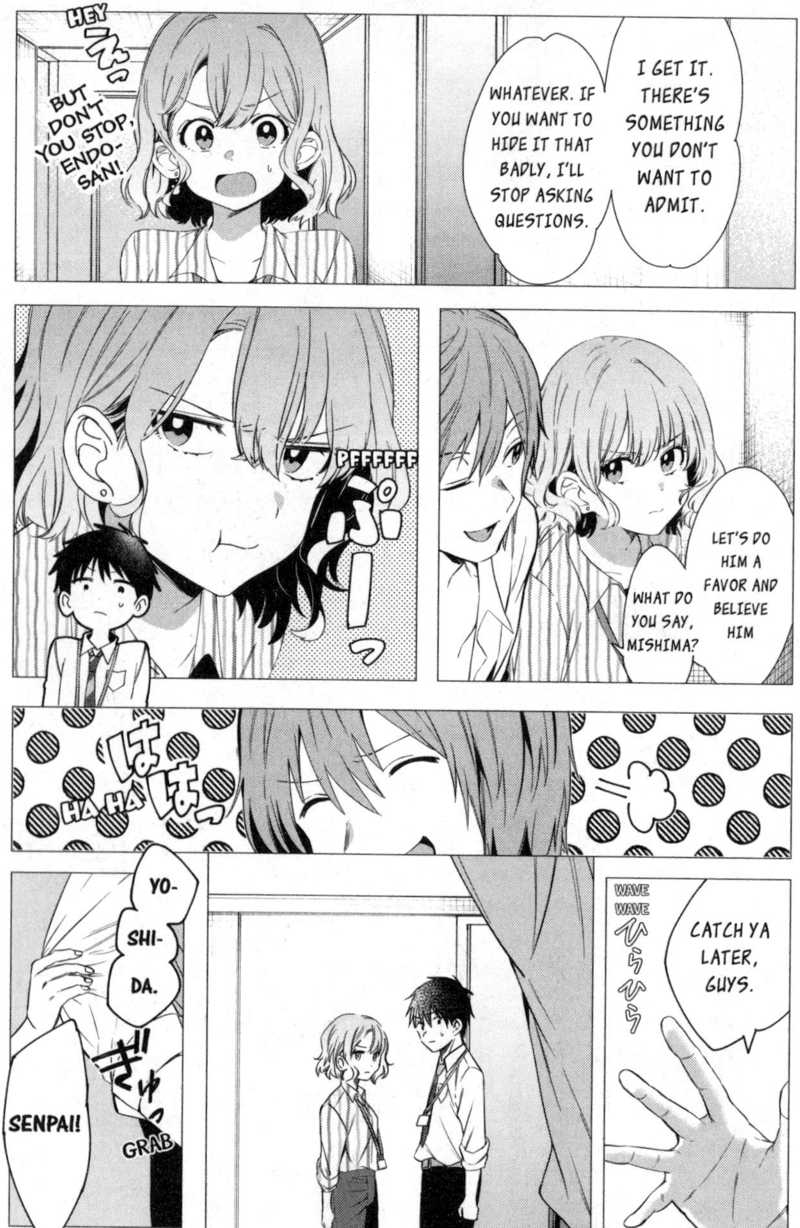
I GET IT. THERE'S SOMETHING YOU DON'T WANT TO ADMIT.
WHATEVER. IF YOU WANT TO HIDE IT THAT BADLY, I'LL STOP ASKING QUESTIONS.
HEY
えっ
BUT DON'T YOU STOP, ENDO-SAN!
LET'S DO HIM A FAVOR AND BELIEVE HIM
WHAT DO YOU SAY, MISHIMA?
PFFFFFF
ぷーっ
ははっ
HA HA
WAVE WAVE
ひらひら
CATCH YA LATER, GUYS.
YO-SHI-DA.
ぎゅっ
GRAB
SENPAI!

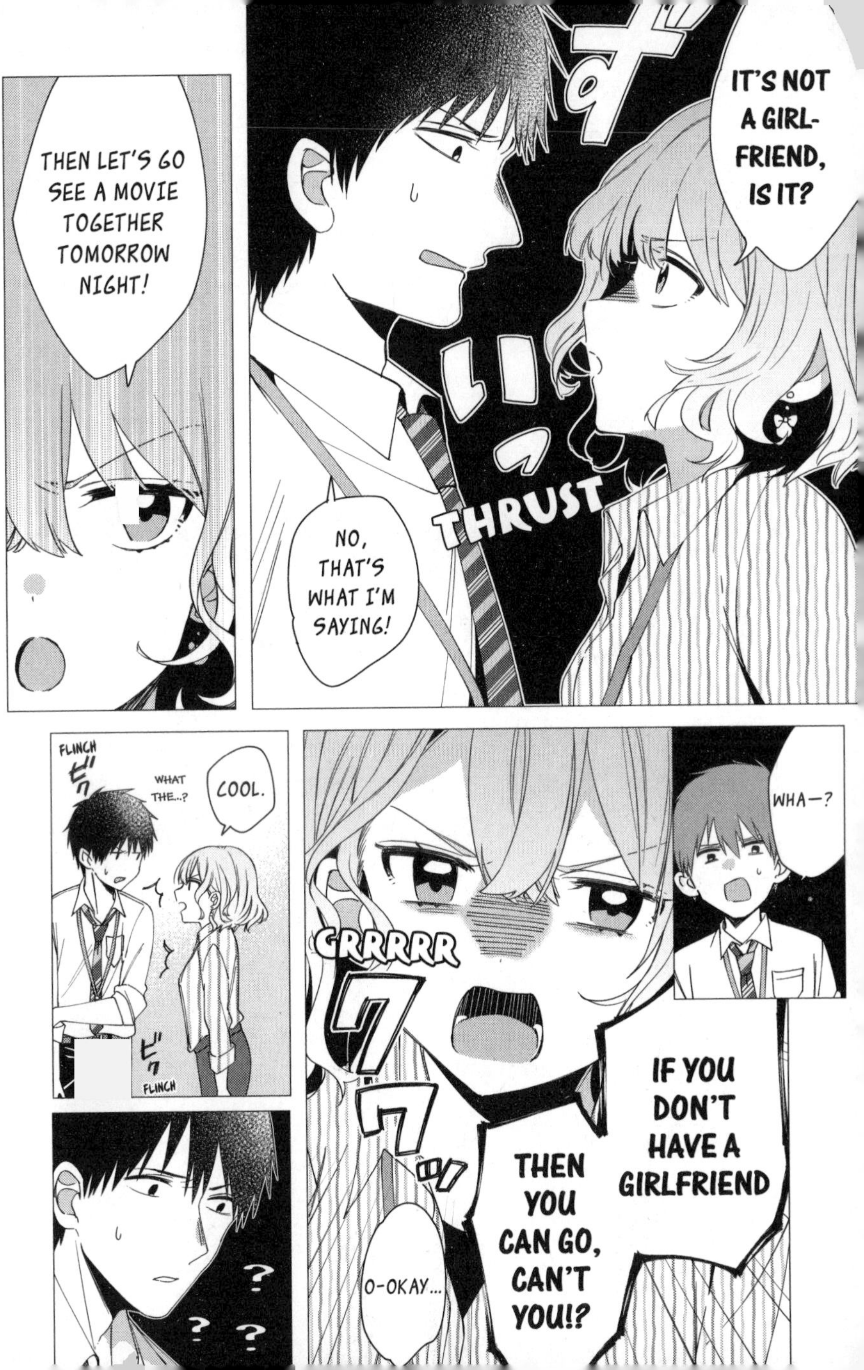
IT'S NOT A GIRL-FRIEND, IS IT?
THRUST
NO, THAT'S WHAT I'M SAYING!
THEN LET'S GO SEE A MOVIE TOGETHER TOMORROW NIGHT!
WHA—?
GRRRRR
IF YOU DON'T HAVE A GIRLFRIEND
THEN YOU CAN GO, CAN'T YOU!?
O-OKAY...
COOL.
WHAT THE...?
FLINCH
FLINCH
? ? ?

milk tea
～運命の温度～
THE FLAVOR OF DESTINY

TICKETS
ロチケット

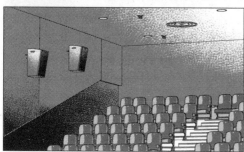

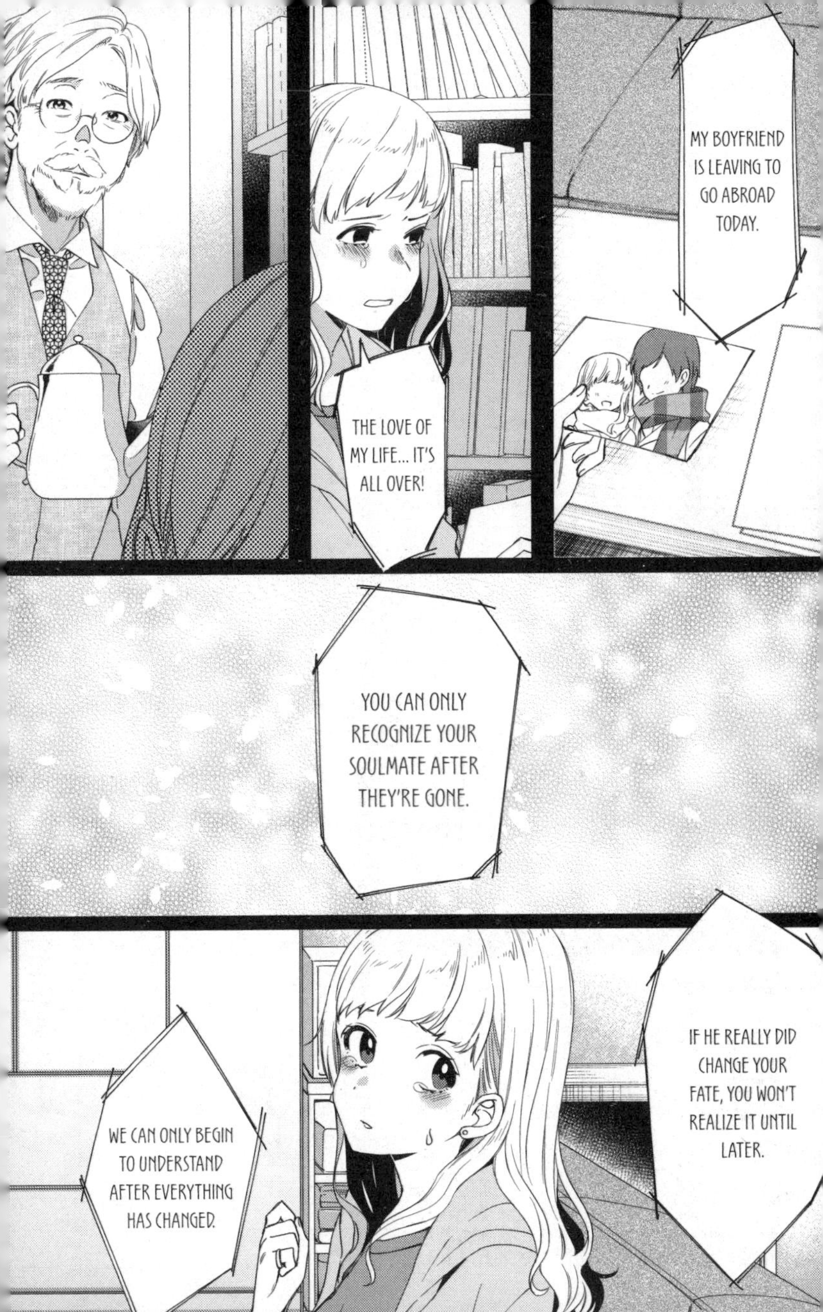

MY BOYFRIEND IS LEAVING TO GO ABROAD TODAY.
THE LOVE OF MY LIFE... IT'S ALL OVER!
YOU CAN ONLY RECOGNIZE YOUR SOULMATE AFTER THEY'RE GONE.
IF HE REALLY DID CHANGE YOUR FATE, YOU WON'T REALIZE IT UNTIL LATER.
WE CAN ONLY BEGIN TO UNDERSTAND AFTER EVERYTHING HAS CHANGED.

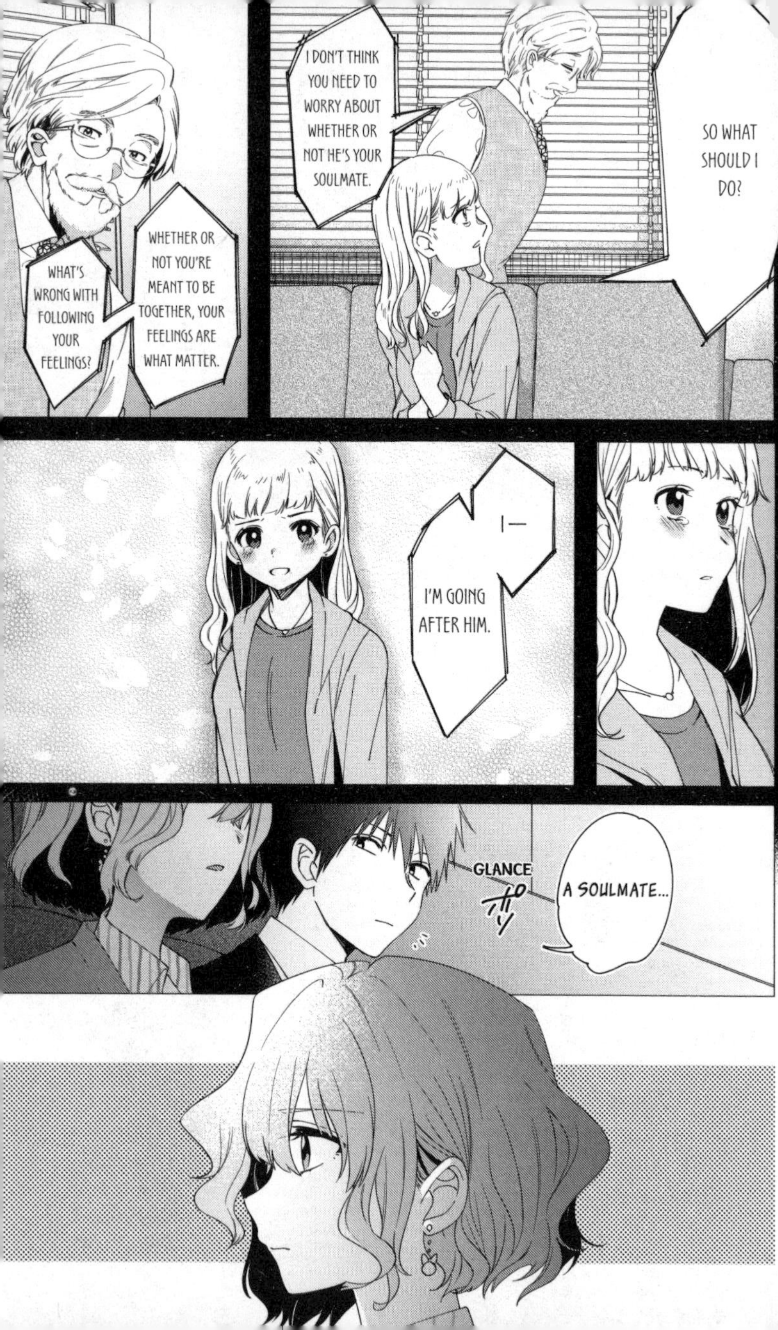
SO WHAT SHOULD I DO?
I DON'T THINK YOU NEED TO WORRY ABOUT WHETHER OR NOT HE'S YOUR SOULMATE.
WHETHER OR NOT YOU'RE MEANT TO BE TOGETHER, YOUR FEELINGS ARE WHAT MATTER.
WHAT'S WRONG WITH FOLLOWING YOUR FEELINGS?
I—
I'M GOING AFTER HIM.
A SOULMATE...
GLANCE

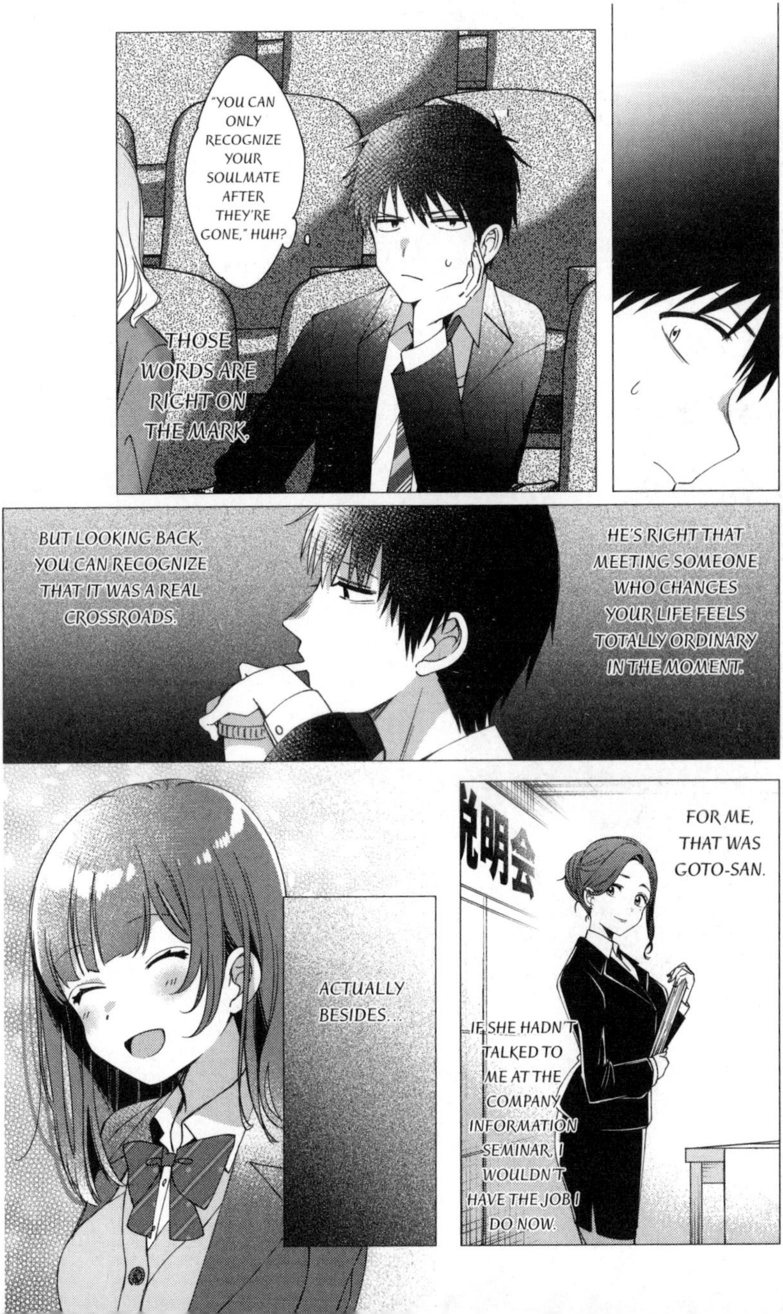
"YOU CAN ONLY RECOGNIZE YOUR SOULMATE AFTER THEY'RE GONE," HUH?
THOSE WORDS ARE RIGHT ON THE MARK.
HE'S RIGHT THAT MEETING SOMEONE WHO CHANGES YOUR LIFE FEELS TOTALLY ORDINARY IN THE MOMENT.
BUT LOOKING BACK, YOU CAN RECOGNIZE THAT IT WAS A REAL CROSSROADS.
FOR ME, THAT WAS GOTO-SAN.
IF SHE HADN'T TALKED TO ME AT THE COMPANY INFORMATION SEMINAR, I WOULDN'T HAVE THE JOB I DO NOW.
ACTUALLY BESIDES...

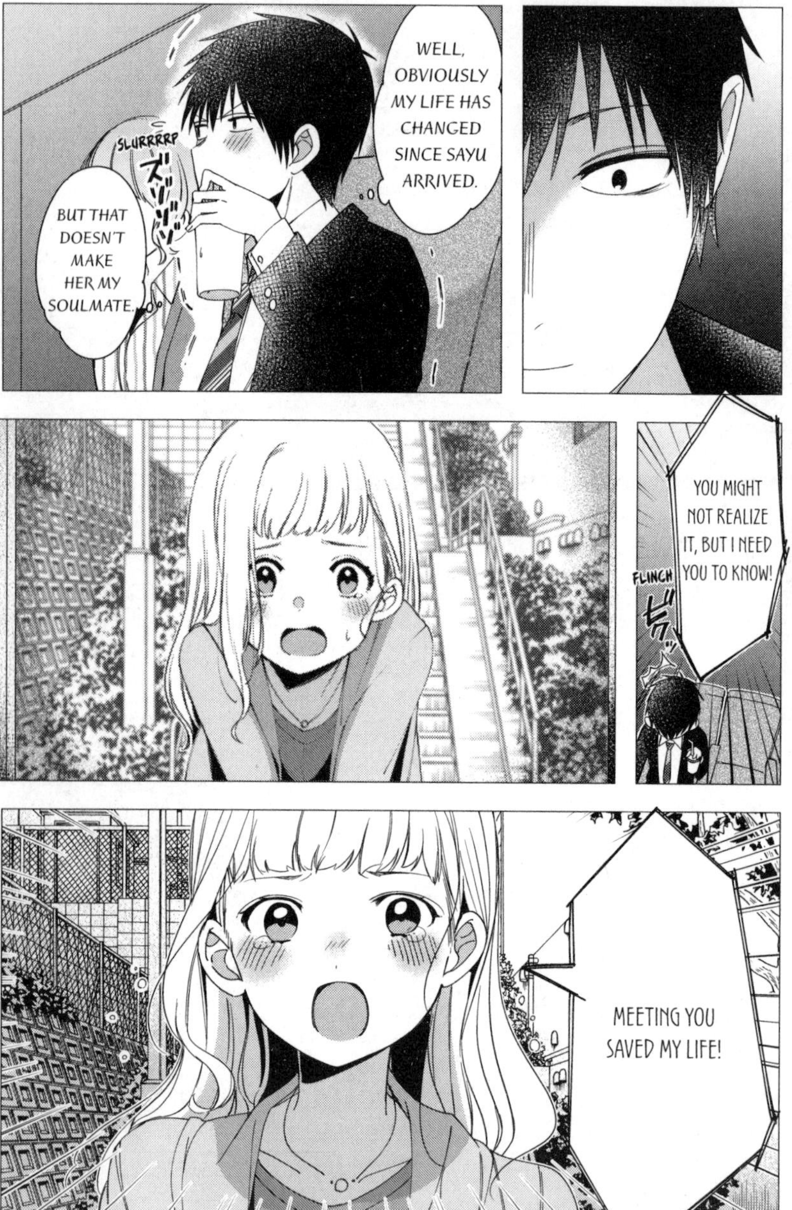
WELL, OBVIOUSLY MY LIFE HAS CHANGED SINCE SAYU ARRIVED.
SLURRRRP
BUT THAT DOESN'T MAKE HER MY SOULMATE.
YOU MIGHT NOT REALIZE IT, BUT I NEED YOU TO KNOW!
FLINCH
MEETING YOU SAVED MY LIFE!

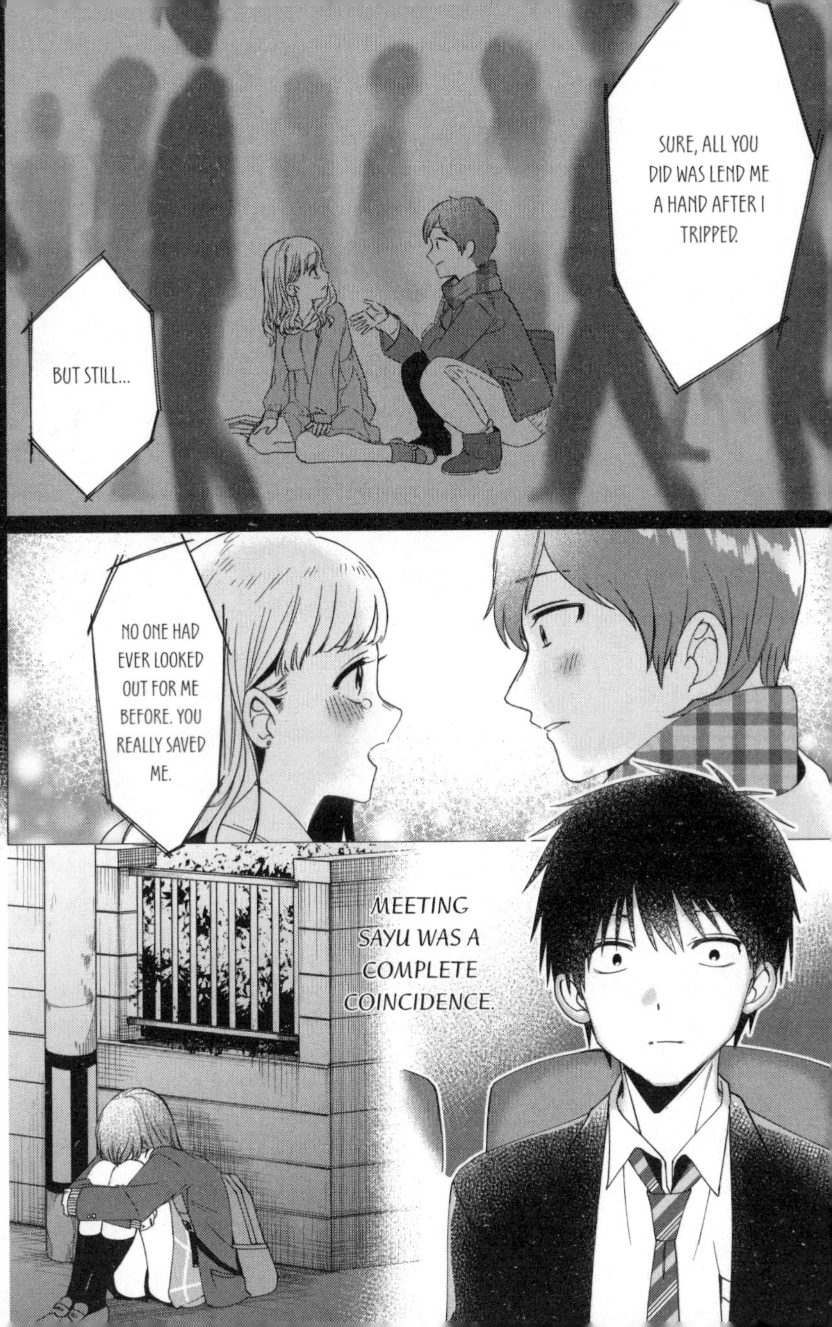
SURE, ALL YOU DID WAS LEND ME A HAND AFTER I TRIPPED.
BUT STILL...
NO ONE HAD EVER LOOKED OUT FOR ME BEFORE. YOU REALLY SAVED ME.
MEETING SAYU WAS A COMPLETE COINCIDENCE.

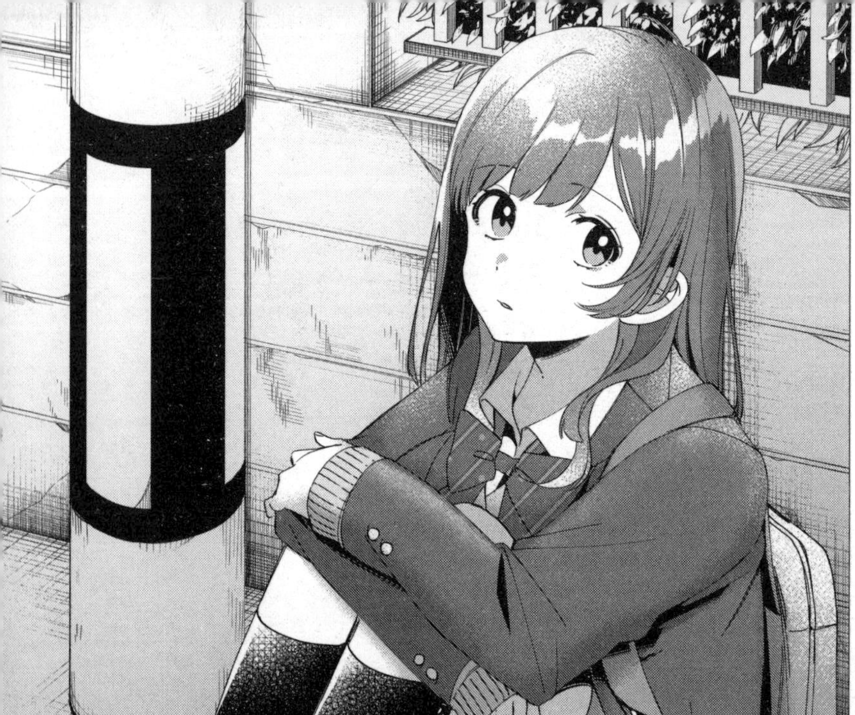

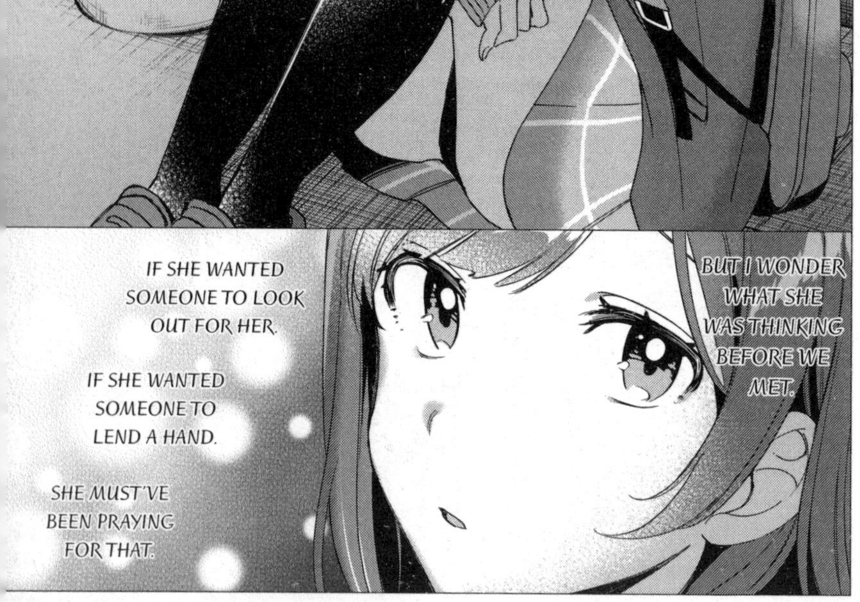
BUT I WONDER WHAT SHE WAS THINKING BEFORE WE MET.
IF SHE WANTED SOMEONE TO LOOK OUT FOR HER.
IF SHE WANTED SOMEONE TO LEND A HAND.
SHE MUST'VE BEEN PRAYING FOR THAT.

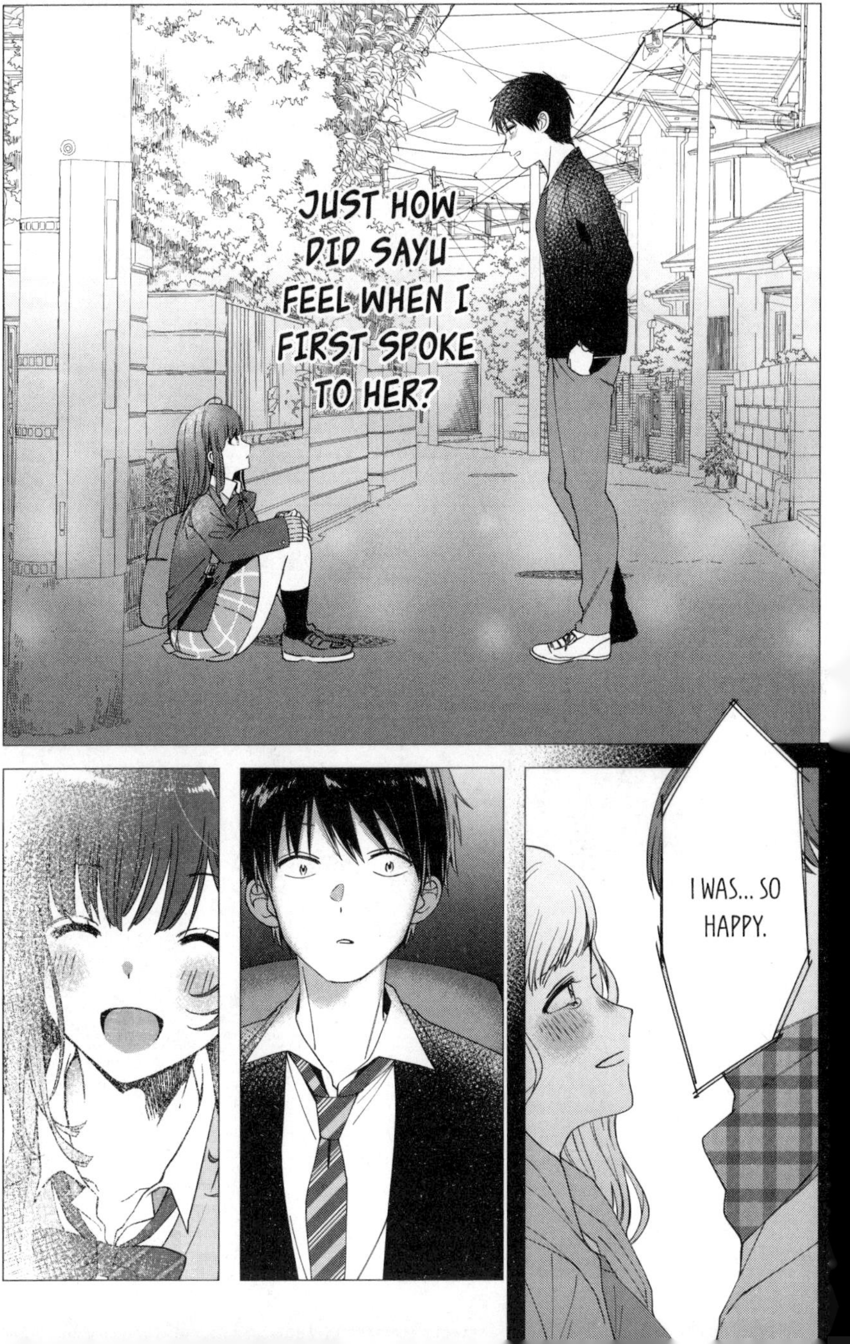
JUST HOW DID SAYU FEEL WHEN I FIRST SPOKE TO HER?
I WAS... SO HAPPY.

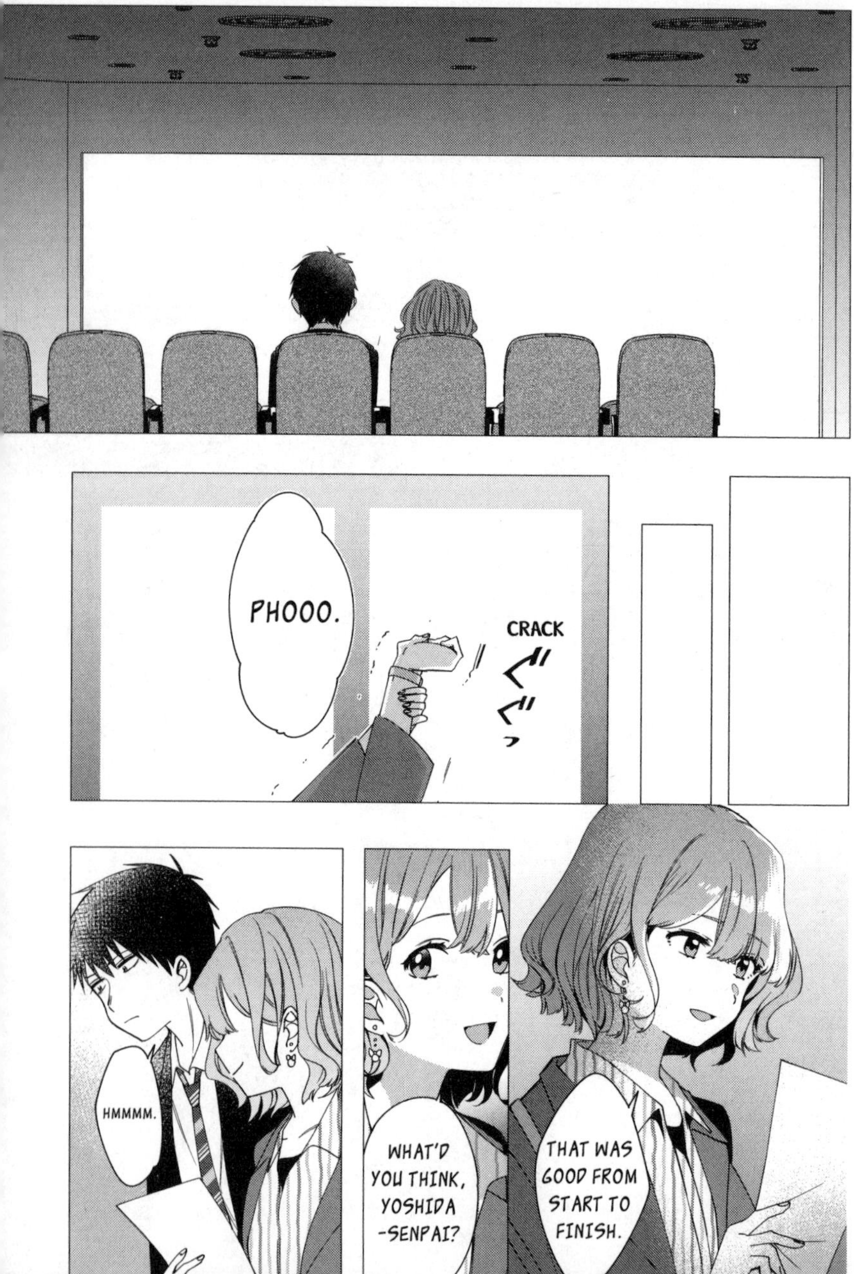
CRACK
PHOOO.
THAT WAS GOOD FROM START TO FINISH.
WHAT'D YOU THINK, YOSHIDA-SENPAI?
HMMMM.

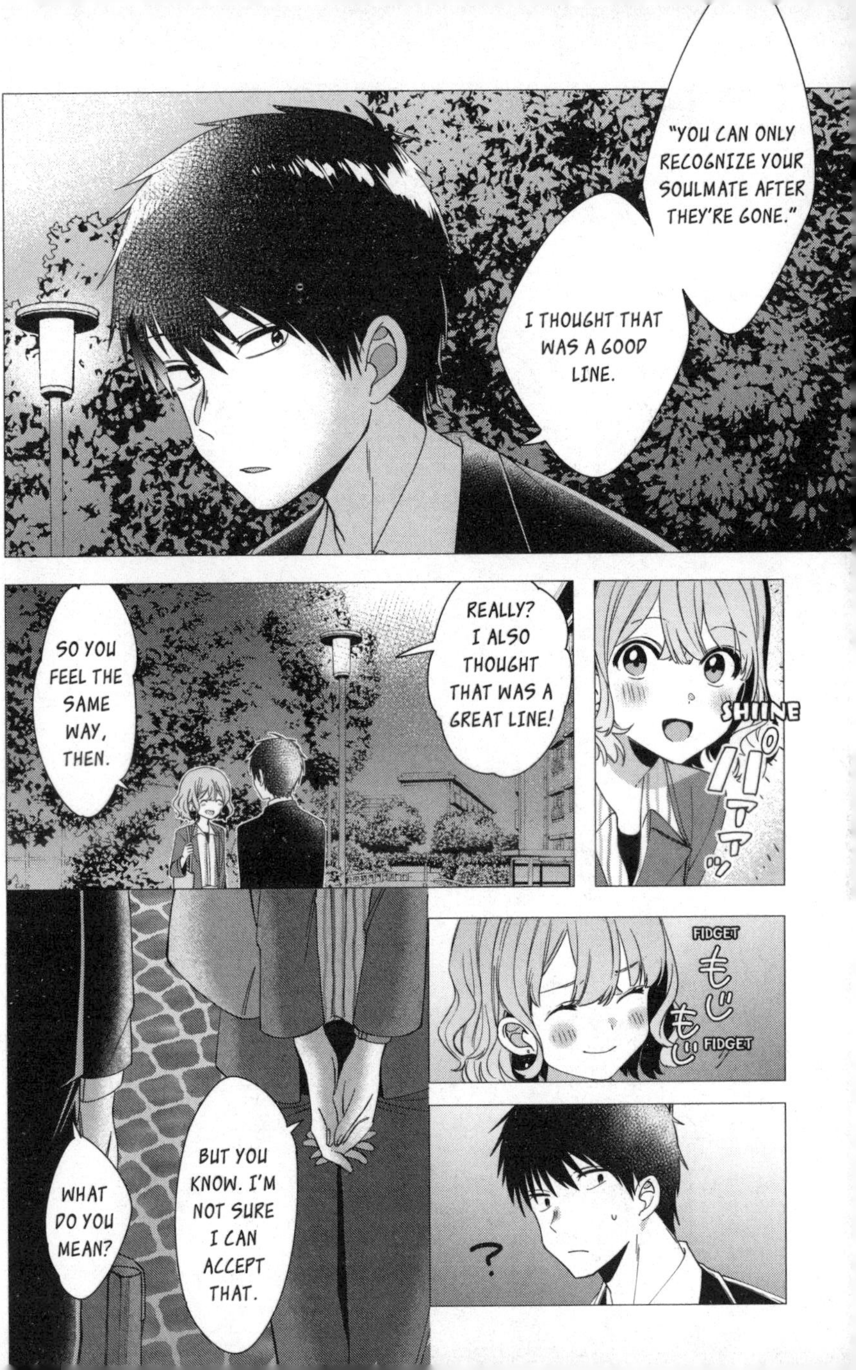
"YOU CAN ONLY RECOGNIZE YOUR SOULMATE AFTER THEY'RE GONE."
I THOUGHT THAT WAS A GOOD LINE.
SHIINE
パァアァッ
REALLY? I ALSO THOUGHT THAT WAS A GREAT LINE!
SO YOU FEEL THE SAME WAY, THEN.
FIDGET
もじもじ
FIDGET
BUT YOU KNOW. I'M NOT SURE I CAN ACCEPT THAT.
WHAT DO YOU MEAN?
?

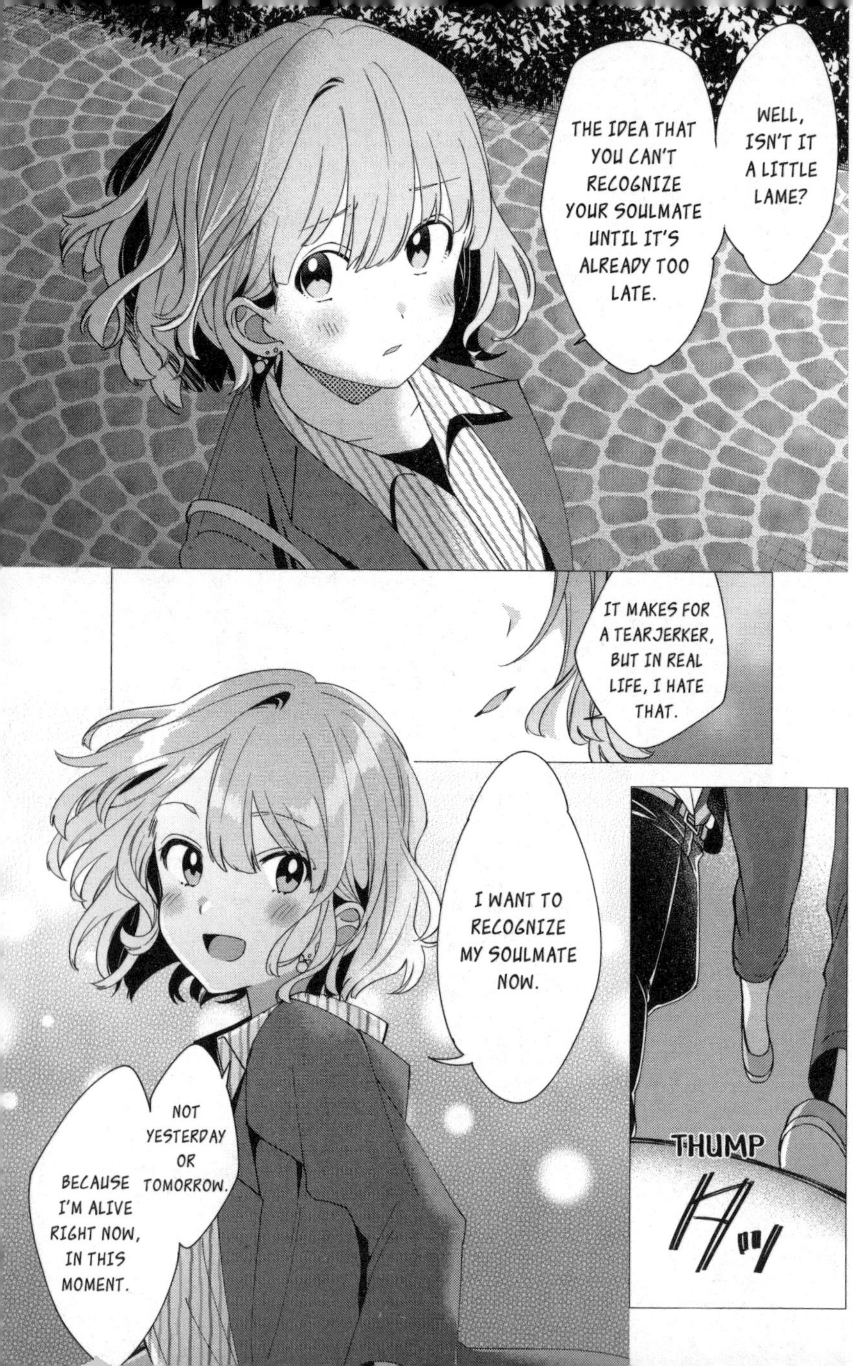
WELL, ISN'T IT A LITTLE LAME?
THE IDEA THAT YOU CAN'T RECOGNIZE YOUR SOULMATE UNTIL IT'S ALREADY TOO LATE.
IT MAKES FOR A TEARJERKER, BUT IN REAL LIFE, I HATE THAT.
THUMP
ハッ
I WANT TO RECOGNIZE MY SOULMATE NOW.
NOT YESTERDAY OR TOMORROW.
BECAUSE I'M ALIVE RIGHT NOW, IN THIS MOMENT.

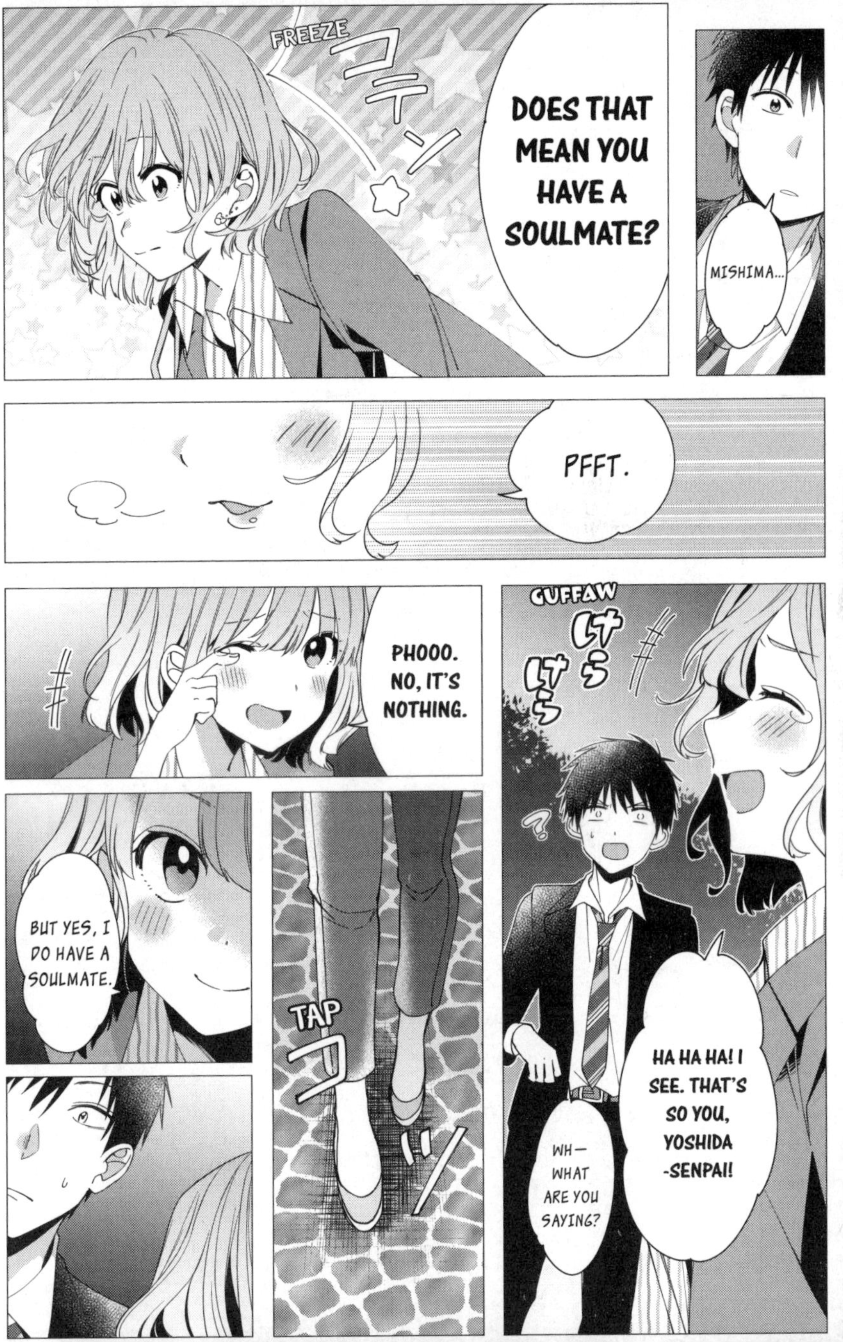
MISHIMA...
FREEZE
DOES THAT MEAN YOU HAVE A SOULMATE?
PFFT.
GUFFAW
HA HA HA! I SEE. THAT'S SO YOU, YOSHIDA -SENPAI!
WH— WHAT ARE YOU SAYING?
PHOOO. NO, IT'S NOTHING.
TAP
BUT YES, I DO HAVE A SOULMATE.

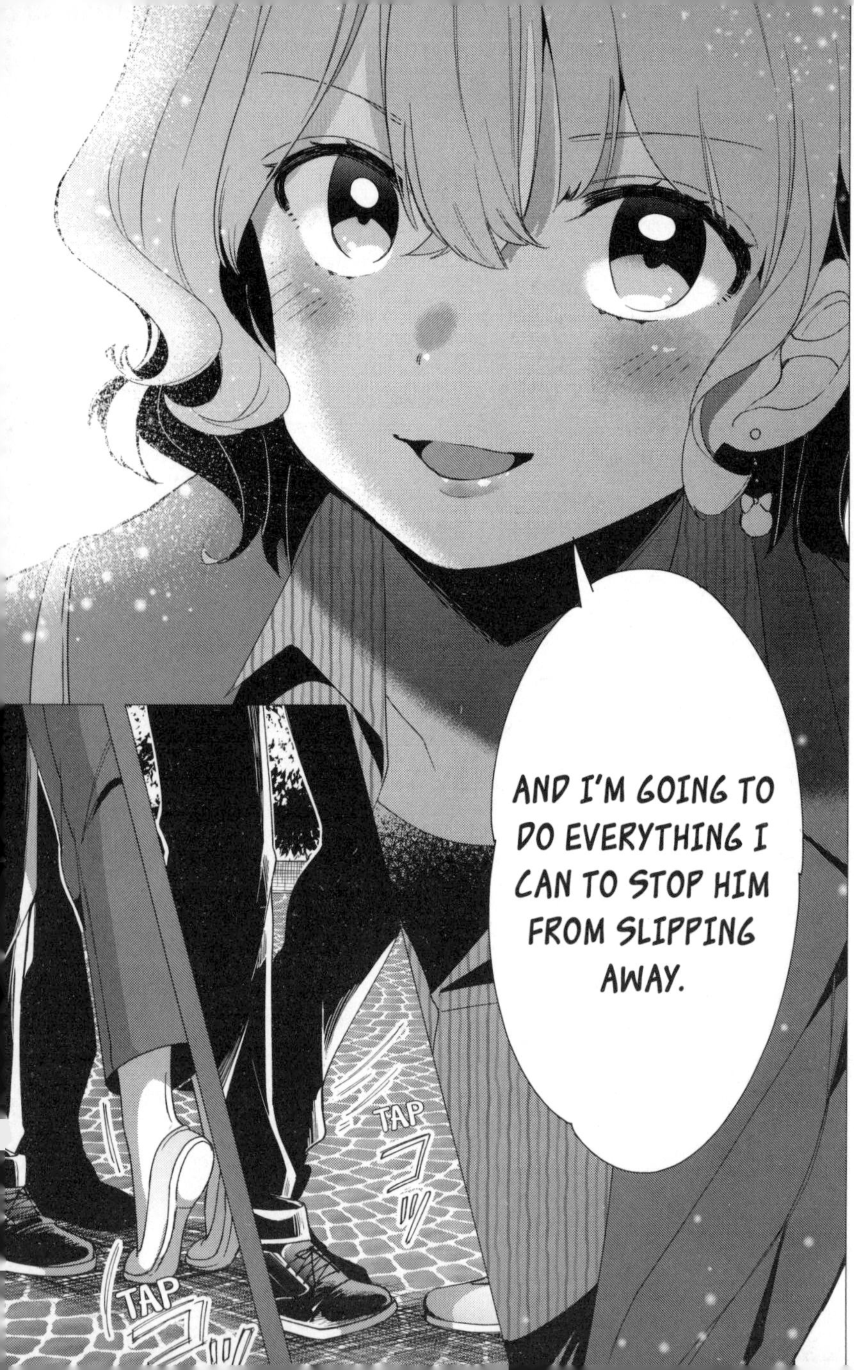
AND I'M GOING TO DO EVERYTHING I CAN TO STOP HIM FROM SLIPPING AWAY.
TAP
TAP

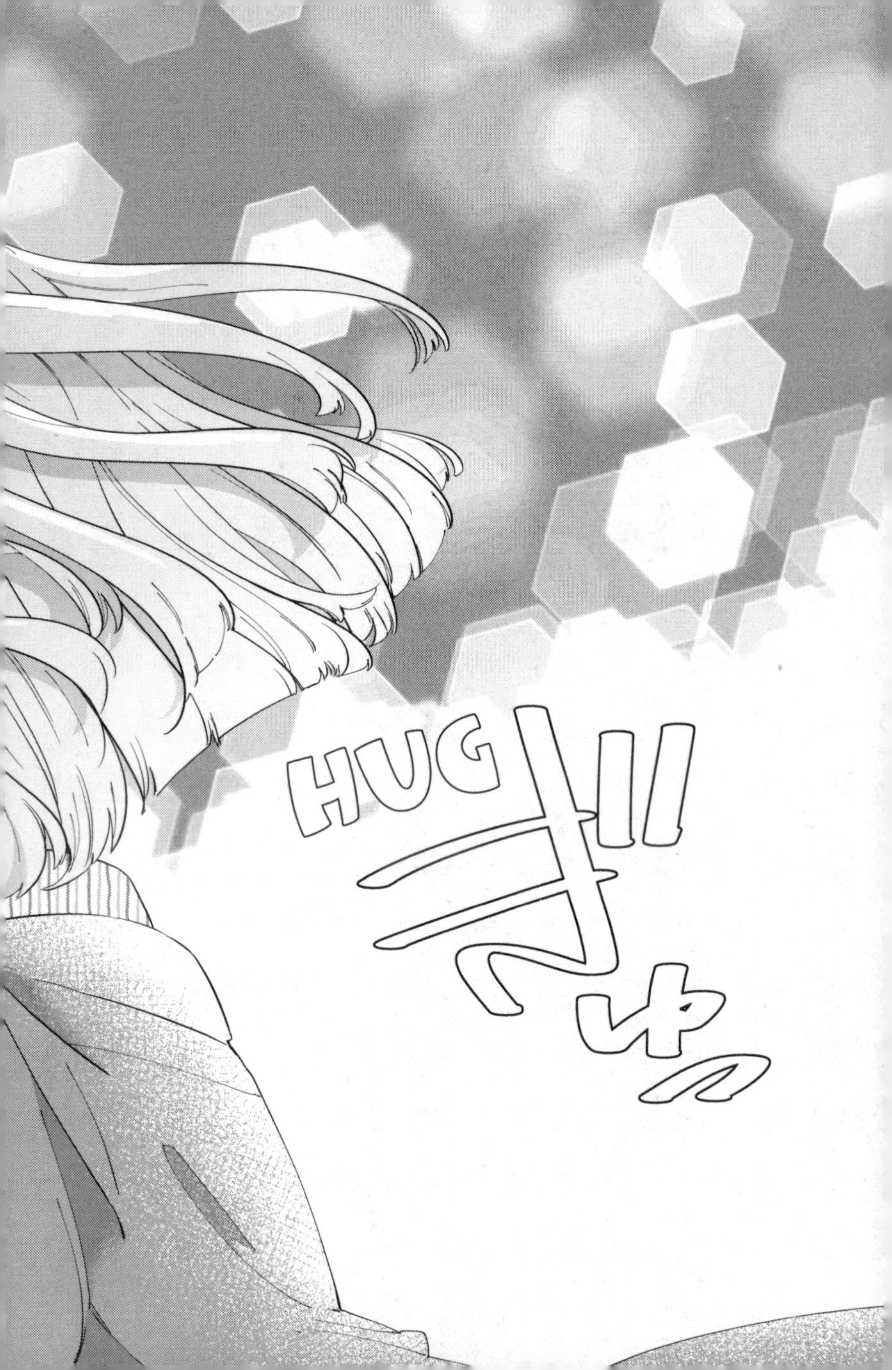
HUG

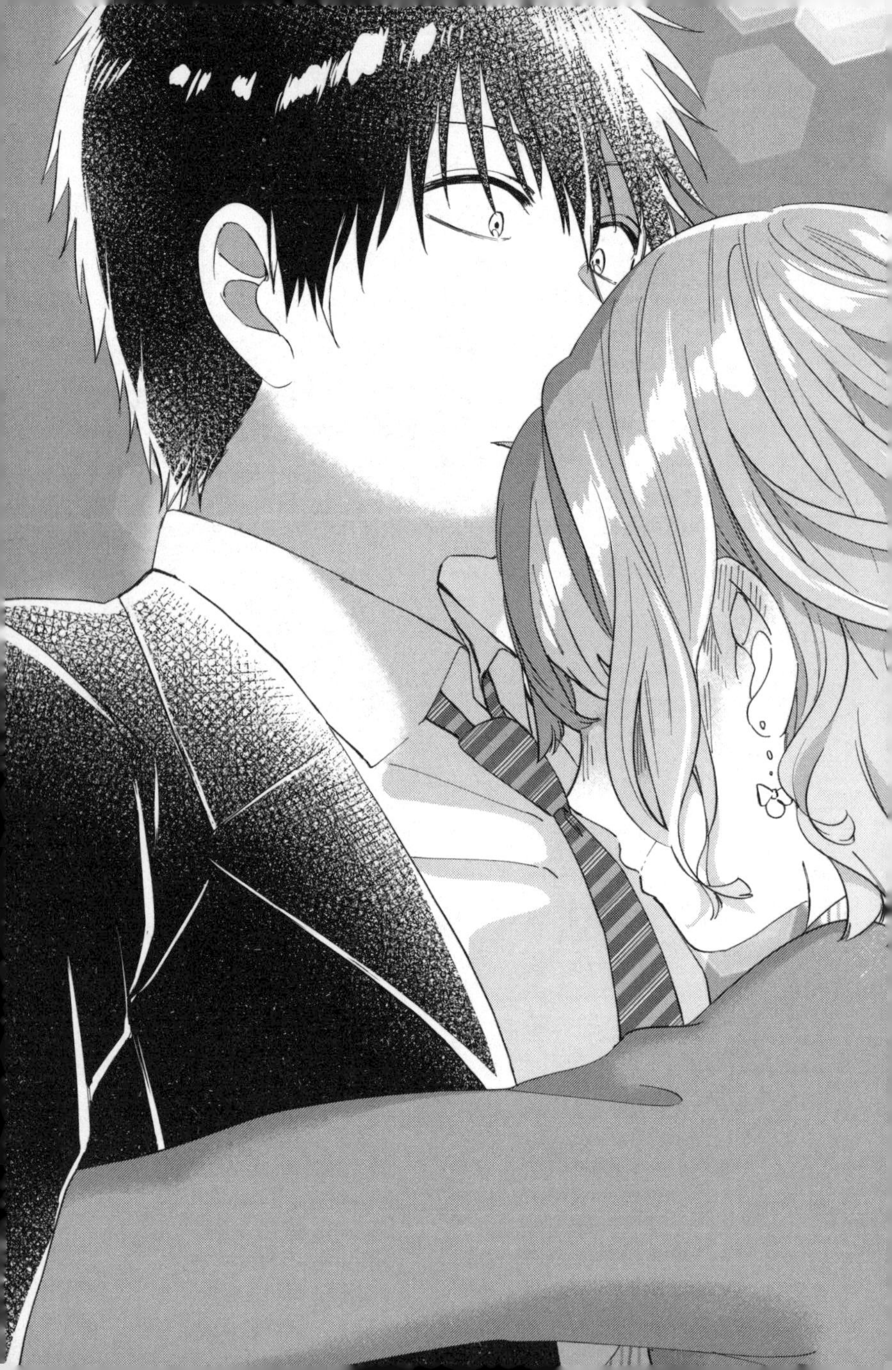

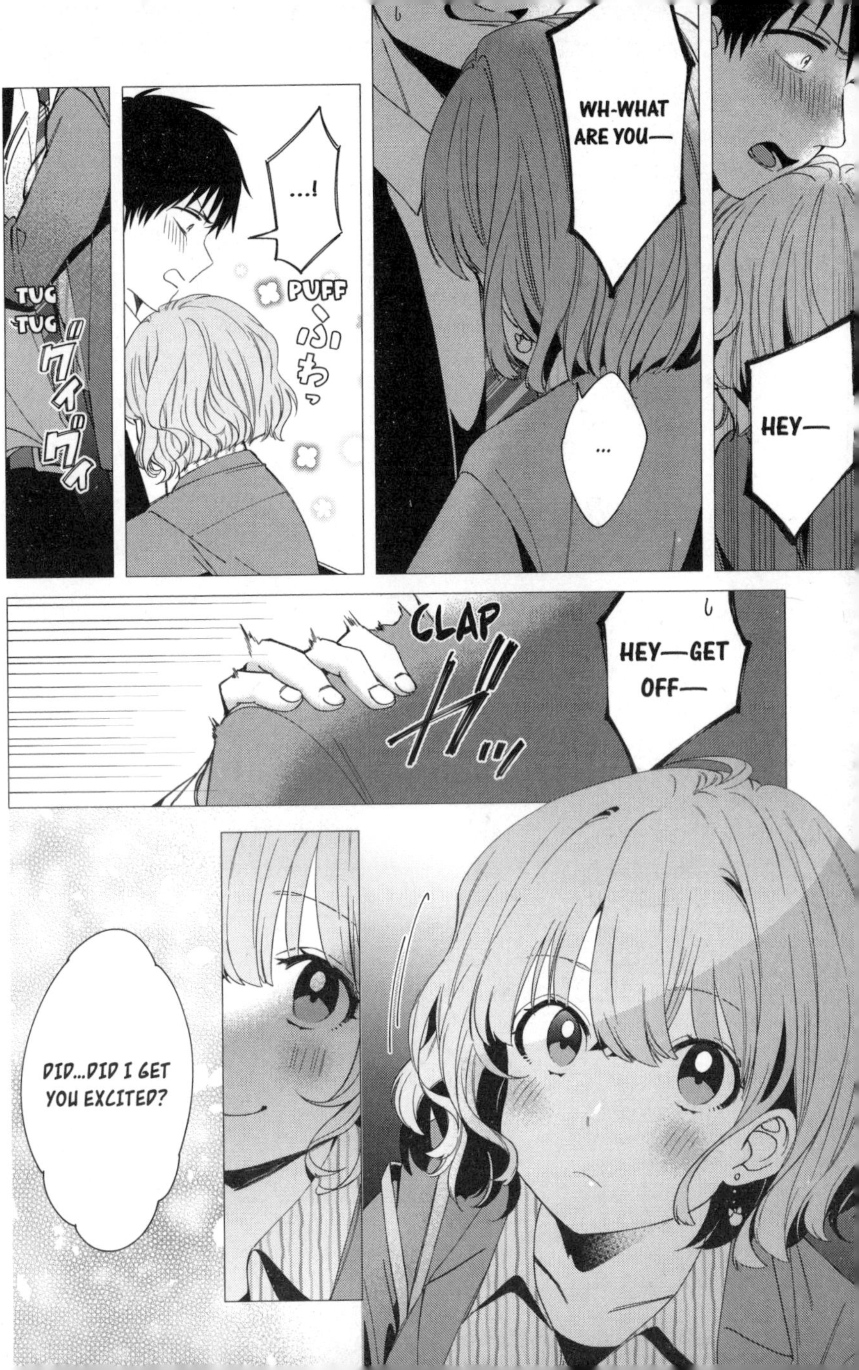
HEY—
WH-WHAT ARE YOU—
...
...!
PUFF
ふわっ
TUG TUG
グィグィ
HEY—GET OFF—
CLAP
ガッ
DID...DID I GET YOU EXCITED?

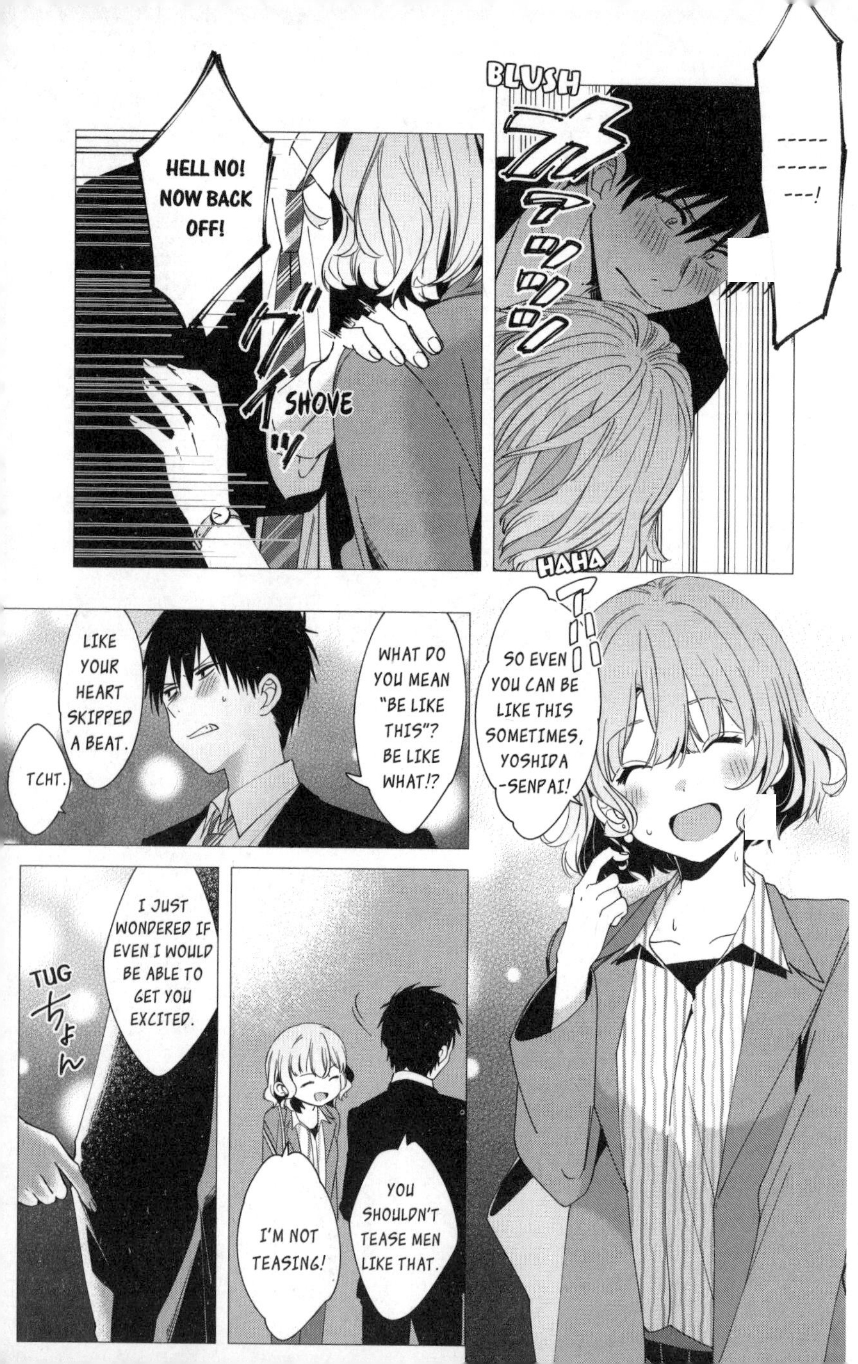

BLUSH

---!
HELL NO! NOW BACK OFF!
SHOVE
HAHA
SO EVEN YOU CAN BE LIKE THIS SOMETIMES, YOSHIDA-SENPAI!
WHAT DO YOU MEAN "BE LIKE THIS"? BE LIKE WHAT!?
LIKE YOUR HEART SKIPPED A BEAT.
TCHT.
YOU SHOULDN'T TEASE MEN LIKE THAT.
I'M NOT TEASING!
I JUST WONDERED IF EVEN I WOULD BE ABLE TO GET YOU EXCITED.
TUG
ちょん

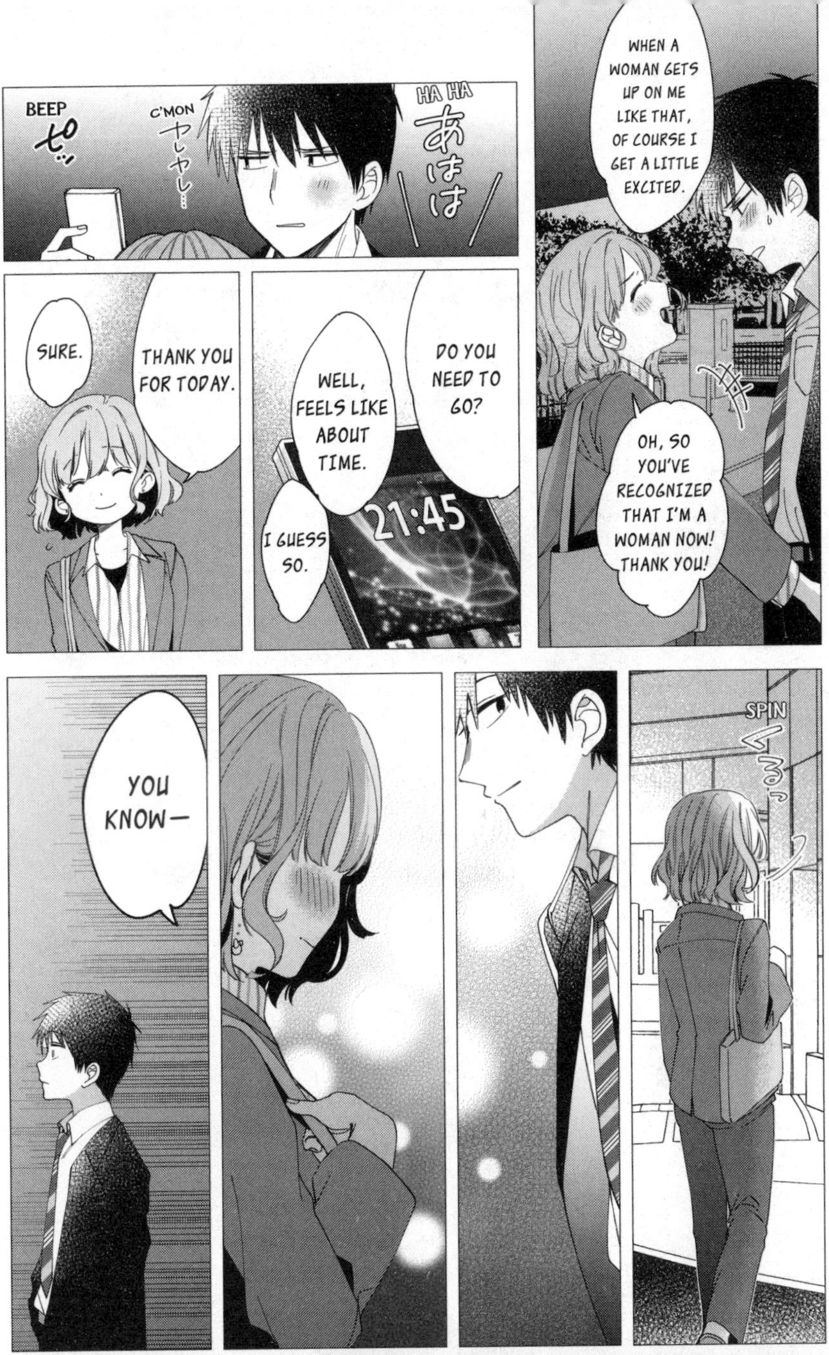
WHEN A WOMAN GETS UP ON ME LIKE THAT, OF COURSE I GET A LITTLE EXCITED.
OH, SO YOU'VE RECOGNIZED THAT I'M A WOMAN NOW! THANK YOU!
HA HA
あはは
C'MON
ヤレヤレ…
BEEP
ピッ
DO YOU NEED TO GO?
WELL, FEELS LIKE ABOUT TIME.
21:45
I GUESS SO.
THANK YOU FOR TODAY.
SURE.
SPIN
くるっ
YOU KNOW—

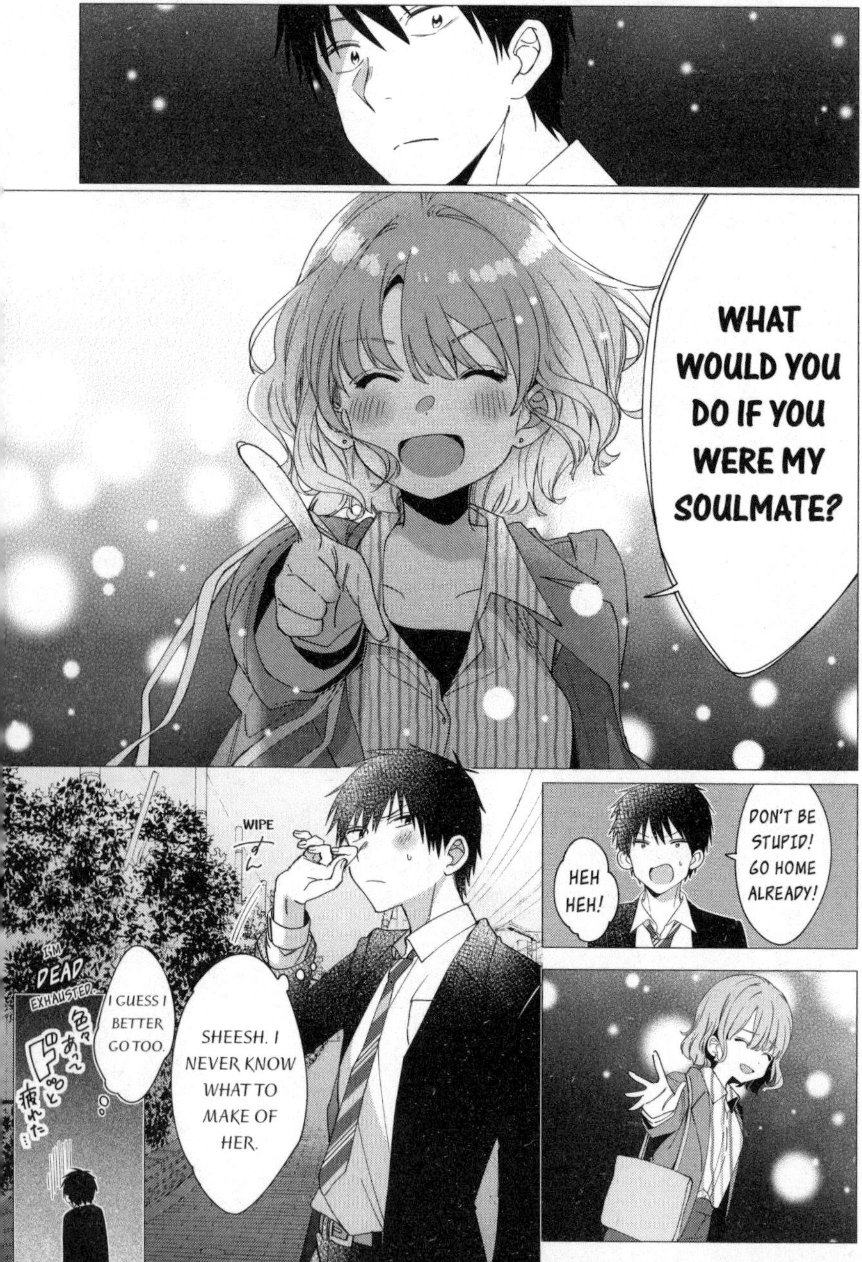
WHAT WOULD YOU DO IF YOU WERE MY SOULMATE?
DON'T BE STUPID! GO HOME ALREADY!
HEH HEH!
WIPE
SHEESH. I NEVER KNOW WHAT TO MAKE OF HER.
I GUESS I BETTER GO TOO.
I'M DEAD EXHAUSTED...
色々あってドっと疲れた…

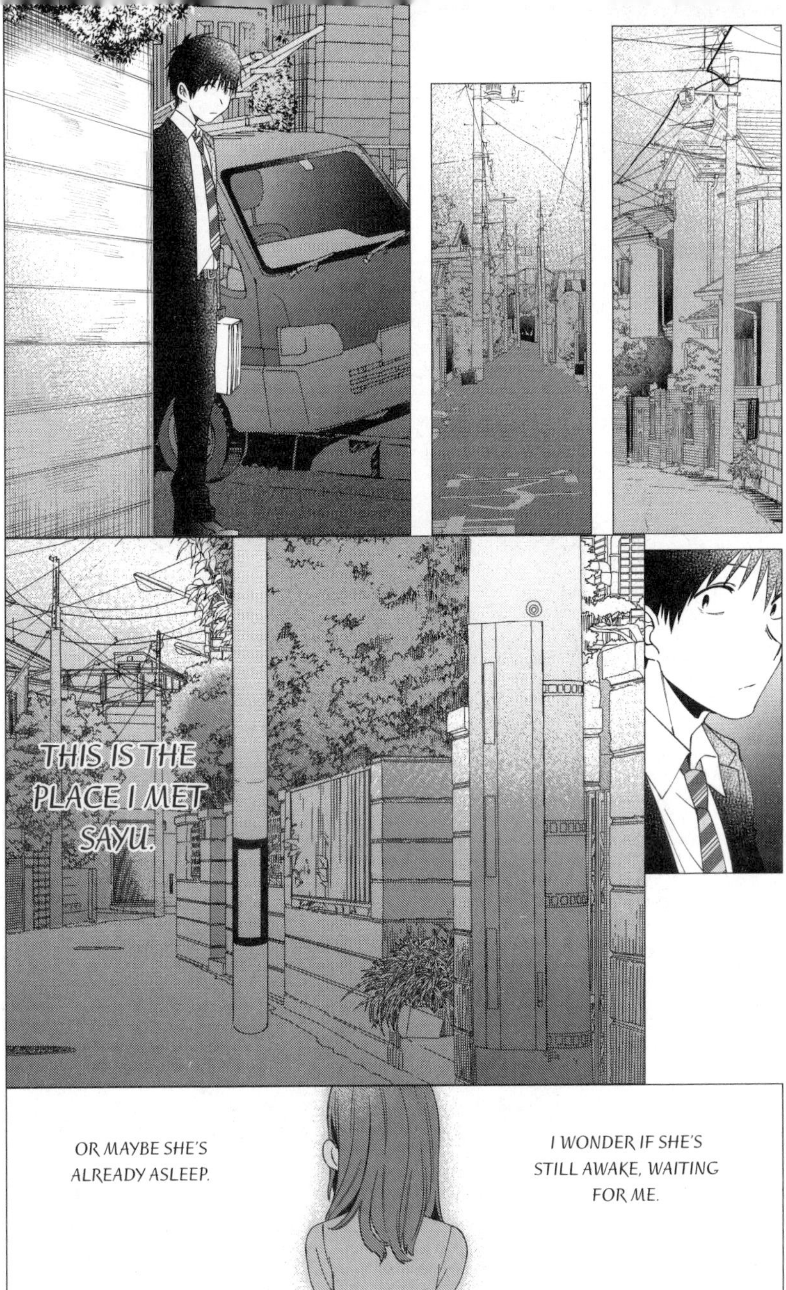
THIS IS THE PLACE I MET SAYU.
I WONDER IF SHE'S STILL AWAKE, WAITING FOR ME.
OR MAYBE SHE'S ALREADY ASLEEP.

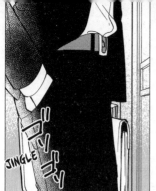

フッ
HEH
カン
CLACK
カン
CLACK
ゴソゴソ
JINGLE
ジャコ
SHK
?
THE DOOR IS OPEN.
CHAK
カチャ…
WHAT'S GOING ON?
YIKES, THAT'S DANGEROUS.
CREAK
ギィ…
HEY, SAYU. THE DOOR'S OPEN!

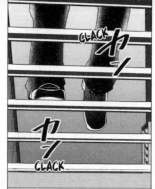

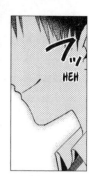

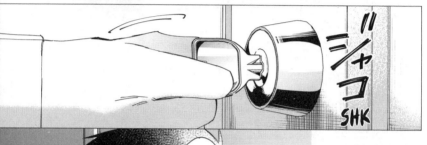

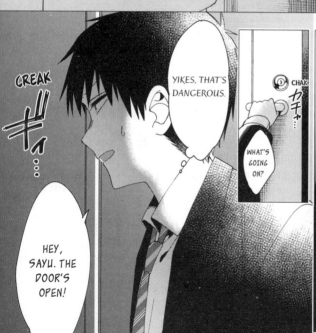

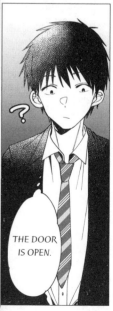

SILENCE

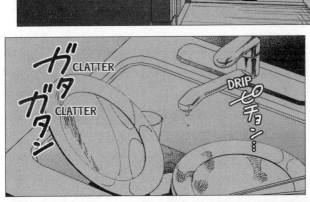

CLATTER
CLATTER
DRIP

IS SHE
ASLEEP?

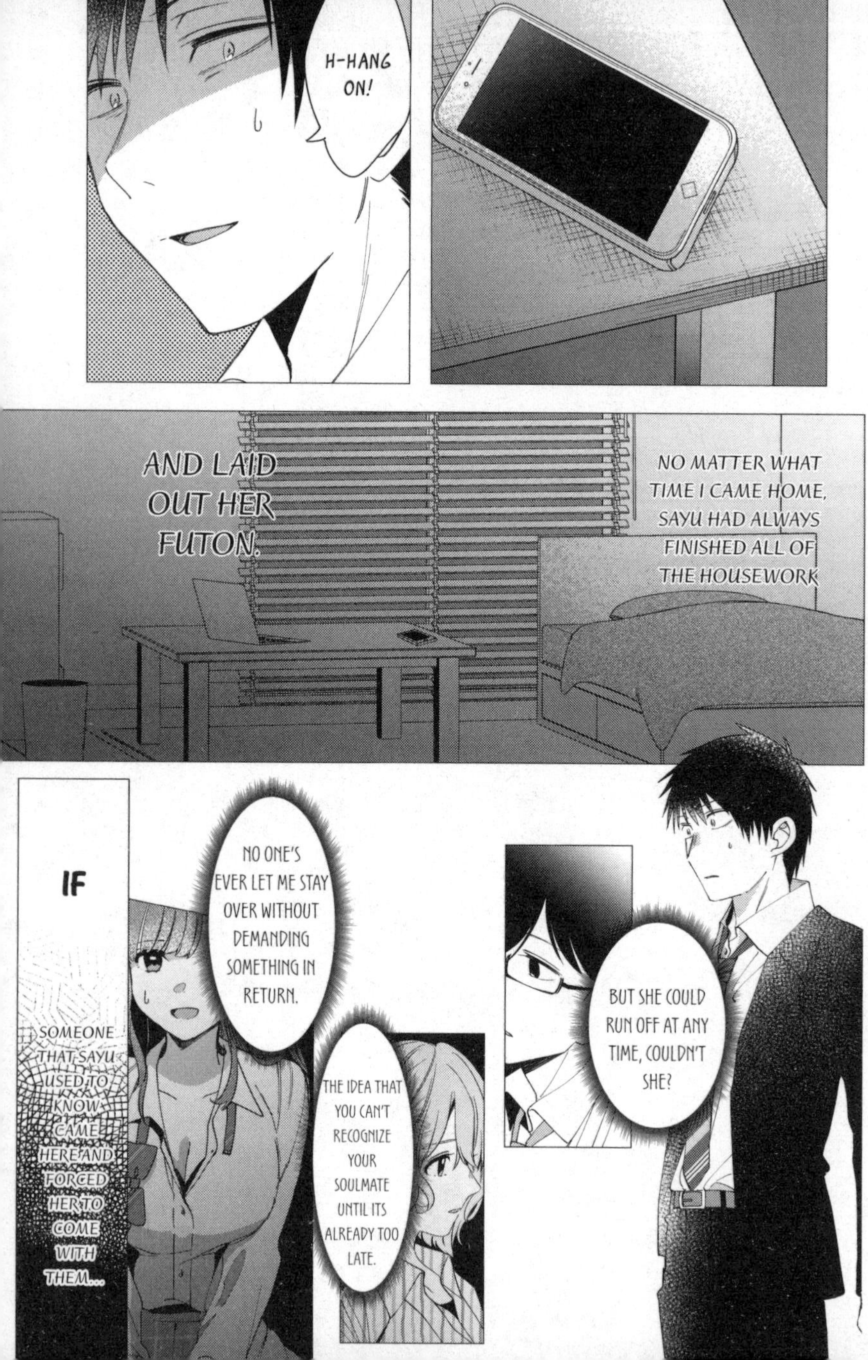
H-HANG ON!
NO MATTER WHAT TIME I CAME HOME, SAYU HAD ALWAYS FINISHED ALL OF THE HOUSEWORK
AND LAID OUT HER FUTON.
BUT SHE COULD RUN OFF AT ANY TIME, COULDN'T SHE?
NO ONE'S EVER LET ME STAY OVER WITHOUT DEMANDING SOMETHING IN RETURN.
THE IDEA THAT YOU CAN'T RECOGNIZE YOUR SOULMATE UNTIL ITS ALREADY TOO LATE.
IF
SOMEONE THAT SAYU USED TO KNOW CAME HERE AND FORCED HER TO COME WITH THEM...

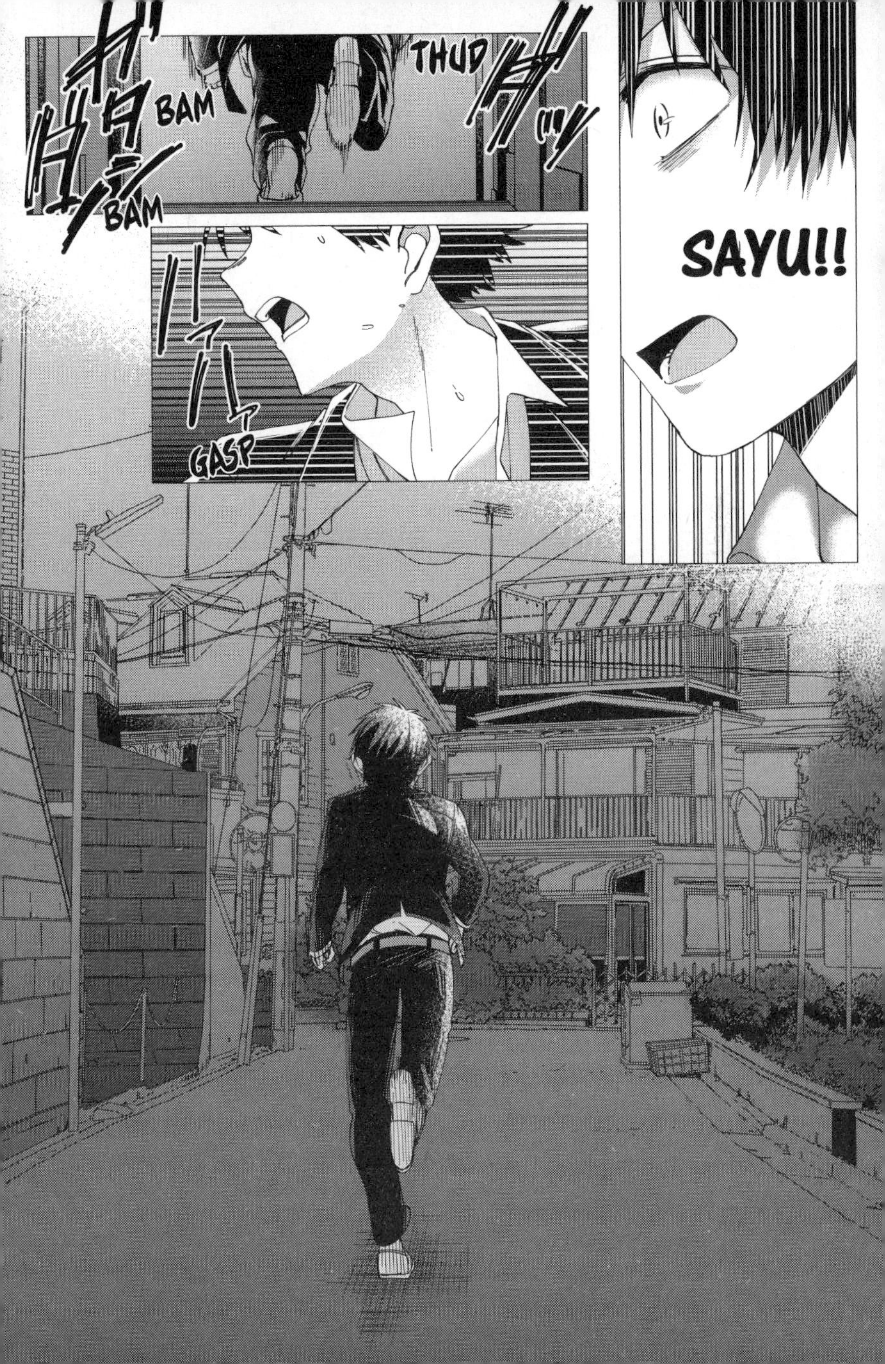
SAYU!!
THUD
BAM
BAM
GASP

HIGEHIRO

After Being Rejected,
I Shaved and Took
in a High School Runaway

AFTERWORD

THANK YOU SO MUCH FOR PURCHASING VOLUME 1 OF HIGEHIRO: AFTER BEING REJECTED, I SHAVED & TOOK IN A HIGH SCHOOL RUNAWAY! WHETHER YOU'RE A FAN OF THE ORIGINAL LIGHT NOVELS OR STARTED OFF WITH THE MANGA, I'M HAPPY SO LONG AS YOU ENJOYED IT.

THANKS TO

SHIMESABA — THE GENTLE BUT HONEST ORIGINAL CREATOR.

KADOKAWA SNEAKER BUNKO, SHONEN ACE
— THANKS FOR ALL YOUR HELP.

MY MANAGING EDITOR
— WITHOUT YOU, I COULDN'T HAVE COMPLETED THIS MANGA. YOU'RE A GENIUS, SUPER-COMPETENT MAN! (RAVE REVIEWS)

BOOOTA — THANKS TO YOUR AMAZING ILLUSTRATIONS IN THE LIGHT NOVEL, I'LL CONTINUE TO CHALLENGE MYSELF AND GET BETTER.

ASSISTANTS CHISE, ARISUN
— THANKS TO YOU, WE SOMEHOW MANAGED TO FINISH A DRAFT.

EVERYONE WHO GAVE THEIR SUPPORT AND FEEDBACK ON TWITTER
— THANKS TO ALL OF YOU, I'M ABLE TO PICK UP THE PEN AND DRAW EVERY DAY.

MY FAMILY, RELATIVES, FRIENDS, EVERYONE ELSE WHO SUPPORTS ME, AND TO ANYONE WHO HAS BEEN INVOLVED IN MAKING THIS WORK A REALITY. AND EVERYONE WHO BOUGHT THIS VOLUME!

THANK YOU FROM THE BOTTOM OF MY HEART!
I'M GOING TO KEEP WORKING HARD, SO PLEASE
CONTINUE TO SUPPORT ME!

IMARU ADACHI

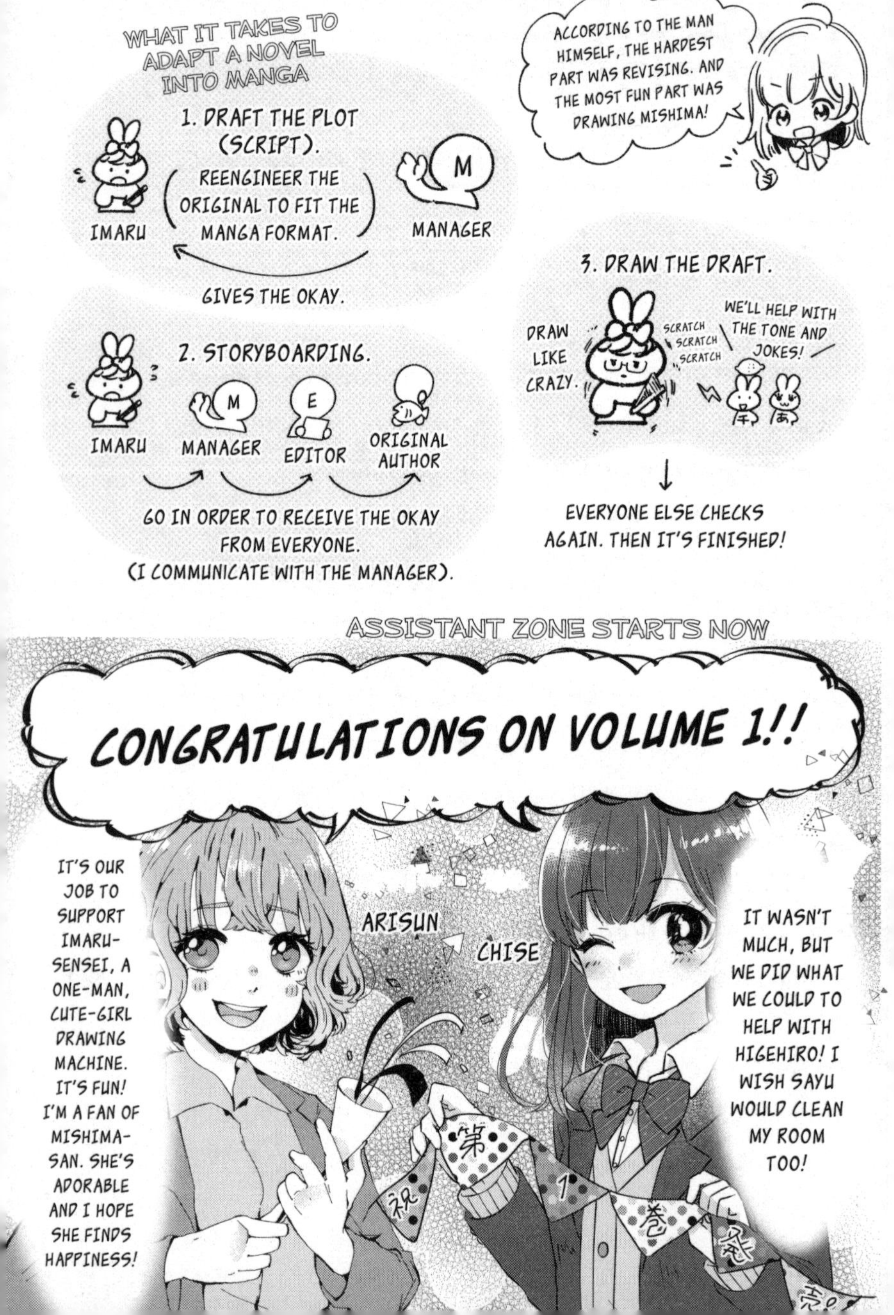
ACCORDING TO THE MAN HIMSELF, THE HARDEST PART WAS REVISING. AND THE MOST FUN PART WAS DRAWING MISHIMA!
WHAT IT TAKES TO ADAPT A NOVEL INTO MANGA
1. DRAFT THE PLOT (SCRIPT).
IMARU
REENGINEER THE ORIGINAL TO FIT THE MANGA FORMAT.
M
MANAGER
GIVES THE OKAY.
2. STORYBOARDING.
IMARU
M
MANAGER
E
EDITOR
ORIGINAL AUTHOR
GO IN ORDER TO RECEIVE THE OKAY FROM EVERYONE. (I COMMUNICATE WITH THE MANAGER).
3. DRAW THE DRAFT.
DRAW LIKE CRAZY.
SCRATCH SCRATCH SCRATCH
WE'LL HELP WITH THE TONE AND JOKES!
EVERYONE ELSE CHECKS AGAIN. THEN IT'S FINISHED!
ASSISTANT ZONE STARTS NOW
CONGRATULATIONS ON VOLUME 1!!
IT WASN'T MUCH, BUT WE DID WHAT WE COULD TO HELP WITH HIGEHIRO! I WISH SAYU WOULD CLEAN MY ROOM TOO!
CHISE
ARISUN
IT'S OUR JOB TO SUPPORT IMARU-SENSEI, A ONE-MAN, CUTE-GIRL DRAWING MACHINE. IT'S FUN! I'M A FAN OF MISHIMA-SAN. SHE'S ADORABLE AND I HOPE SHE FINDS HAPPINESS!
祝
第
1
巻

HIGEHIRO

**After Being Rejected,
I Shaved and Took in a High School Runaway** *1*

Afterword from the original author.

Higehiro: After Being Rejected, I Shaved & Took in a High School Runaway. Congratulations to everyone for publishing the first volume of the manga series!

I still can hardly believe that a novel I wrote was adapted into a manga and that it's actually being sold in bookstores.

I'm the original author, Shimesaba.
When my manager and editor told me that my story was getting a manga adaptation, they told me that the artist was going to be a pretty good one. Imaru Adachi showed me his early character drawings, and I remember well that first time I saw them. I felt like he really understood the characters. The drawings perfectly matched each character's personality, and I could really feel his effort to match the atmosphere evoked by the original illustrator. I knew that letting Imaru run the show would result in a wonderful manga, and I was overcome with excitement.

Once the manga became serialized, the thing that